THE RIGHT TO VOTE

THE RIGHT TO VOTE

Rights and Liberties under the Law

DONALD GRIER STEPHENSON, JR.

A B C ● C L I O

Santa Barbara, California • Denver, Colorado • Oxford, England

Copyright © 2004 by Donald Grier Stephenson, Jr.

All rights reserved. No part of this publication may be reproduced, stored in a re-
trieval system, or transmitted, in any form or by any means, electronic, mechanical,
photocopying, recording, or otherwise, except for the inclusion of brief quotations
in a review, without prior permission in writing from the publishers.

Library of Congress Cataloging-in-Publication Data
Stephenson, D. Grier.
  The right to vote : rights and liberties under the law / Donald Grier Stephenson,
Jr.
     p. cm. — (America's freedoms)
  Includes bibliographical references and index.
  ISBN 1-85109-648-5 (hardback : alk. paper) — ISBN 1-85109-653-1 (e-book)   1.
Suffrage—United States—History.   I. Title.   II. Series.

KF4891.S74 2004
342.73'072—dc22

                                                                2004019717

07 06 05 04 10 9 8 7 6 5 4 3 2 1

This book is also available on the World Wide Web as an e-book. Visit abc-clio.com
for details.

ABC-CLIO, Inc.
130 Cremona Drive, P.O. Box 1911
Santa Barbara, California 93116-1911

This book is printed on acid-free paper.
Manufactured in the United States of America

In memory of
Belle
(1985–2004)
and in honor of
James and Melinda in their new life together

CONTENTS

SERIES FOREWORD

America's Freedoms promises a series of books that address the origin, development, meaning, and future of the nation's fundamental liberties, as well as the individuals, circumstances, and events that have shaped them. These freedoms are chiefly enshrined explicitly or implicitly in the Bill of Rights and other amendments to the Constitution of the United States and have much to do with the quality of life Americans enjoy. Without them, America would be a far different place in which to live. Oddly enough, however, the Constitution was drafted and signed in Philadelphia in 1787 without a bill of rights. That was an afterthought, emerging only after a debate among the foremost political minds of the day.

At the time, Thomas Jefferson was in France on a diplomatic mission. Upon receiving a copy of the proposed Constitution from his friend James Madison, who had helped write the document, Jefferson let him know as fast as the slow sailing-ship mails of the day allowed that the new plan of government suffered one major defect—it lacked a bill of rights. This, Jefferson argued, "is what the people are entitled to against every government on earth." Madison should not have been surprised at Jefferson's reaction. The Declaration of Independence of 1776 had largely been Jefferson's handiwork, including its core statement of principle:

We hold these truths to be self-evident, that all men are created equal, that they are endowed by their Creator with certain unalienable Rights, that among these are Life, Liberty, and the pursuit of Happiness. That to secure these rights, Governments are instituted among Men, deriving their just powers from the consent of the governed.

Jefferson rejected the conclusion of many of the framers that the Constitution's design—a system of both separation of powers among the legislative, executive, and judicial branches, and a federal division of powers between national and state governments—would safeguard liberty. Even when combined with elections, he believed strongly that such structural checks would fall short.

Jefferson and other critics of the proposed Constitution ultimately had their way. In one of the first items of business in the First Congress in 1789, Madison, as a member of the House of Representatives from Virginia, introduced amendments to protect liberty. Ten were ratified by 1791 and have become known as the Bill of Rights.

America's Bill of Rights reflects the founding generation's understanding of the necessary link between personal freedom and representative government, as well as their experience with threats to liberty. The First Amendment protects expression—in speech, press, assembly, petition, and religion—and guards against a union of church and state. The Second Amendment secures liberty against national tyranny by affirming the self-defense of the states. Members of state-authorized local militia—citizens primarily, soldiers occasionally—retained a right to bear arms. The ban in the Third Amendment on forcibly quartering troops in houses reflects the emphasis the framers placed on the integrity and sanctity of the home.

Other provisions in the Fourth, Fifth, Sixth, Seventh, and Eighth Amendments safeguard freedom by setting forth standards that government must follow in administering the law, especially regarding persons accused of crimes. The framers knew firsthand the dangers that government-as-prosecutor could pose to liberty. Even today, authoritarian regimes in other lands routinely use the tools of law enforcement—arrests, searches, detentions, as well as trials—to squelch peaceful political opposition. Limits in the Bill of Rights on crime-fighting powers thus help maintain democracy by demanding a high level of legal scrutiny of the government's practices.

In addition, one clause in the Fifth Amendment forbids the taking of private property for public use without paying the owner just compensation and thereby limits the power of eminent domain, the authority to seize a person's property. Along with taxation and conscription, eminent domain is one of the most awesome powers any government can possess.

The Ninth Amendment makes sure that the listing of some rights does not imply that others necessarily have been abandoned. If the Ninth Amendment offered reassurances to the people, the Tenth Amendment was designed to reassure the states that they or the people retained those powers not delegated to the national government. Today, the Tenth Amendment is a reminder of the integral role states play in the federal plan of union that the Constitution ordained.

Despite this legacy of freedom, however, we Americans today sometimes wonder about the origin, development, meaning, and future of our liberties. This concern is entirely understandable, because liberty is central to the idea of what it means *to be American*. In this way, the United States stands apart from virtually every other nation on earth. Other countries typically define their national identities through a common ethnicity, origin, ancestral bond, religion, or history. But none of these accounts for the American identity. In terms of ethnicity, ancestry, and religion, the United States is the most diverse place on earth. From the beginning, America has been a land of immigrants. Neither is there a single historical experience to which all current citizens can directly relate: someone who arrived a decade ago from, say, Southeast Asia and was naturalized as a citizen only last year is just as much an American as someone whose forebears served in General George Washington's army at Valley Forge during the American War of Independence (1776–1783). In religious as in political affairs, the United States has been a beacon to those suffering oppression abroad: "the last, best hope of earth," Abraham Lincoln said. So, the American identity is ideological. It consists of faith in the value and importance of liberty for each individual.

Nonetheless, a longstanding consensus among Americans on the *principle* that individual liberty is essential, highly prized, and widely shared hardly assures agreement about liberty *in practice.* This is because the concept of liberty, as it has developed in the United States, has several dimensions.

First, there is an unavoidable tension between liberty and restraint. Liberty means freedom: we say that a person has a "right" to do this or that. But that *right* is meaningless unless there is a corresponding *duty* on the part of others (such as police officers and elected officials) not to interfere. Thus, protection of the liberty of one person necessarily involves restraints imposed on someone else. This is why we speak of a *civil* right or a *civil* liberty: it is a claim on the behavior of another that is enforceable through the legal process. Moreover, some degree of order (restrictions on the behavior of all) is necessary if everyone's liberties are to be protected. Just as too much order crushes freedom, too little invites social chaos that also threatens freedom. Determining the proper balance between freedom and order, however, is more easily sought than found. "To make a government requires no great prudence," declared English statesman and political philosopher Edmund Burke in 1790. "Settle the seat of power; teach obedience; and the work is done. To give freedom is still more easy. It is not necessary to guide; it only requires to let go the rein. But to form a *free government;*

that is, to temper together these opposite elements of liberty and restraint in one consistent work, requires much thought; deep reflection; a sagacious, powerful, and combining mind."

Second, the Constitution does not define the freedoms that it protects. Chief Justice John Marshall once acknowledged that the Constitution was a document "of enumeration, and not of definition." There are, for example, lists of the powers of Congress in Article I, or the rights of individuals in the Bill of Rights, but those powers and limitations are not explained. What is the "freedom of speech" that the First Amendment guarantees? What are "unreasonable searches and seizures" that are proscribed by the Fourth Amendment? What is the "due process of law" secured by both the Fifth and Fourteenth Amendments? Reasonable people, all of whom favor individual liberty, can arrive at very different answers to these questions.

A third dimension—breadth—is closely related to the second. How widely shared is a particular freedom? Consider voting, for example. One could write a political history of the United States by cataloging the efforts to extend the vote or franchise to groups such as women and nonwhites that had been previously excluded. Or consider the First Amendment's freedom of speech. Does it include the expression of *all* points of view or merely *some*? Does the same amendment's protection of the "free exercise of religion" include all faiths, even obscure ones that may seem weird or even irritating? At different times questions like these have yielded different answers.

Similarly, the historical record contains notorious lapses. Despite all the safeguards that are supposed to shore up freedom's foundations, constitutional protections have sometimes been worth the least when they have been desperately needed. In our history the most frequent and often the most serious threats to freedom have come not from people intent on throwing the Bill of Rights away outright but from well-meaning people who find the

Bill of Rights a temporary bother, standing in the way of some objective they want to reach.

There is also a question that dates to the very beginning of American government under the Constitution. Does the Constitution protect rights not spelled out in, or fairly implied by, the words of the document? The answer to that question largely depends on what a person concludes about the source of rights. One tradition, reflected in the Declaration of Independence, asserts that rights predate government and that government's chief duty is to protect the rights that everyone naturally possesses. Thus, if the Constitution is read as a document designed, among other things, to protect liberty, then protected liberties are not limited to those in the text of the Constitution but may also be derived from experience, for example, or from one's assessment of the requirements of a free society. This tradition places a lot of discretion in the hands of judges, because in the American political system, it is largely the judiciary that decides what the Constitution means. Partly due to this dynamic, a competing tradition looks to the text of the Constitution, as well as to statutes passed consistent with the Constitution, as a *complete* code of law containing *all* the liberties that Americans possess. Judges, therefore, are not free to go outside the text to "discover" rights that the people, through the process of lawmaking and constitutional amendment, have not declared. Doing so is undemocratic because it bypasses "rule by the people." The tension between these two ways of thinking explains the ongoing debate about a right to privacy, itself nowhere mentioned in the words of the Constitution. "I like my privacy as well as the next one," once admitted Justice Hugo Black, "but I am nevertheless compelled to admit that government has a right to invade it unless prohibited by some specific constitutional provision." Otherwise, he said, judges are forced "to determine what is or is not constitutional on the basis of their own appraisal of what laws are unwise or unnecessary." Black thought that was the job of elected legislators who would answer to the people.

Fifth, it is often forgotten that at the outset, and for many years afterward, the Bill of Rights applied only to the national government, not to the states. Except for a very few restrictions, such as those in section 10 of Article I in the main body of the Constitution, which expressly limited state power, states were restrained only by their individual constitutions and state laws, not by the U.S. Bill of Rights. So, Pennsylvania or any other state, for example, could shut down a newspaper or barricade the doors of a church without violating the First Amendment. For many in the founding generation, the new central government loomed as a colossus that might threaten liberty. Few at that time thought that individual freedom needed *national* protection against *state* invasions of the rights of the people.

The first step in removing this double standard came with ratification of the Fourteenth Amendment after the Civil War in 1868. Section 1 contained majestic, but undefined, checks on states: "*No State* shall make or enforce any law which shall abridge the privileges or immunities of citizens of the United States; nor shall any *State* deprive any person of life, liberty, or property, without due process of law; nor deny to any person with in its jurisdiction the equal protections of the laws" (emphasis added). Such vague language begged for interpretation. In a series of cases mainly between 1920 and 1968, the Supreme Court construed the Fourteenth Amendment to include within its meaning almost every provision of the Bill of Rights. This process of "incorporation" (applying the Bill of Rights to the states by way of the Fourteenth Amendment) was the second step in eliminating the double standard of 1791. State and local governments became bound by the same restrictions that had applied all along to the national government. The consequences of this development scarcely can be exaggerated because most governmental action in the United States is the work of state and local governments. For instance, ordinary citizens are far more likely to encounter a local police officer than an agent of the Federal Bureau of Investigation or the Secret Service.

A sixth dimension reflects an irony. A society premised on individual freedom assumes not only the worth of each person but citizens capable of rational thought, considered judgment, and measured actions. Otherwise democratic government would be futile. Yet, we lodge the most important freedoms in the Constitution precisely because we want to give those freedoms extra protection. "The very purpose of a Bill of Rights was to . . . place [certain subjects] beyond the reach of majorities and officials and to establish them as legal principles to be applied by the courts," explained Justice Robert H. Jackson. "One's right to life, liberty, and property, to free speech, a free press, freedom of worship and assembly, and other fundamental rights may not be submitted to vote; they depend on the outcome of no elections." Jackson referred to a hard lesson learned from experience: basic rights require extra protection because they are fragile. On occasion, people have been willing to violate the freedoms of others. That reality demanded a written constitution.

This irony reflects the changing nature of a bill of rights in history. Americans did not invent the idea of a bill of rights in 1791. Instead it drew from and was inspired by colonial documents such as the Pennsylvania colony's Charter of Liberties (1701) and the English Bill of Rights (1689), Petition of Right (1628), and Magna Carta (1215). However, these early and often unsuccessful attempts to limit government power were devices to protect the many (the people) from the few (the English Crown). With the emergence of democratic political systems in the eighteenth century, however, political power shifted from the few to the many. The right to rule belonged to the person who received the most votes in an election, not necessarily to the firstborn, the wealthiest, or the most physically powerful. So the focus of a bill of rights had to shift too. No longer was it designed to shelter the majority from the minority, but to shelter the minority from the majority. "Wherever the real power in a Government lies, there is the danger of oppression," commented Madison in his exchange of letters with Jefferson in 1788. "In our Government, the real power lies in the majority of the Community, and the invasion of private rights is *chiefly* to be apprehended, not from acts of government contrary to the sense of its constituents, but from acts in which the Government is the mere instrument of the major number of the Constituents."

Americans, however, do deserve credit for having discovered a way to enforce a bill of rights. Without an enforcement mechanism, a bill of rights is no more than a list of aspirations: standards to aim for, but with no redress other than violent protest or revolution. Indeed this had been the experience in England with which the framers were thoroughly familiar. Thanks to judicial review—the authority courts in the United States possess to invalidate actions taken by the other branches of government that, in the judges' view, conflict with the Constitution—the provisions in the Bill of Rights and other constitutionally protected liberties became judicially enforceable.

Judicial review was a tradition that was beginning to emerge in the states on a small scale in the 1780s and 1790s and that would blossom in the U.S. Supreme Court in the nineteenth and twentieth centuries. "In the arguments in favor of a declaration of rights," Jefferson presciently told Madison in the late winter of 1789 after the Constitution had been ratified, "you omit one which has great weight with me, the legal check which it puts into the hands of the judiciary." This is the reason why each of the volumes in this series focuses extensively on judicial decisions. Liberties have largely been defined by judges in the context of deciding cases in situations where individuals thought the power of government extended too far.

Designed to help democracy protect itself, the Constitution ultimately needs the support of those—the majority—who endure its restraints. Without sufficient support among the people, its freedoms rest on a weak foundation. The earnest hope of *America's Freedoms* is that this series will offer Americans a renewed appreciation and understanding of their heritage of liberty.

Yet there would be no series on America's freedoms without the interest and support of Alicia Merritt at ABC-CLIO. The series was her idea. She approached me originally about the series and was very adept at overcoming my initial hesitations as series editor. She not only helped me shape the particular topics that the series would include but also guided me toward prospective authors. As a result, the topic of each book has been matched with the most appropriate person as author. The goal in each instance as been to pair topics with authors who are recognized teachers and scholars in their field. The results have been gratifying. A series editor could hardly wish for authors who have been more cooperative, helpful, and accommodating.

Donald Grier Stephenson, Jr.

PREFACE AND ACKNOWLEDGMENTS

Voting and elections are America's political pastime. Congressional elections occur in every even-numbered year, with all seats in the House of Representatives and approximately one-third of those in the Senate at stake. Presidential elections happen every four years. No year goes by without elections for state and local offices in at least some regions of the country. Superimposed over this beehive of vote-seeking and vote-casting is another frenzy of activity: party primaries, those intra-party contests that select the candidates who contend against each other in the general elections. The pace is feverish and exhausting. Moreover, predictions about the next election begin to be heard almost as soon as the votes in the last election have been counted. For an outside observer, the American way of conducting political business must seem perplexing. A closer look reveals that this pattern flows from choices embodied in the U.S. Constitution and national statutes, plus the laws and constitutions of the fifty states.

Candidates and their campaigns may be fascinating and sometimes even amusing, yet voting and elections are serious business. They are the most tangible and direct means to achieve what the Declaration of Independence called government by "the consent of the governed." It is through the ballot that Americans confer, withhold, or withdraw their consent as to those who govern them. In democracies voting and elections are the principal media for the acquisition and retention of political power.

To some twenty-first century readers, it may come as a surprise to learn that this right to confer, withhold, or withdraw consent—the bedrock device by which the people attempt to control their government—does not belong to everyone, not even to all adults. It never has. The right to vote is a *selective* right because it does not apply universally across the population. In this sense the right to cast a ballot is different from other rights Americans enjoy. For example, everyone in the United States possesses the freedom of speech and the free exercise of religion that are guarded against government interference by the First Amendment in the Constitution. To be sure, there has been unequal enforcement of those guarantees, just as there has long been much debate over exactly what those freedoms encompass and the circumstances in which they may be enjoyed. Still, in the eyes of the law all adults—citizens and non-citizens alike—benefit equally from whatever those freedoms are determined by the courts to mean at any given time. The same has been true of the Fourth Amendment's guarantee of "the right of the people to be secure in their persons, houses, papers, and effects, against unreasonable searches and seizures," or of the Sixth Amendment's assurance that "in all criminal prosecutions, the accused shall . . . have the Assistance of Counsel for his defence." It would have seemed odd during most periods of American history to say that men were entitled to religious freedom but that women were not, or that those with a lot of property were entitled to speak their mind about public affairs but that those with little or no property could be jailed for saying the same thing. For voting, however, such inclusions and exclusions were for a long time the rule, not the exception. Even today, while one's mere presence in the United States places an individual under the umbrella of a host of constitutional safeguards and enablements, the right to vote is not necessarily among them. This is why access to the ballot—called suffrage or the franchise—was not always discussed in terms of a "right" at all. Rather, people spoke of suffrage or the franchise in terms of the *privilege* of voting. Voting was not seen as concomitant with one's humanity or even with citizenship, as was true with many other rights. Instead, access to the ballot was *conferred* on, or given to, an individual by those who already possessed it. The Declaration of Independence spoke of individuals as having been "endowed by their Creator with certain unalienable Rights, that among these are Life, Liberty and the pursuit of Happiness." It did not mention voting. Being able to vote was instead a sign of a special kind of citizenship. Having the franchise was like flying first class or holding membership in an exclusive club.

One of the reasons for this selectivity has been historical: we were launched as a nation with a restricted franchise (although by standards of the day it was enormously generous). In that magic political moment of 1776 when the thirteen colonies declared their independence from Great Britain and established the United States, Americans did not invent the idea of voting. Along with many laws, procedures, and institutions, they inherited voting from England. To one extent or another, voting had been part of the experience with self-government in every colony. But access to the ballot both before and immediately after 1776 was narrow. Most African Americans were excluded from the polls because they were slaves; white women were excluded as well. Among men, only those who possessed a freehold (property worth or yielding a certain amount) or who paid a certain amount in taxes were deemed part of the electorate. Thus the story of voting rights over the course of the past 230 years has been the enlargement of the franchise—making it more rather than less inclusive—albeit with some notable stops, starts, and backsliding along the way.

A second reason for this selectivity is the Constitution itself and the structural principle of federalism that the Constitution contains. At the beginning, the Constitution of 1787 left the definition of the franchise entirely in the hands of the states, even in the case of elections for members of the House of Representatives (the only branch of the national government initially to be filled directly by "the people"). States were thus free from the outset to define the franchise for themselves: no state was subject to voting rules imposed by other states. One state might retain a substantial property qualification for voting; a neighboring state might abolish it altogether. Subsequent modifications by constitutional amendment, and much later by statute, to this practice came by way of limitations on state power, as happened with respect to race, gender, and age. Even today, all elections are administered by state and local governments, whether for county sheriff, school directors, governor, U.S. senator, or president of the United States. Voting and election law in the United States now consists of a bewildering myriad of state and national rules overlaid by a variety of local customs and practices.

The historical anomaly whereby the Constitution initially left the definition of the franchise entirely in the hands of the states was probably a wise tactical decision at the time: it avoided one more obstacle to ratification of the document in 1787 and 1788. But it also demonstrates a positive aspect of the principle of selectivity. Until 1870, removal of barriers to voting was entirely a function of decisions made at the state level. Because each state was free to set its own voting requirements, one state could foster a more inclusive franchise than its neighbor. Had the Constitution of 1787 embodied a definition of the franchise for the nation, it would doubtless have been a restrictive one, and the familiar hurdles to amending the federal Constitution would probably have retarded any relaxation for a very long time. One fourth of the states plus one could have prevented any change whatsoever. Thus the Constitution's complete deferral of the franchise to the states not only allowed states to maintain a narrow franchise but permitted them to enlarge it if they chose, as some surely did, allowing some states to become "political laboratories" or, in James Van Orden's phrasing, political "trailblazers" for their neighbors.

Partisanship—the American system of political parties that developed early in the nation's history—is a third element in the equation of selectivity. Legislators elected on partisan ballots have been responsible for defining the franchise and for writing election laws across the broad sweep of national history. Moreover, in contrast to some other democratic countries, elections in the United States are commonly conducted and overseen by officials usually elected themselves on partisan ballots. Thus there has been a link nearly from the beginning between the outcome of elections (power) and the franchise (those entitled to vote). Indeed, expansion or contraction or maintenance of the franchise at certain points has sometimes occurred precisely because of the perceived advantage or disadvantage that might adhere to one political party or another.

Arguments on the merits, pro or con, as to those who should be allowed to vote have also shaped the pattern of selectivity. Throughout this book, readers will find references to a person's having a valid "stake in society" or "independent will" or being "independent." Emphasis on such qualities usually tilted the voting rights debate away from an expanded franchise. On the other side was the dynamic of the basic American ideology from the Revolutionary era: government by the consent of the governed. Also in play on the expansion side was the example or the prospect of military service: those who risked their lives for the defense of the nation, so the argument went, had earned the right to have a say in its affairs and in the selection of those who made the decisions about peace and war. From one era to the next, similar questions surfaced and were tossed about: why would one favor a narrow franchise over a broad one, or a broad franchise over a narrow one? What were the benefits and risks of each? Were qualifications for voting to be relaxed a little, would any principled way survive to distinguish between those who should, and should not, vote? These are important questions because the answers given to them have helped to determine the allocation of political power. That is profoundly what the franchise is: voting gives one a say in deciding who governs. It is no cause for wonder, therefore, why some who possessed the vote were reluctant to grant the same privilege to others; it is also no cause for wonder why many people who at various periods lacked the vote worked tirelessly to win it. (As with so many parts of the voting rights story, however, there are exceptions to this generalization about the disfranchised, as illustrated by the many women who organized and joined *anti*suffrage societies in the late nineteenth and early twentieth centuries.) Elected officials, if they are responsive at all, respond to those who vote.

Understanding the link between voting and power is the reason why we should discount statements by political candidates to the effect that they want "all Americans to vote." They want no such thing. They want all Americans who favor them to vote, not those who favor the opposition. Candidates who organize get-out-the-vote drives therefore do so very carefully and selectively. They would smile inwardly were a fog-like mood of voter apathy to envelope those individuals inclined to cast ballots for the other side. I had a glimpse of this political truth as a ten-year-old soon after my first dabbling in citizen politics. The Cub Scouts of Pack 58 in Covington, Georgia, were pressed into service for a get-out-the-vote drive in 1952. With brochures in hand urging people to vote, we went from house to house, door to door. We were thorough, or at least as thorough as ten-year-old boys could be on the two Saturdays before November's Election Day. Indeed, apparently we were too thorough. I later learned that our pack leader (*akela* in Cub Scout—and Kipling—nomenclature) had been admonished by the clerk of superior court (the reputed Democratic "boss" in Newton County) because we cubs had also distributed the brochures in the "wrong" part of town.

The interplay of these elements, forces, and factors and the individuals involved with them have guided the development of the right to vote in the United States. That development is the subject of this book and is suggested by the Preamble of the Constitution itself. It opens with the august declaration "We the people of the United States." Who are "We the people"? Which persons have been fully admitted to the political community called "the people of the United States"? The voting rights story is at heart an account of a changing understanding of those words.

The story unfolds in four chapters. Chapter One provides essential theoretical and institutional background in explaining why it makes a difference how the franchise in a country is defined. It seeks to connect voting and elections with the essence of democratic government, particularly in the context of the republican government that the Constitution established. "Democracy," said President Ronald Reagan at Normandy in 1984, "is worth dying for, because it's the most deeply honorable form of government ever devised by man." Yet American notions of what suffices as democracy have changed over the decades, and with it the right to vote.

Chapter Two opens during the English Civil War in the 1640s—significantly a time when some of the English colonies in North America were being settled—and the debates at Putney that occurred within the ranks of Oliver Cromwell's army. These exchanges provide a window into contending ideas that were shaping people's thinking about voting rights, thinking that later influenced the voting rights debate on this side of the Atlantic Ocean. For some very definite reasons, some argued for a restricted franchise; for reasons just as definite, others advocated an expanded franchise that would include virtually all adult males. The focus of the chapter shifts to the franchise in the American colonies on the eve of the Revolution and then among the American states in its aftermath. What happened roughly over the next seven decades was a relaxation or abolition of property qualifications in one state after the other, so that by the middle of the nineteenth century almost all white adult males in the United States were eligible to vote. Amazingly, close attention to debates across this period from 1647 to 1850 yields a catalog of nearly every argument that has been used either for or against expansion of voting rights in the last century and a half. We also begin to gain a sense of the circumstances and factors that typically have encouraged expansion of the franchise and those that have retarded it.

The chronicle of voting rights before the Civil War was largely about which white men would have access to the ballot, but Chapter Two also explores the two voting rights episodes that dominated much of the second half of the nineteenth century. The northern victory in the Civil War resulted not only in the abolition of slavery but in the attempt to absorb all blacks into the American political community, first by conferring national and state citizenship upon them (by way of the Fourteenth Amendment in 1868) and by removing race as a qualification for voting (through the Fifteenth Amendment in 1870). These ambitious undertakings were only partly successful: by century's end most blacks in the South (the region of the country where most blacks lived) had the recently tendered right to vote snatched from their hands. The second episode involved the initial steps to achieve female suffrage. Born in the 1840s, the movement acquired momentum immediately after the Civil War, only to fall short of its objective: a constitutional amendment conferring the vote on women. By century's end, where the chapter concludes, women had won full or partial voting victories in a handful of states and territories but still remained legally uncounted among "We the people" everywhere else.

Chapter Three surveys voting rights developments in the twentieth century. There was first the monumental and swift conclusion to the struggle over female suffrage that climaxed in 1920 with ratification of the Nineteenth Amendment. The right of women, white ones at least, to vote thereafter ceased to be a contentious issue. Firmly securing the vote for African Americans, however, proved to be a different and protracted matter altogether. Especially in most southern states, the right to vote remained more promise than reality until the last third of the century—or about ninety-five years after the Fifteenth Amendment had officially removed race as a criterion for voting. Its promise was eventually realized only after enactment of the Voting Rights Act of 1965. This legislation came about as a result of a rare alignment of the political planets: Supreme Court decisions; partisan forces; presidential leadership; and defiant, violent, and half-witted actions by some state and local officials that were televised to the world. The third chapter also explores a parallel development that occurred about the same time as the revolution in voting rights for blacks: intervention by the federal courts into legislative apportionment and districting. The subject is linked to voting rights because apportionment and districting shape representation and largely determine how much one vote counts relative to another and what difference those votes can make. Contemporaneously, Americans re-thought the age at which a person could be formally allowed to join the national political community.

Chapter Four examines several new and continuing issues in voting rights. During the 1990s, legislative districting to enhance the voting power of African Americans (and occasionally Latinos) engaged the United States Supreme Court on a regular basis. In particular, attempts by the Department of Justice to enforce certain provisions of the Voting Rights Act led state legislatures to construct districts containing heavy concentrations of minority voters. This "packing" would then allow members of a racial minority to determine the outcome of an election in that particular district. Alternatively, if they remained a minority across several districts, their voting strength might be diluted. The validity of these "majority-minority" districts are still an issue after the 2000 census, and their ultimate legal status remains uncertain. The year 2000 also witnessed one of the strangest presidential elections in American history. Aside from controversy over the Supreme Court's intervention in the Florida vote dispute that effectively decided the election, the affair riveted the nation's attention, perhaps for the first time, not on who is entitled to vote, but on the nearly equally important questions of how elections are administered and how votes are counted. (National legislation in the 1990s had significantly expanded the pool of registered voters.) The result has been a series of efforts at both the state and national level to improve ballot design and to provide voting devices that more accurately record a voter's choices.

Finally, the chapter offers a reminder that thousands of Americans are still denied the right to vote in one way or the other. For example, consider the partly enfranchised District of Columbia, the only geographical entity on the American mainland where adult citizens have no vote for a U.S. senator or a voting member of the House of Representatives. And in the District and in most states of the union, there are millions of adult Americans who are temporarily or permanently disfranchised because of crimes for which they have been convicted and for which they have paid with their liberty. Each of these situations raises questions about voting rights, even if neither quite fits into the mold of earlier voting rights debates. Still, each merits attention by a nation that President Abraham Lincoln in 1862 called "the last, best hope of earth."

Chapters Five and Six support the preceding four. For convenient reference Chapter Five contains a series of alphabetically arranged entries on key persons, cases, and events in the voting rights story. Chapter Six reprints excerpts from key documents that are discussed in the preceding chapters. The remaining sections of the book are designed to complement the rest. A chronology of important voting rights events is followed by a table of cases that provides the legal citation to all cases mentioned in the preceding chapters. The annotated bibliography brings together all noncase sources, excepting only brief newspaper articles or editorials, that are referenced in the first four chapters. The bibliography concludes with an overview of resources on the Internet dealing with voting rights.

Throughout the book, emphasis within quotations is in the original unless otherwise noted. In the first four chapters, sources for noncase material such as books and journal articles are noted in brief author-date-page citations. Complete bibliographical data for these sources appear in the end-of-chapter references and in the annotated bibliography. To avoid cluttering the text with too many page citations, the many mainly brief quotations from cases that dot the chapters are identified only by the name of the case from which they were taken and by the year in which the case was decided. This system seems appropriate because the full citation for each case appears in the Table of Cases and because Supreme Court decisions are now readily available on the Internet. Anyone with access to the Internet can easily unearth a particular quoted passage by first locating the case through a database of Supreme Court decisions such as that provided by FindLaw. To access a case on FindLaw, first refer to the Table of Cases near the end of this book for the official citation for the case from the *United States Reports.* The number preceding the "U.S." is the volume number; the number following the "U.S." is the page at which the opinion begins. Next, enter the following Internet address into the web browser: http://laws.findlaw.com/us/000/000.html. (Note: the period following "html" is *not* part of the Internet address.) The volume number should then be inserted *in place of* the first trio of zeros, and the page number *in place of* the second trio of zeros. As an example, the official citation for *Grovey v. Townsend* is 295 U.S. 45 (1935). To access the case using FindLaw, go to http://laws.findlaw.com/us/295/45.html. When the case appears on the screen, use the find function (usually Control-F) to locate a particular passage by entering two or three key words.

Even though the book attempts to be as comprehensive as possible within the space available, no single volume of this length can allot adequate attention to every voting rights issue. The subject is too broad and multifaceted. Our traditions of federalism and localism offer ample exceptions for virtually every generalization. For example, as the second and third chapters demonstrate, racial discrimination has been a powerful impediment to voting in American history. In this context, both because of the length of time involved and the number of people adversely affected over those decades, *The Right to Vote* focuses mainly on the experience of African Americans. This emphasis, however, should not be construed to mean that other racial or ethnic groups have been free of discrimination. Far from it. Native Americans, Asian Americans, and Latinos, to name but three, have also confronted barriers at the polls in various ways and in various places.

There are also less obvious and seemingly more mundane factors that can have a practical effect on one's right to vote. A few of these, such as ballot design, type of voting device, and vote counting are covered in Chapter Four. Others, such as detailed attention to the location of voting places relative to population concentrations, are not. Similarly, there is little room in the book for a comparative perspective on the voting rights experiences of other countries. The campaign for woman suffrage, for instance, was not confined to the United States. Simultaneously, drives to extend the vote to women were occurring in other countries, some moving ahead of and some lagging behind events in this country. These codevelopments were significant because of the possibility they allowed for cross-fertilization: measures adopted in one place toward woman suffrage could be used in voting rights debates elsewhere.

With these and other limitations of coverage in mind, my hope is that the book will do more than to inform. I hope that the book will both spark an awareness of, and quicken, the reader's interest in the subject of voting rights itself, to look beyond the contents of this book to recurring questions about the ballot and about new ones sure to arise.

Moreover, there are issues related to voting rights that the book barely mentions or does not address at all. One of these is the fascinating question of voting behavior itself—why people do or do not vote and, for those who do vote, why they choose one candidate or party over another. Then there are the legal and institutional supports within the political system that allow voters to make meaningful choices at the ballot box. Chapter One briefly touches on some of these supports: free speech, a free press, and the rights of citizens to organize to achieve certain goals. The right to vote is worth little, after all, if there is no right to oppose those currently in power or to propose alternative ways of doing things or to propose doing new things altogether. Also important are the various state and party rules that determine who may vote in party primaries. Broad participation is encouraged by open primaries, which allow all voters to participate, but at a cost to party identity. Closed primaries, which limit voting to persons registered with a particular party, define eligibility far more narrowly, but at a cost to participation. And blanket and nonpartisan primaries offer even more variation and color campaign strategies accordingly. Voter access to primaries is fully a subject all to itself, and, except for discussion of the white primary, largely falls outside the scope of this book. The same is true for other related topics such as campaign finance regulation, the conduct of election campaigns, public opinion formation, and the impact of the news media and the Internet on voting. Their omission entirely from the book or relegation to a brief paragraph should not be taken as an indication that they are unimportant and unworthy of examination. Readers interested in pursuing such cognate subjects should turn to other works, including John H. Aldrich's *Why Parties?*, P. Michael Alvarez and Thad Hall's *Point, Click, and Vote,* Alan Abramowitz's *Voice of the People,*

Doris A. Graber's *Media Power in Politics,* Martin P. Wattenberg's *Where Have All the Voters Gone?,* Jeff Manza and Clem Brooks's *Social Cleavages and Political Change,* Thomas E. Patterson's *The Vanishing Voter,* and Steven E. Schier's *You Call This an Election?* Also pertinent are several volumes in the America's Freedoms series: Ken I. Kersch's *Freedom of Speech,* Robert J. Bresler's *Freedom of Association,* and Nancy Cornwell's *Freedom of the Press.* More information about these and other helpful sources may be found in the annotated bibliography.

No one comes to the end of even a modest undertaking like this one without the help of others, seen and unseen. The end-of-chapter references reflect the debt that I owe to prior scholarship. Those labors of others reveal the rich resources available to anyone exploring the many corners and angles in the development of voting rights in the United States. I am indebted as well to my students in courses on American government and constitutional law at Franklin and Marshall College. I can truly say that they have made it possible for me to say, on most days at least, that I enjoy going to work. They have been partners with me in a classroom dialogue on what democracy, American style, actually means.

For support and counsel throughout this project, I am indebted to Alicia Merritt, senior acquisitions editor at ABC-CLIO. The America's Freedoms series was her idea, and I have been honored to have developed the series and now to be able to contribute a volume. Certainly this book would not have been possible without her guidance and encouragement. My thanks also go to Lauren Arnest, whose skills as copy editor are reflected in the pages that follow. And no author survives very long without the assistance of a talented production editor. In my case, Melanie Stafford provided over many weeks the essential help necessary to convert a manuscript into a book. More than they realize, I also owe much to Robert J. Bresler, formerly of Pennsylvania State University but happily and more recently of Franklin and

Marshall College, to Richard A. Glenn of Millersville University of Pennsylvania, to Peter G. Renstrom of Western Michigan University, to James F. Van Orden of the University of North Carolina School of Law, and to Forrest D. Watson of SAIC. Each read sections of the manuscript and made helpful comments. The book is surely better because of them. Nonetheless, any remaining defects or errors or other sins of omission or commission are my responsibility alone.

Finally, I express my love (and thanks) to Ellen, my wife and best friend for thirty-seven years. Her patience, caring, and understanding have (as always) been invaluable. And, as usual, she is right.

Donald Grier Stephenson, Jr.
Lancaster, Pennsylvania

1

INTRODUCTION

The right to vote, or franchise, is an essential element of democracy. Some have called the right to vote "the first liberty" in that it is foundational for all other rights (Chute 1969). The denotation of those who have access to the ballot goes far in determining those persons who matter politically. A narrow franchise (or none at all) yields a political system where ultimate power is wielded by the few; a broad franchise yields a political system that allows ultimate power to be wielded by the many. Note, however, that the preceding sentence uses the word "allows" rather than "assures" or "guarantees." A broad franchise is the starting point for making sure that people have a firm grip on their government, but it is not the ending point. As will be seen, a broad franchise is a necessary and therefore important condition of democratic government but it is hardly a sufficient condition. Other elements must be in place as well, including (but not limited to) freedom to organize politically, institutions that facilitate political choice, a politically aware voting population, and, above all, citizens who vote.

Largely the handiwork of Thomas Jefferson, the Declaration of Independence of 1776 captured the core of democratic theory as it referred to "[g]overnments . . . deriving their just powers from the consent of the governed." In November 1863, as President Abraham Lincoln dedicated a national cemetery on the battlefield at Gettysburg, Pennsylvania, he restated the principle of consent as "government of the people, by the people, and for the people." However phrased, this founding principle begins with voting and a system of elections—the "dependence on the people" that James Madison in 1788 acknowledged in *The Federalist*, No. 51, as "the primary control on the government" (Brock 1961, 264). Through voting, "the governed" confer (or withdraw) authority on (or from) those who govern as the governed grant (or withhold) their consent. Voting is thus one of the key pillars of constitutional— that is, limited—government. If one of the objectives of constitutional government is the avoidance of absolute or tyrannical rule that would imperil individual liberty, voting allows the people to wield a potent check on power.

Yet, because voting empowers a majority, constitutional government ironically also requires limits on what a majority of the voters may do by way of the officials whom they elect. This was the foremost problem the framers faced "[i]n framing a government which is to be administered by men over men." As Madison continued to explain in *The Federalist*, No. 51, "the great difficulty lies in this: you must first enable to government to control the governed; and in the next place oblige it to control itself" (Brock 1961, 264). Otherwise, the rights of minorities are in danger. "Wherever the real power in a Government lies, there is the danger of oppression," he wrote in the same year in correspondence with Jefferson over the desirability of a bill of rights. "In our Government," he noted, "the real power lies in the majority of the Community, and the invasion of private rights is chiefly to be apprehended, not from acts of government contrary to the sense of its constituents, but from acts in which the Government is the mere instrument of the major number of the Constituents" (Mason and Stephenson 2002, 422). That "experience," he insisted, "has taught mankind the necessity of auxiliary precautions" (Brock 1961, 264); hence, the Constitution's chief structural characteristic: separate institutions (Congress, the presidency, and the judiciary) that share some powers through an intricate system of checks and balances, enabling power to counter power.

Furthermore, majorities are in flux. Groups that compose a majority today may be but a minority tomorrow. By imposing limits on what any majority may do and by dividing and juxtaposing power, constitutional government thus serves to protect the interests of all, majority and minorities alike.

THE CRITICAL POLITICAL MOMENT OF 1865

America's experiment in constitutional government met its severest test in 1861 when eleven states refused to accept the outcome of the presidential election of 1860. The result was the Civil War, which, as Justice Robert C. Grier wrote in its midst, "all the world acknowledges to be the greatest civil war known in the history of the human race" (*Prize Cases,* 1863). The conflict lasted four years and inflicted combined casualties on the Union and Confederate forces that exceeded 900,000. A political process designed to channel, manage, and contain conflict within the bounds of peaceful action utterly failed in coping with the sectionally and morally divisive issue of slavery.

After the guns of the Civil War fell silent in April 1865 at Appomattox Courthouse, Virginia, and at Durham Station, North Carolina, the United States encountered no shortage of dilemmas and problems. Among the most pressing was the one precipitated by the abolition of slavery: the insistence by many people that the political community of the reunited nation be redefined. The Preamble of the Constitution had declared that "We the people . . . do ordain and establish this CONSTITUTION." But exactly who were "We the people"? Who was included within the American political community?

The answers to those questions had long been indeterminate. The reason stemmed from certain omissions the framers made in the plan of government they devised at the Constitutional Convention in Philadelphia in 1787. Their objective was ambitious: to construct a system of government for the country that would replace the Articles of Confederation, which had proven inadequate for the exigencies that the new nation had encountered. Above all, the framers wanted to strengthen the national government by giving it the authority to tax and to regulate trade between the states, among other things. (Unofficially since its drafting in 1777, and officially since its adoption by all the states in 1781, the Articles had served as the governing charter for the United States. Members of its congress—there was no separate executive or judiciary—were elected by state legislatures. Thus under the Articles no direct electoral link existed between the people and the national government.) But the proposed Constitution that emerged from the Philadelphia convention still had to be ratified, and during the summer's proceedings that shaped it, ratification was never far from the forefront of the framers' minds. "It has been frequently remarked," wrote Alexander Hamilton in *The Federalist*, No. 1, literally as the state ratifying conventions began their work in the fall of 1787, "that it seems to have been reserved to the people of this country, by their conduct and example, to decide the important question, whether societies of men are really capable or not of establishing good government from reflection and choice, or whether they are forever destined to depend for their political constitutions on accident and force" (Brock 1961, 1).

The framers' "reflection and choice," however, avoided the potentially disruptive subject of deciding who could vote. Establishing a uniform policy for the nation might have thrown the convention into turmoil, given the variations in voting rights already in place in the former British colonies that in 1776 had become the thirteen American states. Most certainly such a policy would have endangered approval of the Constitution by the ratifying conventions in the states during late 1787 and 1788. As it was, because the Constitution already contained an ample number of provisions that opponents of the Constitution, called Antifederalists, could view with alarm, there seemed little point in handing them yet one more target at which they might take aim.

So, strangely enough for a new national political system founded on the principle of government by the consent of the governed, the Constitution established no national right to vote. The Constitution granted or denied the right to vote to no one. Instead, it entrusted the conduct of elections for congressional offices to the governments of the pre-existing states, subject to modifications that Congress might make. "The Times, Places and Manner of holding Elections for Senators and Representatives," declared Section 4 of Article I, "shall be prescribed in each State by the legislature thereof; but the Congress may at any time by Law make or alter such Regulations."

Moreover, those persons in each state eligible to vote for "the most numerous Branch of the State Legislature"—a right conferred not by Congress but by the legislature of each state—elected members of the U.S. House of Representatives, the lower house of Congress. These representatives were the only officials of the new national government directly elected by "the people." Until the Seventeenth Amendment mandated popular election of U.S. senators in 1913, state legislatures chose members of the Senate. Electors, "appoint[ed], in such Manner as the Legislature [of each state] . . . may direct," were to choose the president and vice president, as they continue to do today. Thus each state was left to define the political community for itself. Through its own laws, each state controlled access to the ballot not only for state elections but for national elections, too. Thus at the outset the American constitutional system enshrined what the Preface calls the principle of selectivity, that reflected both the influence of federalism and localism and the view that access to the ballot was to be conferred, not assumed. And states would be the entities who did the conferring.

As will be explored in detail in the following chapter, state laws during the first years of government under the Constitution generally, but with a few exceptions, limited the franchise to white adult males who owned at least modest amounts of property. By standards today, this was hardly a broad franchise. Yet it was the broadest franchise at the time in a world where examples of anything resembling republican—that is, representative—government were few and far between. Nonetheless, the effects of the earliest state voting laws were to exclude a sizeable majority of the adult population (white women, African Americans of both genders, and some white males) from the franchise. The next half century witnessed a change. States relaxed various barriers to voting so that on the eve of the Civil War, the United States had achieved nearly universal white adult-male suffrage. This democratization was fully consistent with American ideology that had emerged during the 1820s and 1830s. This in turn had been energized by President Andrew Jackson and his followers, who preached popular sovereignty and did battle against the privileged and moneyed elites. This process reflected the positive aspect of the principle of selectivity. Until 1870, removal of barriers to voting was entirely a function of decisions made at the state level. Because each state was free to set its own voting requirements, one state could foster a more inclusive franchise than its neighbor. Had the Constitution of 1787 embodied a definition of the franchise for the nation, it would doubtless have been a restrictive one, and the hurdles to amending the federal Constitution would probably have retarded any relaxation for a very long time. One fourth of the states plus one could have prevented any change whatsoever. Although the Constitution's complete deferral of the franchise to the states was a historical curiosity, it was probably not only a tactically wise decision at the time but in many respects a fortuitous step for the future.

Wars frequently set in motion revolutionary ideas, movements, and transformations or push to the forefront pre-existing ones. Proposals once deemed improbable, unreasonable, or even almost unthinkable may come to seem possible, reasonable, and worthy of discussion. The Civil War was no exception. Thus the critical political moment of 1865: The end of the war and ratification of the Thirteenth Amendment in December 1865 brought about the abolition of slavery. There were now some 4 million former slaves, some of whom had fought on the Union side during the war. These people stood on the verge of citizenship for the first time, a citizenship that would be conferred statutorily by Congress in the Civil Rights Act of 1866 and made more secure constitutionally by the Fourteenth Amendment in 1868. There were in addition 488,000 other persons of color, many residing in the middle Atlantic states, who had never been slaves or who had gained their freedom prior to the war. Nearly all of this group had also been barred from voting. Would the franchise now be redefined to include nonwhite males as well? Moreover, as they had in each war beginning with the Revolution, women in the most recent conflict had sacrificed and contributed to the war efforts of both North and South. Were they to continue to be denied the basic participatory right of voting?

Then there was a third group whose hold on a place in the political community appeared tenuous: immigrants, or the foreign-born. The industrial revolution demanded workers for factories, the construction of railroads, lumbering, and mining. Such opportunities were like magnets that drew unprecedented numbers of people to American shores. And the Civil War had only accelerated industrial and other forms of economic growth. But the most recent arrivals tended to come not from countries to which old-stock Americans traced their origins. Nor did many of the most recent arrivals share the same religious traditions as the old stock. Instead, they were more heavily Roman Catholic and, later, Jewish. Wholly aside from the question whether the franchise should be extended to women and to African Americans, such demographic and cultural changes posed a more fundamental question: Would the nearly universal adult male suffrage that was in place by the 1850s itself survive? The nativist and anti-Catholic "Know-

Nothing" movement (which came together briefly as the American Party) in the mid-1850s had expressed dismay over the political power exerted by the influx of newcomers and proposed various measures that would reduce their influence and even block them from the polls. By 1865 the Know-Nothings had vanished as an organized entity, but many of their ideas had not.

Into this mix was one additional change wrought by the Civil War. To a degree unknown in earlier American history, people began to think *nationally*. In 1865, for the first time the continued existence of the Union was no longer a subject for serious discussion. For decades before 1865, the survival of the American nation had overshadowed and colored nearly every national political issue for the president, the Congress, and even the Supreme Court. That era was now gone. "The Constitution, in all its provisions," declared Chief Justice Salmon Chase, "looks to an indestructible Union, composed of indestructible States" (*Texas v. White,* 1869). The precise balance between the authority of the national government and the states would remain unfixed, but the supremacy of the national government and the perpetuation of the Union were now assumed to be accomplished facts.

Furthermore, victory in the war had been possible only because of a vigorous harnessing of energies in the North and by the assumption and exercise of unprecedented powers by the national government. The idea of states' rights seemed linked to the defeated Southern cause and so, temporarily at least, was out of favor. And this tendency to speak of national solutions for national problems carried over to voting. Thus for the first time there were large numbers of people who argued that the national government should have a role in defining the franchise and, just as important, in protecting the right to vote.

President Lincoln had proclaimed a "new birth of freedom" in his address at Gettysburg in 1863. Even earlier, in a speech at Springfield, Illinois, on June 26, 1857, he had insisted that the promises of the Declaration of Independence established a "standard maxim for free society, which should be familiar to all, and revered by all; constantly looked to, constantly labored for, and even though never perfectly attained, constantly approximated. . . . Its authors meant it to be a stumbling block to all those who in after time might seek to turn a free people back into the hateful paths of despotism" (Basler 1953, vol. 2, 406).

Now American democracy truly found itself at a crossroads. In one direction lay maintenance of the status quo: a white adult-male franchise. In another direction lay a modified white adult-male suffrage with restrictions to bar or at least to discourage "undesirable" white males from voting. In a third direction lay an expanded franchise that included white women and African American men and women. Although the social, political, and intellectual ferment sparked by the Civil War and its conclusion gave great impetus to efforts to lead the country down the third road, decades would pass before so expanded a franchise became an accomplished fact. Even then, voting in America would retain influences from the second road as well.

Consider the Fifteenth Amendment, ratified in 1870, that formally removed race as a criterion for voting. It embodied a pledge that took decades to realize in practice. For example, some states soon developed ingenious devices to sidestep the Constitution. One of these—the grandfather clause—was not invalidated by the U.S. Supreme Court until the second decade of the twentieth century (*Guinn v. United States,* 1915). It typically exempted from a literacy test for voting all persons and their lineal descendants who had voted on or before January 1, 1866, a date that excluded virtually every black. Even more persistent than the grandfather clause was the white primary. The primary—an election *within* a political party to choose the party's candidates—took hold in many areas of the United States early in the twentieth century as a means of democratizing parties, by transferring the selection of candidates from party leaders to the party rank and file. In states where one party was dominant, as the Democratic Party was in southern states, the primary in effect became the election because Republicans by this time could mount only token opposition or no opposition at all in the general election. So even when blacks were allowed to vote in the general election, rules in some states barred them from voting in the primary, thus totally negating their influence on local and state races. Not until almost eight decades after ratification of the Fifteenth Amendment did the Supreme Court hold definitively that the right to vote free of racial discrimination, guaranteed by the Fifteenth Amendment, applied to primaries as well as general elections (*Smith v. Allwright,* 1944).

Nonetheless, as the 1960s began, no more than one in four eligible black persons in the South were registered to vote, and actual turnout for elections was considerably less than that. Moreover, those statistics masked wide variations within the region. In some places, voting by blacks was not that uncommon; in a few cities, such as Atlanta, black voters were sufficiently numerous to affect the outcome of local elections. In many other places voting by African Americans was practically nonexistent. Action on two fronts brought remarkable changes within a decade, allowing voting by blacks to approach rates comparable to that for whites. First came successful assaults on the poll (or head) tax, still in use in a few places, which discouraged the poor, especially blacks, from voting. The Twenty-fourth Amendment (1964) prohibited use of a poll tax in federal elections, and two years later the Supreme Court invalidated the tax as a requirement in state elections (*Harper v. State Board of Elections,* 1966). Second, the Voting Rights Act of 1965—the most important voter legislation ever enacted by Congress—largely overcame the more subtle ways in which African Americans had long been kept from the polls. Through measures such as federal oversight of elections and a ban on literacy tests, black voter registration by 1967 had doubled in Georgia, nearly tripled in Alabama, and jumped almost 800 percent in Mississippi.

In contrast, the female suffrage movement, dating from the 1840s, took longer to achieve formal voting rights but, once secured, needed no further protective legislation. In 1869, the Wyoming Territory became the first political unit in the United States to extend the vote to women, but others were slow to follow, especially because the Supreme Court had ruled that states could continue to bar women from the polls without violating the Fourteenth Amendment (*Minor v. Happersett*, 1875). By the end of the nineteenth century, four other states had fully enfranchised women. The Nineteenth Amendment did so nationally in time for the elections of 1920.

In retrospect, the critical political moment of 1865 seems in part both accomplishment and missed opportunity. An altered national mood about voting resulted in the first steps to include within the definition of the political community a whole class of people who barely a few years before had, in the eyes of the law, been a category of property at worst and an object of discrimination at best. Yet the ferment of the immediate post–Civil War era brought about far less change in voting than many thought achievable, thus keeping several generations of millions of Americans still well outside the boundaries delineating "We the people."

DIMENSIONS OF VOTING RIGHTS

By determining peacefully those who shall govern and by bestowing legitimacy on the decisions they make, voting and elections provide answers to crucial questions faced by any political system. Today, most agree that these goals are more easily achieved when the characteristics of an electoral system encourage a widely shared perception that it is both free and fair. That perception in turn is encouraged when an electoral system meets several standards: (1) a franchise and an access to the ballot that are more inclusive than exclusive; (2) an equality of votes so that no vote counts more than another; (3) and election outcomes determined by rules established in advance, with minimal cheating and fraud in the casting and counting of votes. Each of these in turn assumes a stable and secure voting environment where citizens can cast their votes without fear of violence or retribution and with confidence that their votes will be counted accurately. These assumptions have been made all the more poignant in light of threats by al Quaeda terrorists to disrupt the U.S. elections in 2004.

Standards for free and fair elections have not been static over American political history. Their evolution has reflected each generation's experience in grappling with the several dimensions of voting rights: the nature of political community, the latitude of lawful dissent, representation, and electoral structures and procedures. Each of these dimensions are explored to varying degrees in the remainder of this book.

Who May Vote

The preceding section and the chapters that follow demonstrate that suffrage, or access to the ballot, in America "has expanded slowly, grudgingly, and by compromising steps" (Porter 1971, vii). Deciding who may vote, therefore, is central to understanding voting rights. This is because voting is the medium for government by consent of the governed. Moreover, voting facilitates empowerment. Although the right to vote does not guarantee that a particular person or a group will have political influence, its permanent denial to a class of persons virtually guarantees their political impotence. Thus voting is a first step toward power. It also offers the enfranchised a platform from which to demand the protection of the government to safeguard their liberty, property, and personal security. Conversely, those denied the vote are at the mercy of everyone else.

Who May Run for Office

A second dimension of voting rights and political community—the right to stand for public office, or the right to receive the votes that others cast—is a corollary of the first. To the degree that classes of people are excluded from those designated as eligible to hold public office, the right to vote itself is diminished. The field of possible candidates—reflecting various perspectives, positions, and backgrounds—from whom voters may choose is narrowed.

Laws setting qualifications for public office in the United States, therefore, have had to balance two competing values. On the one hand, states have traditionally preferred an inclusiveness that has reflected the scope of the franchise in a given era. Those eligible to vote could also usually run for office. That is, once someone has met qualifications that might be imposed for age, residency, and citizenship, that person has had a right to try to gain access to the ballot so that his or her name might be considered by the voters. But not always. Pennsylvania's Constitution of 1776, for instance, required legislators to take an oath that they were professing Christians, a stipulation not imposed on voters themselves. The United States Constitution through its Article VI has always forbidden such a religious test for national office, and the Supreme Court held in 1961 that states were forbidden to do so as well (*Torcaso v. Watkins*, 1961).

On the other hand, the evolution of state election laws reflects the conclusion that it is wise to discourage an excessive number of candidates and political parties, even as most classes of adults themselves are deemed eligible to run. (The California gubernatorial recall election of 2003, with 135 candidates on the ballot was both an obvious and rare exception to that principle.) This is because parties aggregate and accommodate interests. The preference, therefore, has been for a governing majority that is formed by coalitions *within* a party, not a governing majority that depends upon coalitions *among* parties, as is the case today in many other countries, especially those with a parliamentary form of government. In the United States, election laws instead favor arrangements that increase the likelihood that the person who wins an election will win with a majority of the votes or at least with a substantial plurality, objectives less likely to be met with a multiplicity of candidates and parties.

These objectives can be achieved, for example, by requiring someone entering a party primary to collect a certain number of signatures on a petition, as well as by paying a filing fee, with the number of signatures and size of the fee often being higher for statewide offices and considerably lower for local races. This requirement signals that the individual already enjoys at least modest support in the electorate. The filing fee in turn helps to assure that she or he has not entered into the candidacy lightly or as a frill but is probably sufficiently serious about what is being undertaken. (And the fee may be applied to compensating the public or party treasury for the costs of the election or primary.) Similarly, to have its candidates' names placed on the ballot, a party may be required to demonstrate a modicum of preexisting support—whether through signatures on petitions or by the number of votes received in the previous election.

The fact that each state sets its own rules for a candidate's or a party's access to the ballot creates special burdens for anyone seeking the presidency as the candidate of a minor or "third" party—that is, any party in addition to the two major ones, such as the Republican and Democratic Parties today. Candidates must meet the ballot qualification rules in each state to be on the ballot in that state. This is an easy enough task for both major parties, but can be a daunting challenge for a third party. In the presidential election of 1924, for example, Robert La Follette, running as the nominee of the Progressive Party, did well in many midwestern and western states and received nearly 17 percent of all popular votes cast nationally, an unusually large share for a third-party candidate. However, because his name was not on the ballot in some states, millions of Americans were denied the right to cast a vote for him. Consequently, his vote count fell far short of the total number he might have acquired.

Dominance by one or the other of two major parties over most of American history, however, has not confined voter choice as much as it might first seem. This has been true for at least three reasons: (1) the parties themselves have changed over time both in terms of their bases of support within the electorate and in terms of what they advocate; (2) minor parties, especially at the state level, have alerted the major parties to changing views among voters or potential voters; and (3) any policy put into effect by the ruling party may be subject to constitutional challenge in the Supreme Court.

Latitude of Lawful Dissent

Voting is a meaningless exercise without choice, and so another dimension of voting is the freedom of those seeking office or influence in an election to present choices to the electorate. An election without at least one plausible opposition candidate is a farce. Citizens opposed to those in power must also be allowed to publicize their views, to criticize policies, and to attract and organize supporters, as well as to run as opposition candidates. Free and fair elections are thus impossible to maintain where officials have authority to silence their critics. This may be a difficult lesson for any nation to learn, but it is an even harder lesson to put into practice.

Wide latitude has usually been accorded dissent in the United States, but notable exceptions demonstrate that liberties are sometimes in greatest danger when they are needed most. At different periods of American history, there have always been those who believed that the safety of the republic depended upon stamping out noxious views and ideas deemed dangerous. Examples range from the Sedition Act of 1798, which for three years criminalized scandalous criticism of the president or Congress, through suppression of abolitionist literature in the South and attempts to bar use of the Post Office everywhere by abolitionist publications in the 1850s, to enforcement of the Smith Act during the Cold War in the 1950s that criminalized advocacy of the violent overthrow of the government.

In contrast, others have asserted that security is best maintained through freedom. This has been the prevailing interpretation of the First Amendment's guaranties of free speech and free press since the 1960s. "Freedom to differ is not limited to things that do not matter much," wrote Justice Robert H. Jackson for the Supreme Court in 1943. "That would be a mere shadow of freedom. The test of its substance is the right to differ as to things that touch the heart of the existing order" (*West Virginia Board of Education v. Barnette,* 1943). Debate on public issues, advised Justice William J. Brennan Jr. in 1964, "should be uninhibited, robust, and wide-open, and . . . may well include vehement, caustic, and sometimes unpleasantly sharp attacks on government and public officials" (*New York Times Co. v. Sullivan,* 1964). In short, while government today may validly curtail inciteful speech when violence is imminent (*Brandenburg v. Ohio,* 1969), there is under the Constitution no such thing as an illegal *idea.* "If there be time to expose through discussion the falsehood and fallacies, to avert the evil by the processes of education," declared Justice Louis D. Brandeis in 1927, "the remedy to be applied is more speech, not enforced silence" (*Whitney v. California,* 1927, concurring opinion). Much later Justice Brennan echoed Brandeis in defending even the constitutional right to burn an American flag as an act of political protest: "If there is a bedrock principle underlying the First Amendment, it is that the government may not prohibit the expression of an idea simply because society finds it offensive or disagreeable" (*Texas v. Johnson,* 1989).

Just as important as explicit constitutional safeguards for free expression are restrictions in other provisions of the Bill of Rights. The framers knew firsthand the dangers that the government-as-prosecutor could pose to freedom. Even today, authoritarian regimes in other lands routinely use the tools of law enforcement—arrests, searches, detentions, as well as prosecutions—to squelch political opposition. Limits in the Bill of Rights on government's crime-fighting powers thus also help safeguard democracy.

Representation

Voting results in the selection of officials who act on behalf of the people. Voting thus forms the basis of republican, or representative, government. This link is most obvious in a state legislature or in the Congress where officials in their lawmaking role represent an entire state or part of a state called a district. The system of representation employed in a state or nation is important because it affects the allocation of power not only among geographical regions but among contending interests. In Congress, for example, the apportionment of senators set by the Constitution is two per state, while in the House of Representatives the apportionment by state varies according to population. Thus Wyoming, with hardly a half million residents, has exactly the same representation in the Senate as does California, with nearly 34 million residents. In the House, however, Wyoming has but one representative, while, as a result of the 2000 census, California has fifty-three. This plan—representation by political unit in one house and by number of people in the other—allows small states, as well as the interests they contain, to matter more politically than would be true were representation in Congress based entirely on population. The reverse is also true: the most populous states and the interests they contain matter somewhat less politically in Congress as a result.

State legislatures have the responsibility for creating their own legislative districts as well as the districts for the delegates from their states to the U.S. House of Representatives. The overwhelming preference in the United States has been for single-member districts—if a state sends ten members to the House, then the legislature carves the state into ten congressional districts, with one representative being elected by each district. If a state senate consists of fifty members, then the legislature carves the state into fifty senatorial districts, and so on.

Single-member districts may also greatly diminish the influence of a large political minority. This is because the drawing of district lines can be done to exaggerate or to diminish the strength of a party, a process called gerrymandering. If carried to an extreme and persisting for a period of years, the Supreme Court might find such arrangements a violation of the Constitution, but since the decision in *Vieth v. Jubelirer* (2004), judicial intervention now seems highly unlikely. Short of that, gerrymandering has been a time-honored, if not altogether savory, practice in American politics. This is why the election in the year of, or immediately following, a decennial census is especially important: the party that controls the state legislature at the dawn of the new decade draws the district lines for state legislative and congressional seats that remain until after the next decennial census. Americans usually perceive the partisan use of districting as unfair only if the same political party is advantaged again and again. As a happy counterbalance to the temptation to gerrymander, legislators are sometimes as interested in protecting incumbency (that is, assuring their own reelection regardless of party) as they are in securing partisan advantage over the opposition party.

However, as will be explained in more detail in Chapter Three, the Supreme Court long ago put an end to another districting arrangement that yielded substantial inequalities in representation. By the 1950s, noticeable numerical disparities among state legislative and congressional districts were commonplace in nearly every state. As people moved from farms to the cities and from the cities to the suburbs, districting did not keep pace. Some sparsely populated rural areas were more heavily represented than heavily populated urban and suburban areas. Incumbent legislators from less populated areas understandably were not eager to adjust representation so that it more approximately reflected population centers. The result was a pattern of representation that meant a person's vote was worth more or less—sometimes much more or less—than another's, depending on where that person resided within a state.

A series of decisions by the Supreme Court in the early 1960s invalidated such districting plans, requiring instead that all districting be done on a one-person, one-vote basis. That is, the number of people within a district must now be equal to the population of the state divided by the number of districts. Before the end of the 1960s, this new interpretation of the Constitution worked a revolutionary change in representation in the United States, transferring political power from rural to urban and especially to suburban regions. Such decisions brought the judiciary ever closer to the day-to-day operation of partisan politics. As Chapter Four explains, current controversies often turn on the use of majority-minority districts to enhance the representation of racial minorities.

Electoral Structures and Procedures

Wholly apart from outright fraud—"Vote Early and Vote Often" was for years the mantra of Chicago politics—electoral rules and practices may also affect what voting rights mean in practice. Consider voting impediments and vote counting.

One conspicuous fact about elections in the United States during the past several decades is the widespread phenomenon of nonvoting. (Voting in the United States is voluntary, not legally required as it is in some countries.) Even in high visibility presidential elections, voter turnout in recent years has hovered at or just above 50 percent. That is, fully half of the voting age population (almost all citizens over 17 years of age) does not vote. This rate contrasts with a turnout of about 65 percent—a modern day high—in the presidential election of 1960, when Democrat John F.

Kennedy eked out a narrow win over Republican Richard M. Nixon. Operationally, low turnouts can reveal surprising realities. For example, when President Bill Clinton won reelection in 1996 with 49 percent of the popular vote in an election in which the turnout was only 49 percent, he was the choice of slightly less than one quarter of those persons of voting age. In other words, three-quarters of the eligible electorate either voted for someone else or did not vote at all. Turnouts in midterm national elections and in state elections in odd-numbered years are typically even more dismal, often dropping to 25 to 45 percent. (Midterm elections are those held in even-numbered years not divisible by four. All members of the House of Representatives are subject to election every two years, as are one-third of U.S. senators.) Turnout in some primaries and elections for state and local offices may plummet into even lower double digits.

At the same time, as Chapter Four explains, there are millions of Americans of voting age who for different reasons are not eligible to vote. If one bases turnout rates on the pool of eligible voters, instead of the total number of persons of voting age, turnout rates are somewhat improved, even though the trajectory has still been generally downward (Patterson 2002). Yet, however they are cast, these percentages stand in sharp contrast to turnouts in the second quarter of the nineteenth century, as state voting laws quickly shifted toward universal adult-male suffrage. Some estimates suggest that as many as 75 percent of eligible voters or more routinely cast ballots (Rogers 1992, 3). Political campaigns were more like entertainment; voting then was truly the American pastime.

What has been responsible for the trend toward nonvoting? Factors such as a decline in a sense of civic and community obligation, voter apathy stemming from a perception that elections do not make a difference in one's life, and an increase in the percentage of two wage-earner households may depress turnout. Perhaps even excessive frequency of elections, particularly when they dominate the airwaves, may dampen interest. Primaries and/or elections of some kind take place in most states every year. Excessive frequency may not breed contempt, just yawns.

Recent campaigns have also been marked by heavy emphasis on negative direct mail and email, as well as negative thrusts via the Internet and through television, radio, and print campaign ads. Reliance by campaign managers on negativity points to a fundamental difference between those running campaigns and those selling products and services. Whether the total vote in an election is high or low is meaningless in the sense that elections do not normally require a certain turnout percentage in order for the results to be valid. Instead, what matters is a candidate's share of whatever number of votes are cast. But in commercial marketing, what matters is both share *and* the number of goods sold. This is why one rarely sees an ad for one make of sport utility vehicle depicting a rival SUV's tendency to roll over in a sharp turn and then burst into flames. That might depress the market for SUV's altogether. But in politics, if an ad sours voters on politics generally, that is not necessarily bad. What matters is the candidate's share of the vote, regardless whether the turnout is 60 percent or 30 percent.

It is also important to keep in mind that voting in the United States entails three different decisions. Aside from deciding to vote and deciding for whom to vote, the prospective voter usually must also have registered to vote ahead of time. Registration laws themselves were latecomers to American voting, being adopted by most states only after the Civil War. Prior to their introduction, prospective voters merely arrived at the polls with whatever documentation or witnesses that might be necessary to establish eligibility (Keyssar 2000, 151). In any event, registration even today may impede some voting because registration rolls usually close weeks before the election itself. Moreover, because registration is done by state and within states by counties, and within counties is organized by precincts, persons who have recently relocated almost always have to reregister or at least make sure, in advance of election day, that their existing registration has been transferred. So the mobility of the American population suggests that there is always a certain number of would-be voters who are kept from the polls because of registration requirements. As discussed in Chapter Four, recent experiments such as automatic registration, as when one applies for or renews a driver's license (the so-called motor voter plan), have increased the number of registered voters but do not seem to have improved turnout. Nonetheless, the fact remains that registration rules a half century ago were more stringent than is the case today, and voter turnouts were usually higher.

As for those who both register and vote, legal safeguards have been developed over the years to minimize error and to assure fairness in the counting of ballots. Voting means little if votes are not accurately counted. "The people who vote don't decide an election," Joseph Stalin, once premier of the old Soviet Union is supposed to have said. "The people who count the votes do." The chilling truth in those words is why the laws of all states provide for recounts in certain instances and permit the initial apparent loser to contest the election. Otherwise, doubts about the accuracy of the vote count might undermine public confidence in the integrity of elections and subtract from the legitimacy of the declared winner. As discussed in Chapter Four, no better example exists than the extended presidential election of 2000 that highlighted all too clearly problems that can arise in the usually mundane and unglamorous process of counting votes.

VOTING AND POLITICAL PARTIES:
LINKS BETWEEN THE RULERS AND THE RULED

Possibly no institution has both reflected and forged voting and elections in America as much as the political party. Defined as an organization that seeks to shape public policy by placing its members into positions of authority within the government, a party presents to the voters a slate of candidates who promise, if victorious, to translate the party's positions on issues into law and public policy. As they cast their votes, citizens thus choose among competing visions of the future as advanced by the parties. If parties function effectively, they promote popular government by enabling the electorate to make choices about the nation's future and by injecting responsibility into government. The notion of "the consent of the governed," after all, presumes an opportunity for voters to hold their rulers accountable. If parties are identified in the voters' minds with certain policies and proposals, parties become a kind of label or political shorthand, making it easier for the electorate to control government by rewarding or punishing candidates at the polls. In effect, parties may function as linkage institutions between the rulers and the ruled, the governors and the governed.

Parties have long been so ubiquitous on the electoral landscape that most Americans would have difficulty thinking or talking about politics and government for more than a few seconds without mentioning or thinking about parties. This is so even though political parties receive not a single mention in the Constitution, a fact that makes the party system the most remarkable extraconstitutional feature of the American political system.

The Constitution's official silence on the subject of parties was hardly accidental. Many of the framers of the Constitution, including James Madison and George Washington, actually feared political parties (or factions, as they sometimes called them). In a government in which ultimate political power lay in the hands of the people, they feared that a concerted and overbearing majority might run roughshod over the rights of a minority. Accordingly, one of the arguments advanced in support of the proposed Constitution was that the charter would minimize the influence of factions that might form in the new government. As Madison shrewdly explained in *The Federalist*, No. 10, "Among the numerous advantages promised by a well-constructed Union, none deserves to be more accurately developed than its tendency to break and control the violence of faction. The friend of popular governments never finds himself so much alarmed for their character and fate as when he contemplates their propensity to this dangerous vice" (Brock 1961, 41).

In his Farewell Address in September 1796, with embryonic national parties just beginning to churn around him, President Washington was even more direct. The "spirit of party," he warned,

> serves always to distract the Public Councils and enfeeble the Public administration. It agitates the Community with ill-founded jealousies and false alarms, kindles the animosity of one part against another, foments occasional riot and insurrection. It opens the door to foreign influence and corruption, which find a facilitated access to the government itself through the channels of party passions. . . . A fire not to be quenched; it demands a uniform vigilance to prevent its bursting into a flame; lest instead of warming it should consume. (Richardson 1917, vol. 1, 219)

His message, in short, was that parties were inimical to free government.

In spite of this aversion to parties, political groupings emerged early in American national history and have persisted. Indeed they were probably inevitable: if the right to rule rests on obtaining a majority of the votes, it comes as no surprise that rulers and would-be rulers form organizations to marshal votes and win elections (Aldrich 1995, 28–29). Moreover, some of the same devices built into the Constitution to thwart factions or parties, plus the practicalities of governing, actually encouraged their growth. The functional horizontal division of powers among the three branches of the national government and the vertical division of control between the national and state governments, combined with a large land area for which and over which public policy would have to be formulated and implemented, created hurdles for effective government right from the start. Parties soon formed to help overcome the fragmentation of authority caused by these divisions. Through parties, like-minded individuals could, by holding enough offices, move public policy in a common direction, giving concrete realization to the preferences of the voters. Thus one irony of the Constitution: a document crafted in part to minimize political parties could probably not have functioned successfully over any considerable period of time without them.

Like the nation itself, parties and voter preferences have changed over the decades to reveal as many as six major party "systems." These systems are periods "with characteristic patterns of voting behavior, of elite and institutional relationships, and of broad system-dominant decisions" (Burnham 1967, 289). Once parties were established, each party system evolved from its predecessor following a few years of political turmoil that is commonly termed "realignment" (see Table 1.1). In a realigning (or "critical") election, voters perceive a distinct difference between political parties that not only gives them a "choice" but shifts voters from the ranks of one party to another and hands control of most machinery of government—the presidency, Congress, and most state offices—to the victorious party for some span of years across several presidential terms. According to one of the classic studies of party change, realignments

> arise from emergent tensions in society which, not adequately controlled by . . . politics as usual, escalate to a flash point; they are issue-oriented phenomena, centrally associated with these tensions and more or less leading to resolution adjustments; they result in significant transformations in the general shape of policy; and they have relatively profound aftereffects on the roles played by institutional elites. They are involved with redefinitions of the universe of voters, political parties, and the broad boundaries of the politically possible. (Burnham 1970, 10)

26

Table 1.1 American Party Systems, 1789–Present

Party System	Period*	Defining Characteristics	Significant Minor Parties**
First	1792–1820	Competition between Federalists and Democratic-Republicans; Federalists do not run a presidential candidate after 1816.	n/a
Second	1824–1856	Democratic-Republican party is reshaped by Andrew Jackson into the Democratic party; opposed initial by National Republicans, then by Whig party	Anti-Masonic (1832); Free Soil (1848, 1852); Whig-American (Know-Nothing) (1856)
Third	1856–1896	Whig party disintegrates and is replaced by the new Republican party; after the Civil War, the era is defined by close competition between Democrats and Republicans for control of the presidency and the Congress.	Constitutional Union (1860); Southern Democratic (1860); Populist (1892)
Fourth	1896–1932	Competition between Democrats and Republicans continues, but, with only few exceptions, Republicans dominate presidential and congressional elections.	Socialist (1912); Bull Moose (1912); Progressive (1924)

| Fifth | 1932–1968 | As a result of the Great Depression, Democrats gain ascendancy and dominate almost all presidential and congressional elections. | States-Rights Democratic (1948); American Independent (1968) |
| Sixth | 1968–present | Era marked by close competition between Democrats and Republicans for the presidency. Divided government is the rule rather than the exception; except for six years of Republican control of the Senate (1981–1987), Democrats control Congress from 1968 until Republicans regain control of both houses in 1994 elections; Republicans maintain control in most subsequent years. | Perot/Patriot (1992, 1996) |

* Because the shift from one party system to another often occurred over several years, the dates shown here are approximate.

** Minor (or "third") parties receiving at least 5 percent of the popular vote in one or more presidential elections, and/or winning electoral votes in one or more presidential elections.

Party realignment is revolution, American style. Realignment may involve not only the major parties of the day but minor ones, too. Sometimes the latter have had a sizeable influence on one or both major parties, although only once has a new or third party displaced a major one altogether. Although there is not universal agreement on which elections qualify as realigning events, many scholars include the elections of 1828, 1860, 1896, 1932, and some count 1800 and 1968.

As depicted in Table 1.1, an initial grouping of political forces took shape by the late 1790s. In the first party system, Federalists combated Antifederalists, called Democratic Republicans by 1800 or just Republicans. By 1828, some years after disappearance of the Federalists as an organized party, the second party system featured clashes between Democrats (formerly called Republicans) and Whigs. The latter were the spiritual descendants of the Federalists; many Whigs had also comprised the short-lived National Republican Party. The second party system, as well as the Whig Party itself, dissolved by 1860 over the issue of slavery, and in its place for most of the rest of the century was an arrangement characterized by relatively close competition between Republicans and Democrats. Republican ascendancy, along with a significant alteration in the nature of the Democratic Party, marked the fourth party system from 1896 until 1932. The calamity of the Great Depression ushered in an era of Democratic rule in the fifth party system that persisted until 1968.

Compared to the fifth party system, the years since 1968 have presented no clear picture. A majority of voters, apparently tightly wedded to neither party, has entrusted the executive branch sometimes to one party and the legislative branch sometimes to the other, and only occasionally have both branches been firmly under the dominance of the same party at the same time. Some have called this recurring pattern of divided government "de-alignment." Hence there is a sixth party system in the sense that the pattern is one of inconclusiveness and stands in contrast to what prevailed in the fifth party system.

CONCLUSION

Voting in free and fair elections is essential in assuring the consent of the governed, the bedrock of democratic politics. Elections are at once both power- and legitimacy-conferring instruments, just as unfair and dishonest elections, or elections based on a narrow franchise, may cast doubt on any official's claim to office and diminish her or his ability to govern. The point of democracy, after all, "is the legitimacy of its judgments, not their unerring character" (Anders 2004, D-8).

Few argue that electoral politics in the United States is perfect. Over the years, some of its features have hindered, deflected, muted, or distorted the people's consent. Yet, for several reasons most Americans believe that overall their electoral system today meets at least minimal standards for fairness and honesty. For instance, with the noticeable and instructive example of the Civil War nearly a century and a half ago, elections in the United States operate effectively: by determining winners and losers they accomplish what elections are designed to do. Defeated candidates and their supporters willingly, if not cheerfully, defer to the victors and acknowledge their right to rule. This is no small achievement. Such acceptance presupposes an electoral system where ultimate values and interests are rarely, if ever, at risk. Few would voluntarily submit to an election in which their life or death, slavery or freedom, hinged on the outcome.

Moreover, lessons emerge from America's democratic experience that point to characteristics that are probably essential to the maintenance of a stable democratic process both here and abroad. First, access to the vote and the ballot should be widely available, with no vote worth more than any other vote. To restrict the political community on the basis of gender, political beliefs, ethnicity, or religion, for instance, undercuts any regime's legitimacy. An inclusive franchise, by contrast, encourages all elements of a society to perceive a stake in the existing order because each has a chance eventually to prevail. Second, encouraging high turnouts of voters in elections should be a priority. Low voting turnouts should be cause for concern, if not alarm. Not only may they result in election of officials without the support of a majority of the eligible electorate, but they exaggerate the influence of well-organized and intensely motivated interests. Third, restricting the perimeter of lawful dissent not only inhibits electoral politics by stifling opponents, but may drive dissidents from legitimate channels of political participation into violent means of protest. Fourth, elections and the system of representation must enable a majority of the people to control the government, yet safeguards must be in place to prevent a majority from overwhelming and destroying a minority. Nonetheless, arrangements that assign undue electoral weight to minority interests may frustrate a central element of consent of the governed: legislation that efficiently reflects the will of the majority. Otherwise, minority views displace those of the majority or so cripple the decision-making process that the government becomes incapable of acting at all. Fifth, because elections function effectively only if most people perceive them to be free and fair, procedures must be in place to respond quickly to allegations of voting irregularities. Without such remedial devices, electoral politics may quickly be perceived as a fraud.

"Democratic institutions are never done," observed future president Woodrow Wilson over a century ago. "[T]hey are like living tissue—always a-making. It is a strenuous thing, this living of the life of a free people" (Wilson 1893, 116). Voting and elections can promote the civic health of the polity. Yet, awareness of the flaws in an electoral system is as important as appreciation of its virtues.

References

Aldrich, John H. 1995. *Why Parties?* Chicago: University of Chicago Press.

Anders, George. 2004. "Common Knowledge." *Wall Street Journal,* May 25, D-8.

Basler, Roy P., ed. 1953. *The Collected Works of Abraham Lincoln.* 9 vols. and supp. New Brunswick, NJ: Rutgers University Press.

Brock, W. R., ed. 1961. *The Federalist.* New York: E. P. Dutton.

Burnham, Walter Dean. 1967. "Party Systems and the Political Process." In William Nisbet Chambers and Walter Dean Burnham, eds., *The American Party Systems.* New York: Oxford University Press.

———. 1970. *Critical Elections and the Mainsprings of American Politics.* New York: W. W. Norton.

Chute, Marchette. 1969. *The First Liberty: A History of the Right to Vote in America, 1619–1850.* New York: E. P. Dutton.

Keyssar, Alexander. 2000. *The Right to Vote: The Contested History of Democracy in the United States.* New York: Basic Books.

Mason, Alpheus Thomas, and Donald Grier Stephenson Jr. 2002. *American Constitutional Law: Introductory Essays and Selected Cases.* 13th ed. Upper Saddle River, NJ: Prentice Hall.

Patterson, Thomas E. 2002. *The Vanishing Voter.* New York: Knopf.

Porter, Kirk Harold. 1971 [1918]. *A History of Suffrage in the United States.* New York: AMS Press.

Richardson, James D. 1917. *A Compilation of Messages and Papers of the Presidents, 1789–1902.* 20 vols. New York: Bureau of National Literature.

Roche, John P. 1961. "The Founding Fathers: A Reform Caucus in Action." *American Political Science Review* 55: 799–816.

Rogers, Donald W. 1992. "Introduction—The Right to Vote in American History." In Donald W. Rogers, ed., *Voting and the Spirit of American Democracy: Essays on the History of Voting and Voting Rights in America.* Urbana: University of Illinois Press.

Wilson, Woodrow. 1893. *An Old Master and Other Political Essays.* New York: Scribner's.

2

ORIGINS

The search for beginnings, no matter how far pressed, usually serves only to open more distant vistas of earlier developments. Origins recede as historical inquiry advances; ancient beginnings tend to become but the proximate ends of remoter outposts. (Mason 1964, 3)

American thinking and laws about voting rights and elections have been no exception to this general rule. As important as were the ideas about consent of the governed enshrined in the Declaration of Independence and the Gettysburg Address, those wellsprings of American political thought have antecedents that reach into ancient and medieval times. Yet their immediate origins are probably more instructive and influential in understanding the shaping of the politics and policy that prevail today. These origins drew from widespread intellectual ferment in England slightly less than 400 years ago. Moreover, the timing of this political churning was propitious: the establishment of all but one of the original thirteen British colonies that became the United States of America in 1776 had been substantially completed, was underway, or was about to begin by the mid-1600s. Thus ideas in play in England sooner or later found their way to the east coast of North America. Consider the wide-ranging debates that occurred at Putney, near London, between October 28 and November 11, 1647.

THE DEBATES AT PUTNEY

Much of the seventeenth century was anything but a happy time in England. Armed conflict had broken out during the reign of King Charles I (1625–1649) over fundamental religious and constitutional questions. Variously arrayed on one side by 1642 were nobles and other supporters of the king, royal prerogatives, and episcopacy (that is, church polity dominated by appointed bishops). On the other side were gentry such as Oliver Cromwell who advocated the supremacy of Parliament and the abolition of episcopacy (and, for some, the substitution of the more egalitarian Presbyterianism in place of the latter). Charles surrendered in 1646, and he would lose his head, literally, in 1649.

With the parliamentary army thus victorious by 1647 in what historians of English history call the Civil War, Parliament attempted to disband its army without either appropriating funds to pay the troops or passing legislation to protect the political rights of the people. As evidence of the notions that were being shared not only by philosophers but by ordinary people, some rank-and-file soldiers came under the sway of militants called "Levelers," who believed that all men should be made politically "level" or equal. "Democratic religious ideas were yielding their fruit in political democracy" (Lunt 1957, 432). The Levelers had been unpersuaded by the "Declaration of the Army," a document addressed to Parliament and prepared by a moderate faction within the military. This declaration was drafted mainly by senior officers under the leadership of Commissary (Lieutenant) General Henry Ireton and contained more modest demands. To counter the declaration, and to proffer new foundations for liberty and authority, the radical elements composed the "Agreement of the People." Although it was never submitted to Parliament for consideration, Cromwell, Ireton, and other officers agreed to discuss the agreement with spokespersons from the ranks. The result was a wide-ranging give-and-take that highlighted both some consensus and highly divergent views. To one extent or another, every voting rights debate for more than 200 years afterwards echoed the debates at Putney.

Although both sides accepted the existence of a higher law embodying what they called "natural" or "native" rights, they disagreed over precisely what those rights were. Those rights were natural or native in that they derived not from the sovereign or the government but from the fact of one's humanity. Both sides also agreed that civil government was to be based on compact—an agreement among those to be governed concerning the laws by which they would be governed—even as they disagreed over the identity of those entitled to take part in making the compact. Finally, if to varying degrees, all recognized the sanctity of private property as basic to organized society (Mason 1964, 5).

One of the demands of the agreement called for equal electoral districts for Parliament and a nearly universal adult-male suffrage. And it was particularly over this latter point that the participants in the debates at Putney were most sharply divided. (The call for equal electoral districts would echo much later, especially at the Virginia constitutional convention of 1829–1830 and in the United States Supreme Court in the 1960s.) Ever since enactment of a statute in 1430, Parliamentary electors (those entitled to vote for a member of the lower house called the House of Commons) had been confined mainly to forty-shilling freeholders. (The functional division of Parliament between the knights and the burgesses, functioning as "the commons," and the nobility and ecclesiastical leaders, sitting as "the lords temporal and spiritual," seems to have been in place by the middle of the fourteenth century [Lunt 1957, 227–228].) This freeholder class included owners of land that produced at least forty shillings a year in rentals or other income, as well as certain equivalents. Also included were

lessees of land yielding forty shillings a year, but their leases had
to be of an indeterminate, not a specified, length. Thus under this
nomenclature, a freeholder was the owner (or sometimes the
lessee) of a freehold; property in turn qualified as a freehold when
it yielded a statutorily specified minimum income. Some merchants and others could vote if they lived in certain "open" boroughs (incorporated municipalities) and met a taxpaying qualification. But the overwhelming majority of male subjects had no
voice in the selection of members of the lower (and elected) house
of Parliament (Williamson 1960, 5).

Historians are not entirely sure of the reasons for the 1430
statute, but the theory of a suffrage based on freehold is consistent
with the emergence of the House of Commons as a separate part
of Parliament. Kings needed money to pay for the extraordinary
expenses of government, especially war. If landowners and others
with substantial incomes outside the nobility provided much of
the tax revenue, then it seemed reasonable to place selection of the
Commons in their hands (Williamson 1960, 6). Yet, whatever the
origins and justifications for the forty-shilling freehold in 1430,
when viewed alongside maintenance of this status quo more than
two centuries later, the agreement's call for abolition of the freehold requirement was plainly radical.

To this Commissary General Ireton objected. If the agreement
meant "that every man that is an inhabitant is to be equally considered, and to have an equal voice in the election of the representors [or representatives], . . . then I have something to say against
it. . . . I think that no person has a right to an interest or share
in . . . determining . . . the affairs of the Kingdom, and in choosing
those that shall determine what laws we shall be ruled by here, . . .
that has not a permanent fixed interest in this Kingdom." Being
born in England, he continued, was, without something else more
substantial, insufficient basis for such an interest. Instead, "those
that choose the representors for the making of Laws by which this
State and Kingdom are to be governed are the persons who taken

together do comprehend the local interest of this Kingdom, that is, the persons in whom all land lies, and those in Corporations in whom all trading lies." To convey political power to those with little or no property carried great risk, he warned. "If we shall go to take away this fundamental part of the civil constitution [the property-based franchise] we shall plainly go to take away all property and interest that any man has." If "one man must have as much voice as another, then show me . . . why," by the same principle of equality, "one man may not claim another's property as well?" Furthermore, Ireton observed, "those who shall choose the law makers shall be men freed from dependence upon others." That is, a narrow property-based franchise assured that those who chose the lawmakers would themselves be able to act independently, without undue pressure from others on whom they might otherwise be dependent (Firth 1891, 299–303).

"I confess [there is weight in] that objection that the Commissary General Ireton has insisted upon," added a Colonel Rich, "for you have five to one in this Kingdom that have no permanent interest. Some men [have] ten, some twenty servants, some more, some less." Therein lay a difficulty. "If the Master and servant shall be equal Electors, then clearly those that have no interest in the Kingdom will make it their interest to choose those that have no interest." Referring to elections in the Roman Republic, Rich reminded his audience that "the people's voices were bought and sold, and that by the poor, and thence it came that he that was the richest man . . . made himself a perpetual dictator." The risk was not the tyranny of the few over the many, but the tyranny of the many over the few. "[I]f we strain too far to avoid monarchy in Kings, [let us take heed] that we do not call for Emperors to deliver us from more than one Tyrant" (Firth 1891, 315).

"We judge that all inhabitants," retorted a Mr. Pettus, "that have not lost their birthright should have an equal voice in Elections." "Really," emphasized Colonel Thomas Rainboro, "I think that the poorest he that is in England has a life to live as the richest he, and therefore truly, Sir, I think it's clear, that every man that is to live under a Government ought first by his own consent to put himself under that Government. . . . I do not find anything in the law of God, that a Lord shall choose 20 Burgesses, and a Gentleman but two, or a poor man shall choose none. . . . But I do find, that all Englishmen must be subject to English laws, and I do verily believe, that there is no man but will say, that the foundation of all law lies in the people" (Firth 1891, 300, 301, 304).

What particularly troubled Rainboro and others was the justification for a narrow franchise. "I would fain know how it [the franchise] comes to be the property [of some men but not of others]." Presumably, military service itself demonstrated that many of the disfranchised in fact had a permanent "interest" in the affairs of the realm. "I would fain know what we have fought for, and this is the old law of England and that which enslaves the people of England that they should be bound by laws in which they have no voice at all." If Ireton stood fast on the importance of possession of a permanent interest, supporters of the agreement stressed the role of consent. "Every person in England has as clear a right to elect his Representative as the greatest person in England," insisted a Mr. Wildman. "I conceive that's the undeniable maxim of Government: that all government is in the free consent of the people. . . . And therefore I should humbly move, that if the Question be stated . . . it might rather be this: whether any person can justly be bound by law, who does not give his consent that such persons shall make laws for him?" (Firth 1891, 311.)

Yet even those aligned with the agreement believed that the franchise could not be truly universal among adult males. (No one advocated voting by women—that would have been unthinkable.) "I conceive the reason why we would exclude apprentices, or servants, or those that take alms," explained Pettus, "is because they depend upon the will of other men and should be afraid to displease [them]. For servants and apprentices, they are included in their masters, and so for those that receive alms from door to door" (Firth 1891, 342).

Thus, while the two sides accepted the revolutionary principle of government by consent, they differed markedly concerning those whose consent mattered. For most of the senior officers at Putney, only a substantial interest in the realm—a freehold—placed one in a position to give consent. For the more radical element, adult English males who were not paupers, apprentices, or (perhaps) servants possessed a sufficient interest to cast an equal vote with others by virtue of their birthright.

To be sure, the debates at Putney were influenced by certain realities, such as the material interests of the participants. But the participants also attempted to mesh ideas about voting with deeply held beliefs and values. That is, there was both a self-interested and an ideological component to the debates. A narrow franchise would naturally work to the advantage of those it encompassed; they would thereby be able more easily to preserve rights and privileges they already possessed. An expanded franchise would transfer considerable influence to the large majority of English males who in 1648 (and for nearly two centuries afterward) had no vote. And both the franchised and the unfranchised were well aware of the fact that any expansion of the franchise would come only at the behest of the former; the empowered few would have to be content with, and agree to, power sharing with the many.

Those who favored maintenance of a narrow franchise—and in early English usage, recall that the word *franchise* meant a privilege or immunity or entitlement that the government could grant at its pleasure—stressed the link between one's stake in society and the right to vote. Only those with sufficient property (usually defined as real estate) were judged to be sufficiently attached to the community and affected by the laws of the realm to have earned the *privilege* of having a voice in public affairs.

Coupled with this view was the understanding that the franchise could be entrusted only to those who were independent in some substantial way, that is, who possessed an independent will. This was, after all, the theoretical basis of the freehold. The freehold provided the independence, so that one's vote could not be dictated by another. The "independence" theory would thus partly explain why no one made a serious argument to include women in the franchise. Legally, a married woman was an extension of her husband and so was dependent on him. Yet the independence theory would not account for denying the vote to widows and other single women, any of whom even then could legally own vast amounts of property.

Moreover, the view that those with little or no property should not be allowed to vote because they possessed no independent will of their own was made alongside another, seemingly contradictory, claim. As the debates at Putney illustrated, the enfranchised propertied class feared that a newly enfranchised nonpropertied class would threaten the holdings of the former. That might be true, but the claim also would have to assume that the nonpropertied had too much (not too little) will of their own (Keyssar 2000, 10–11).

Those favoring a broad franchise typically rested much of their case on natural rights, which all possessed equally. A right to vote flowed from one's existence as a human being, not from the property that might be owned. That egalitarian claim blended well with the antimonarchial attitudes in the England of the 1640s. Yet it, too, was not free of difficulty. If voting derived from natural rights, and if all possessed those rights as equals, then the franchise would have to be universal. If so, on what basis could women, youth, or others logically be denied the vote? Even most of the radicals at Putney seemed to agree that a franchise defined as adult males would not include *every* adult male. Such questions would continue to shape the voting rights debate as the English colonies developed along the Atlantic seaboard of the North American continent.

VOTING RIGHTS IN AMERICA AROUND THE TIME OF THE REVOLUTION

The debates at Putney occurred after English colonization in the New World—a process that stretched over a 126-year period—was well underway. The first permanent colony in Virginia had been established in 1607, that in Massachusetts in 1620. Settlements continued to multiply, with the last of the seaboard colonies, Georgia, taking root in 1733.

Just as the debates at Putney resulted in no immediate expansion of the franchise in England, the franchise in the colonies that would compose the United States after 1776 tended to reflect the prevailing English practice. Except for the imperial expectation that voting had to be tied to a freehold, the definition of the franchise was not dictated from London and forced on unwilling colonial subjects. Instead, colonial assemblies merely tended to mimic the property-based system with which they were already familiar. For them, that was essential to good government. Britons and colonists alike accepted "the concept that the freeholders were and should remain the backbone of state and society" because they had a stake in both and "were the repository of virtues not found in other classes" (Williamson 1960, 3). Yet, by the late eighteenth century two important realities were in place.

First, because there were thirteen colonies, each with its own local law-making body, the franchise differed in some respects from one colony to another. Thus the significant decision by the framers of the Constitution in 1787 to leave the definition of the franchise in federal elections to the states, as discussed in the first chapter, drew on a decades-old colonial tradition. Just as there had been no uniform rule for voting in colonial times, there continued to be none under the Articles of Confederation after 1777 and even after the new government under the Constitution got underway in 1789.

Second, variations in voting among the colonies stemmed not merely from the absence of dictates by a central authority but from the dictates of local situations. In other words, the English practice was modified in light of different conditions encountered in different parts of the New World. This was true not only with respect to voting. In a major departure that affected the distribution of wealth as well as the breadth of the vote, by the eve of the Revolution the legal systems of most of the colonies had abandoned primogeniture, the English rule whereby an estate passed exclusively to the eldest son, with his brothers and sisters receiving nothing. This had been a cornerstone of the old feudal structure because it ensured the perpetuation of an undivided estate (Plucknett 1956, 527). With an absence of large, pre-existing feudal estates, and with land in many areas in abundant supply, primogeniture came to be seen in America as inapposite (Friedman 2002, 30–31). By the time of the Revolution, primogeniture remained the rule in only four colonies—Georgia, North Carolina, Virginia, and Rhode Island— and was abolished even there before 1800. The effect of the abolition of primogeniture on voting was direct. Because primogeniture left most male offspring without property, it encouraged a tightly restricted franchise that continued to be based on property. In contrast, if male heirs inherited property on a more equitable basis, the result would not only be a division of property but an increase in the number of freeholders.

Table 2.1 illustrates both the lack of complete uniformity across the colonies in terms of property qualifications for voting and the adaptation of the freehold to reflect local needs and conditions. As for the first, some colonies based the franchise on the value of the real property, others on the income it produced, and still others on the acreage itself. Indeed, the picture was even more variegated than Table 2.1 depicts. This was because, within some colonies, some cities possessed charters issued by the Crown. Thus the franchise in them was set by royal decree, not by the colonial assembly, and tended to reflect the different types of property that city-dwellers might own. Still the charter-based definitions of the franchise were generally neither more strict nor more lax than the

Table 2.1 Property Qualifications for Voting on the Eve of the Revolution, as Established by Colonial Assemblies or Charters

Colony	Real Estate Required	Alternative
Real Estate in Terms of Acres		
Georgia	50 acres	None
New Jersey	100 acres	Combination of other real or personal property worth 50 pounds
North Carolina	50 acres	None
Virginia	50 acres vacant, or 25 acres cultivated and a house, or a town lot and house	None
Real Estate in Terms of Value		
New Hampshire	Worth 50 pounds	None
New York	Worth 40 pounds	None
Rhode Island	Worth 40 pounds, or yielding 40 shillings in annual income	None
Real Estate with an Alternative		
Connecticut	Yielding 40 shillings annual income	Other property worth 40 pounds
Delaware	50 acres (12 cleared)	Other property worth 40 pounds
Maryland	50 acres	Other property worth 40 pounds
Massachusetts	Yielding 40 shillings annual income	Other property worth 40 pounds
Pennsylvania	50 acres	Other property worth 50 pounds
South Carolina	100 acres on which taxes were paid, or town lot and house on which taxes were paid, worth 60 pounds	Payment of 10 shillings in taxes

Source: Adapted from Porter 1971, 12.

assembly-derived definitions that governed voting in other towns and in the countryside (Keyssar 2000, 6). The substitution of acreage for property worth or income in some colonies reflected the differences in land availability and value. A relatively small acreage in Connecticut, for instance, might yield the requisite forty shillings or in New Hampshire be worth fifty pounds because New England was more densely populated and the price of land was higher. In other colonies, such as Georgia or South Carolina, where land was more plentiful (and less valuable) and where the population was more scattered, acreage was preferred as a measure of the freehold in place of value. It was easier to acquire a lot of land than it was to acquire land worth a lot.

Voting in the late colonial period was also varied because of other requirements that might be found in one colony but not another. Although Massachusetts had dropped its seventeenth-century stipulation that only members of the Congregational Church could vote, Jews were excluded in four colonies and Catholics in five. The latter group ironically included Maryland, which had been initially chartered in 1632 as a haven for Catholic as well as Protestant émigrés. Some colonies allowed Native Americans and free blacks to vote; others did not. Statutes in a few places expressly barred women from the polls, while custom barred them in others, but in a few New York and Massachusetts towns, widows who possessed the requisite property could vote. In Virginia some landowners could cast more than one vote if they owned sufficient property in more than one voting district (Keyssar 2000, 6). And this crazy-quilt pattern was probably even more complex due to variation in enforcement of the rules that did exist.

Still, given that property remained the most important voting qualification, what percentage of the adult male population was legally eligible to vote? No definitive answer to that question exists, although several studies have offered estimates based on sampling techniques. Perhaps the most thorough of these studies found variations among the colonies, as one might expect, but in nearly every instance the property qualification proved to be more inclusive than exclusive. Consequently, a substantially higher percentage of adult males in colonial America met the free-hold requirement than did their counterparts in England during the same period. Among New Hampshire towns, freeholding ranged from a low of 50 percent to a high of 90 percent of adult males, while in Rhode Island the figure was about 75 percent. Freeholding in Connecticut towns fell between 51 and 79 percent, numbers similar to freeholding in New York State where the picture was complicated by the prevalence of leaseholds, many of which qualified as freeholds. A rate of half to three-quarters also characterized New Jersey. About half of adult white males in Virginia probably met the property requirement (Williamson 1960, 25–30). And within each colony, the percentage of enfranchised males often varied by region.

The figure for Virginia was lower than those in colonies to the north in part because of primogeniture. As noted, under that rule, if a landowner had four sons, the estate passed to the eldest. So, the younger sons, say in their twenties, would have no land, yet by the time they had reached their thirties or forties they might well have had the resources to purchase some on their own. A failure to qualify to vote initially, therefore, did not necessarily mean that they were forever disfranchised (Sydnor 1962, 41). Moreover, because Virginians could cast a vote in any county in which they owned sufficient property, a man could vote two or three times provided he could overcome the handicaps of distance and primitive transportation. This practice continued well into the nineteenth century. "There is a tradition that in the late antebellum period a Virginian prided himself on voting in four counties, a feat which he accomplished by arranging relays of horses at county seats" (Sydnor 1962, 40).

Freeholding was apparently more widespread in North Carolina than in Virginia. Although qualifying property owners amounted to less than half the adult males in a few counties, freeholding ranged from about half to as much as 86 percent in most of the others that were sampled (Williamson 1960, 30–31). In Georgia, where English settlement had begun less than a half century before the Revolution, generous land-grant policies encouraged a high rate of freeholding, especially in the inland counties where the rate probably exceeded 75 percent. "One Georgian said in 1757 that the people claimed as a right at least 50 acres of land for every person in a family, whether white or black" (Williamson 1960, 31). Commenting on the diffusion of land ownership in the colony, James Wright, Georgia's last royal governor, observed that "by far the great number of voters, are the most Inferior Sort of People" (Williamson 1960, 31).

Thus a conservative estimate, overall, would count as many as 60 percent of adult white males among those eligible to vote in the thirteen colonies (Keyssar 2000, 7). Had voting requirements remained static over the next seventy-five years (and they did not), this percentage would doubtless have declined decade by decade. As cities grew in population, thanks to factory jobs, and as fewer Americans proportionally earned their livelihoods on farms, a smaller fraction of the population would have been able to qualify. In the period between 1820 and 1850, for example, U.S. census data show that the ratio of persons engaged in agriculture to persons engaged in commerce and manufacturing dropped from 5.4:1 to 1.7:1 in New Hampshire, from 3.6:1 to 1:1 in New York, from 2.1:1 to 0.8:1 in Pennsylvania, and from 3.4:1 to 0.6:1 in Maryland.

The actual casting of votes usually occurred in a manner that Americans today would find thoroughly unfamiliar and possibly intimidating. Whether votes are cast by paper ballot, machine, electronic device, or through another medium, a voter's choices at the polling place are made in private. The voter alone knows the person or persons for whom he or she has voted. Although a record is kept of who votes, no record connects voters with the votes they cast. Although some colonies such as North and South Carolina experimented with secret voting, secrecy was not always prized, even where ballots were sometimes used. Ballots for certain offices in Rhode Island, for instance, could not be accepted unless they had been signed by the voter. New Jersey law required that a record be kept not only of those who voted but the candidates for whom they voted, and under certain circumstances that information could become public knowledge. But the most common procedure followed the English practice: *viva voce,* or an election by voice vote in which voters publicly declared the name of the candidate(s) for whom they were voting. For any single freeholder, this was not a time-consuming event: In contrast to the situation today, there were not only fewer government offices in general but fewer filled by election.

In his classic study of voting practices in Virginia during George Washington's day, both before and after the Revolution, Charles Sydnor explained that "an election would be held at a single place in each county and that place by law was the courthouse." The day chosen ordinarily would be on county-court days when men would be coming together in any event "to transact business connected with the court, to buy and sell land, slaves, and other commodities, to catch up on the news, and to enjoy the excitement and activity of court day." Eighteenth-century elections could be accompanied by "plentiful supplies of liquor, occasional fights, and 'drunken loungers at and about the Courthouses'" (Sydnor 1962, 27). Elections ordinarily took place in the courtroom or, in good weather, outside. The county sheriff presided, in the company of the local magistrates. Each candidate had a clerk who transcribed the votes on a poll sheet.

> The paper was ruled and the lines numbered so that one could tell at a glance at any moment in the election exactly how many votes each candidate had. . . . When the sheriff thought that all was in readiness, . . . he opened the election by reading the writ which ordered it. In case there were no more candidates than there were places to be filled or in case sentiment was very one-sided, the law allowed the

election to be determined "by view." Whether the decision was reached in such a case by a show of hands or by some other method is not revealed in the records. . . .

When a poll was taken—and election by poll seems to have been more frequent than by view—the voters presented themselves one by one before the table where the election officials sat. Voters were not registered before elections, and there were no officials to turn back nonqualified men before they reached the polling place. However, the sheriff could refuse to take the vote of a man whom he knew to be disqualified, and each candidate had the right to challenge any voter and to require that he swear that he met the legal requirements. The most common objection was "no freehold." . . .

As each freeholder came before the sheriff, his name was called out in a loud voice, and the sheriff inquired how he would vote. The freeholder replied by giving the name of his preference. The appropriate clerk then wrote down the voter's name, the sheriff announced it as enrolled, and often the candidate for whom he had voted arose, bowed, and publicly thanked him. (Sydnor 1962, 27–29)

Voting was thus an unfolding process. Candidates, voters, and onlookers alike could easily tell at a given hour who was ahead and who was behind, giving the latter an opportunity to round up supporters among those who had not yet voted. Moreover, candidates were not often disposed to challenge those whose right to vote was in doubt, unless much was at stake or unless the election appeared very close. Rigid adherence to the law, after all, might generate ill will and cost the candidate some support, either at the moment or in the future. In one instance, in Lunenburg County "some forty men who could not qualify were allowed to vote in an election held in 1771. By common consent and contrary to the law, a local movement toward universal manhood suffrage was on foot" (Sydnor 1962, 29).

At one level, the system of *viva voce* meshed perfectly with the theory of the freehold. The latter was justified in part because it assured that the electorate was confined to the ranks of those of independent means—that is, possession of the freehold assumed that a man was not beholden to, or dependent on, another who could influence his vote. It therefore made no difference that the casting of a vote took place in front of one's fellow citizens. Yet at another level, *viva voce* and the principle of the freehold were at odds. It takes barely a moment's reflection to realize that few individuals, then or now, are truly independent and not subject to another's influence, whether that influence be familial, social, economic, political, or intellectual. It strains credulity to believe that most voters could publicly declare their choice in an election, oblivious to the opinions and reactions of their neighbors, who, for instance, might also be their creditors.

If these were the rules and practices in place on the eve of the Revolution, what change in the franchise did the Revolution bring about? In the near term, the answer was very little. In large part this was because of the nature of the American Revolution itself. In at least three meaningful ways, the Revolution was fundamentally different from other great revolutions of the modern age, such as the French Revolution that boiled up in 1789 or the Russian Revolution that began in 1917. First, the radical minority of 1774–1776 who instigated the colonies' break with England was actually able to maintain control of things until a largely younger generation took over to complete the formative period with the Philadelphia Convention of 1787 and the launching of the new government under the Constitution it devised. The American experience thus stands in contrast to the more common pattern, whereby the initial instigators of a revolution are sooner or later liquidated by their successors.

Second, a system of rule of law and experience with self-government were already in place and so did not have to be constructed from scratch after 1776. "We began with freedom," Ralph Waldo Emerson would later write (Morison 1965, 270), not with the authoritarian traditions that had characterized prerevolutionary France and Russia. "Experience must be our only guide. Reason may mislead us," announced John Dickinson, who had been principal drafter of the Articles of Confederation, to the delegates at the Philadelphia Convention in 1787 (Mason 1962, 8–9). What the colonials had known firsthand before 1776 became the starting point for new institutions once independence had been declared.

Third, the purpose of the break with England was therefore not to create something wholly new, as the French and Russians attempted to do. Rather, it was to reaffirm liberties the colonials had enjoyed but lately had been put in peril by an overreaching imperial policy from London, and then to fashion governments to safeguard those freedoms. Before the Revolution, after all, colonial Americans enjoyed more liberty and self-government than any other people on earth. Indeed, this was a prominent theme of the Declaration of Independence:

> [W]hen a long train of abuses and usurpations, pursuing invariably the same Object evinces a design to reduce them under absolute Despotism, it is their right, it is their duty, to throw off such Government and to provide new Guards for their future security.—Such has been the patient sufferance of these Colonies, and such is now the necessity which constrains them to alter their former Systems of Government. The history of the present King of Great Britain is a history of repeated injuries and usurpations, all having in direct object the establishment of an absolute Tyranny over these States. To prove this, let Facts be submitted to a candid world.

The concept of "abuses and usurpations" is meaningless without reference to a norm of accepted substance and procedure. The bulk of the Declaration, therefore, is not a display of pie-in-the-sky reaching for a new regime or social upheaval. Rather, three-quarters of the text of the Declaration is a recitation of excesses by the Crown—each characterized as a departure from *existing* law and practice and a violation of rights that the colonists assumed had been theirs. In short, the primary purpose of the American Revolution was to secure true self-government: to make good the break with Great Britain and to make Americans custodians of their own destiny and rights.

These objectives would account for the relatively small number of immediate changes in the franchise after fighting ended. As Table 2.2 shows, in comparison with Table 2.1, each former colony, now a state, retained a link between voting and a person's financial circumstances, usually defined in terms of property.

Some state requirements reflected a relaxation over the colonial period, with Pennsylvania's moving the furthest from a strict property condition. There, payment of a "head tax" on all heads of households apparently enfranchised a large majority of adult males. Qualifications in other states remained about the same. Indeed, the requirement in Massachusetts became more demanding. And, when the Congress under the Articles of Confederation enacted the Northwest Ordinance in 1787, to govern the territory that now comprises the states of Ohio, Indiana, Illinois, Michigan, and Wisconsin, a fifty-acre freehold was imposed. Thus, as late as the era of the Philadelphia Convention, most states were comfortable with either a freehold stipulation or some other financial threshold. When the Declaration of Independence declared that "all political connection between" the colonies "and the State of Great Britain, is and ought to be totally dissolved," that dissolution hardly entailed immediate abandonment of the historic link between voting and property. To be sure, rumblings of a broader franchise that echoed the thoughts expressed at the Putney Debates were heard, but those ideas fell well short of commanding a majority in the newly established state legislatures. Thus the principle of "government by consent of the governed," that had infused the Declaration of Independence and inspired the Revolution, was initially honored more in the transgression than in the observance. In most states it was still a matter of government by the consent of *some* of the (white male) governed. Added to this

Table 2.2   Property Qualifications for Voting Immediately after the
Revolutionary War

State	Real Estate Required	Alternative
Real Estate in Terms of Acres		
North Carolina	50 acres for state senate elections*	None
Virginia	50 acres uncultivated, or 25 acres cultivated, and a house or a town lot and house	None
Real Estate in Terms of Value		
New York	Worth 20 pounds, or yielding 40 shillings annual income, and payment of state tax	None
Rhode Island	Worth 40 pounds, or yielding 40 shillings annual income	None
Real Estate with an Alternative		
Connecticut	Yielding 40 shillings annual income	Other property worth 40 pounds
Delaware	50 acres (12 cleared)	Other property worth 40 pounds
Maryland	50 acres	30 pounds in money
Massachusetts	Yielding 30 pounds annual income	Other property worth 60 pounds
South Carolina	50 acres, or a town lot	Payment of a tax equal to a tax on 50 acres
No Real Estate Required		
Georgia	Property worth 10 pounds	None
New Hampshire	Payment of poll tax	None
New Jersey	50 pounds "proclamation money"	None
Pennsylvania	Payment of taxes	None

* But only payment of taxes was required for state house elections.
Source: Adapted from Porter 1971, 13.

mixture was the slogan popularized on the eve of the Revolution: "no taxation without representation." With far-reaching potential, a blossoming American ideology was already at war with the facts.

Consider the situation in revolutionary Massachusetts, for example. A constitution drafted in 1778 was rejected by the state's citizens in part because it did not tilt far enough toward popular government. After delegates to another constitutional convention—themselves selected in voting that included all freemen (Keyssar 2000, 19)—had actually stiffened the Bay State's colonial-era property requirement in the Constitution of 1780, they candidly explained the reasons for their actions:

> Your Delegates considered that Persons who are Twenty-one Years of age, and have no Property, are either those who live upon a part of a Paternal estate, expecting the Fee thereof, who are but just entering into business, or those whose Idleness of Life and profligacy of manners will forever bar them from acquiring and possessing Property. And we will submit it to the former class, whether they would not think it safer for them to have their right of Voting for a Representative suspended for [a] small space of Time, than forever hereafter to have their Privileges liable to the control of Men who will pay less regard to the Rights of Property because they have nothing to lose. (Handlin and Handlin 1966, 437)

Aside from the details of the particular franchise requirement, the Massachusetts example illustrates a notable development after 1776: the franchise was viewed as worthy of *constitutional* status. (The Massachusetts Constitution of 1780 was also the first in the former colonies to be ratified by vote by the electorate.) The break with England necessitated the creation in each new state of some legal foundation to replace the previous governance authorities; by 1775, all were royal colonies except for the corporation colonies of Connecticut and Rhode Island, and the proprietary colonies of Maryland and Pennsylvania. Except for Connecticut and Rhode Island, which merely carried over and adapted their charters as constitutions (minus the royal connections, of course), the remaining eleven each drafted a constitution.

That flurry of constitution writing might be said to be the beginning of what was initially a two-tiered, now three-tiered arrangement, that legally describes the structure of both American state and national governments. For a given state, its constitution occupied the highest tier, the "supreme Law of the Land," as Article VI of the federal Constitution of 1787 described its own place in the new political order. A constitution established the essential framework for the political system, laid down ground rules, and conferred authority and set limits on those who governed. A constitution, declared Justice William Paterson in 1795, "is the form of government, delineated by the mighty hand of the people, in which certain first principles of fundamental laws are established" (*Van Horne's Lessee v. Dorrance*, 1795). On the authority of the constitution, therefore, the legislature of a state would pass laws. This statutory law comprised the second tier, and the theory was that the statutes enacted by the legislature were to be in conformity with the constitution. The lowest tier— administrative law—did not begin to take shape in any meaningful way until nearly a century later. Statutory law might authorize certain government officials to make rules to carry out purposes contained within a statute. Indeed, the bulk of law today derives from the third tier, as illustrated by the host of regulations emanating from federal agencies such as the Consumer Product Safety Commission, the Federal Election Commission, the Environmental Protection Agency, the Federal Communications Commission, and so on.

Typically, constitutions are much more difficult to change than statutes. The latter may be altered by majority vote of the legislature and usually the executive's approval; the former are alterable only through a much more cumbersome process, and deliberately so. If a constitution embodies a state's ground rules and expresses its basic values, it would defeat the purpose of having a fundamental law if it could be amended on a whim, much like changing the rules in the middle of a game. Otherwise, the rules might be changed by one group today to its advantage and then twisted tomorrow to serve the ends of a different group that had come to power. Accordingly, constitution writers place within its text those things they do not want easily altered, much like placing an object on the highest shelf so as not to be easily reached. The object is not completely out of reach, but it is reachable only with extraordinary effort. So it was significant that provisions in most states regarding who could vote from the outset were often ensconced in the constitutions of those states, although sometimes the provisions could be augmented by statute.

Then there was the special case of Vermont. The only New England state today without an Atlantic seacoast, Vermont was not one of the original thirteen colonies and so does not appear in Tables 2.1 and 2.2. During the colonial period, the territory that is now the Green Mountain State was claimed first by New Hampshire and then by New York. When the colonies declared independence from England, Vermonters in effect launched a revolution within the Revolution and established themselves as an independent state in 1777. Its constitution not only was the first to abolish slavery; it eliminated the property-owning requirement altogether and, going beyond Pennsylvania, removed any taxpaying stipulation as well. When Vermont became the fourteenth state in 1791, all adult males who took the Freeman's Oath were eligible to vote. (Called the Voter's Oath since 1794, this requirement originally excluded any prospective voter who opposed the validity of land grants under New Hampshire authority during the colonial era.) However, one scholar suggests that eliminating even a taxpaying requirement may have stemmed as much from practical considerations as from democratic convictions. With no existing state tax-collecting machinery in Vermont, "a taxpaying qualification would have disfranchised every inhabitant" (Williamson 1960, 99).

TOWARD A (NEARLY) UNIVERSAL
WHITE MANHOOD SUFFRAGE

As described in the previous section, the limited objectives of most leaders of the American Revolution moderated short-run changes in the franchise. Yet there was another reason why, once freed of British control, most state governments at first were hesitant to relax the link between voting and property. That reason had to do with the fact that the framers of the new governments were venturing into uncharted territory. Their new governments were fundamentally without model. Moreover, compounding the unknown was a threat of potentially great magnitude.

Recall the governance structure with which political leaders in the last quarter of the eighteenth century were familiar. Their British origins reminded them that political power was divided three ways. In this balanced or mixed arrangement, as the English constitutional system had evolved, laws were made upon the agreement of the three components of the realm: the monarch, the nobles who sat in the House of Lords, and the elected members of the House of Commons. (The judiciary had not yet been conceived as a third branch of government; judges were agents of the King's justice. Even today in Great Britain, the House of Lords sits as the highest court of the realm.) Thus debates about expanding the franchise, as occurred at Putney, were debates about expanding the electorate for one of three elements in the system. Even had the radicals at Putney had their way in broadening the electoral base for the House of Commons, there presumably still would have been a monarch (at least after the Restoration of the monarchy in 1660) and a House of Lords who would have had to give their assent to anything Commons chose to do. That was true even though England's "Glorious Revolution" of 1688 had established the supremacy of Parliament over the Crown.

Then consider the structure of government in most of the colonies, where an analogous balance prevailed. Whether the colony was royal, corporative, or proprietary at its core, there was typically an appointed governor, an elected assembly with its members selected by those meeting the prevailing property requirement, and an appointed council that served both as an upper legislative house and usually as the highest adjudicatory body within the colony. Thus, again, the elected element (the assembly) could be checked by the governor and council. Furthermore, colonial legislative enactments required the approval of the King's Privy Council, to make sure they conformed to imperial policy. In no sense, therefore, was the entire administration of a colony's affairs lodged in the hands of delegates elected by "the people," even in the limited colonial meaning of that term.

In theory and usually in practice, such balance—whether in England or in the colonies—had much to recommend it. But in the late 1760s and early 1770s the British government attempted to recoup through various taxes part of the costs of the Seven Years' War with France (1755–1763), the conflict that in America was called the French and Indian War. (Wars, then and now, are expensive.) Colonial Americans objected strenuously to the taxes, not because they resented the defense of their homeland or rejected the idea of balanced government, but largely because they had been left out of the balanced decision-making arrangement entirely.

The right to vote, that a substantial number of colonials possessed, extended only to their colonial assemblies. Electorally, the House of Commons—one of the three components of balanced government that was supposed to protect the liberties of the British subjects—was beyond their reach. In their cry of "no taxation without representation," they rejected the notion of "virtual representation" whereby even regions sending no delegates to a

legislative body were presumably represented by other representatives. By that theory, legislators elected in England by English
freeholders would be solicitous of the interests of the colonists in
the same way as if the latter had elected the former. So, the list of
abuses in the Declaration of Independence was thus not a rejection of, but a justification of, inclusiveness in a system from which
colonials had been excluded.

Compare that view of the ideal political world against the reality that prevailed after 1776 and especially after it became apparent in 1781 that the war for independence was ended and the
break with England had been made secure. In a system premised
upon government by the consent of the governed, what had been
one-third of the balanced structure now seemingly composed it
all. There was no executive appointed from without, and no appointed upper house or council equally unanswerable to the electorate. Suddenly, the balance seemed to have been lost. Political
power, depending on the actual structure, lay directly or indirectly with the electorate. What did this actually mean? Perhaps
James Wilson, one of the first six justices on the U.S. Supreme
Court, answered that question most eloquently. In an early case
having to do not with voting but with jurisdiction of the federal
courts, he explained,

> To the Constitution of the United States the term *sovereign* is totally
> unknown. There is but one place where it could have been used with
> propriety. But, even in that place it would not, perhaps, have com-
> ported with the delicacy of those who ordained and established that
> constitution. They might have announced themselves "sovereign"
> people of the United States: But serenely conscious of the fact, they
> avoided the ostentatious declaration. . . .
>
> With the strictest propriety, therefore, classical and political, our
> national scene opens with the most magnificent object which the na-
> tion could present. "The people of the United States" are the first per-
> sonages introduced. Who were those people? They were the citizens

of thirteen states, each of which had a separate constitution and government, and all of which were connected together by articles of confederation. (*Chisholm v. Georgia*, 1793)

Put more directly, if less eloquently, the cartoonist Walt Kelly captured the essence of the same problem in the remark he credited to his character Pogo on Earth Day in 1971: "We have met the enemy and he is us" (Kelly and Crouch 1982, 163). The notion of "power to the people," at least for those people who could vote, had come home to roost.

Who would constitute "the people" who now had, in one way or the other, sovereignty, or ultimate authority? And they did possess that authority. "The people," with apparently no outside constraints, could make over their political systems in any way they chose. This was unprecedented. Even at the federal level, where the Constitution of 1787 allowed direct election only of members of the U.S. House of Representatives, voters still elected the members of their state legislatures, who then in turn elected members of the U.S. Senate and determined how presidential electors from their state would be selected. That, coupled with the amendment procedures that the Constitution provided in Article V, meant that, as Justice Wilson acknowledged, sovereignty in America now lay with the people.

Little wonder there was concern at the outset over the vast potentialities of such an untried system. If political power now resided in a majority of the people, it became highly significant how "the people" were defined. At the Philadelphia Convention in the summer of 1787, James Madison was particularly alert to the political consequences of the demographic changes he anticipated: "[I]n future times a great majority of the people will not only be without land but any other sort of property. These will either combine under the influence of their common situation; in which case, the rights of property and the public liberty will not be secure in their hands; or which is more probable, they will become the tools of opulence and ambition, in which case there will be equal danger on another side" (Farrand 1966, vol. 2, 203–204).

The growth of industry (and signs of the industrial revolution were already present) would mean a change in the social structure. If propertyless males became the majority and possessed the franchise, they would be politically dominant and therefore a danger to those with property. As John Adams warned in Massachusetts, "an immediate revolution would ensue" (Adams 1856, vol. 10, 268). Hence the value of linking the vote to property: "Property qualifications, in effect, would function as a bulwark against the landless proletariat of an industrial future" (Keyssar 2000, 12).

Besides, once the vote was unyoked from property, there might be no logical stopping point. "The same reasoning which will induce you to admit all men who have no property, to vote, with those who have," argued Adams in 1776, in words that would be variously repeated by others for decades,

> will prove that you ought to admit women and children, for, generally speaking, women and children have as good judgments, and as independent minds, as those men who are wholly destitute of property; these last being to all intents and purposes as much dependent upon others, who will please to feed, clothe, and employ them, as women are upon their husbands, or children on their parents.... Depend upon it, Sir, it is dangerous to open so fruitful a source of controversy and altercation as would be opened by attempting to alter the qualifications of voters, there will be no end of it. New claims will raise; women will demand the vote; lads from twelve to twenty-one will think their rights not enough attended to; and every man who has not a farthing will demand an equal voice with any other, in all acts of state. It tends to confound and destroy all distinctions, and prostrate all ranks to one common level. (Adams 1856, vol. 9, 377–378)

Were the comments like those of Madison and Adams merely reflective of a class bias or did they reveal a genuine concern about stability and liberty? From the perspective of more than two centuries later, it would be easy to classify such remarks as nothing more than expressions of self-interest. Those with property presumably would not want to adopt policies that would open up the possibility that what they possessed might be taken from them. The same might be said of those who argued for an expanded franchise; they wanted the vote because they wanted to acquire the influence that came with it. But men like Adams and Madison probably had deeper considerations in mind as well. They were beginning to grapple with the conundrum of how a system that encouraged economic inequality, which they took for granted, could coexist with a system founded on political equality. And property itself was centrally linked to liberty. Indeed, it was widely believed that a person could not truly be free without owning property (Price 2003, 3). Thus, if property was imperiled, liberty was imperiled too. And if "the people" were defined too broadly, might they not pose the danger of tyranny of the majority?

Such concerns probably explain the product of the Philadelphia Convention itself: a constitutional structure premised on a division and juxtaposition of powers among the legislative, executive, and judicial branches, augmented by an overlapping arrangement (called checks and balances) whereby power could limit power. In effect, the framers anticipated the threat posed by majority rule, and as they created a new national government, they hemmed it in. If the pre-1776 problem had been to protect the many (the people) from the few (the Crown), the new post-1776 problem became one of figuring out how to protect the few (those who possessed more wealth) from the many (those who possessed less). Madison acknowledged as much in *The Federalist*, No. 10, which he published in November 1787 in the campaign for ratification of the proposed Constitution in New York State. On the premise that a propensity of popular government was to succumb to the "dangerous vice" of faction, he advanced as a reason for favoring the Constitution that it would "break and control the violence of faction." And what did he mean by "faction"? "By a faction, I understand a number of citizens, whether amounting to a majority or minority of the whole, who are united and actuated by some common impulse of passion, or interest, adverse to the rights of other citizens, or to the permanent and aggregate interests of the community."

And the principal cause of factions was "the various and unequal distribution of property. Those who hold and those who are without property have ever formed distinct interests in society." Where a faction constituted only a minority of the population, the principle of majority rule could contain it. The real danger would arise when the faction constituted the majority. There, at the national level at least—the problem of factions *within* an individual state would remain a cause for concern—the Constitution's features would reduce the nationwide damage any such faction could wreak. "[W]e behold a republican remedy for the diseases most incident to republican government" (Brock 1961, 41–43, 48).

Despite the modest short-run changes in the franchise that took effect in the wake of the Revolution, developments and various arguments had already begun both to undercut the views of those like Adams who insisted on the social necessity of a limited franchise and to highlight the significance of Madison's theory of the Constitution with its built-in checks on majority rule. Still, the journey "from property to democracy" (Williamson 1960) took decades.

It is, therefore, worthwhile first to ask what accounted for the voting modifications that occurred before examining the particulars of the modifications themselves. The question of "why" or "how" is important because of a basic reality: the disfranchised could not enfranchise themselves. That could take place only if a sufficient number of those who were already franchised decided to broaden the suffrage. Explanations for the growing willingness of those who could vote to enlarge the electorate fall generally into four categories: the power of ideas, socioeconomic changes, self-interest, and the rise of national political parties.

Recall that the first small but important step toward divorcing formal political rights from property ownership had already been taken by 1776 in a few colonies, where property other than real estate qualified one to vote. Although possession of a certain amount of personal property was still consistent with the concept of "independence" that the freehold was supposed to assure, the move was nonetheless noteworthy because it expanded on the concept of "stake in society" that entitled one to a voice in its affairs. That stake was no longer land, but could be something else instead. The second step in the divorce was the substitution of payment of taxes for possession of a certain amount of property. As Table 2.2 shows, in South Carolina this substitution was still tied to real estate in its value, but in New Hampshire and Pennsylvania it was uncoupled from property altogether. Thus step two was a significant movement away from ownership of a stake in society. For instance, if paying a head tax was sufficient qualification, then it was entirely possible that one could vote without owning any property at all; being employed would suffice. Indeed, step two no doubt reflected the influence of the Revolution's captivating slogan regarding taxation and representation.

That slogan had helped to energize public opinion against Great Britain just before the Revolution. It branded as an inequity the situation in which those persons who were taxed (the colonists) had no say in the selection of those persons (members of the House of Commons in London) whose assent was necessary for imposition of the taxes. After the break with the Crown, this homegrown idea was effectively applied to American suffrage. If it was unacceptable for the British government, in which the colonists had no direct voice, to impose taxes on the colonies, then how could the legislatures of the American states rightly impose taxes on those citizens who were ineligible to take part in the selection of their legislators? (The Congress under the Articles of Confederation had no power to tax; instead, it depended for its sole revenue on requisitions to the state legislatures, which in turn were to tax their inhabitants to provide the money to fund the national government.)

There was a second idea at work, too, that had the potential to extend the franchise even further: the concept of "government by the consent of the governed." In terms of intrinsic appeal, it rivaled and perhaps even surpassed that of "no taxation without representation." "The elected, not the electors, were henceforth the subject of intimidation and coercion. Political power was changing sides" (Williamson 1960, 77). "The people . . . should be consulted in the most particular manner that can be imagined," asserted a group of Pennsylvanians on the eve of the Revolution (Williamson 1960, 77). The idea of consent found its way into public documents long after the ink on the Declaration of Independence was dry. "All power being originally vested in, is derived from, the people," proclaimed Pennsylvania's constitutional convention of 1789, "and all free governments originate from their will, are founded on their authority, and instituted for their peace, safety, and happiness; and for the advancement thereof; they have, at all times, an unalienable and indefeasible right to alter, reform, or abolish their government in such manner as they may think proper" (Porter 1971, 28).

Yet, states governed not merely property owners and taxpayers, but all within their domain. If political legitimacy rested on consent, and if elections were the medium by which that consent was conferred or withheld, then on what proper grounds could the propertyless and the nontaxpayer be excluded from the polls?

Coupled with consent was the concept of natural rights, which also pointed to an inclusive suffrage. The Declaration of Independence had insisted that "all men are created equal" in that they were "endowed by their Creator with certain unalienable Rights, that among these are Life, Liberty and the pursuit of Happiness. That to secure these rights, Governments are instituted among Men, deriving their just powers from the consent of the governed." Those claims echoed the debates at Putney. In terms of one's status in civil society, therefore, no person counted more than another. With such notions having captured the American mind, it was hardly surprising that a natural rights objection was raised to the property requirement imposed by the Massachusetts Constitution of 1780: "Ye right of election is not a civil; but it is a natural right," declared a resolution passed by one town, "which ought to be considered as a principle [sic] cornerstone in ye foundation for ye frame of Government" (Williamson 1960, 102).

The war for independence itself added another push for a broader franchise, in a pattern that would repeat itself after the second war for American independence (otherwise known as the War of 1812). Beginning with the fighting at Lexington and Concord in 1775, the militia that opposed the Redcoat regulars was composed not only of taxpayers and the propertied but those of meager means as well (Fischer 1994, 319–320). Indeed, during the war some of the propertied were able to pay some of the latter to serve in their stead (Whichard 2000, 33–34). If a person risked his life for his country, on what proper grounds, the question was posed, could he be denied the right to have a say in its affairs? Angered that the Constitution of 1780 did not allow all taxpayers to vote for governor and the lower house of the state legislature, officers in the state militia bluntly told Massachusetts Governor John Hancock, as they resigned their commissions, that they could no longer encourage their troops "who are so poor as to be thus deprived of their fundamental Rights, that they are fighting for their own freedom" (Williamson 1960, 103). Some of the enfranchised would also perceive their own self-interest at stake, whether their concern was the British, restless Indians on the frontier, or the possibility of slave rebellions. Military preparedness would be more easily achieved and maintained if the poorer men in the population felt obliged to serve. During the Massachusetts constitutional convention of 1820, one delegate worried aloud that the "ardor" of the unfranchised "would be chilled ... when called upon to defend their country" (Keyssar

2000, 38). Why would they feel disposed to defend a government in which they had no say?

Other social and intellectual forces combined eventually to create a political climate more receptive to fewer barriers to voting. Reformers in the new world not only quoted from the same philosophers who had inspired the Revolution, but were also in touch with contemporary democratic movements and writers in the Old World. Trans-Atlantic traffic in ideas moved in both directions. Then there was the nature of the change in the American population in the first half of the nineteenth century. Economic and technological innovations hastened the growth of factories and commercial agriculture in the north and midwest, as it did the spread of plantation slavery across the south and toward the southwest. With ranks of factory and mill workers, owners and managers, those who constructed and operated canals and railroads, in addition to small farmers, planters, and financiers, the social order was becoming more complex. With these changes came new local elites "who came from outside the established gentry—urban and country merchants, manufacturers, lawyers, newspaper editors, and other professionals" who comprised "an articulate stratum of ambitious men who owed little or nothing to the old ideal of a landed freeholder citizenry and ... patrician leadership. In state after state, these new men of the market revolution played critical roles, either in mobilizing support for reforms or in helping broker these reforms in state legislatures and constitutional conventions" (Wilentz 1992, 35–36).

Below the new professional class were large numbers of ordinary people, those whom President Andrew Jackson in the 1820s called the "real people" as he emphasized the virtues of popular sovereignty. As Daniel Rodgers described them, these were "men of little property shut out of the early political arrangements of power, farmers and petty planters from the malapportioned back countries, debtors far from the seats of legal justice, urban mechanics grown restless with the politics of deference and the injuries of merchant capitalism" (Wilentz 1992, 36). Those who spoke for Jackson's "real people," and they spoke up in every state in the union, demanded a war on privilege and a fair chance for every man to rise. Essential to those objectives was the vote. And they responded positively to Benjamin Franklin's oft-quoted mockery of property as a precondition for the franchise.

> Today a man owns a jackass worth fifty dollars and he is entitled to vote; but before the next election the jackass dies. The man in the mean time has become more experienced, his knowledge of the principles of government, and his acquaintance with mankind, are more extensive, and he is therefore better qualified to make a proper selection of rulers—but the jackass is dead and the man cannot vote. Now gentlemen, pray inform me, in whom is the right of suffrage? In the man or in the jackass? (Zall 1980, 149–150)

Moreover, not coincidentally did a system of national political parties begin to take shape and then to take hold at the same time states were enlarging their electorates. Political parties at heart were (and are) organizations to mobilize voters behind candidates in pursuit of victory at the polls. Thus it was only natural for parties to think of expanding their ranks of supporters by enfranchising the unfranchised. In other words, a party might insist on expansion of the franchise not solely as a matter of political philosophy but as a source of new voters. Similarly, another party might oppose relaxation of voting requirements if the change seemed likely to cut into its chances to win. Democrats tended to favor alien suffrage (voting by noncitizens), for example, because immigrants felt more comfortable in their ranks. Even if a party thought that an expanded franchise might work to its short-term disadvantage, there was a longer-term concern that the party risked alienating a whole new bloc of voters if it remained obsessively opposed to relaxed criteria. Prudence, therefore, dictated moderating its stance, thus assuring passage. "The newly enfranchised," explained political scientist E. E. Schattschneider, "had about as much to do with the extension of the suffrage as the consuming public has had to do with the expanding market for toothpaste. The parties, assisted by some excited minorities, were the entrepreneurs, took the initiative, and got the law of the franchise liberalized" (Elliott 1974, 34).

Also at work within the party system was a peculiarity of some franchise rules: a partial franchise. That is, a state might allow taxpayers to vote for some officials, but impose a property requirement for election of other officials. Once one party or faction within a party trumpeted an expanded franchise, some on the other side took a risk if they advocated the status quo: the partially franchised might seek vengeance at the polls. This is essentially how North Carolina finally abandoned its property requirement. According to Alexander Keyssar's account, politics in the Tar Heel State in the late 1840s had been dominated by the Whigs,

> until David S. Reid, a long-shot Democratic candidate for governor, embraced the cause of suffrage reform. . . . In the election of 1848, Reid did much better than expected (there was no property requirement in gubernatorial elections) and aided by a wave of support from the landless was elected governor in 1850, promising . . . to eliminate the property qualification for senatorial voting. Once elected (and re-elected), Reid pursued that goal, declaring that the "elective franchise is the dearest right of an American citizen" and complaining that 50,000 free white men were disfranchised by the state's constitution. Sobered by political reality, the Whigs abandoned their opposition to suffrage reform: by the early 1850s, they saw the wisdom of tacitly approving a measure that they had denounced in 1848 as "a system of communism unjust and Jacobinical." (Keyssar 2000, 41)

Throughout self-interest for a party could easily be disguised as pursuit of principle, then as now. Consider, for example, an event that occurred much later in the nineteenth century when efforts were made at Pennsylvania's constitutional convention of 1872–1873 to repeal the taxpaying requirement. Democrats and some progressive Republicans favored the repeal, insisting in the debate that "the right of suffrage" was a "natural social right" that belonged "to a man because he is a man" and not "because he is a taxpayer." It was repulsive to exclude "from the right of suffrage any man on the face of the earth because he is poor." Regular Republicans, however, were opposed to repeal. The proposal would permit "those to vote . . . who have no manner of stake in the government." They rejected any measure "by which vagabonds and stragglers shall have a right to step up to the election polls and cast a vote which will count just as much as the man whose property is taxed thousands of dollars." Yet it was common knowledge that the dominant Republican party organization in the state routinely paid the taxes for its poorer supporters (including, presumably, even the "vagabonds and stragglers") in order to have their votes. Democrats, being less well-heeled as a party, wanted to be able to reap votes from poorer supporters in their ranks and so favored the change. The Republicans prevailed on this issue, and the taxpaying requirement remained a feature of Pennsylvania politics until 1931 (Keyssar 2000, 131–132).

Self-interest might apply across party divisions, as in the case of the concern about sufficient numbers of available men in the militia. But self-interest was also connected to settlement itself. As noted below in connection with voting by aliens, allowed in a few states, no state entered the Union after 1800 with a property qualification, although some did with a taxpaying requirement. More than ideology was probably at work in such instances. There was an inducement, too: white males settling in those developing regions acquired the right to vote.

The interaction of all these ideas, forces, and factors led to a further democratization in most of the states between 1800 and 1860, so that by the eve of the Civil War property and taxpaying requirements had either disappeared entirely or, where they hung on in one form or another as in Pennsylvania, posed no major barriers for voting by white men. However, after the Civil War many states instituted a poll tax of one or two dollars a year as a precondition for voting, often with a stipulation that the prospective voter had to present proof of payment of the tax. This was a useful device to discourage voting by the poor and especially by poor persons of color.

As can be gleaned from Table 2.3, the prewar broadening of the franchise occurred in roughly four waves (Wilentz 1992, 33). The first twelve years of the nineteenth century witnessed elimination of the property requirement in Maryland and South Carolina, and a reduction in New Jersey. Efforts to do the same in Massachusetts, New York, Rhode Island, and Connecticut failed to make headway. Minus Rhode Island, reform efforts succeeded in the other three states between the end of the War of 1812 and 1828. A third wave began with a reduction in Virginia's property requirement through that state's constitutional convention of 1829–1830 and resulted in relaxed voting requirements in other states as well. A revolt in Rhode Island in 1842 marked the beginning of the fourth stage that led to the virtual elimination of property tests where they remained.

Removal or reduction of the property requirement was not accomplished easily, especially in states such as New York and Virginia. Probably at no other time in American history has there been such an exhaustive series of debates on suffrage as occurred in the New York constitutional convention of 1821 and the Virginia constitutional convention of 1829–1830. In the New York convention, the Empire State's legal luminary, Chancellor James Kent, sulfurously described the risks of reform:

> The tendency of universal suffrage is to jeopardize the rights of property and the principles of liberty. . . . [O]ur governments are becoming downright democracies. . . . The principle of universal suffrage, which is now running a triumphant career from Maine to Louisiana, is an

Table 2.3   The Decline of Property and Taxpaying Voter
Qualifications, 1776–1860

State	Entered Union	Property Qualification Ended	Taxpayer Qualification Ended
Connecticut	1776	1818	1845
Delaware	1776	1792	continuing
Georgia	1776	1789	continuing
Indiana	1816	n/a	n/a
Kentucky	1792	n/a	n/a
Louisiana	1812	n/a	1845
Maryland	1776	1810	n/a
Massachusetts	1776	1821	continuing
Mississippi	1817	n/a	1832
New Hampshire	1776	1784	1792
New Jersey	1776	1844	n/a
New York	1776	1821[a]	1826[a]
North Carolina	1776	1856	continuing
Ohio	1803	n/a	1851
Pennsylvania	1776	1776	continuing
Rhode Island	1776	1842[b]	continuing
South Carolina	1776	1810[c]	1810
Tennessee	1796	1834	n/a
Virginia	1776	1850	n/a
Vermont	1791	n/a	n/a

[a] except for a "man of color"

[b] for native-born male citizens only

[c] if residency requirement met

NOTE: After Mississippi in 1817, no state entered the union with a property or taxpaying requirement. However, property tests persisted in some states for special elections, such as those involving bond issues, even after the test had been dropped for elections generally. Taxpayer requirements could be of at least three kinds: (1) that one pay any taxes that might be owed; (2) that one pay a head tax to qualify; and (3) that one owe (and pay) taxes.

awful power, which, like gunpowder, or the steam engine, or the press itself, may be rendered mighty in mischief as well as in blessings. We have to fear inflammatory appeals to the worst passions of the worst men in society; and we have greatly to dread the disciplined force of fierce and vindictive majorities, headed by leaders flattering their weaknesses and passions, and turning their vengeance upon the heads and fortunes of minorities, under the forms of law. . . . We must ingraft something like quarantine laws into our constitution to prevent the introduction and rage of this great moral pestilence. . . . Who can undertake to calculate with any precision how many millions of people this great state will contain in the course of this and the next century . . . ? The disproportion between the men of property and the men of no property will be in every society in a ratio to its commerce, wealth, and population. We are no longer to remain plain and simple republics of farmers. . . . Universal suffrage once granted is granted forever, and never can be recalled. There is no retrograde step in the rear of democracy. (Mason and Leach 1959, 233–235)

Kent's objections were countered by advocates such as David Buel. His vision was a land of diverse property ownership, where property was sacrosanct among the poor as well as the rich. "The supposition that, at some future day, when the poor shall become numerous, they may imitate the radicals of England, or the Jacobins of France; that they may rise, in the majesty of their strength, and usurp the property of the landholders, is so unlikely to be realized that we may dismiss all fear rising from that source" (Mason and Leach 1959, 240).

Still, in predicting that commercial development would exacerbate class differences, Kent's insights into the future were profound, and he said so nearly three decades before publication of Karl Marx's *Communist Manifesto*. Yet his protestations were in vain. The convention handed the vote to men who paid taxes, served in the militia, or worked on the public highways. Moreover, neither Kent nor Buel could anticipate that the judiciary would soon begin to play a larger role in overseeing public policy. Initially, with the contract clause of Article I in the Constitution and later with the due process clauses of the Fifth and Fourteenth Amendments, federal and state courts reined in runaway majorities that, in the judges' view at least, tampered too severely with rights of property and other fundamental liberties (Mason and Stephenson 2002, 336–344).

In Virginia, the question of voting was also linked, as it was in a few other states, to imbalances in representation. Settled first, coastal counties were heavily weighted in the apportionment of seats in the legislature. More inland regions—called the up-country or the backcountry, depending on the state—were underweighted even though their populations had grown. Thus the matter of voting rights was doubly important: easing access to the polls would diminish the political clout of the low-country counties even more were legislative seats to be distributed more evenly on a population basis.

At the Virginia convention, John Randolph waged a campaign against change of either the franchise or the apportionment. Echoing Chancellor Kent nearly a decade before, he believed that "king numbers" had to be avoided at all costs. Why? Because the principle of equality itself was false: "Sir, my only objection is that these principles, pushed to their extreme consequences—that all men are born free and equal—I can never assent to for the best of all reasons, because it is not true." There were two kinds of majorities: a majority of interests and a majority of numbers. Those with property composed the former and were therefore entitled to control the machinery of government.

Will you go into joint stock with those "vagabonds" and that "rabble" ... who never mean to have a freehold? ... the profligate, the homeless ... who ... hang very loosely on society, but stick very closely to her skirts, and who are determined to pick up their vile and infamous bread by every despicable means? I call on the young non-

freeholders, the sons of freeholders . . . to wait, and not to unite themselves with those who, in the nature of things, can have no permanent
interest in the Commonwealth. (Mason and Leach 1959, 247)

For Randolph, substituting other restrictions on suffrage in
place of the freehold was misguided. "[Y]ou can place no restriction on it [the franchise]. When this principle [of population as the
basis for representation] is in operation, the waters are out. It is as
if you would ask an industrious and sagacious Hollander that you
may cut his dykes, provided you make your cut only of a certain
width. A rat hole will let in the ocean. Sir, there is an end to the security of all property in the Commonwealth" (Mason and Leach
1959, 248).

With parallels to the debates at Putney, part of the case for a
more inclusive franchise came in the form of "a memorial from a
numerous and respectable body of citizens, the nonfreeholders of
the city of Richmond." They could not have had a more respected
delegate to present their ideas to the delegates: Richmond resident
(and property owner) Chief Justice John Marshall, then seventy-
four years old. What he read amounted to a catalog of arguments
for liberalizing the suffrage. To deny the vote to a class of citizens
was to weaken their claim to all other rights because to be disfranchised was to be disempowered. With no vote, they were "like
aliens or slaves, as if destitute of interest, or unworthy of a voice,
in measures involving their future political destiny." Moreover,
Marshall read on, if no "invidious distinctions" based on property
were drawn among citizens in time of war, in terms of who had an
obligation to serve, why should such distinctions be drawn with
respect to voting?

We have been taught by our fathers that all power is vested in and derived from the people; not the freeholders: that the majority of the
community, in whom abides the physical force, have also the political
right of creating and remoulding at will their civil institutions. . . . The

generality of mankind, doubtless, desire to become owners of property: left free to reap the fruit of their labours, they will seek to acquire it honestly. It can never be their interest to overburthen, or render precarious, what they themselves desire to enjoy in peace. . . . To deny to the great body of the people all share in the Government on suspicion that they may deprive others of their property, is to rob them in advance of their rights; to look to a privileged order as the fountain and depository of all power is to depart from the fundamental maxims, to destroy the chief beauty, the characteristic feature, indeed, of Republican Government. (Mason and Leach 1959, 250–251)

As eloquent as was their plea, the nonfreeholders of Richmond and elsewhere in the Old Dominion had to wait another twenty years for the eventual demise of the property requirement.

Virginia's turning point fell into the fourth wave of prewar suffrage reform that had been initiated by the Dorr Rebellion in Rhode Island. Given the extent of the expansion of the franchise after 1776, that event in the Ocean State is noteworthy: it marked the only time in American national history in which a statewide dispute over the franchise led to organized insurrection, violence, and death.

The uprising merits a brief review. Recall that Rhode Island (officially "The State of Rhode Island and Providence Plantations," the smallest state in the union possesses the longest name) was one of only two former colonies not to write a constitution following the break with Great Britain. Instead, it carried over its existing charter, complete with property stipulations, that had been granted by King Charles II in 1663. Only freeholders and their eldest sons could vote. By the 1840s, after Andrew Jackson's presidency, such narrow suffrage was under attack as it had been in Virginia. Many of the disfranchised organized themselves as the Rhode Island Suffrage Association and, after a state constitutional convention had rejected reform proposals, held a convention in 1841 to write a "People's Constitution." Under that substitute charter, which was ratified in an impromptu referendum, voters elected a prominent Providence attorney named Thomas Wilson Dorr as governor. Meanwhile, the existing charter government passed laws to criminalize the actions of anyone acting under the People's Constitution. There were now two governors claiming legitimacy in Rhode Island. Nationally, Democrats tended to side with Dorr, Whigs with the charter government. On May 18, 1842, Dorr and some followers assembled at the state arsenal (a symbol of power and legitimacy) and attempted to seize it. Dorr and his men were driven off, and Dorr fled the state and took refuge in states in the hands of Democrats. Other quasi-military adventures by Dorr supporters over the next few months resulted in several deaths. But throughout, the charter government remained in control, thanks in part to President John Tyler's dispatch of federal troops to assist in rounding up renegades that remained at large.

The Dorr Rebellion remains constitutionally significant because it occasioned the U.S. Supreme Court's first decision in what at heart was a voting rights dispute. After the raid on the arsenal, a state military official named Luther Borden arrested Martin Luther, one of Dorr's followers. Martin Luther sued Luther Borden on the grounds that the Dorr government was the lawful government of Rhode Island and therefore Borden's arrest of Luther had been a trespass. The question in the case turned on the clause in Article IV of the U.S. Constitution that guarantees for every state "a republican form of government" (sometimes referred to as the guarantee clause). Luther's claim was that the charter government was not "republican" and that a majority of the people within a state, drawing on principles from the Declaration of Independence, therefore had a right to replace a bad government with a good one. By the time the Supreme Court decided the case in 1849, the Dorr Rebellion had entered the history books, but *Luther v. Borden* remains significant because Chief Justice Roger B. Taney, speaking for the Court, used the case as a vehicle to announce the political question doctrine. Effectively affirming the lower court's decision for the charter government, Taney tossed the basic questions in the case into the hands of the president and Congress. He explained that determining the lawful government of a state (and whether a state had a republican form of government) was the responsibility of the "Political Department" and not the judiciary. Thus, by dispatching troops to shore up the charter government, Tyler had made the decision; by admitting Rhode Island's delegation to the House and the Senate, Congress had affirmed the legitimacy of the charter regime. In other words, the answer to the question whether a state was "republican" lay not with the courts but with the legislative and executive branches.

What happened to Dorr? He returned to Rhode Island in 1843 and was promptly arrested, tried, and sentenced to life imprisonment at hard labor in 1844. The U.S. Supreme Court refused to hear an appeal from Dorr (*Ex parte Dorr,* 1844) because the habeas corpus jurisdiction of federal courts did not at that time encompass state courts. For whatever reasons, his former adversaries shortly released him from jail.

What effects did the rebellion have on the franchise in Rhode Island? The charter government acted prudently to include all native-born men—a significant enlargement—within the franchise after 1842. Rhode Island's relaxation of suffrage rules came relatively late, especially for the New England and Mid-Atlantic states. What the charter government obviously noted was that the makeup of the state's citizens had been changing. It was now noticeably an industrial and partially foreign-born population—in other words, working class. Alexander Keyssar's thesis is that the "reforms of the antebellum era were not designed or intended to enfranchise" such people (Keyssar 2000, 76). So one draws two conclusions: Had relaxation of suffrage restrictions in other industrializing and immigrant-friendly states not occurred as early as they did, they may well have been delayed for a longer time. And had those relaxations in voting requirements been delayed, the United States would likely have experienced more Dorr-type rebellions.

Still, as troubling as were the circumstances of Rhode Island's revolution, one fact surely by that time had begun to sink into the minds of even the Kents and the Randolphs and others who resolutely had opposed a relaxation of suffrage requirements—a fact that itself furthered relaxation of the rules. At least since Putney, the dire prediction had been that the admission of the unpropertied into the ranks of the electorate would endanger private property itself. In those states that had moved toward universal manhood suffrage by the 1840s, there had been no leveling, no broadscale assaults on the citadel of property. Even in Rhode Island that had not been one of Thomas Dorr's objectives. Thomas Babinton Macaulay had made a similar point in the British Parliament on March 2, 1831, in a debate on suffrage: "Universal suffrage exists in the United States without producing any very frightful consequences" (Platt 1989, 357).

Indeed, by the 1840s, the word "democracy"—government by the people, as opposed to government by the people's betters—had actually become respectable, in most quarters at least. Statistics reflected the change that was underway. In 1832 when President Andrew Jackson won a second term, he and his opponents received a total 1.29 million votes. Eight years later, when General William Henry Harrison denied a second term to President Martin Van Buren, the voting electorate had nearly doubled, to 2.4 million, an increase far outpacing the rate of population growth. And there was a second dimension to this democratization: election of the president by an appeal to the people. The Constitution had placed election of the president in the hands of unique electors (constituting the electoral college) whom "[e]ach State shall appoint, in such Manner as the Legislature thereof may direct." For the early elections most state legislatures picked these electors. Indeed, it was not until the election of 1824, when enough states had switched to the current practice of allowing the voters to elect the electors, that the custom developed of reporting the "popular vote" for president and vice president, in addition to the electoral vote. By the 1840s, this trend had accelerated so that popular election of presidential electors was the rule in nearly every state.

The fading of property as a precondition for voting by mid-century, however, by no means led to an abandonment of requirements altogether. Age had always been a criterion, and nearly every state by statute or through its constitution barred felons or others convicted of specific crimes from the polls. But as states made more people eligible to vote after 1800, additional criteria were added. Especially after 1830, states began to experiment with voter registration—official lists of those eligible to vote. For the voter, this meant that the act of voting actually consisted of two acts. First, the would-be voter would have to become registered, usually by some predetermined date in advance of election day; with his name on the roll, only then would he be allowed to vote. Ordinarily, registration would be a one-time act, unless the voter moved to another state or election district when the process would have to be completed again. Justified as a guard against fraud by assuring eligibility and discouraging multiple voting, registration was typically opposed by Democrats because it discouraged poorer and newly arrived citizens from voting. For the same reason Whigs usually supported registration.

States adopted various residency rules as well. Voter eligibility commonly required one-year residency within the state (although some expected two), with a shorter residency mandated within the county or election district. From one perspective, such conditions were consistent with the stake-in-society concept that had underlain the freehold for so long. Being part of a state or community gave one an interest in its affairs, and duration of residency was seen as a proxy for that commitment. Like registration, however, residency rules invariably barred some people from voting, and not merely those who had recently moved into a new community with intentions to put down roots. A residency rule more or less permanently disfranchised anyone who moved frequently, such as migrants and transients, and that of course was one of its purposes. (As for paupers, however, and often for inmates of nonpenal institutions, some states expressly barred them from the polls, no matter how long they had been present in a specified location.)

A third pattern that one sees in the various state definitions of eligibility is the consensus in the first half of the nineteenth century that voting was a privilege for white men only, or, depending on the wording of the exclusion, not a privilege that free African Americans could enjoy. In 1790, just three of the thirteen states formally excluded voters based on race. By 1820 such exclusions were present in fourteen of the twenty-three states, and by 1840 in twenty-one of the twenty-six states. By 1860, the prohibition was found in twenty-six of the thirty-one states. In other words, across the United States, among states old and new, free blacks could vote only in New England (minus Connecticut, which had imposed a racial test in 1818). But even there the privilege rang hollow, as only 6 percent of northern blacks in 1850 lived in those five states. (New York allowed them to vote only if they met a property requirement.) And in the few places where formal barriers did not exist, blacks might have been excluded for other reasons, as might happen if they disproportionately fell among the poor and those who did not pay taxes.

A double irony existed in this all-but-uniform racial exclusion. Blacks, free and slave, counted in determining the size of a state's delegation in the House of Representatives. According to Section 2 of Article I, population for purposes of representation "shall be determined by adding to the whole Number of Free Persons, including those bound to Service for a Term of Years, and excluding Indians not taxed, three fifths of all other persons." Thus free blacks were counted like any other person. Three-fifths of enslaved blacks—those euphemistically referred to as "all other Persons" by the Constitution (although it countenanced slavery, the

Constitution of 1787 never used the word "slave")—were then added to the total. So African Americans, slave or free, male or female, enhanced to some measure a state's clout in Congress, as did white women, all the while those same states largely barred them from the polls. The same formula was used in setting the number of electoral votes assigned to each state in the electoral college. A state's electoral vote was a function of the size of its congressional delegation (its representatives plus its two senators). Thus a large slave population or the presence of many free blacks amplified the power of white men in presidential contests. Indeed, without that electoral anomaly, Thomas Jefferson—the first successful opposition candidate for the White House—probably would not have won the presidency in 1800 (Wills 2003, xiii).

If antiblack sentiment was widespread, less consensus existed with respect to citizenship as a criterion for voting—that is, whether alienage should be a disqualifying factor. Beginning with its colonial heritage, the United States has always been a nation of immigrants. They have usually been welcomed into the economic life of the country, but not necessarily into its political life, as the two decades before the Civil War illustrate. What historians refer to as the "old migration" picked up speed between 1820 and 1850 and consisted heavily of Irish, Germans, and Scandinavians. (The "new migration" was a hallmark of the late nineteenth and early twentieth centuries, consisting largely of eastern and southern Europeans.) During the 1830s, there were 552,000 arrivals, 1.5 million in the 1840s, and 2.7 million in the 1850s. It was surely a challenge for the nation to absorb them all, especially when one recalls that the national population in 1830 was but 12 million (Kleppner 1992, 46). Indeed, by 1850 more than one-fifth of those living in Boston and New York had been born in Ireland.

The recent arrivals tended to fall into one of two categories: settlers and workers (Hoerder 1985, 3–31). The former reached America with skills and wherewithal. They often ventured into the upper midwest and the newly settled areas of the northwest, bought land, and were absorbed into the middle class. The latter were typically impoverished, Catholic, and Irish, and had been peasants in the Old World. They usually settled in the cities of the northeast and got jobs in factories or in railroad construction projects. Although many states excluded immigrants from the polls until they had been naturalized, some thinly populated states deliberately tried to encourage growth, especially by the agrarian-disposed settler class. Between 1848 and 1859, for instance, declarant noncitizens (those who had affirmed that they intended to become citizens) were awarded the vote after only a brief residency period in Indiana, Kansas, Michigan, Minnesota, Oregon, Wisconsin, and the Washington territory (Keyssar 2000, 83).

It was the worker class, concentrated in the cities of the east, that ignited American nativism on a grand scale for the first time. Just as voting and legislative apportionment had been linked in Virginia in the late 1820s, voting and immigration came to be linked in the minds of those who wanted to preserve America for old-stock Americans. The Order of the Star-Spangled Banner was founded in New York State in 1849 as a secret, oath-bound fraternal order. Its members came to be called "Know-Nothings" because of the response they gave when questioned by outsiders about the society. By 1854, the order claimed a million members and had lodges in every northern state. It drew members from across the political spectrum. Know-Nothings were highly suspicious of immigrants, especially Catholic ones, believing that the large influx of Catholics would lead to "Romanism"—nothing less than papal control of the United States. Anti-Catholicism was hardly original with the Know-Nothings, but with a surge in the number of Catholic immigrants with no end in sight, they capitalized on feelings already well ingrained into Protestant America. Immigrants were also suspect because their values were not perceived to be "American." Irish Catholics especially were thought to drink too much and to have questionable morals and criminal tendencies. And immigrants were said to fuel political corruption.

Their votes could be bought with liquor or money, it was claimed, and there were stories passed around of mass naturalizations in cities just prior to elections to swell the turnout.

The order burst onto the political scene in 1854, appropriately calling itself the American Party. Along with the Anti-Masonic, Liberty, and Free-Soil parties, it was among the first of the so-called third parties (minor parties that function alongside the major parties) in the United States. It went its own way as a separate party because pragmatic politicians among Democrats and Whigs, in their struggle for votes, could hardly allow their parties to be branded with nativism. Democrats and Whigs alike could do the arithmetic. There was too much to lose (Kleppner 1992, 51). Nonetheless, the Know-Nothings had an astonishing, if brief, run of successes. Not surprisingly, they were strongest in states and cities of the east with large immigrant populations. Within two years the new party could claim eight governors, more than one hundred members of Congress, the mayors of Boston, Philadelphia, and Chicago, and hundreds of local officials (Annbinder 1992, ix-xiv). But the Know-Nothings disappeared as a distinct political party almost as suddenly as they had appeared. By 1857, the party was in control of ex-Whigs more focused on preserving the union than on immigrants, and soon, with the rise of the new Republican party, the American Party disintegrated as a national political force (Holt 1973, vol 1., 575–620).

The startling arrival and departure of the Know-Nothings is a fascinating, even revealing, political story, but the organization deserves space in a book on voting rights both because of what the American Party tried to do and what it accomplished. Along with some Whigs, and later Republicans, the Know-Nothings advocated legislation to prevent aliens from voting (where that was allowed), to set up tough registration systems, and to impose literacy tests (from which property holders would be excused). Moreover, they had plans to address the immigrant issue directly. Never going so far to call for closing the borders, they instead wanted Congress to enact long residency periods before aliens would be eligible for naturalization, to ban state judges (who might be tied too closely to local political organizations) from conducting naturalizations, and to mandate a long waiting period *after* naturalization before new citizens would be eligible to vote. Depending on the particular proposal, the time between a man's disembarkation on the east coast and the casting of his first ballot would be more than twenty years (Annbinder 1992, 253).

The most extreme proposals got nowhere. Elected officials were wary of alienating recent immigrants who were already part of the electorate. But some proposals were enacted even after the American Party disappeared as a discrete unit of national politics. For example, Connecticut in 1855 and Massachusetts in 1857 enacted literacy tests that required prospective voters to write their names and to read a passage from the Constitution. Know-Nothings claimed the measures would reduce the number of "ignorant, imbruted Irish" at the polls (Keyssar 2000, 86). (Massachusetts, however, compromised its test to exempt men over sixty and anyone who had previously voted.) The Bay State also imposed a two-year postnaturalization waiting period on immigrants before they would be eligible to vote—a stipulation that was later repealed during the Civil War, probably for enlistment reasons. And the same state and Maine specified that, in order to qualify, immigrants would have to present their naturalization papers to election officials three months ahead of the election. In New York the legislature in 1859 passed a stringent registration bill to "purify" the ballot box that applied only in New York City and New York County. Four states in New England and a few elsewhere prohibited state judges from conducting naturalizations. Alongside all that had been advocated as policy for the nation, these steps did not amount to a colossal retrogression in voting rights. Yet each of the Know-Nothing-inspired measures, in one way or the other, placed obstacles on the path to the polls. Most significant perhaps was resort to the literacy test, which would later figure prominently in wholesale efforts to discourage voting by African Americans. The nativistic tsunami of the 1850s showed that many Americans were distinctly uncomfortable with the nearly universal regime of white manhood suffrage that was now a reality. That expansion of the suffrage had taken roughly eight and a half decades to achieve. But the Civil War with its cataclysmic effects was about to reposition the voting rights debate.

THE RECONSTRUCTION AMENDMENTS

Two great questions dominated the voting-rights debate in the last third of the nineteenth century: the status of African American men and the status of women, white and black alike. Those subjects loomed large after the Civil War (1861–1865), and both are treated in the last two sections of this chapter. But voting rights for African American men became salient not merely after, but *because* of the outcome of, that conflict. And so it is to the legal fallout of that war—the Reconstruction amendments in particular and the attitudes that accompanied them—that this book now turns.

In U.S. history, the Civil War remains the landmark event that dwarfs all others in the nineteenth century. Especially with respect to black men, it is impossible to know with certainty when they would have gained access to the ballot box had the conflict between the states not occurred. Because voting eligibility was entirely a matter for each state to define, one supposes—if the earlier expansion of the franchise to include almost all while adult males is any guide—that voting rights would have been conferred grudgingly and gradually over several decades. This would have been true even in the South as changed economic realities made slavery unprofitable and brought about its abandonment by century's end. What one does know for certain is that, without the war, neither the end of slavery nor the enfranchisement of African American men would have occurred so soon.

On the eve of the Civil War, attitudes of white Americans on
the subject of race reflected both widespread disagreement as well
as agreement. Seen through the prism of slavery—virtually all
slaves were African American, and the overwhelming majority of
African Americans were slaves—no consensus on race existed.
Legally after 1830, the nation was divided in half: with few exceptions, slavery had been made illegal everywhere except the South,
the border states, and some territories. Accordingly, attitudes toward correct public policy fell into five categories, but of these,
only one called for an immediate elimination of slavery.

Among the other four, the position most favorable to slave
owners insisted on their absolute right to possess slaves anywhere
in the United States. Legally at least, this would allow slavery to
expand into new areas and take root. Consistent with this view, as
stressed by statesmen such as John C. Breckenridge, vice president in the presidency of James Buchanan and the southern
Democratic candidate for president in 1860, any escaped slave re-
captured in a free state remained a slave and was to be returned to
his or her master or mistress. Moreover, anyone abetting the es-
cape was to be prosecuted under the Fugitive Slave Act. Anchor-
ing the opposition at the other end of the spectrum were aboli-
tionists such as James G. Birney and Charles Sumner who called
for immediate emancipation, although among antislavery groups
there was no consensus as to how that would be accomplished
within the Union. In between were other convictions. Less
friendly to the slavocracy, but not intrinsically antislavery, some
believed that slavery was a matter to be determined by each state
or territory for itself. This application of "popular sovereignty" to
the status of slavery in the United States was thought by persons
such as Senator Stephen A. Douglas, regular Democratic presidential candidate in 1860, to be the only way to prevent the slavery dispute from splitting the Union. Abraham Lincoln, the successful Republican presidential candidate in 1860 (who had

unsuccessfully challenged Douglas for the Senate in 1858), and other members of his party insisted on the prerogative of Congress to ban slavery in the territories as a way to prevent slavery's spread and eventually to choke it off as a sectional anachronism. It was Lincoln's theory that the Supreme Court deemed constitutionally unacceptable in the infamous *Dred Scott Case* of 1857, which held that a congressional (or territorial legislative) ban on slavery in a territory violated the property rights of slave owners (*Scott v. Sandford*). Then there was the theory of persons like Senator and future Chief Justice Salmon P. Chase. They enraged slave owners in their belief (also rejected by the Supreme Court in *Jones v. Van Zandt,* 1847) that slavery could not exist outside a state that allowed it; consequently, slaves ceased to be slaves once they set foot on free soil, regardless of whether they had escaped; accordingly, the national Fugitive Slave Act itself was unconstitutional.

In contrast to that array of opinion, a broad consensus existed on the status of free blacks: they were not deserving of the full blessings of citizenship. Indeed, most whites believed that assimilation was both undesirable and impossible, notions that had driven establishment of the American Colonization Society that promoted resettlement of free blacks in Africa. Deprivations went beyond the denial of the right to vote in almost all states. Attitudes of white supremacy and black inferiority prevailed. In calling for slaves not only to be freed but to "share an equality with the whites, of civil and religious privileges," the views of the American Anti-Slavery Society, founded in 1833, were very much the exception (Kraditor 1973, vol. 1, 741). "The major political parties, whatever their position on slavery, vied with each other in their devotion to that doctrine [of white supremacy], and extremely few politicians of importance dared question them" (Woodward 1966, 18). It was no southern slave owner but Abraham Lincoln who made the following statement in Illinois in 1858:

I will say then that I am not, nor ever have been in favor of bringing about in any way the social and political equality of the white and black races [applause]—that I am not nor ever have been in favor of making voters or jurors of negroes nor of qualifying them to hold office, nor to intermarry with white people, and I will say in addition to this that there is a physical difference between the black and white races which I believe will forever forbid the two races living together on terms of social and political equality. (Basler 1953, vol. 3, 247–248)

In the context of his debates with Senator Douglas, Lincoln's appeal to Illinois voters was understandable. Indiana, Illinois, and Oregon had provisions in their constitutions restricting the admission of blacks within their borders. Several other states required blacks to post bond upon entrance to assure good behavior. By custom or by law, blacks were excluded from jury service almost everywhere and in some states could not testify in court against a white person. As one historian depicted the full prewar development of this third-class treatment,

[w]hile statutes and customs circumscribed the Negro's political and judicial rights, extralegal codes—enforced by public opinion—relegated him to a position of social inferiority.... In virtually every phase of existence, Negroes found themselves systematically separated from whites. They were either excluded from railway cars, omnibuses, stagecoaches, and steamboats or assigned to special "Jim Crow" sections; they sat, when permitted, in secluded and remote corners of theaters and lecture halls; they could not enter most hotels, restaurants, and resorts, except as servants; they prayed in "Negro pews" in the white churches, and if partaking of the sacrament of the Lord's Supper, they waited until the whites had been served the bread and the wine. Moreover, they were often educated in segregated schools, punished in segregated prisons, nursed in segregated hospitals, and buried in segregated cemeteries. (Litwack 1961, 97)

Perhaps Alexis de Tocqueville, the close French observer of Jacksonian America, said it most directly:

> In that part of the Union where the Negroes are no longer slaves, have they come closer to the whites? Everyone who has lived in the United States will have noticed just the opposite. Race prejudice seems stronger in those states that have abolished slavery than in those where it still exists, and nowhere is it more intolerant than in those states where slavery was never known. (de Tocqueville 1966, 315)

Appreciation of this pervasive prejudice is helpful in grasping the fact that the decision to move forward on black voting rights in the postwar period rested on little more than a thin veneer of conviction. Understandably, then, extending the franchise to blacks was one of the last policies to be pursued during the postwar Reconstruction.

The Civil War provided a military answer to questions about the legitimacy of secession and the supremacy of the national government. A long-running debate in American federalism thus was settled, if not entirely silenced. Generated but not resolved by the war were many other issues, chief among which was the status of the newly freed slave population that numbered about 4 million. Along with a series of statutes, the Thirteenth, Fourteenth, and Fifteenth Amendments to the U.S. Constitution—ratified between December 1865 and March 1870—addressed that matter directly. They remain today the constitutional legacy of the Republic's greatest domestic crisis. Some attention to the scope of those amendments, as well as to the circumstances of their creation, will help in understanding the fate of black voting rights, especially when those issues arrived at the U.S. Supreme Court for review. As will be seen, the broad consensus that had formed by the close of the war that slavery should be abolished soon dissipated as the discussion shifted to other aspects of status.

The Thirteenth Amendment, which ended slavery, was therefore the least surprising of the three amendments, even if its human consequences were vast. In granting freedom to one class, it imposed a huge and unprecedented economic penalty on another. No compensation was paid to the slave owners, most of whom lived in the states of the late Confederacy and now faced financial ruin. "The legal authority of the United States was thus used for an annihilation of individual property rights without parallel (outside of modern communism) in the history of the Western world" (Palmer 1960, 543). Proposed four months before General Robert E. Lee's surrender at Appomattox Courthouse in April 1865, ratification of the Thirteenth Amendment in December made permanent and national a major Union war objective born in President Lincoln's Emancipation Proclamation two years earlier. The amendment quickly accomplished its immediate objective, as slavery vanished from the fields and from the political agenda.

More than either of the other two amendments of this period, the Fourteenth Amendment, proposed in June 1866 and ratified in July 1868, signaled a new relationship between national and state governments that had been decreed by the Union victory. In contrast to the single objectives of the Thirteenth and Fifteenth Amendments (the latter to be discussed shortly), the Fourteenth was actually five amendments rolled into one. The first sentence of Section 1 addressed citizenship: "All persons born or naturalized in the United States and subject to the jurisdiction thereof, are citizens of the United States and of the State wherein they reside." Those twenty-eight words constitutionally consigned to the trash heap the Supreme Court's holding in the *Dred Scott Case* (1857), that the framers of the Constitution never intended African Americans to be included within the meaning of the word "citizens" and so could "claim none of the rights and privileges which that instrument provide[d] for and secure[d] to citizens of the United States." Those twenty-eight words were also the Constitution's first definition of state and national citizenship.

Additionally, the second sentence of Section 1 proclaimed new, broad, but undefined restrictions on state power: "No State shall make or enforce any law which shall abridge the privileges or immunities of citizens of the United States; nor shall any State deprive any person of life, liberty, or property, without due process of law; nor deny to any person within its jurisdiction the equal protection of the laws."

The first clause borrowed language from Article IV of the Constitution: "The Citizens of each State shall be entitled to all Privileges and Immunities of Citizens in the several States." The second clause drew verbatim from the due process limitation on the national government in the Fifth Amendment. The words of the third clause were new to the Constitution, and seemed to tweak the guaranties of the first and second clauses. Taken together, the three evidenced a strong antidiscriminatory purpose.

Most immediately, both parts of Section 1 erased any lingering doubts about the constitutionality of the Civil Rights Act of 1866. This comprehensive statute, designed to augment the Thirteenth Amendment's abolition of slavery, had declared all persons born in the United States to be national citizens. The statute also sought to remove various discriminations against blacks in contractual rights and in the criminal justice system. As with the Fourteenth Amendment itself, these statutory bans were designed to apply throughout the United States, not merely within the states of the late Confederacy.

[S]uch citizens, of every race and color, without regard to any previous condition of slavery or involuntary servitude . . . shall have the same right, in every State and Territory . . ., to make and enforce contracts, to sue, be parties, and give evidence, to inherit, purchase, lease, sell, hold, and convey real and personal property, and to full and equal benefit of all laws and proceedings for the security of persons and property, as is enjoyed by white citizens, and shall be subject to like punishment, pains, and penalties, and to none other, any law,

statute, ordinance, regulation, or custom, to the contrary notwith-
standing.

By constitutionalizing as well as codifying both these guaranties and a new relationship between national and state governments, Congress greatly reduced the chance that lawmakers of a
later day might undo its work. Little wonder that the Fourteenth
Amendment has sometimes been called the "Second Constitution."

Section 3 of the Fourteenth Amendment politically disabled
former Confederate leaders, Section 4 foreclosed any attempt by
nation or state to assume the Confederate debt or to pay compensation to former slave owners, and Section 5 empowered Congress
to enforce the terms of the amendment. Yet it is only in Section 2
that an oblique and curious reference to voting rights appears. It
eliminated the "three-fifth's compromise" (discussed earlier in this
chapter, this provision in the Constitution of 1787 counted three-
fifths of the slave population for purposes of determining representation in the House of Representatives and votes in the electoral college). But Section 4 also dictated that a state's
representation in Congress would be reduced in proportion to the
number of males twenty-one years of age and older who were denied the right to vote. In so doing, the Fourteenth Amendment indirectly recognized the principle of adult *manhood* suffrage that
had become the norm in the late prewar years. But the hand that
gave also took away. Although that penalty has never been exacted from a state, the amendment directly anticipated, and indirectly allowed, albeit at a cost, racially based disfranchisement.

The origins of the Fifteenth Amendment ("The right . . . to vote
shall not be denied or abridged by the United States or by any
State on account of race, color, or previous condition of servitude.") thus rest in the Fourteenth. For the first time the Constitution embodied a limitation on how the states defined the franchise within their borders. This innovation was a major break

with the way in which Americans had conducted their elections. The last dictates on suffrage from without predated the Revolution: the Crown-imposed freehold, which colonial leaders had accepted as customary and unobjectionable.

The Fifteenth Amendment also derived from complex political realities at a time when the future of the Republican Party was at stake. With the prospect of Democratic inroads at the polls in the North, Republican control of Congress and the White House, dating from the elections of 1860, was in danger. This was a matter of concern, especially in view of an increase by some fifteen seats in southern representation in the House as a result of the elimination of the three-fifths compromise. Blacks in the South would surely vote Republican if they were allowed to vote. Yet the difficulty in 1866 in providing security for black voters in the South was compounded by the fact that blacks in northern states voted freely only in New England. Indeed, voters in eleven northern states expressly rejected black suffrage between 1865 and 1869 (Gillette 1965, 25–26). An extension of the vote to blacks by way of a provision in the Fourteenth Amendment at the time it was proposed in 1866, therefore, might have been costly to Republicans at the polls. Besides it may well have doomed ratification of the amendment itself. Awareness of this reality would probably explain the complete absence of the word "race" in the Fourteenth Amendment. Section 2 thus represented a compromise between doing a lot for black suffrage and doing nothing. If southern states excluded blacks from the polls, they did so at the risk of losing representation in the House and votes in the electoral college, thereby also diminishing somewhat the impact of a Democratic resurgence in the old Confederacy. The Fourteenth Amendment thus tacitly recognized the widespread unacceptability among whites, almost everywhere, of voting by black men.

Also part of the equation that yielded the Fifteenth Amendment was a series of congressional enactments in 1867 requiring black suffrage in some territories and the District of Columbia and as a condition for Nebraska's admission to the Union. In addition, the Reconstruction Act of that year required black voting as a condition for readmitting the former states of the Confederacy to the Union and reseating their delegations in Congress. An ironic double standard was now in place. Black voting was the law of the land except in most northern states, all of which had been free soil before the war.

Republican setbacks among northern white voters in the elections of 1868, however, stimulated a rethinking of this policy of voting rights incrementalism. If there were political risks in promoting black voting, there were perhaps greater risks in failing to protect it. Only a constitutional amendment would open the polls fully to blacks in the North. "You need votes in Connecticut, do you not?" asked Massachusetts Republican Senator Charles Sumner, an architect of Reconstruction policy and Congress's chief abominator of all things associated with the white South. "There are three thousand fellow-citizens in that State ready at the call of Congress to take their place at the ballot box. You need them also in Pennsylvania, do you not?" he went on. "There are at least fifteen thousand in that great State waiting for your summons. Wherever you most need them, there they are; and be assured they will all vote for those who stand by them in the assertion of Equal Rights" (Stephenson 1988, 51).

Various versions in Congress of what became the Fifteenth Amendment would have guaranteed the right of blacks to hold political office; directly conferred the vote on all males twenty-one years of age and older; and eliminated poll taxes, literacy tests, and property qualifications. These would have been monumental achievements had they been incorporated, perhaps avoiding problems of titanic proportions in later years. In the interests of passage and ratification, however, all were eliminated from the final version that was proposed to the states on February 26, 1869—not an affirmative extension of the franchise but an injunction against the use of race in setting qualifications for voting. Questionable prospects for ratification—some West and East Coast Republicans feared it would give the Chinese and too many Irish access to the polls—may explain why there was so little discussion in the Fortieth Congress on Section 2 of the amendment—the enforcement clause. That involved the consensus-splitting issue of federal control over state election laws, best left wrapped in silence. As it was, Tennessee, Kentucky, Delaware, and Maryland (former slave states not covered by the Reconstruction acts) rejected the amendment, as did California and Oregon. Ohio rejected it initially, until Republican leaders, including Supreme Court Justice Noah Swayne, intervened and persuaded enough state legislators to change their minds (Stephenson 2003, 68). New York rescinded its ratification. Nonetheless, the requisite number of states signed on to make the amendment officially a part of the Constitution on March 30, 1870.

Make no mistake about it: the Thirteenth, Fourteenth, and Fifteenth Amendments were ambitious measures. As the first shots were fired in the Civil War in April 1861, hardly anyone imagined either the severity or the length of the conflict to come or the changes that the war's outcome would bring. Within a span of only fourteen years, the Republican Party had gone from calling for a ban on slavery in the territories to the achievement of goals that the party's center had not even contemplated with respect to African Americans when Republicans ran their first candidate for president in 1856 and when their second candidate won the presidency in 1860. The amendments gave constitutional protections for equality an unprecedented jumpstart.

Yet each amendment was also restrained. Given the total collapse of the Confederacy and the unconditional surrender by the South, much that might have been done in the wake of so great a defeat was not. None of the amendments provided for reparations to former slaves or guaranteed a redistribution of land to them. No new political system was enshrined. Federal power could now check state power in certain new respects, but did not truly displace it. States still retained the primary responsibility for legislating with respect to the lives of their citizens, including voting and elections. Exactly what balance would ultimately be struck between the competing objectives of ambition and restraint would be left to the Supreme Court.

Three weeks before the death of Chief Justice Salmon Chase, the Supreme Court examined the Thirteenth and Fourteenth amendments for the first time in the *Slaughterhouse Cases* (1873). The circumstances of the litigation seemed about as remote as could be from the presumed purpose of the amendments: racial justice (Labbé and Lurie 2003, 245). Moreover, the tight five-to-four decision symbolized the lack of consensus over precisely what the amendments, especially the Fourteenth, were supposed to accomplish. The case warrants attention here for two reasons: first, it cast a long shadow on the Supreme Court for a number of years with respect to voting rights; second, it was an astonishing decision to be rendered by a bench of eight justices that had been appointed by *Republican* presidents (five by Lincoln and three by Ulysses Grant).

In 1869 the carpetbag legislature of Louisiana chartered the Crescent City Livestock Landing & Slaughter-House Company and gave it a monopoly over the slaughtering of animals in three parishes, including the city of New Orleans. As many as 1,000 butchers were adversely affected. Barred from slaughtering on their own premises, they had to use the Crescent City facilities at a fee. In three separate cases, the Butchers' Benevolent Association and others unsuccessfully sought an injunction in the state courts to block the monopoly. When the cases reached the U.S. Supreme Court, their attorney, former Justice John A. Campbell, argued that the legislation was constitutionally defective on four counts: (1) that it created "an involuntary servitude forbidden by the thirteenth article of amendment," (2) that it abridged "the privileges and immunities of citizens of the United States," (3) that it denied them "the equal protection of the laws," and (4) that it deprived them "of their property without due process of law; contrary to the provisions of the first section of the fourteenth article of amendment."

"This court," Justice Samuel Miller momentously observed for the majority, "is thus called upon for the first time to give construction of these articles." Miller continued,

> On the most casual examination of the language of these amendments, no one can fail to be impressed with the one pervading purpose found in them all, . . . and without which none of them would have even been suggested, we mean the freedom of the slave race, the security and firm establishment of that freedom. . . . It is true that only the fifteenth amendment, in terms, mentions the negro [sic] by speaking of his color and his slavery. But it is just as true that each of the other articles was addressed to the grievances of that race, as designed to remedy them as the fifteenth.

As for the constitutional objections alleged by the aggrieved butchers, Miller thought counts one, three, and four merited only the briefest attention. To regard the Louisiana regulation as "involuntary servitude" within the meaning of the Thirteenth Amendment "requires an effort, to say the least of it." Miller also perfunctorily dispensed with the butchers' due process objection: "Under no construction of that provision that we have ever seen, or any that we deem admissible, can the restraint imposed by . . . Louisiana . . . be held to be a deprivation of property within the meaning of that provision." As for the equal protection claim, Miller "doubt[ed] very much whether any action . . . not directed by way of discrimination against the negroes as a class, or on account of their race [neither of which applied in this instance], would ever be held to come within the purview of this provision."

Regarding the second count, Miller seized on the first sentence of Section 1 as a means of virtually dispatching the privileges and immunities clause from the Fourteenth Amendment. That sentence spoke of state citizenship and national citizenship. The second sentence spoke of "the privileges and immunities of citizens of the United States," leading Miller to conclude that one possessed certain privileges and immunities by virtue of state citizenship and others by virtue of national citizenship. The latter consisted of rights created by the national government. The remaining (and larger) category of rights either flowed from state citizenship or predated formation of the national government. These were "fundamental" rights that belonged "to the citizens of all free governments," as Justice Bushrod Washington had written in an 1823 circuit court opinion construing the privileges and immunities clause of Article IV. Although declining to enumerate them, Washington suggested "several general heads: protection by the government, with the right to acquire and possess property of every kind, and to pursue and obtain happiness and safety, subject, nevertheless, to such restraints as the government may prescribe for the general good of the whole" (*Corfield v. Coryell* 1823). Accordingly, Miller insisted that any liberties claimed by the butchers—such as a right to pursue a lawful calling—derived from state citizenship and so fell outside the protection of the Fourteenth Amendment. To read the clause more generously, Miller contended, would make the Supreme Court "a perpetual censor upon all legislation of the States" and "radically change the whole theory of the relations of the State and Federal governments to each other and of both these governments to the people."

If shoring up constitutionally the Civil Rights Act of 1866 was the most widely understood purpose of the Fourteenth Amendment when it was proposed and ratified, as seems today to be generally conceded (Currie 1985, 347), the Court both undershot and overshot the mark in the *Slaughterhouse Cases*. Miller resisted a broader reading to avoid altering the federal balance, but a strong case can be made that the amendment was indeed supposed to alter that balance. Although the framers and ratifiers of the amendment may not have had local monopolistic legislation in mind when they used the words "privileges and immunities," they presumably intended the amendment to prevent penalties that a state might impose on some of its residents in the exercise of basic rights, just as Article IV had always enjoined a state from denying basic rights to nonresidents that it afforded to its own residents. On the other hand, by emphasizing the racial purpose of all three amendments, Miller made abundantly clear what the authors of the amendments had sought to obscure for partisan reasons. Still, it would be Miller's narrow view that frequently dictated the Supreme Court's application of the Reconstruction amendments in civil rights cases after Morrison R. Waite of Ohio assumed the chief justiceship on March 4, 1874.

RACE AND VOTING: A PROMISE UNFULFILLED

The Fifteenth Amendment ushered in a new phenomenon: voting by African Americans. With overt opposition to black voting in so many parts of the nation, however—recall the Fourteenth Amendment's timidity on the question—would blacks truly be able to exercise their newly acquired constitutional right? If local officials or private persons attempted to impede their voting, how would the courts view vigorous enforcement efforts to make the right a reality? The answers to those questions reveal that it took many decades to fulfill the promise of the Fifteenth Amendment in a saga that divides itself roughly into four periods: (1) from 1870 until 1893, (2) from 1893 until 1927, (3) from 1927 until 1965, and (4) from 1965 until the present. The status of black voting rights in the first period may fairly be characterized by the word "irresolution," by "retreat" in the second, by "restoration" in the third, and by "clarification" in the fourth.

The *Slaughterhouse Cases* had revealed a bench sharply divided over the breadth of the Fourteenth Amendment. Yet as racially tinted civil rights cases involving one or more of the Reconstruction amendments arrived at the Supreme Court, one might have expected the justices, remembering what Justice Miller in the *Slaughterhouse Cases* had called the "persuasive purpose" of the amendments, to have had an easier time deciding them than the Chase Court had had with the butchers' lament. As it happened, dissents were few, but racially driven voting rights claims only rarely prevailed.

Yet the fact that voting rights cases would now begin to be part of the Supreme Court's docket was itself a novelty. The Supreme Court held its first session in 1790, more than eight decades before Waite became chief justice. Yet in all that time, voting rights cases were not part of the Court's business, largely because the franchise had been a matter the Constitution reserved exclusively for the states to determine. As an earlier section of this chapter explained, the closest the prewar Court had gotten to the ballot box had been in foreswearing any desire to become entangled in Rhode Island's Dorr Rebellion, itself chiefly a revolt over voting rights (*Luther v. Borden*, 1849). But congressional steps to implement the Reconstruction amendments had moved closer to forever changing the Court's relationship with the electoral process.

That fact became apparent when the Supreme Court decided *United States v. Reese* and *United States v. Cruikshank* in 1876. Both involved the Enforcement Act of 1870, which Congress passed soon after ratification of the Fifteenth Amendment. Each tested the meaning of this newest amendment as well as Congress's authority to make that meaning a reality. Each decision foreshadowed a bleak future for black voting rights.

Section 1 of the statute declared a right to vote free from racial discrimination. Section 2 made it unlawful for an official, on account of race, to refuse to permit citizens to perform actions required for voting, such as payment of a poll tax. Section 3 specified that if an official violated Section 2, the aggrieved citizen could present an affidavit to that effect to those in charge of an election and that the affidavit would qualify him to vote. Section 4 made it unlawful for any person to prevent another from voting or from doing those things necessary to qualify for voting. When *Reese* reached the Supreme Court for argument in January 1875, at issue were indictments based on Sections 3 and 4.

The facts in the case were revealing as to ways in which blacks could be kept from voting. William Garner, a black man residing in Lexington, Kentucky, was denied the right to vote in January 1873. The city charter required payment of a head tax of $1.50 before one could vote. The tax was due on or before January 15, but when Garner attempted to pay the tax, the collector refused to accept it. When Garner later produced the affidavit as set forth in Section 3, Hiram Reese and Matthew Foushee, two of the three election inspectors in Lexington, refused to allow him to vote. Garner claimed that the tax collector and the inspectors acted as they did solely because of his race.

According to Chief Justice Waite, the Court's principal task was to determine at the outset what the Fifteenth Amendment had done. It "does not confer the right of suffrage upon anyone," he wrote. Rather, it prevented states from conditioning the vote on race. "It follows that the amendment has invested the citizens of the United States with a new constitutional right which is within the protecting power of Congress." But the right granted was not the right to vote, but the right to vote free of discrimination based on race. To be "appropriate legislation" within the meaning of Section 2 of the amendment, therefore, Sections 3 and 4 of the statute needed to refer explicitly to "wrongful refusal . . . because of race." Unlike the first two sections of the statute, however, Sections 3 and 4 did not explicitly refer to race when criminalizing the refusal to accept the affidavit or the obstruction of someone's attempt to vote. The Court refused to accept the government's contention that Section 3 was merely the next step to cope with the racially discriminatory act proscribed in Section 2. Moreover, both Sections 3 and 4 contained the word "aforesaid," referring presumably to the racially based denial of the vote in Sections 1 and 2. Instead, the Court concluded that the Sections 3 and 4 on which the indictments were based were severed from the Fifteenth Amendment because the sections omitted reference to race and because the amendment authorized no general protection of the right to vote, only protection of the right to vote free of racial discrimination. Sections 3 and 4 were deemed "inappropriate" and therefore unconstitutional.

Only Ward Hunt, a New Yorker and the most junior associate justice, dissented. He rejected outright the reading the majority gave to the 1870 Act. The "intention of Congress on this subject is too plain to be discussed. . . . Just so far as the ballot to . . . the freedmen is abridged, in the same degree is their importance and their security diminished. . . . Punishment is the means, protection is the end," he continued. "The arrest, conviction and sentence to imprisonment of one inspector, who refused the vote of a person of African descent on account of his race, would more effectually secure the right of the voter than would any number of civil suits in the state courts, prosecuted by timid, ignorant and penniless parties against those possessing the wealth, the influence and the sentiment of the community." For Hunt, the law in question was not only appropriate within the terms of the amendment, but the most effectual means of achieving its objective: a franchise free of racial discrimination. Echoing the petition of the unfranchised residents of Richmond at Virginia's constitutional convention of 1829–1830, noted earlier in this chapter, Hunt also perceptively identified the implications for power and personal security that accompanied access to the ballot. Conversely, those denied the vote were at the mercy of everyone else.

What seemed implausible about *Reese* was not the majority's reading of the Fifteenth Amendment. Theirs had become the mainstream Republican view. It conformed to what Waite had written a year earlier in *Minor v. Happersett* (1875), discussed later in this chapter and which tested whether the privileges and immunities clause of the Fourteenth Amendment barred states from excluding women from the polls. The provision "did not add to the privileges and immunities of a citizen," he wrote. "It simply furnished an additional guaranty for the protection of such as he already had." Except by conferring national and state citizenship on those who lacked it, "no new voters were necessarily made by it." The Fourteenth Amendment, then, did not make voting a privilege and immunity of citizenship. Rather, *Reese* seemed implausible because of the majority's reading of the statute. Not only did Hunt make the stronger argument, but the concurring opinion by Nathan Clifford of Maine, a Democrat and the sole surviving prewar member of the Court, found the racial nexus obvious between the first and last pair of sections. His conclusion that the indictments were defective rested not on constitutional, but factual, grounds. (The other Democrat on the Court, Lincoln-appointee Stephen J. Field of California, joined Waite's opinion.)

Why might the Court have resorted to such a tortured reading of the statute? One explanation is partisan. According to this view, the six Republican justices in the majority reflected their party's dismay at the losses they suffered in the congressional elections of 1874, where Democrats gained a majority in the House of Representatives for the first time since the Buchanan administration in the late 1850s. By largely defanging a prominent piece of Reconstruction legislation, the bench did the party a favor by making the link between Republicans and civil rights more distant, therefore making the party more appealing to white voters, all the while leaving open opportunity for Congress to correct the statutory deficiencies if the political climate changed (Maltz 1996, 76–77).

Yet one would think that party leaders and Republican legislators would be more attuned to that need than the Court. Besides, *Reese* would appear to be a carom shot at best for that objective. Moreover, such partisan motivation seemed wholly out of character for at least some of the majority, especially Miller and Joseph Bradley, and Waite himself. To be sure, these three were faithful

Republicans, but little in their backgrounds would lead one to expect party-driven behavior on the bench. Besides, if the *Reese* Court was moved mainly by partisan concerns, why did Justice Field, a truly partisan Democrat in the majority, cooperate with his colleagues' supposed attempt to rescue the Republican Party? A more probable explanation was the spirit that animated the decision in the *Slaughterhouse Cases* that had evidently enveloped most of the bench: suspicion of an enlarged federal authority, unless both the Constitution and the relevant statute spoke unequivocally. Also served was a related objective: insisting on specificity and clarity in the criminal law, and construing criminal statutes narrowly, had long been seen as a way to avoid injustices. Among other things, the Waite bench seemed to be reminding Congress as it embarked on its new civil rights adventure to dot its "i's" and to cross its "t's."

At about the same time that Garner was denied the right to vote in Kentucky, a violent event occurred in Louisiana. Because of a disputed election, Democrats and Republicans both laid claim to local offices. A posse composed of black men authorized by the state's carpetbag Republican governor occupied the Grant Parish Courthouse in Colfax. (In Louisiana, the parish fills the position in local government that the county does in other states.) Whites representing the rival Democratic group stormed the building, and at least sixty blacks were killed. The Justice Department (Congress had established this newest unit in the cabinet in 1870) sought to indict more than 100 whites under the Enforcement Act of 1870, Section 6 of which prohibited the banding together of persons "with the intent to violate any provision of this Act, or . . . to prevent or hinder [an individual's] free exercise and enjoyment of any right or privilege granted or secured to him by the Constitution or laws of the United States." Indictments were returned against only eight whites, including William Cruikshank, charging that they had conspired to deprive two citizens "of African descent and persons of color" of a number of rights, all of which "were secured to them by the constitution and laws of the United States."

At the trial in circuit court, Justice Bradley sat with Circuit Judge (later Justice) William Woods, but the two disagreed over the validity of the indictments. (Until 1891, justices of the Supreme Court spent part of each year "riding circuit," that is, sitting as trial judges in the various circuit courts of the United States.) Woods saw ample federal authority; Bradley did not. Although Bradley had dissented in the *Slaughterhouse Cases,* now in his circuit court opinion he professed a more constricted view of national power and constitutionally protected rights. Protection of fundamental rights "does not devolve upon . . . [the federal government], but belongs to the state government as a part of its residual sovereignty." Although the Fifteenth Amendment admittedly created a right to be free from racial discrimination in voting and provided for congressional enforcement of this right, the indictments in the Colfax killings were unauthorized because neither action by the state government nor racial basis for the attack was shown. Because of the division between Bradley and Woods, the case moved to the Supreme Court on certification. That had been the grounds for the Court's consideration of *Reese* as well. Otherwise the High Court at this time would have had no appellate jurisdiction over an ordinary federal criminal case.

For the full Court (with Clifford again concurring on very different grounds), Chief Justice Waite adopted Bradley's view of the case. Similarly, it was not Bradley's dissent in the *Slaughterhouse Cases* but Justice Miller's majority opinion from that case that carried the day. Cruikshank also profited from effective advocates. Counsel included former Justice John Campbell, who had pressed for an enlarged national jurisdiction on behalf of the Louisiana butchers in the *Slaughterhouse Cases.* Also present was David Dudley Field, brother of sitting Justice Stephen Field. This time Justice Field, who had been persuaded by Campbell's earlier advocacy on behalf of the butchers, was persuaded by Campbell again, and adopted the restricted understanding of national rights shared by his brethren.

"To bring a case within the operation of that statute," Waite explained, "it must appear that the right, the enjoyment of which the conspirators intended to hinder or prevent, was one granted or secured by the Constitution or laws of the United States." So, when the indictments read that the defendants had hindered others in their right peaceably to assemble, Waite was quick to point out that the First Amendment secured that right against infringement by Congress but that it did not create the right. "For their protection in its enjoyment, . . . the people must look to the States. The power for that purpose was originally placed there, and it has never been surrendered to the United States." Because the rights claimed to have been violated did not inhere in national citizenship, they lay outside the amendment's—and therefore the statute's—protection. Consistent with the doctrine laid down in the *Slaughterhouse Cases,* the Reconstruction amendments had not given the national government a new responsibility in protecting those rights. Nor was there sufficient basis to charge the Colfax defendants with interfering with the right to vote. According to Waite, "the right of suffrage is not a necessary attribute of national citizenship [but] exemption from discrimination in the exercise of that right on account of race . . . is. The right to vote in the States comes from the States; but the right of exemption from the prohibited discrimination comes from the United States. The first has not been granted or secured by the Constitution; but the last has been." Implicit was a sharp distinction that Waite drew between private action that was under state, not national, control and state action in violation of federally protected rights that was. The Colfax mob lay under the former's, not the latter's, jurisdiction.

Because the indictments in *Cruikshank* did not rest on racially motivated conduct, whatever had occurred did not interfere with a right protected by the national government. "We may suspect that race was the cause of the hostility; but it is not so averred." Consistent with *Reese,* the Waite Court would not infer even that which seemed plainly apparent. Yet, without a racial component, would there have been a riot?

Taken together, *Reese* and *Cruikshank* are an astounding pair of decisions. By voiding two sections of the Enforcement Act of 1870 and dismissing indictments under another section, the Court in effect was saying that the Reconstruction amendments had amended very little—that Congress had acquired no general authority to protect the political rights of Americans. Recall the minimal point of common ground among the justices in the *Slaughterhouse Cases* had been that the amendments were intended to guard the rights of black Americans. Yet that objective, thanks to *Reese* and *Cruikshank,* now seemed largely out of reach. Fearing the consequences of momentous change, the Court held back from acknowledging that a radical change had occurred in the nature of the Union.

Viewed narrowly, the decisions by themselves did not have to cripple civil rights enforcement. Congress might have corrected the deficiencies in Sections 3 and 4 of the Enforcement Act that had proven fatal in *Reese.* Indeed, the Senate did in 1876, but a House in the hands of the Democrats refused to go along. Likewise, more carefully crafted indictments were surely possible. But already the conviction rate for prosecutions brought under the Enforcement Act had dropped sharply, from about 74 percent in actions brought in 1870 to less than 10 percent in 1874 and after (Cummings and McFarland 1937, 238). These figures, coupled with a growing local hostility to prosecutions, made indictments hard to come by, even as violations were on the rise. Practically, then, the 1870 act had become nearly a dead letter by the time *Reese* and *Cruikshank* were decided (Swinney 1962, 217–228). The decisions of 1876 obviously compounded the difficulty of obtaining both indictments and convictions and no doubt further demoralized federal prosecutors.

The Court was not prepared, however, to negate federal supervision entirely. Perhaps the consequences of a diminished federal presence were becoming more obvious. In a voting fraud case not involving race that came before the Justices in 1880 (*Ex parte Siebold*), Justice Bradley went out of his way to insert in his opinion a reference to federal authority. "It seems to be often overlooked that a National Constitution has been adopted in this country, establishing a real government therein, operating upon persons and territory and things." That was an astonishing statement, more of a confession of weakness than a reminder of strength. There was evidently no large or effective federal presence in voting rights disputes.

Justice Bradley's concern bore fruit four years later in *Ex parte Yarbrough* (1884). This was the only Supreme Court decision in the nineteenth century in full support of federal protection of voting rights where race was a factor. Jasper Yarbrough and eight other white men in Georgia had brutalized a black man named Berry Saunders because he had voted in a congressional election. Incarcerated in the Fulton County jail in Atlanta after their convictions, they overcame the Supreme Court's lack of jurisdiction to review federal criminal convictions through the usual route of a writ of error, by which the Court routinely examined decisions by the U.S. circuit courts in noncriminal cases. Instead, they petitioned the Court for a writ of habeas corpus to ascertain the lawfulness of their confinement. Even so, Justice Miller acknowledged that this form of pleading allowed only a narrow opening through which to examine the case. The Supreme Court had no authority, he explained, to "convert the writ of habeas corpus into a writ of error, by which the errors of law committed by the court that passed the sentence can be reviewed here; for if that court had jurisdiction of the party and of the offense for which he was tried and has not exceeded its powers in the sentence which it pronounced, this court can inquire no further."

Whether the U.S. circuit court for the northern district of Georgia that had tried and convicted the defendants had jurisdiction was a function of the validity of their indictments. That question, in turn, rested on the constitutionality of two sections of the Enforcement, or Ku Klux Klan, Act of 1871, the second act Congress had passed in implementation of the Fifteenth Amendment. Among other things, the statute banned various forms of voter intimidation. Neither section, however, referred to intimidation based on race. To suggest that the government "has no power . . . to secure this election from the influence of violence, of corruption, and of fraud, is a proposition so startling as to arrest attention and demand the gravest consideration," declared Miller. *Reese* was not to be read, he said, as arguing otherwise. The Fifteenth Amendment "does . . . substantially confer on the negro the right to vote, and Congress has the power to protect and enforce that right." Neither was congressional power confined to cases involving racial discrimination. "The principle . . . that the protection of the exercise of this right is within the power of Congress is as necessary to the right of other citizens to vote as to the colored citizen, and to the right to vote in general as to the right to be protected against discrimination." He was at pains to sidestep the formal "state action" doctrine that lay at the core of the *Civil Rights Cases* (1883), decided the year before. (That decision had invalidated part of the Civil Rights Act of 1875 that criminalized racial discrimination in privately owned places of public accommodation, such as restaurants, hotels, and theatres.)

[W]hile it may be true that acts which are mere invasions of private rights, which acts have no sanction in the statutes of a State, or which are not committed by any one exercising its authority, are not within the scope of [the Fourteenth] amendment, it is quite a different matter when Congress undertakes to protect the citizen in the exercise of rights conferred by the Constitution of the United States essential to the healthy organization of the government itself.

Without such authority, Miller declared, "the country [is] in danger." Thus Yarbrough and his cohorts could constitutionally be tried because they interfered with another's exercise of the right to vote, even though the interference lacked a racial predicate. Regardless of Miller's insistence to the contrary, the basis of the holding in *Yarbrough* did seem difficult to square with *Reese*.

Still, despite the potentially broad sweep of *Yarbrough,* it was abundantly clear that the Court maintained a highly circumscribed view of the power of Congress under the Reconstruction amendments to protect voting rights. By the 1880s, the chances that Congress would enact additional civil rights legislation to meet the Court's objections were slim. The Court's decision in this and most other civil rights cases blended with the so-called Compromise of 1877, to be discussed below. Moreover, the Court's position was consistent with mainstream opinion. *Harper's Weekly* approvingly editorialized that since the "long and terrible Civil War sprang from the dogma of State sovereignty, invoked to protect and perpetuate slavery, it was natural that, at its close, the tendency to magnify the National authority should have been very strong, and especially to defend the victims of slavery. . . . In a calmer time, the laws passed under the humane impulse are reviewed, and when found to be incompatible with strict constitutional authority, they are set aside." "The Court has been serving a useful purpose in thus undoing the work of Congress," added the *New York Times.* "The fact is, that, so long as we have State governments, within their field of action we cannot by National authority prevent the consequences of misgovernment. The people of the State," the *Times* concluded, "are dependent on their own civilized ideas and habits for the benefits of a civilized administration of laws" (Mason and Stephenson 2002, 649). In fact, Congress did not again pass a civil rights bill of any kind until 1957.

The Supreme Court's posture in most voting rights cases during this period obscured an important dynamic at work in the protection of civil rights. Prosecutions under any of the Reconstruction-era civil rights laws would be brought by a United States attorney in the appropriate judicial district. The U.S. attorney occupied the same place with respect to a federal criminal law as a local district attorney or county prosecutor occupied with respect to a state criminal law. Upon observance of a crime or on the complaint by a victim, the U.S. attorney could bring to bear the full prosecutorial resources of the Department of Justice. An offense against a person became an offense against the American people: hence the case name *United States v. Reese.* To the degree that the Court narrowed or otherwise invalidated federal civil rights laws, the role of the U.S. attorney was severely marginalized.

Lawsuits to challenge state laws or practices that arguably were in conflict with the Constitution were exactly that: actions instituted by individuals, not by the United States government. In the late 1800s, such challenges would be developed by counsel that defendants were able to employ. It would not be a challenge propelled by the full weight of the federal government. Moreover, the hostility of local community opinion might effectively discourage a lawsuit. A heavy price in terms of intimidation might be exacted on any plaintiff who dared bring suit. That prospect alone might incline someone to accept second-class citizenship instead of challenging it. And without litigation, a court could not act.

Thus the myopia of the Waite Court on voting lay in believing that a person's rights would be properly vindicated through the ordinary workings of the judicial process, relying on the Reconstruction amendments alone, without the help of Congress. That would have been appropriate had state legislators been dim-witted enough to pass a statue that plainly said that blacks were to be excluded from the polls. But such was rarely the case. Instead, the Court shared a latent suspicion of an enlarged federal presence. Whatever benefit the latter might bring seemed not to be worth the cost, in most instances at least, of destruction of a widely shared vision of the Union as it was before the Civil War in which the states had been the dominant players. The irony was that individuals would feel free to vindicate their rights only in the absence of the very intimidation that the federal statutes, gutted in some instances by the Court, had been designed to prevent.

A second part of this dynamic involved the results of litigation. Successful prosecutions brought by the government against persons violating the legal rights of another would mean fines and/or jail sentences for the individuals found guilty. Not only would these perpetrators be punished, but the punishments would perhaps make others think twice before committing similar offenses. In contrast, the effects of an individual's success in convincing the Supreme Court that a particular state law or policy violated constitutionally protected rights were often far more limited. No official would be fined or imprisoned. True, the courtroom victory became a precedent that was to govern litigation in similar cases from that time forward. Yet if a trial judge failed to heed the precedent, there was little an individual could do beyond an appeal on that point to a higher court on the hope that the law would be applied correctly. The difference was between vindication of individual rights by government and vindication of the same rights by individuals.

Still a third part of this dynamic involved power. Especially with respect to voting rights under the Fifteenth Amendment, energetic enforcement backed by a generous construction of federal civil rights statutes would have translated into a franchise generally free of racial discrimination and so open to all otherwise eligible males. Then as now, voting is empowerment. Denial of the right to vote condemns a person to the mercies of those who do vote. This was Justice Hunt's point in his *Reese* dissent: "Just so far as the ballot to . . . the freedmen is abridged, in the same degree is their importance and their security diminished. . . . Punishment is the means, protection is the end." The truth of that comment became especially evident not long after the last of the federal troops were withdrawn from the South in 1877—the first of two political developments that, by the turn of the century, resulted in a monumental decline in black voting. The withdrawal of the remaining troops was the essence of what is usually called the Compromise of 1877. Thereafter, mainly white-dominated state governments were once again in full control of their own affairs and had little to fear from federal supervision. The compromise stemmed from discussions that had been going on for months between conservative northern Republicans and southern Democrats about an end to Reconstruction, but the compromise itself was a product of the disputed presidential election of 1876.

In the race against Ohio Republican Rutherford B. Hayes, Democrat Samuel J. Tilden of New York comfortably won the popular vote, with an edge of about 250,000, out of over 8 million votes cast. That statistic surely pleased Democrats: it was the first presidential election since 1856 in which they out-polled the Republicans and the first since 1852 in which their party received at least 50 percent of the vote. Their euphoria, however, was tempered by one sobering fact. Although Tilden seemed certain of 184 electoral votes to Hayes's 165, 20 electoral votes remained in play because of competing returns from Florida, Louisiana, Oregon, and South Carolina. From that pool of 20, Tilden needed only 1 to reach the minimum majority of 185, and thus the White House. To reach the same magic number, Hayes required all 20. Democrats were acutely aware of the fact that in 3 of those states Hayes's hopes rested on the legitimacy of actions taken by local canvassing officials who were themselves part of the Reconstruction governments that Republican congressional majorities had imposed on a vanquished South.

To avert civil strife, Democrats and Republicans (the former held a majority in the house, and the latter a majority in the Senate) agreed to a commission composed of three Democratic and two Republican representatives, three Republican and two Democratic senators, and five Supreme Court justices, two of whom turned out to be Democrats and three Republicans. Members of the commission voted along party lines in each case to accept the Hayes electors, thus handing Hayes the presidency by a margin of one vote. Democrats in Congress believed that the election had been stolen from them, but enough of them acquiesced in Hayes's election—another part of the compromise—to allow his inauguration to proceed. For their part, in return for home rule, conservative southern Democrats (who became known as the "redeemers" because they had "redeemed" the South from northern occupation) promised to protect the rights of the freedmen. (Yet another part of the compromise, that congressional Republicans would support the rebuilding of southern infrastructure, never came to pass.)

The formal end of Reconstruction did not immediately bring an end to black voting and sometimes blacks were elected themselves. As had been true since early in Reconstruction "[b]lack faces continued to appear at the back door, but they also [appeared] in wholly unprecedented and unexpected places—in the jury box and on the judge's bench, [and] in council chamber and legislative hall" (Woodward 1966, 26). As late as 1890, sixteen African Americans were members of the Louisiana legislature that passed a law requiring separate cars for blacks and whites on trains operating within the state. This was the same statute that led to the Supreme Court's endorsement of the "separate but equal" standard for racial segregation in *Plessy v. Ferguson* (1896) (Woodward 1966, 54). Indeed, black voters were courted by Republicans, the redeemers, and agrarian-oriented Greenbackers who later became part of the Populist movement. Yet the security of southern blacks now rested principally in the hands of white-dominated state governments, given the withdrawal of a true federal presence and a Supreme Court hostile to much of Congress's postwar civil rights agenda.

The second major political development that affected African Americans in the South capitalized on the potential created by the Compromise of 1877. This episode largely unfolded during the

1880s and 1890s through a complex series of moves and counter-moves. The prestige that conservative Democrats had earned in the Redemption gave them a strong hold on power, a hold that they tightened by portraying themselves to blacks as the latter's protectors from predations by lower-class whites. But the redeemers' command of the moral high ground was undercut in the 1880s when financial scandals came to light, giving the agrarian radicals ammunition to use against the conservatives. Then the late 1880s and early 1890s witnessed a sharp and persistent economic downturn that resulted in a collapse of financial markets throughout the country in 1893. Hard times on the farm only got worse, and poor whites and blacks probably had to endure more than their share of hardships. Agrarian factions used the economy as a wedge to try to lure black voters into their ranks. Feeling threatened, conservatives, all the while still trying to retain black support, dropped their usual display of racial noblesse oblige and played the race card against the radicals, accusing them of attempting an alliance with blacks against everyone else. Blacks became the scapegoat: the sacrifice for uniting southern whites in a cause. And the cause was that of white supremacy. The crass maneuvering largely succeeded, especially after 1896, as conservatives consolidated their holds on power (Woodward 1966, 67–82).

But those holds on authority had to be made secure, and the method chosen in state after state was the near-total disfranchisement of African Americans. Neutralizing blacks politically would prevent them from being pawns in any group's grab for power in the future. Besides, such drastic measures could be justified as a way to prevent corruption or as a purification of the electoral process. The Fifteenth Amendment, of course, would seem to present a formidable obstacle to any such objective, but the objective was accomplished through clever means that will be described in the next chapter. If any public policy can ever be said to have been effective, it was this one. Numbers tell the story. In Louisiana in 1896, 130,334 black men were registered to vote. By the presidential election of 1904 that count had shriveled to 1,342 (Woodward 1966, 85).

The short- and long-term costs to the people of the United States of disfranchisement of blacks in the South may well be incalculable. Not only did they lose the leverage to protect themselves, but they lost any tangible claim on public services. Disfranchisement was followed by a harsh system of racial segregation that entrenched itself in southern legal systems and that was mimicked by private discrimination elsewhere in the nation.

Moreover, the loss of the right to vote translated into loss of other rights as well, as *Williams v. Mississippi* (1898) illustrates. A black man named Henry Williams had been convicted of murder in Washington County, in the delta region of Mississippi. He claimed that his conviction violated the equal protection clause of the Fourteenth Amendment because only white men sat on the grand jury that had indicted him. Eighteen years earlier, the Supreme Court had invalidated a West Virginia statute on equal protection grounds that barred African Americans from service on juries and grand juries (*Strauder v. West Virginia,* 1880). But Mississippi had no such racial exclusion in its law. Rather, grand jurors were chosen from the list of registered voters, which in the operation of Mississippi's voter registration laws that placed enormous discretion in the hands of local officials in determining eligibility, virtually guaranteed an all-white pool of prospective jurors. The Supreme Court, unanimously, was unmoved by Williams's plea. This was so even in light of *Yick Wo v. Hopkins* (1886) that had invalidated a fiendishly clever scheme that discriminated against Chinese laundries in San Francisco because the racially neutral ordinance had been "administered by public authority with an evil eye and an unequal hand." Those words, wrote Justice Joseph McKenna, are "not applicable to the Constitution of Mississippi and its statutes. They do not on their face discriminate between the races, and it has not been shown that their actual administration was evil, only that evil was possible under them." So, loss of the franchise to blacks as a class effectively eliminated them as jurors and possibly cost Williams his life.

Finally, reference to the voting rights of Native Americans merits attention in this section. As is true today, some Native Americans in the nineteenth century sought assimilation into the dominant culture, while others remained members of tribes and resided on tribal lands. The legal status of a tribe has been that of a "domestic dependent nation" exercising quasi-sovereign authority over its members and territory (*Cherokee Nation v. Georgia,* 1831); ordinarily only federal and tribal law applies on a reservation. (Only since 1924, by act of Congress, have tribal Indians born in the United States been deemed American citizens.) With respect to voting, a pattern emerged shortly before and after the Civil War, especially as states and territories were settled in regions of the continent where most Native Americans then lived. States commonly included Native Americans in their electorates if they had blended into the general population, but excluded those who retained tribal allegiance or who were not subject to taxation. Michigan's constitution of 1850, for example, conferred the franchise on "civilized male inhabitants of Indian descent, native of the United States and not a member of any tribe." The word "civilized" appeared in the statutes and constitutions of other states as well, and typically meant assimilation or at least disassociation from the tribe.

GENDER AND VOTING: INITIAL STEPS

Most Americans today probably believe that voting by women came about relatively late in American history. That is generally true. However, from the outset of the Revolutionary War, some women who met the property requirement were allowed to vote in New Jersey, apparently at the discretion of local election officials—until 1807 at least. In that year the law was changed to exclude all but "free, white male citizen[s]" from the polls (Chute 1969, 289–290). Thereafter, voting was exclusively a prerogative for otherwise qualified men across the United States until the late 1800s when a few spotty exceptions began to appear. Not until ratification of the Nineteenth Amendment in 1920 was full female suffrage the law of the land.

Thus women and African Americans alike both gained the vote by way of constitutional amendment. Yet, the process of expanding the franchise to include women stands in sharp contrast in at least two ways to the formal eradication of racial barriers that was explored in the previous section. First, blacks went from slavery to freedom to the polls (for the men at least) within a five-year period. This was a revolution: even the eradication of slavery did not itself become a major objective of the North until the second half of the Civil War. Emancipation of all slaves, accomplished by the Thirteenth Amendment, was followed by the Civil Rights Act of 1866 that sought to grant the freedmen some measure of contractual and civil equality, but not the right to vote. Elevation of black men to full political equality still seemed fanciful to mainstream opinion. Even the Fourteenth Amendment's oblique reference to voting was only by way of a penalty to be exacted from any state that denied the vote to "male inhabitants" over twenty-one years of age, but the amendment directly conferred the right to vote on no one. Not until ratification of the Fifteenth Amendment in 1870 was race officially disallowed as a criterion in establishing voter eligibility. The journey toward a gender-neutral franchise across the United States, however, extended over more than seventy years. Nationally, women were allowed to join the electorate a full half century after black males. In language parallel to that of the Fifteenth Amendment, Section 1 of the Nineteenth Amendment reads: "The right of citizens of the United States to vote shall not be denied or abridged by the United States or by any State on account of sex."

Second, once that amendment was in the Constitution, voting by women ceased to be seriously controversial. No legislation or federal prosecutions were needed to protect them as they exercised this new right. Opponents of female suffrage acquiesced in the new order of things, even if it distressed them. But as the previous section demonstrated, such was not the case with black suffrage. The Fifteenth Amendment was only the beginning, not the end, of efforts to banish the color barrier at the polls. As the following chapter will show, that objective took nearly a century to be realized.

Achievement of female suffrage stood in contrast as well both to the drive to eliminate the color line and the drive for white manhood suffrage. With minor exceptions, the system of political parties did not advance the goals of the suffragists, as those who advocated the right to vote for women were called. But the existence of political parties did help black men: achieving partisan advantage, not principle, was probably the primary driving force for a race-neutral franchise, as Republicans sought to secure their base against inroads by Democrats. Party competition had also contributed to a broader franchise in the 1830s and 1840s for white men. This earlier phenomenon may have been what leading suffragist Elizabeth Cady Stanton had in mind when she addressed the National Woman Suffrage Convention in 1869.

Women's Suffrage, in 1872, may be as good a card for the Republicans as Gen. Grant was in the last election. It is said that the Republican party made him President, not because they thought him the most desirable man in the nation for that office, but they were afraid the Democrats would take him if they did not. We would suggest, there may be the same danger of Democrats taking up Woman Suffrage if they do not. God, in his providence, may have purified that party in the furnace of affliction. (Buhle and Buhle 1978, 251)

But party competition and the lure of votes did not serve the cause of suffrage for women as it did for men. Neither major party evidently saw an advantage in gender inclusiveness, particularly because the idea of women voting struck most men as utterly preposterous. Politics in the nineteenth century was a man's business.

The campaign for female suffrage was also different from the campaign for white manhood suffrage. To be sure, both movements took about the same length of time to achieve success. If one dates the beginnings of an expanded suffrage for men from 1776, then the goal had been largely reached roughly eighty years later. Similarly, the genesis of the crusade for female suffrage in the early 1840s preceded the Nineteenth Amendment by about eighty years. The expansion of male suffrage, however, progressed as enfranchised men with some means made concessions to include those with little or no property. In other words, in 1776 those who could vote consisted of what today would be called the middle, upper-middle, and upper classes. The unfranchised ordinarily consisted of the lower-middle and lower classes. Unrelenting demands by the latter, plus the possible advantages that their votes might afford for candidates and parties, eventually wore down the resistance. In contrast, the women's suffrage movement existed because of the labors and arguments of women from the middle and upper-middle classes. Typically these were educated, politically aware people in New England, upstate New York, and the states of the old northwest—women from families of some means with connections to the professions through their husbands.

To a point, arguments for and against women's suffrage shared common ground with the campaign for manhood suffrage. Familiar references to natural rights, consent of the governed, and taxation without representation were heard throughout the eighty-year period. Like the radicals at Putney two centuries earlier, proponents of universal suffrage stressed that one's humanity entitled one to vote. As phrased by one Ohioan shortly after the Civil War, "Each individual on entering a state of society surrenders a portion of natural rights, and in return therefore receives, among others, the political right of the elective franchise. A woman is an individual, and when she enters into a state of society and thereby surrenders a portion of her natural rights, she receives in return therefore the right of the elective franchise, equally with man" (Keyssar 2000, 188).

Opponents countered by insisting that voting was a privilege, not a right. As illustrated by an exchange in the Ohio constitutional convention of 1912, voting was either conferred by the government on the basis of one's place in society, or it was not.

> Mr. [James] Halfhill: Now, gentlemen, this question of franchise is not, as has been sometimes delegated and urged, an inalienable right; it is a conferred right, and it must be conferred under our theory of government and under our organization of society.
>
> Mr. [John] Fackler: If suffrage is a conferred right and not a natural one, who conferred that right on us? (Keyssar 2000, 172)

Opponents also drew upon notions of virtual representation, contending that women did not need the vote because men who could vote would protect them. "I deny, Mr. Chairman," spoke James Caples at California's constitutional convention in 1879, "that there is one scintilla of truth in the assertion that woman is oppressed. Men shield and protect and defend her as a being better than themselves. . . . The male, at least in all species which form unions of any degree of permanence . . . defends and protects the female and her young ones" (Keyssar 2000, 183–184). Just as male nonfreeholders rejected the notion that their rights and interests could properly be cared for by freeholders, suffragists rejected the view that men were suitable guardians for women's interests. The latter drew on the empowerment theory—that the franchise was the basis of individual liberty. Accordingly, they deserved the vote because their interests would not be fully secure so long as men possessed a monopoly of political power (DuBois 1978, 41–46). For the purpose of securing equal rights, "the Right of Suffrage for Women is," resolved the Second National Convention in 1851, " . . . the corner-stone of this enterprise, since we do not seek to protect woman, but rather to place her in a position to protect herself" (Buhle and Buhle 1978, 112).

In a kind of cross-fertilization, the spirit of democratization that fueled the expansion of manhood suffrage during the Jacksonian era energized women, too. Ideas supporting a broad franchise for men seemed to include women as well. The suffragists' reliance on natural rights, consent, and empowerment, however, gave the remaining defenders of a more restrictive male franchise additional reason to oppose votes for women, especially before the Civil War. If even some women were to be admitted to the polls as a matter of right and because they were citizens, then, for the same reasons, it would be impossible not to include all adult white men, and perhaps others, too. As Samuel Young argued at New York's constitutional convention of 1821, abolishing the freeholder requirement would lead to absurd results—"it would end with Negro women having the right to vote" (Chute 1969, 316). And after ratification of the Fifteenth Amendment, southern whites typically opposed female suffrage on a similar ground: it would double the number of black voters, a result to be avoided. (White men failed to appreciate the fact that in many locales the number of white women exceeded the number of black men and women combined.)

Yet the debate was energized by unique arguments as well. Rarely does one find claims, widely heard with respect to other groups, that women were to be kept from the polls because they were unintelligent or untrustworthy or because their participation in politics would threaten rights of property. Instead, men and many women opposed female suffrage because it defied the natural order, because it threatened the family, and because it threatened women. According to Caples at the 1879 California convention,

This fungus growth upon the body of modern civilization is no such modest thing as the mere privilege of voting, by any means. . . . The demand is for the abolition of all distinctions between men and women, proceeding upon the hypothesis that men and women are all the same. . . . Gentlemen ought to know what is the great and inevitable tendency of this modern heresy, this lunacy, which of all lunacies is the mischievous and most destructive. It attacks the integrity of the family; it attacks the eternal decrees of God Almighty; it denies and repudiates the obligations of motherhood. (Keyssar 2000, 192)

Caples presumably was entirely comfortable with U.S. Supreme Court Justice Joseph Bradley's admonition six years earlier. The Illinois Supreme Court had denied Myra Bradwell's admission to the bar because she was a woman. The exclusion was thoroughly reasonable and therefore constitutional, wrote Bradley. "The paramount destiny and mission of woman are to fulfill the noble and benign offices of wife and mother," he advised. "This is the law of the Creator. . . . [I]n view of the peculiar characteristics, destiny, and mission of woman, it is within the province of the legislature to ordain what offices, positions, and callings shall be filled and discharged by men" (*Bradwell v. Illinois*, 1873). If this was an example of women's interests being safeguarded by men, Ms. Bradwell obviously was unimpressed.

Female suffrage threatened the family as well and upset male notions of both masculinity and femininity. If the woman's place was in the home as mother and caregiver, then the franchise would divert her attentions elsewhere. There would be familial upheaval. "I provide a home for my wife, and I expect her to do her share in maintaining it," argued New York Assemblyman James Shea. "If we give women the vote our wives will soon be absorbed in caucuses instead of in housekeeping. They will be drafted on juries, too. When I come home at night I expect my wife to be there, and not in a political caucus or locked up in a jury room with eight or ten men" (Keyssar 2000, 196).

Moreover, the rough and tumble of political involvement would endanger women themselves. This, presumably, was what

Finley Peter Dunne's saloon-keeping character Mr. Dooley had in mind as he philosophized late in the century: "'Politics,' he says, 'ain't beanbag. 'Tis a man's game; an' women, childher, an' pro-hybitionists'd do well to keep out iv it'" [sic] (Dunne 1898, xiii). "I believe that women occupy in many respects a higher position than men," asserted a delegate to California's constitutional convention of 1879, "and I, for one, do not wish to drag them down from the exalted sphere" (Keyssar 2000, 191). Two scenarios, equally undesirable, seemed likely: either women generally would be debased by the political process or the better women would not vote, leaving only the worst sort of their gender who did.

Finally, perhaps the most unusual argument to be made against female suffrage—one that would resurface in various forms in later years—materialized in New Jersey during the brief period after the Revolution when that state experimented with a gender-neutral franchise. An author named William Griffith tied his objection firmly to urban versus rural influence: "The great practical mischief . . . resulting from their admission . . . is that the towns and populous villages gain an unfair advantage over the country, by the greater facility they enjoy over the latter, in drawing out their women to the election" (Chute 1969, 289–290). In other words, women in rural areas of the state, in contrast to women in the more settled areas, would have a more difficult time leaving their homes to make the trip to the polls and so would likely vote in fewer numbers, thus strengthening the influence in the legislature of cities and towns.

Except for arguments like Griffith's, suffrage advocates tried to turn male-female similarities and differences to women's advantage. "I think it was Wendell Phillips, who said something like this," spoke Carrie Chapman Catt to Delaware's constitutional convention in 1897. "[I]f women are like men, then they certainly possess the same brain and that should entitle them to the ballot; if they are not like men, then they certainly need the ballot, for no man can understand what they want" (Keyssar 2000, 196).

The crusade for female suffrage passed through three phases. The first, that might be called *opinion formation*, began in the 1840s and lasted until the Civil War. The second—the *legal-constitutional* stage—encompassed the war years and most of Reconstruction. That stage had faded into the third—the *organizational* phase—by about 1875 and lasted until ratification of the Nineteenth Amendment.

The women's rights tradition in the United States traces its origins to the early American national period and to ideas emanating from the French Revolution (1789–1799). For women such as Abigail Adams, wife of the first vice president and the second president, politics was very much in their blood. "I cannot say that I think you are very generous to the ladies," she wrote her husband John during the Revolution, "for whilst you are proclaiming peace and good will to men, emancipating all nations, you insist upon retaining an absolute power over wives. . . . [W]e have it in our power, not only to free ourselves, but to subdue our master, and, without violence, throw both your natural and legal authority at our feet." During his term as president, she expressed similar thoughts to her sister. "I will never consent to have our sex considered in an inferior point of light. Let each planet shine in their own orbit. God and nature designed it so—if man is Lord, woman is *Lordess*—that is what I contend for" (Smith 1962, vol. 1: 225–226, vol. 2: 1006).

Political involvement by women moved ahead on multiple fronts in the early nineteenth century. In particular, organizational, speaking, and writing skills were honed in various reform movements—especially temperance and (outside the South) anti-slavery societies—often in conjunction with mainline Protestant churches. There were also efforts to minimize certain economic inequities. For example, in 1839 Mississippi became the first state to grant women the right independently to own and control property after marriage, without fear of being liable for their husbands' debts. To achieve the same advantage, Alabama women were advised to use all their powers of persuasion: "your smiles and your graces are irresistible," counseled one reformer (Eaton 1964, 206). But it was not until the 1840s that calls for full political equality were widely articulated. "Although early feminists demanded economic rights and intellectual equality, the widespread conviction of women's fundamentally domestic nature kept them from . . . imagining women voting, the ultimate public act" (DuBois 1992, 69).

Among the first recognitions and assertions of that ultimate act appeared in a declaration adopted by the Women Rights Convention in Seneca Falls, New York, in 1848. Led by women such as Lucretia Mott and Elizabeth Cady Stanton, the declaration was modeled in its style and phrasing on the Declaration of Independence. "The history of mankind is a history of repeated injuries and usurpations on the part of man toward woman, having in direct object the establishment of an absolute tyranny over her. To prove this, let facts be submitted to a candid world." And the first such fact "submitted" dealt with voting: "He has never permitted her to exercise her inalienable right to the elective franchise" (Buhle and Buhle 1978, 94).

What had become plainly obvious was that voting was the quintessential political right. Whether the cause was antislavery, temperance, or equal treatment under the law, goals that women wanted to achieve would be far easier to reach with the franchise than without it. Understandably, therefore, in whatever cause they might be engaged, women leaders sprinkled references to voting rights throughout their essays and addresses during the opinion formation stage. At the Seventh National Woman's Rights Convention, held in New York City in 1856, for example, Lucy Stone noted both progress that had been made and steps that still needed to be taken: "Ohio, Illinois, and Indiana have also materially modified their laws. And Wisconsin . . . has granted almost all that has been asked *except the right of suffrage.* And even this, Senator Sholes, . . . said 'is only a question of time, and as sure to triumph as God is just.'" At the Tenth National Convention in New York in 1860, Susan B. Anthony reminded her audience that the Empire State would be revisiting its constitution within a few years. "These should be years of effort with all those who believe that it is the right and the duty of every citizen of a State *to have a voice in the laws that govern them.* . . . We who have grasped the idea of woman's destiny, her power and influence, the trinity of her existence as woman, wife, and mother, can most earnestly work for her elevation to that high position that it is the will of God she should ever fill" (Buhle and Buhle 1978, 157, 159, 162, emphasis added).

The second, or legal-constitutional, stage of the campaign for voting rights for women was propelled by the Civil War. That holocaust left no part of the country untouched, the women's suffrage movement included. Women contributed to the war effort, North and South, in both unprecedented ways and numbers. Short of actual combat, they were engaged from Fort Sumter to Appomattox Courthouse. Moreover, they were probably aware that the cause of white manhood suffrage had been advanced after the Revolutionary War and the War of 1812 because of the military service of many nonfreeholders (and because freeholders wanted to be assured of their loyalty in future crises). And so they seized the opportunity that national crisis provided. "At this eventful hour the patriotism of woman shone forth as fervently and spontaneously as did that of man," wrote Matilda Joslyn Gage at war's end. "The evils of bad government fall ever most heavily on the mothers of the race, who, however wise and far-seeing, have no voice in its administration, no power to protect themselves and their children against a male dynasty of violence and force" (Buhle and Buhle 1978, 195–196). Stanton and Anthony headed the Woman's National Loyalty League that backed Senator Sumner's insistence that the war be made a battle for freedom—universal emancipation. They helped to marshal support for the Union and exerted pressure upon the Lincoln administration to expand the national commitment to democracy. The question before us," asked Anthony at a League meeting in 1863, "is: Is . . . it possible for this Government to be a true democracy, a genuine republic, while one-sixth or one-half of the people are disfranchised?" The League and its causes thus acquired a stature that the prewar woman's movement had lacked. The League, declared Gage "voiced the solemn lessons of the war: liberty to all; national protection for every citizen under our flag; [and] universal suffrage" (Buhle and Buhle 1978, 203, 197.) The effects of the war upon the woman's suffrage movement was thus galvanic: while the vote had been *a* principal prewar concern for women, the labors of the League narrowed the focus practically to the franchise alone.

Most suffragists therefore linked their cause with the right of blacks to vote. In their mind, one would be secured in the process of securing the other. The result would be a national Reformation, the achievement at last of the goals of the Declaration of Independence and American democracy.

Republican men in Congress—that party held tight control of the legislative branch after 1860—however, did not share the same vision, or for those who did, the vision may have seemed far-fetched. The urgency prompted by the end of the war was the status of the freedmen: what their rights would be and how those rights would be protected. Recall that the idea of a racially neutral franchise seemed so precarious when the Fourteenth Amendment was drafted that its framers included no guarantee of a right to vote, only a penalty for those states who denied the vote to "male inhabitants" over twenty-one years of age. From that perspective, to have blended female suffrage into the amendment might have invited a failed ratification. Such practical considerations did little to impress suffragists who now believed they had been spurned. The amendment constitutionalized the presumption that it was proper for states to bar women from the polls. Nor did suffragists take solace when Wendell Phillips cautioned, "One question at a time. This hour belongs to the negro" (Keyssar 2000, 177).

Nor, despite dozens of petitions to Congress, were suffragists any happier with the Fifteenth Amendment, then pending, that proposed to remove race, but not gender, as a criterion for voting. That provision combined with the "male inhabitants" of the Fourteenth Amendment established what Stanton labeled in an address in 1869 "an aristocracy of sex on this continent." "It will be no enviable record for the Fortieth Congress [the Congress that crafted the Fifteenth Amendment], that in the darkest days of the republic it placed our free institutions in the care and keeping of every type of manhood, ignoring womanhood, all the elevating and purifying influences of the most virtuous and humane half of the American people" (Buhle and Buhle 1978, 251, 250).

The causes of black and women's suffrage were now decisively severed. Stanton and others urged Congress speedily to send to the states for ratification a new amendment that would parallel the Fifteenth by removing sex as a criterion for voting. Republican Representative George Julian of Indiana promptly introduced in Congress an amendment that would have done exactly that (and more). What might have become the Sixteenth Amendment provided: "The right of suffrage in the United States shall be based on citizenship, and shall be regulated by Congress; and all citizens of the United States, whether native or naturalized, shall enjoy this right equally, without any distinction or discrimination whatever founded on sex." Julian's amendment, however, was well ahead of its time, was never formally proposed by Congress to the states, and otherwise made little headway (DuBois 1978, 172–173; Flexner and Fitzpatrick 1975, 143).

With Congress unwilling affirmatively and expressly to endorse a woman's right to vote, suffrage leaders adopted a new tactic with respect to the Fourteenth Amendment called the "New Departure." Bypassing the negativeness of Section 2, they focused positively on the vague guaranties of Section 1, especially the clause prohibiting states from "abridg[ing] the privileges or immunities of citizens of the United States." Voting was the preeminent act of citizenship, so they maintained that one of the "privileges or immunities" of American citizens was the right to vote. Properly understood, therefore, the Fourteenth Amendment, without any further effort by Congress, enshrined female suffrage. This was true because the Constitution itself was not the primary source of rights, but instead was a document to protect rights the people already and naturally possessed. As for rights generally, that theory squared with American tradition about rights. But was voting a right or a privilege? If the former, was it a right adhering in *national* citizenship? This part of the argument was novel. How would it fare in the courts?

The answer came after a St. Louis woman named Virginia Minor in 1869 insisted that the Fourteenth Amendment, along with a few other provisions in the Constitution, overrode Missouri's restriction of the suffrage to men. When her case reached the U.S. Supreme Court, the bench unanimously rejected her reasoning. Citizenship, the Court held, had to do with "conveying the idea of membership of a nation, nothing more." It certainly did not include voting. In conferring citizenship, as the Fourteenth Amendment did, the Constitution "did not necessarily confer the right of suffrage." Just because a person was counted as a "member" of a country did not presuppose a right to participate in its affairs by voting. That right adhered in one's state citizenship, and according to the *Slaughterhouse Cases,* discussed previously, rights one possessed by virtue of state (as opposed to national) citizenship were not among those that the Fourteenth Amendment safeguarded against state interference (*Minor v. Happersett,* 1875).

Meanwhile, other advocates of the New Departure took direct action by trying to cast votes en mass—"storming the polls," it was sometimes called (Isenberg 2001, 836). Even if their votes were not counted (and they almost always were not), suffragists believed that they had dramatized their cause and made a point. In 1868, some 200 women in Vineland, New Jersey, cast ballots in a separate ballot box and then tried to get election officials to include their votes in the official tally. That ballot box is still a prized possession of the Vineland Historical Society. According to one study, such voting attempts accelerated in 1871 and 1872. "Evidence exists of hundreds trying to vote and most likely there were more. Most of these women were not prominent outside of their own towns" (DuBois 1992, 74).

Probably the highest profile New Departure action was Susan B. Anthony's, when she cast a vote in the presidential election of 1872 and was arrested soon afterward for illegal voting. Her defense was that she was exercising a right protected by the Fourteenth Amendment. Assigned to her case in the litigious Second Circuit was recently confirmed U.S. Supreme Court Justice Ward Hunt (who would write the strong and perceptive dissent in *United States v. Reese*, that defended federal efforts to protect voting rights of African Americans). Excluding women from the franchise did not violate the Fourteenth Amendment, Hunt explained, because voting was a right that derived from state, not national, citizenship. "If the state of New York should provide that . . . no person having gray hair, or who had not the use of all his limbs, should be entitled to vote, I do not see how it could be held to be a violation of any right derived or held under the Constitution of the United States [even though] [w]e might say that such regulations were unjust, tyrannical, unfit for the regulation of an intelligent state" (Kutler 1969, vol. 2, 1225). Accordingly, Hunt directed the jury to find her guilty and imposed a fine of $100 (*United States v. Anthony*, 1873). One writer states that "Anthony was prohibited from appealing her case" (DuBois 1992, 77), as if there were something unusual or invidious about that. The truth is that appeals in criminal cases from a U.S. circuit court (the principal federal trial court at that time) to the U.S. Supreme Court were not allowed until 1891.

The organizational phase of women's suffrage took shape once it became clear that no satisfactory voting rights amendment would soon be forthcoming from Congress. Founded in 1869, the

National Woman Suffrage Association (NWSA) was headed by suffrage veterans Stanton and Anthony and in membership was limited to women. Based in New York, it attempted to succeed precisely on the ground where the earlier movements had failed. By focusing on Congress, the NWSA hoped to enfranchise women through the most efficient means available: a constitutional amendment. The NWSA was also involved in the Bradwell and Minor litigation at the Supreme Court and supported dramatic and confrontational measures like poll storming that had resulted in Anthony's arrest and trial for illegal voting. For a decade or more, the NWSA adopted a non- or bipartisan outlook. It was aligned with neither major party but was prepared to work with, and support, candidates and officeholders who promised to advance its cause. Leaders of the NWSA routinely vocalized resentment over the enfranchisement of black men, reminding audiences of the "superiority" of white women over black males as potential voters.

At about the same time that the NWSA appeared, other suffragists including Lucy Stone and Antoinette Brown Blackwell (the first ordained woman minister in the United States) organized the American Woman Suffrage Association (AWSA). Based in Boston, it differed from the NWSA in several important respects. It maintained ties to the Republican Party and admitted men both to its membership and into its leadership positions. Less overtly racist than the NWSA, the AWSA proudly reminded its members of the prewar link between antislavery and rights for blacks and women. But the most important difference between the two groups was on strategy. The AWSA's was state oriented, focusing battle by battle, contest by contest, on legislatures and constitutional conventions to include women within the electorate. The AWSA was also more interested in a related objective—partial or limited suffrage—whereby women were allowed to vote in specific types of elections, such as those dealing with schools, liquor licensing, or taxes.

Competing with both the NWSA and the AWSA for the energies and time of women was the Women's Christian Temperance Union (WCTU), founded in 1874 by educator Frances Willard. The WCTU preached a broader gospel of "Home Protection" that muted demands for equal rights in favor of emphasis on the special needs of women because of their domestic role (Isenberg 2001, 836–837). Yet because of its emphasis on the home, the WCTU vigorously campaigned for partial suffrage rules that would allow women to vote on matters relating to the sale of alcoholic beverages. For the WCTU, the link with the family was obvious: drunkenness created economic hardships and sparked violence toward women.

In 1890 the NWSA and the AWSA merged to form the National American Woman Suffrage Association (NAWSA) that was headed initially by Stanton and Anthony and then by a younger cadre of leaders such as educator and journalist Carrie Chapman Catt. By the end of the decade, the NAWSA had chapters in every state; hardly any elected state or federal official escaped their attention.

Despite the organizational changes during this period, the movement for female suffrage remained very much a middle- and upper-middle-class endeavor. In their literature, traditional equal rights themes (if men could vote, then women should be allowed to as well) gave way to other class- and gender-specific arguments. Muting equal rights themes had the advantage of avoiding touchy subjects like protecting black voters in the South or enfranchising immigrants in cities everywhere. Instead, the reasoning went, including women in the electorate would inject desirable feminine and family-oriented qualities into public life, qualities that most men lacked. A second point echoed a theme that was heard even in the prewar years: that women had unique economic and social interests that would be adequately addressed only if they could vote. Yet another argument emphasized that the enfranchisement of women would have a positive effect on the electorate, as a counterbalance to the votes of undesirable males, immigrants and otherwise, from the lower class. "Today there has arisen in America a class of men not intelligent, not patriotic, not moral, nor yet not pedigreed," declared Catt. "In causes and conventions, it is they who nominate officials, at the polls through corrupt means, it is they who elect them and by bribery, it is they who secure the passage of many a legislative measure" (Keyssar 2000, 198). In 1889, a Universalist minister named Olympia Brown had done her homework and was even more precise with the numbers.

> There are in the United States three times as many American-born women as the whole foreign population, men and women together, so that the votes of women will eventually be the only means of overcoming this foreign influence and maintaining our free institutions. There is no possible safety for our free school, our free church, or our republican government, unless women are given the suffrage and that right speedily. (Keyssar 2000, 198)

Six years later, Henry Blackwell made the same point at the NAWSA Convention: "[I]n every State, save one, there are more educated women than all the illiterate voters, white and black, native and foreign" (Buhle and Buhle 1978, 337).

Perhaps in light of the adoption of literacy tests in some states, a trend that would persist into the twentieth century, the reasoning of Catt, Brown, and Blackwell assumed that only the "better" women would or could vote. This, presumably, is what Stanton had in mind when she referred to an "educated suffrage." Testifying before a Senate committee in 1898, she acknowledged that "the popular objection to woman suffrage is that it would 'double the ignorant vote.' The patent answer to this is 'abolish the ignorant vote'" (Keyssar 2000, 199). Otherwise, adding ignorant and/or otherwise "undesirable" women to the voting pool would, from their perspective, seem counterproductive. In Stanton's view, the "ignorant" vote was against female suffrage, in any case.

Given the great expenditure of so much energy by so many people on female suffrage, how much had suffragists achieved by century's end? With the state of things in 1865 as a benchmark, the results were promising. But alongside the objective of full women's suffrage across the United States, the movement still had a long way to go. The most encouraging signs were those states where some form of limited or partial suffrage had been extended to women. By 1900, some twenty-five states or territories permitted women to vote in elections dealing with schools. Two of these, Kentucky and Michigan, had qualified women to vote in such elections before the Civil War. Of the twenty-five, four (Kansas, Montana, Michigan, and Iowa) as well as Louisiana permitted women to vote either in municipal elections and/or in elections concerning bond or tax issues. Probably reflecting the romantic image of womanhood that prevailed in the South longer than elsewhere in the United States, no state of the old Confederacy, except Louisiana, granted any form of limited suffrage for women before 1900. As for full enfranchisement—the right to vote in all elections—the list was short. As of 1900, women were fully enfranchised only in Wyoming (since 1869), Montana (since 1887), Colorado (since 1893), Utah (since 1896), and Idaho (since 1896). Washington is not on the list; it had adopted full female suffrage in 1883, only to have it invalidated by the supreme court of the territory in 1887 (Keyssar 2000, 387–390).

Utah is a special case. As a territory, it adopted full female suffrage in 1870. But this policy fell victim to a war by the United States government against the Church of Jesus Christ of Latter-Day Saints (the Mormons), members of which had settled Utah in the late 1840s. Because of their well-known practice of polygamy, Mormons became pariahs. As the platform of the newly organized Republican Party proclaimed in 1856, "it is both the right and the imperative duty of Congress to prohibit in the Territories those twin relics of barbarism—Polygamy, and Slavery" (Stephenson 1999, 86). Among other pieces of anti-Mormon legislation,

Congress in 1882 imposed the first de facto religious test for voting since colonial days when it disfranchised polygamists and their wives, a ban that was upheld by the Supreme Court in *Murphy v. Ramsey* (1885). Congress had plenary authority over how territories would be governed, explained Justice Stanley Matthews.

> [N]o legislation can be supposed more wholesome and necessary in the founding of a free, self-governing commonwealth than that which seeks to establish it on the basis of the idea of the family, as consisting in and springing from the union for life of one man and one woman in the holy estate of matrimony; the sure foundation of all that is stable and noble in our civilization, the best guaranty of that reverent morality which is the source of all beneficent progress in social and political improvement. And to this end, no means are more directly and immediately suitable than those provided by this Act, which endeavors to withdraw all political influence from those who are practically hostile to its attainment.

Congress formally repealed the territory's provision for female suffrage in 1887, a move that affected Mormons and non-Mormons alike. Only with statehood in 1896 was female suffrage in Utah restored.

CONCLUSION

If an American living in 1776—the year of the Declaration of Independence—had fallen into a deep, Rip Van Winkle-styled sleep, only to awaken at the end of the nineteenth century, that person would gaze amazed at many changes. Not only was the United States a vastly larger country, not only had there been astonishing progress in transportation and communication, but there had been astounding, even mind-boggling changes in the political world.

Nearly all white men could vote. Black men, who in 1776 had been electorally inert, had been given the vote by constitutional command after a huge loss of life in a civil war of unprecedented proportion. In some places that constitutional command had been made a reality for them, but in other places, especially where they lived in greatest numbers, it was being withdrawn. Women, although certainly not all of them, demanded the right to vote. In some places they had acquired it partly, and in a very few places held it fully. These were changes that few could have contemplated in 1776.

The Declaration of Independence had held out a promise of political equality. It echoed values asserted in debates at Putney, England. Even with the cross-currents and contradictions on voting that abounded in late nineteenth-century America, President Abraham Lincoln's characterization of the Declaration seemed still to be apt. That document, he said in 1857, set up "a standard maxim for free society, which should be familiar to all, and revered by all; constantly looked to, constantly labored for, and even though never perfectly attained, constantly approximated. . . . Its authors meant it to be a stumbling block to all those who in after time might seek to turn a free people back into the hateful paths of despotism" (Basler 1953, vol. 2, 406). The question for the new century would be the extent to which the promises of 1776 would be realized or abandoned.

REFERENCES

Adams, Charles Francis. 1856. *The Works of John Adams, Second President of the United States.* Boston: Little, Brown.

Annbinder, Tyler. 1992. *Nativism and Slavery: The Northern Know-Nothings and the Politics of the 1850s.* New York: Oxford University Press.

Basler, Roy P. 1953. *Collected Works of Abraham Lincoln.* 9 vols. New Brunswick, NJ: Rutgers University Press.

Brock, W. R., ed. 1961. *The Federalist.* New York: E. P. Dutton.

Buhle, Mari Jo, and Paul Buhle, eds. 1978. *The Concise History of Woman Suffrage: Selections from the Classic Work of Stanton, Anthony, Gage, and Harper.* Urbana: University of Illinois Press.

Chute, Marchette. 1969. *The First Liberty: A History of the Right to Vote in America, 1619–1850.* New York: E. P. Dutton.

Cummings, Homer S., and Carl McFarland. 1937. *Federal Justice: Chapters in the History of Justice and the Federal Executive.* New York: Macmillan.

Currie, David P. 1985. *The Constitution in the Supreme Court: The First Hundred Years, 1789–1888.* Chicago: University of Chicago Press.

de Tocqueville, Alexis. 1966. *Democracy in America.* J. P. Mayer and Max Lerner, eds.; George Lawrence, trans. New York: Harper and Row.

DuBois, Ellen Carol. 1978. *Feminism and Suffrage: The Emergence of an Independent Women's Movement in America.* Ithaca, NY: Cornell University Press.

———. 1992. "Taking Law into Their Own Hands: Voting Women during Reconstruction." In Donald W. Rogers, ed., *Voting and the Spirit of American Democracy: Essays on the History of Voting and Voting Rights in America.* Urbana: University of Illinois Press.

Dunne, Finley Peter. 1898. *Mr. Dooley in Peace and War.* Boston: Small, Maynard.

Eaton, Clement. 1964. *The Mind of the Old South.* Baton Rouge: Louisiana State University Press.

Elliott, Ward E. Y. 1974. *The Rise of Guardian Democracy: The Supreme Court's Role in Voting Rights Disputes, 1845–1969.* Cambridge, MA: Harvard University Press.

Farrand, Max, ed. 1966. *The Records of the Federal Convention of 1787.* 4 vols. New Haven, CT: Yale University Press.

Firth, C. H., ed. 1891. *The Clarke Papers.* New series XLIX, vol. 1. London: The Camden Society.

Fischer, David Hackett. 1994. *Paul Revere's Ride.* New York: Oxford University Press.

Flexner, Eleanor, and Ellen Fitzpatrick. 1975. *Century of Struggle,* enl. ed. Cambridge, MA: Harvard University Press.

Friedman, Lawrence M. 2002. *Law in America: A Brief History.* New York: Modern Library.

Handlin, Oscar, and Mary Flug Handlin. 1966. *The Popular Sources of Political Authority: Documents on the Massachusetts Convention of 1780.* Cambridge, MA: Harvard University Press.

Hoerder, Dick. 1985. *Labor Migrations in the Atlantic Economies: The European and American Working Classes during the Period of Industrialization.* Westport, CT: Greenwood Press.

Holt, Michael F. 1973. "The Antimasonic and Know-Nothing Parties." In Arthur Schlesinger, Jr., ed., *History of U.S. Political Parties.* 4 vols. New York: Chelsea House.

Isenberg, Nancy. 2001. "Women's Rights Movements." In Paul S. Boyer, ed., *The Oxford Companion to United States History.* New York: Oxford University Press.

Kelly, Selby, and Bill Crouch Jr., eds. 1982. *The Best of Pogo.* New York: Simon and Schuster.

Keyssar, Alexander. 2000. *The Right to Vote: The Contested History of Democracy in the United States.* New York: Basic Books.

Kleppner, Paul. 1992. "Defining Citizenship: Immigration and the Struggle for Voting Rights in Antebellum America." In Donald W. Rogers, ed., *Voting and the Spirit of American Democracy: Essays on the History of Voting and Voting Rights in America.* Urbana: University of Illinois Press.

Kraditor, Aileen S. 1973. "The Liberty and Free-Soil Parties." In Arthur M. Schlesinger, ed., *History of U.S. Political Parties.* 4 vols. New York: Chelsea House.

Kutler, Stanley I. 1968. "Ward Hunt." In Leon Friedman and Fred L. Israel, eds. *The Justices of the United States Supreme Court 1789–1969: Their Lives and Major Opinions.* 4 vols, ed. New York: Chelsea House.

Labbé, Ronald M., and Jonathan Lurie. 2003. *The Slaughterhouse Cases: Regulation, Reconstruction, and the Fourteenth Amendment.* Lawrence: University Press of Kansas.

Litwack, Leon F. 1961. *North of Slavery: The Negro in the Free States, 1790–1860.* Chicago: University of Chicago Press.

Lunt, W. E. 1957. *History of England.* 4th ed. New York: Harper and Brothers.

Maltz, Earl M. 1996. "The Waite Court and Federal Power to Enforce the Reconstruction Amendments." In Jennifer M. Lowe, ed., *The Supreme Court and the Civil War.* Washington, DC: Supreme Court Historical Society.

Mason, Alpheus Thomas. 1962. *The Supreme Court: Palladium of Freedom.* Ann Arbor: University of Michigan Press.

———. 1965. *Free Government in the Making: Readings in American Political Thought.* 3d ed. New York: Oxford University Press.

Mason, Alpheus Thomas, and Donald Grier Stephenson Jr. 2002. *American Constitutional Law: Introductory Essays and Selected Cases.* 13th ed. Upper Saddle River, NJ: Prentice-Hall.

Mason, Alpheus Thomas, and Richard H. Leach. 1959. *In Quest of Freedom: American Political Thought and Practice.* Englewood Cliffs, NJ: Prentice-Hall.

Morison, Samuel Eliot. 1965. *The Oxford History of the American People.* New York: Oxford University Press.

Platt, Suzy. 1989. *Respectfully Quoted: A Dictionary of Quotations from the Congressional Research Service.* Washington, DC: Library of Congress.

Plucknett, Theodore F. T. 1956. *A Concise History of the Common Law.* 5th ed. London: Butterworth.

Porter, Kirk Harold. 1971. *A History of Suffrage in the United States.* New York: AMS Press (reprint of 1918 edition).

Price, Polly J. 2003. *Property Rights.* Santa Barbara, CA: ABC-CLIO.

Smith, Page. 1962. *John Adams.* 2 vols. Garden City, NY: Doubleday.

Stephenson, Donald Grier, Jr. 1999. *Campaigns and the Court: The United States Supreme Court in Presidential Elections.* New York: Columbia University Press.

Swinney, Everette. 1962. "Enforcing the Fifteenth Amendment, 1870–1877." *Journal of Southern History* 1962: 202–218.

Sydnor, Charles S. 1962. *American Revolutionaries in the Making: Political Practices in Washington's Virginia.* New York: Collier.

Whichard, Willis P. 2000. *Justice James Iredell.* Durham, NC: Carolina Academic Press.

Wilentz, Sean. 1992. "Property and Power: Suffrage Reform in the United States, 1787–1860." In Donald W. Rogers, ed., *Voting and the Spirit of American Democracy: Essays on the History of Voting and Voting Rights in America.* Urbana: University of Illinois Press.

Williamson, Chilton. 1960. *American Suffrage from Property to Democracy 1760–1860.* Princeton, NJ: Princeton University Press.

Wills, Garry. 2003. *"Negro President": Jefferson and the Slave Power.* Boston: Houghton Mifflin.

Woodward, C. Vann. 1966. *The Strange Career of Jim Crow,* 2d rev. ed. New York: Oxford University Press.

Zall, Paul M. 1981. *Ben Franklin Laughing: Anecdotes from Original Sources by and about Benjamin Franklin.* Berkeley: University of California Press.

3

TWENTIETH-CENTURY
ISSUES

Voting in the United States at the beginning of the twentieth century was a vastly different affair than it had been at the start of the nineteenth. A franchise that excluded some white adult males in 1800 had expanded in all the states to such an extent by 1900 that the phrase "universal manhood suffrage" was practically a reality, at least in law. Women, whose high hopes were dashed in the immediate post–Civil War period when neither Congress nor the states extended the vote to them, had achieved partial access to the ballot in some states by 1900. Yet they enjoyed full access in barely a handful. Advocates for female suffrage were convinced that victory was only a matter of time, but it remained unclear at the dawn of the new century how quickly or by what means full female suffrage would be accomplished. It was even in doubt whether that goal could be reached within the lifetimes of those who then had been most active in the cause. Then there was the matter of race—"an American dilemma" (Myrdal 1944). In practice, any reference to universal manhood suffrage obscured the fact that African American men, having acquired the vote nationally by virtue of the Fifteenth Amendment in 1870, and having widely exercised that right for a time, were actually having the right cleverly taken from their hands, particularly in those parts of the country where their numbers were greatest.

Among all the developments in voting rights in the United States in the twentieth century, five stand out from the rest. One involves the relatively rapid progression of female suffrage. Another embraces the near-total disfranchisement of blacks around 1900 and the long and sometimes brutal struggle to regain what the Fifteenth Amendment said was rightfully theirs. This is a story not only about blacks but about white Americans in their effort to reconcile a general belief in equality with powerful individual and group racial prejudices.

The remaining three developments are related to the first pair in that they have provided added dimension to the right to vote. Of these, the most important has been representation. Government in the United States is republican in character in that, through elections, voters choose those who will make decisions for them—those who will represent them and act in their stead. Probably no system of representation has ever been devised that can perfectly reflect the views, values, and preferences of the electorate. Still, one model of representation may come closer to an accurate reflection by weighing votes the same, while another system may inject some distortion by effectively giving added weight to some votes at the expense of others. A great legal battle over exactly this issue was fought in the second half of the twentieth century that literally changed the political map of the United States.

The outcome of that battle had hardly been determined when the nation underwent another adjustment in voting rights. A new consensus emerged concerning the minimum voting age, a consensus that resulted in ratification of the Twenty-sixth Amendment in 1970. It admitted no one new to the franchise in the ways that the Fifteenth and Nineteenth amendments had done; rather it opened the franchise to all otherwise qualified persons at an earlier point in their lives.

The fifth noteworthy development in the twentieth century affecting voting is most closely identified with the first two decades of the century and was largely institutional in nature. Significant modifications in the way Americans conducted their politics started to take hold that offered voters new ways to influence the political system—new venues through which Americans could express themselves at the ballot box. Ironically those changes embodied a partial rejection of the idea of representation itself, in favor of a greater emphasis on direct democracy. This development was largely initiated, though hardly completed, by a broad-based movement called Progressivism.

PROGRESSIVISM

Progressivism was an intellectual movement that also spawned a short-lived political party that fielded candidates for president and vice president in the elections of 1912 and 1924. (The movement had little or nothing to do with another political party by the same name that nominated Henry Wallace for president in 1948.) With origins dating into the 1880s but most effective between about 1900 and 1920, the movement loosely included three kinds of political reformers: agrarian, social, and political. Each element had its own set of goals that sometimes overlapped with those of one of the other two elements. Lying outside the scope of this book was a cultural component of Progressivism as well that eventually infused education, scholarship, architecture, journalism, and the arts in ways illustrated by the work of individuals as varied as John Dewey, Charles A. Beard, Frank Lloyd Wright, Lincoln Steffens, Upton Sinclair, and Charles Ives. Some historians even compare the essence of Progressivism to a religious phenomenon, almost like a third "Great Awakening." "Most Progressive leaders came from Protestant and often clerical families, they had learned Christian moral principles from an early age, and they tended to assume that sin was somehow at the core of social problems. Sin implied sinners; sinners needed to repent; and thus the period comes increasingly to look like a massive revival effort, with journalists, professors, lawyers, social workers, and clergy exhorting their audiences in sermons, secular or otherwise" (Crunden 2001, 623). (As used here, "Progressive," "Progressivism," or "Progressives" is capitalized when referring to the movement, to its beliefs, to the political party—known in 1912 as the Bull Moose Party— or to persons active in this movement or party. Thus capital-P Progressives included many people who retained ties to the Democratic and Republican Parties as well as others who were specifically active for a time in the Progressive or Bull Moose Party itself.)

One component of the Progressive movement consisted of followers of Williams Jennings Bryan (Democratic presidential nominee in 1896, 1900, and 1908) and their converts from the heyday of the Populist Party in the 1880s and 1890s. These agrarians pursued an antimonopoly and soft-money debtor-relief agenda designed mainly to help farmers particularly and rural America generally at a time when agriculture in the United States was still dominated by the family farm and not the "agribusiness" that was to come. A second group of reformers had in mind a variety of social objectives primarily to ameliorate problems associated with cities and an expanding industrial base. Inspired by the efforts of Jane Addams and Ellen Gates Starr who opened Hull House in Chicago in 1889, they labored to abolish child labor and to improve adult literacy, public health, immigrant assimilation, and workplace hours and conditions. Some also supported the rights of working people, although leaders of organized labor such as Samuel Gompers pursued their own separate agenda. Overlapping somewhat with the first two elements, still other Progressives were most interested in "honest government" or "good government" issues. They sought to give voters greater control over their governments. Accordingly, they fought entrenched political organizations (they pejoratively called them "machines") and the "bosses" who headed those organizations. Such machines, held together by the patronage that rewarded the faithful, were thought to be corrupt and in unholy alliance with local monopolies such as transit companies and utilities. On national issues, like other Progressives the good-government crowd favored a national income tax, popular election of United States senators, antitrust action, and other regulatory measures to rein in or to eliminate corporate conglomerates. Combined, their efforts wrought the greatest era of constitutional change since Reconstruction. Within a period of seven years, the Progressive movement resulted in ratification of four amendments to the United States Constitution.

Women suffragists had long hoped that the first amendment to be added to the U.S. Constitution after the Fifteenth would be one erasing gender distinctions at the polls. It was not. The Sixteenth Amendment (1913) in fact had nothing to do with the franchise but instead overturned a decision by the Supreme Court in 1895 that had invalidated an income tax of 2 percent that Congress had imposed in 1894 on annual incomes above $4,000 (*Pollock v. Farmers' Loan & Trust Co.*, 1895). Voting five to four, the Court considered a tax on income to be a direct tax, and under the stipulations of the Constitution, one that had to be apportioned among the states on the basis of population—as obviously an income tax could not equitably be apportioned. Thus the Sixteenth Amendment reaffirmed Congress's authority to tax incomes "from whatever source derived, without apportionment among the several States, and without regard to any census or enumeration."

Rapidly on the heels of the Sixteenth, the Seventeenth Amendment (1913) inaugurated direct popular election of United States senators. This change discarded the previous arrangement, as spelled out in Article II of the Constitution, whereby state legislatures, not the electorate, had elected senators. The Seventeenth was more than a cosmetic alteration. Under the original design, senators literally represented the *governments* of the states from which they came, while members of the House of Representatives represented the *people* of the districts or states that had chosen them. As a result of the Seventeenth, both houses of Congress would henceforth be directly accountable to the electorate. Excepting only the Fourteenth Amendment's enhancement of national power at the expense of the states, the Seventeenth Amendment represented the most significant alteration of the plan of government the framers had devised at the Philadelphia Convention of 1787. In shifting power from state legislatures to the people, the amendment was itself an enlargement of the franchise, at least for the election of senators. In the face of obvious resistance in the Senate, such drastic change was possible only because of the new Progressive mind-set. By 1912, the year that Congress proposed the amendment to the states, thirty-seven states already provided for some popular input in the selection of senators by the state legislatures, and twenty-eight of those states allowed direct nomination of senators by popular vote. The amendment thus finalized everywhere a small revolution that was already underway (Rotunda 1996, 207–209). And as explained in the next section, the Seventeenth Amendment also followed a pattern that helped to propel female suffrage: Washington's most vocal and persistent advocates of popular election of U.S. senators were those members of the Senate who themselves had effectively been chosen by popular will (Kobach 1994, 1979).

Six years later, the temperance movement, in which women had played the leading role for at least eighty years, succeeded in convincing enough people that a "dry" nation would be a better nation. Accordingly, the Eighteenth Amendment (1919) banned the "manufacture, sale, or transportation of intoxicating liquors" within the United States, with its prohibition taking effect one year after ratification. Not coincidentally, as will be seen, the Prohibition Amendment was followed one year later by the Nineteenth Amendment (1920) that embodied the long-awaited grant of full suffrage to women.

In one way or another each of these amendments was inspired and fueled by Progressivism. The degree of change was both breathtaking and unprecedented. Excepting only the first ten amendments that were ratified together in 1791 as the Bill of Rights, no other seven-year period in American history has seen as many as four textual alterations in the fundamental law of the land take place.

In addition to the obvious impact of the Seventeenth and Nineteenth amendments on voting, good-government Progressives pushed other proposals that affected voting by placing more political power in the hands of the voters. Recall from the previous chapter the emphasis during the Jacksonian era on an expanded franchise for white men and on popular sovereignty generally as a vehicle to attack privilege. Progressives carried this idea one step further: "[T]he first essential in the Progressive programme," declared Theodore Roosevelt in his campaign for the presidency on the Bull Moose ticket in 1912, was "the right of the people to rule" (Roosevelt 1912, 2223). Democrat Woodrow Wilson expanded on the idea with his "New Freedom" agenda for his presidential campaign. The power that lay with the people must be released, and to do this was the function of leadership. Leadership would liberate the "people's vital energies" and return to the people "in very trust the control of [their] government" (Wilson 1913, 277).

Progressives, whether in Bull Moose or Democratic garb, advocated devices that allowed "the people to rule." Among these were the recall, the initiative, the referendum, and, for some, the short ballot. All were designed to transfer political power from the hands of legislators, party leaders, and others into the hands of the voters. Such "good government" measures were at heart antiparty in purpose and orientation, and, as a window into the political minds of Progressives themselves, may partly explain why Progressives were never able to organize sufficiently along party lines to become a permanent fixture in American politics. (Along with most white

Americans, many Progressives were not particularly bothered about the shrinking ability of blacks to vote in many states of the union, a contraction that ironically proceeded contemporaneously with the constitutional and other legal reforms of the period.)

The recall allowed voters to remove elected officials, judges included, before their terms expired. The initiative was an electoral device that converted voters into legislators. With a sufficient number of signatures on a petition, a proposed statute or constitutional amendment would be placed on the ballot for voters to enact or reject, thus bypassing the legislature altogether. The referendum allowed voters, again contingent on the requisite number of signatures on a petition, either to act on proposed legislation placed on the ballot for their approval or disapproval, or to repeal bills already enacted by a legislature. The short-ballot movement was designed to remedy complexities of voting that had been a by-product of the Jacksonian era. As more and more state and local offices became elective, not appointive, voters required greater knowledge and attention to detail in dealing with what had truly become a long ballot. By reducing the number of official positions filled by voters, short-ballot advocates hoped to empower voters through informed voting and thus to reduce the influence of party leaders and their organizations who otherwise might exploit ballot complexity by telling voters for whom to vote. During the Progressive era and afterwards, most states adopted one or more of these devices in one form or another for state and/or local elections, with states in the West or Midwest typically being more receptive to such Progressive innovations than the older states of the Northeast and South. However, recall, initiative, and referendum by the people all remained unknown to federal law, as is still the case today. As for the short ballot, the Constitution has always kept the number of elective federal offices to a minimum. In federal elections voters in any given state choose at most presidential electors (by casting a vote for president), a representative, and never more than two senators.

Probably aside from the Nineteenth Amendment itself, no electoral reform from the Progressive era has had a greater impact on voting and the political system than the direct primary and its cousin the presidential primary. Typically scheduled several months before the general election, a primary election is a device to select candidates. At heart it is a "first" election *within* a party to choose the party's candidates for various offices, whereas the general election is an election *between* or *among* candidates who have been slated by the parties as a result of the primary. In a direct primary, the candidate who gets the most votes is the party's nominee for a particular office, although sometimes a runoff might be necessary between the top two vote getters if party rules require that the nominee receive a majority, not merely a plurality, of the vote. In a presidential primary, at least as it has evolved today, voters do not directly choose presidential candidates but rather vote for delegates usually pledged to a particular presidential candidate. The delegates chosen in each state then gather at the party's national nominating convention in the summer of the presidential election year. The candidate who receives a majority of the votes cast by these delegates then becomes the party's nominee for president. Compared to the direct primary, then, the presidential primary can be seen as an *indirect* primary. But with both the direct and presidential primaries, the selection of candidates is a function of voter preference. Overall, adoption of the primary system of nomination has virtually doubled the number of elections in the United States.

Voter eligibility in a primary, however, is not necessarily the same as voter eligibility in a general election. As will be seen later in this chapter, this difference allowed some states to circumvent the Fifteenth Amendment as a way of largely disfranchising African Americans. But for now, consider the primary in terms of what it permits those who in fact vote in primaries to do.

Understanding the significance of the primary begins by asking how a party might choose candidates without a primary. (The premise of that question is that the names of candidates appear on ballots by virtue of decisions made by parties. Indeed, that has been the case since the development of a mainly two-party system early in American history, although one may also enter an election as an "independent" candidate outside the party rubric.). Without a primary, the decision about those who will be a party's candidates would rest in the hands of the party's leaders, whether the medium for that selection was through a caucus or convention. This difference explains why Progressives found the idea of the primary so attractive. It empowered the people. A ballot presents choices in the form of candidates. Rather than having party leaders define those choices for the electorate, the primary enabled the electorate to define those choices for the party leadership. Thus the idea of the primary was that the selection of candidates would reflect popular, not elite, sentiment.

The significance of this difference—and the profound effect Progressivism eventually had on voting and the channels through which voters made their choices—becomes apparent by briefly examining the evolution of the process by which candidates for the presidency have been selected. Progressive era ideas eventually succeeded in turning that process upside down.

The winter and spring of 2004 witnessed a replay of the uniquely American political drama called "How to Nominate a Presidential Candidate." With changing rules, sets, and casts of characters, that drama has been playing for more than 200 years. Early nominating procedures, however, were vastly different from the pattern that is familiar today. By 1800, party caucuses in Congress recommended presidential nominees to the state legislatures, which in most states in turn selected members of the electoral college. Soon the Federalist Party declined as a national political force, leaving the Democratic-Republicans as the dominant faction in the first party system (as shown in Chapter One). As a result, the members of the surviving party in Congress were, in effect, selecting the next president.

By 1824, this system of nomination by congressional caucus began to break down as the surviving party broke up into factions. Candidate William Crawford, the choice of the Democratic caucus, found himself with anything but full party support in the nation. Alongside Crawford appeared others such as Andrew Jackson, John Quincy Adams, and Henry Clay designated by state legislatures and state party conventions. The failure of the congressional caucus to unite Democratic factions explains why no candidate received a majority of the electoral vote in that year. The decision fell to the House of Representatives, which chose John Quincy Adams as the next president, even though Andrew Jackson received more popular and electoral votes. (Jackson and his followers were convinced that the House verdict in 1824 had been the product of a "corrupt bargain" and, with the emergence of the second party system, wrested the presidency from Adams in the election of 1828 [Stephenson 1999, 55].)

In 1832, a new party called the Anti-Masonic Party tried an alternative nominating device—the convention. Necessity was truly the mother of invention. Having no real congressional representatives, they resorted to a meeting outside Congress. Their site was a Baltimore saloon. Some 116 delegates from 13 states filled the room. Representatives of the new Whig Party did the same thing. They even met in the same saloon. A convention composed of delegates of the state parties who had been selected by local party leaders impressed many observers as a ideal way of choosing a candidate who could rally widespread support. Democrats were convinced and so also convened in Baltimore to renominate Jackson for a second term.

The convention as a nominating device persisted. Party rank and file—that is, ordinary voters—had little if nothing to do directly with selection of presidential nominees. Every four years, delegates to the national conventions of both major parties would be selected by state party chieftains. Conventions often required multiple ballots before a nominee emerged, sometimes as the result of efforts made behind the scenes by brokers in the proverbial smoke-filled room. To no one's surprise, this system made presidential candidates acutely sensitive to the needs and wishes of state party organizations. (The record for multiple balloting remains held by the Democratic convention of 1924, at which John W. Davis was nominated for president on the 103rd ballot.)

It was against this backdrop of leadership-directed conventions that the presidential primary emerged. Progressive leaders such as Senators Robert La Follette of Wisconsin and Hiram Johnson of California demanded a larger role for the people in the nomination process. Under their proposal, the voters would be empowered to select delegates to the national convention and to express a preference for their party's presidential nominee. The idea was contagious. As early as 1912, nearly one-third of the states provided for some kind of popular election of convention delegates. By 1916 half the states had a Democratic or Republican presidential primary, and a few had both. Among Democrats, 54 percent of the convention delegates were chosen by primaries in 1916—a figure that would not be surpassed until 1972. For Republicans, 59 percent of the delegates were the products of primaries, a proportion not exceeded until 1976 (Wayne 1997, 6–14).

Still, popular participation went only so far. Most primaries did not generate binding results. That is, delegates were not legally obligated by primary results to vote for a particular candidate. Party leaders influenced how delegates actually voted. Theodore Roosevelt learned this fact the hard way. In 1912, 42 percent of the delegates for the Republican national convention were chosen in primaries. "TR" won nine of the ten primaries he entered, including the one in incumbent President William Howard Taft's home state of Ohio, but Taft got the nomination.

Partly because influence by party leaders continued to overshadow preferences of the rank and file in presidential primaries, voter turnout in primaries declined. And Progressivism itself waned nationally as a movement after 1920. States began to abandon the primary as a delegate-selection device. By 1936 only 40 percent of the convention delegates of the two major parties were chosen in primaries. Thus, during the first two-thirds of the twentieth century, primaries were *a* route to the nomination, but by no means *the* route. They were no substitute for careful cultivation of state party leaders. For example, in 1952 Tennessee Senator Estes Kefauver entered thirteen of the seventeen Democratic primaries, a large number for that day. He won twelve of the thirteen, and the party nominated Illinois Governor Adlai Stevenson.

The strategy became one of picking and choosing primaries carefully. In 1960 John Kennedy entered and won the primary in West Virginia, an overwhelmingly Protestant state, as a way of refuting the conventional wisdom that a Roman Catholic could not be elected president. Until the 1970s primaries mainly were seen by both candidates and state party leaders as devices to confirm consensus within a party. Few viewed the primary as a tool to forge such a consensus. That had to be done before the primary season. Except for Thomas E. Dewey in 1940 and Kefauver in 1952, the front-runner before the first primary was the convention choice in every contest between 1936 and 1968.

A different world of presidential campaign politics emerged after 1968. Hubert H. Humphrey, the Democratic nominee in 1968, was the last presidential candidate of either major party who did not enter a single presidential primary in the year he was nominated. The old La Follette-Johnson notion of popular control of the candidate-selection process was reborn. New rules adopted first by Democrats and then by Republicans in the 1970s transformed the nomination process into one by which candidates competed for delegates in state presidential primaries (or in local presidential caucuses) in every state in the land. What began in the Progressive era as a means to transform presidential politics by empowering voters finally swept the nation (Stephenson 1989, 15–18).

Thus the effects of Progressivism lingered long after the Progressive movement itself had faded. As noted, except for its incarnation as the Bull Moose ticket in the presidential election of 1912, and its reemergence as a separate entity in the election of 1924, Progressivism as a movement did not establish itself as a permanent political party. American politics remained mainly a contest between Democrats and Republicans. Why? A realignment, whereby Progressives might have displaced one of the other parties, was averted partly because Progressives themselves reflected such diversity. No single central organization ever succeeded in combining the many elements into a new national party behind a single electoral strategy. Moreover, there were Progressive-minded people in both major parties, which in turn were therefore responsive at different times to Progressive concerns. Democrats with a Progressive orientation could be pleased by their party's nomination of Woodrow Wilson for president in both 1912 and 1916, just as Progressive Republicans could approve the nomination of Supreme Court Justice (and former New York governor) Charles Evans Hughes to oppose Wilson in 1916, after former president Theodore Roosevelt, the Bull Moose contender in 1912, withdrew his name from consideration.

GENDER: ACCESS TO THE BALLOT AT LAST

The crusade for female suffrage passed through three phases, as the previous chapter explained. The first, the *opinion formation* stage, began in the 1840s and lasted until the Civil War. The second, the *legal-constitutional* stage, encompassed the war years and most of Reconstruction. That stage blended into the third, the *organizational* phase, by about 1875 and lasted until ratification of the Nineteenth Amendment in 1920.

During the first few years of the third stage, the suffrage movement was driven mainly by two organizations with different strategies: The National Woman Suffrage Association was riveted on Congress in an attempt to achieve full suffrage by constitutional amendment. Alternatively, Congress might be induced to pass a "federal suffrage bill," extending the vote to women in elections for national office (Norgen 1999, 37). Because such legislation would be constitutionally dubious, the NWSA preferred the foolproof route of suffrage by amendment. In contrast, the American Woman Suffrage Association thought speedier results could be achieved by working at the state level. The theory was that victories in a few states would build momentum that would sweep through other states. "Go, get another state," President Theodore Roosevelt challenged the movement in 1908. The aging Susan B. Anthony agreed: "I don't know the exact number of States we shall have to have[,] . . . but I do know that there will come a day when that number will automatically and resistlessly act on the Congress of the United States to compel the submission of a federal suffrage amendment. And we shall recognize that day when it comes" (Catt and Shuler 1923, 227). Each strategy had its advantages and disadvantages. The NWSA's allowed concentration of resources at the national level, but at the cost of sacrificing some of the very grassroots work that might make its congressional offensive more effective. The AWSA's realized the importance of mobilizing support at the grassroots, but at the cost of spreading resources across numerous battleground states—those states where their message stood the best chance of taking hold.

What a twenty-first-century reader should find noticeably absent from the previous paragraph is any mention of the judiciary. Americans today are accustomed to turning to the courts to vindicate their rights. But a century ago there could be no voting right to vindicate unless a state or a new federal constitutional amendment created it and provided for its protection. This was because, with respect to woman suffrage, the Supreme Court had made the existing U.S. Constitution irrelevant. Rejecting Virginia Minor's claim that the recently ratified Fourteenth Amendment implicitly enfranchised women, the Court ruled in *Minor v. Happersett* (1875) that the amendment did no such thing. That 1868 addition to the Constitution was not a source of voting rights and so guaranteed no one's right to vote. With the exception of the Fifteenth Amendment that banned the use of race as a criterion for voting, the franchise remained, as it had always been, entirely a matter for the states to define.

By 1890, when the AWSA and the NWSA merged to form the National American Woman Suffrage Association, it appeared that the former's approach had borne some fruit. The NWSA had made no headway at all with an amendment to the U.S. Constitution or a federal suffrage law, but some states had granted the vote to women in school elections (on the grounds that education did not involve "politics" and so voting on such measures would not tarnish women), and some states permitted women to vote in municipal elections or in elections concerning taxes and bond issues. A handful of territories and states had even accorded women full suffrage. But after Idaho came into the Union in 1896 with full suffrage, little progress was made anywhere else until 1910. The exceptions were few: Delaware extended partial suffrage in 1898 in school elections, and New York in 1906, and Michigan in 1909 did so with respect to some tax and/or bond issues. Just six referenda were held on full suffrage during this period, and all of them failed. Thus, for nearly fifteen years, the momentum that seemed to have been achieved by 1890 had dissipated. It was a frustrating time for suffragists who, looking back, called it "the doldrums" (Keyssar 2000, 200; Flexner 1975, 230–271).

This was so despite the fact that suffragists were making some progress abroad. New Zealand had enacted female suffrage in 1893. Married women had been given the right to vote in England in local, but not parliamentary, elections in 1894. During the doldrums, several Australian states extended the vote to women, as did several Scandinavian countries. In 1918 England would grant the vote to women above the age of twenty-nine and to all men above twenty. Not until 1928 were women above twenty fully enfranchised in England.

Before turning to the factors that allowed the movement to regain its momentum, it will be helpful first to examine the reasons why the movement stalled. In 1900, the suffrage movement still had a limited social basis. Indeed, although it may seem incredible to contemporary readers, evidence indicates that most women still remained opposed to receiving the franchise. This opposition did not mean that women were focused only on matters inside the home, however. By 1900, over a million women, mainly Protestant and middle class and whose husbands were in business or the professions, were organized in a variety of clubs in every state of the Union. With roots extending back into the pre–Civil War period, these clubs or voluntary associations had broad benevolent and reform agendas, ranging from temperance to health to improved educational opportunities for women. Many of these societies were associated with the Women's Christian Temperance Union or united with the General Federation of Women's Clubs. Such connections kept each club abreast of activities elsewhere (Blair 2001, 835). Lacking the vote, members used indirect measures to influence policy makers: petitions, delegations, and letter-writing campaigns (Graham 1996, xiii).

Yet the bulk of women's clubs in the country still refrained from endorsing, much less campaigning for, suffrage. Some women even believed that they could be more effective politically without the vote than with it. Perhaps some accepted the truth of Russell H. Conwell's assessment that voting did not really confer power. "You [won't] get anything that is worth while," he explained, because "this country is not run by votes. . . . It is run by influence. It is government by the ambitious and the enterprises which control votes" (Mason and Leach 1959, 354). (A Baptist minister who was also the first president of Philadelphia's Temple University, Conwell was a highly influential orator in the late nineteenth and early twentieth centuries. Through his lecture "Acres of Diamonds," which he delivered more than 6,000 times on the Chautauqua circuit and elsewhere, Conwell preached "the gospel of wealth" that sought to harmonize Christianity with rampant capitalism. "You have no right to be poor," he admonished his hearers [Crossen 2004, B1]. Cynical about politics, he insisted that individual betterment would come through one's own endeavors, not the government's [Burr 1926].)

Moreover, some women acted directly by organizing antisuffrage groups to counter the suffragists. Boston had had its Woman's Anti-Suffrage League since 1882, and its endeavors were reinforced by the National Anti-Suffrage Association and the Woman's Anti-Suffrage Association, both of which pressed their status-quo views on state and federal legislators. "The proportion of women who desire the suffrage seems to be smaller in America than in England," wrote British statesman and historian James Bryce, who was an astute observer of American culture, politics, and government in the late nineteenth and early twentieth centuries:

> Of the many American ladies whose opinion I have from time to time during forty years inquired, the enormous majority expressed themselves hostile.... They support journals also, which press upon women the desirability of their continuing in the sphere they have hitherto occupied, and dwell upon the greater and better influence which, so it is thought, they may exert on legislation and administration if they remain "outside politics." ...Woman suffragism, has been, though less so now than formerly, thought "bad form," and supposed to betoken a want of culture and refinement. (Bryce 1921, vol. 1, 610–611)

Not only were most women probably opposed to the franchise during this period, but many women who possessed it voted infrequently. Suffragists must surely have found some of the data discouraging or even demoralizing. Massachusetts held a nonbinding referendum in 1895 on suffrage for women in municipal elections, but only 23,000 of 600,000 women cast a vote (Keyssar

2000, 200). The *New York Times* had already used evidence of low turnout as an argument against women suffrage, citing school elections in Connecticut where less than 3 percent of women voted, with half the towns reporting no votes by women at all. "If women do not care for suffrage, why should it be thrust upon them?" asked the editors (Editorial 1893, 4). Of course the argument was spurious: the absence of voting by *some* women could hardly be justification for denying the vote to *all* women. Besides, it was an argument unlikely to be applied to any subset of male voters.

Such attitudes were reinforced by the inertia of the prevailing male ideology. As Bryce explained, "There is a widespread apprehension that to bring women into politics might lower their social position, diminish men's deference for them, harden and roughen them, and, as it is expressed, 'brush the bloom off the flowers'" (Bryce 1921, vol. 1, 610). Moreover, to enfranchise women would "strike a blow at the harmony . . . of the home," as one Delawarean delegate warned at his state's constitutional convention (Keyssar 2000, 201). Coupled with those fears was the religiously based perspective that men were supposed to occupy a higher place in the social order. Accordingly, political equality would upset the divine plan. "[T]he head of the woman is man. . . . [W]oman is the glory of man. For man did not come from woman, but woman from man; neither was man created for woman, but woman for man" (I Corinthians 11:3, 7–9). St. Paul's prescription for first-century Christians was presumed by many to be applicable to Americans 1,900 years later. Even without any reference to a divine plan, the male editorial board at the *New York Times* as late as 1908—well into the Progressive era—nonetheless found arguments for female suffrage wholly vacuous:

If the women would gain nothing for themselves by the use of the ballot, if communities would not be better governed, and if, as certainly now appears to be the case, a great majority of the women do not want the ballot, the cause of the suffragettes and of the suffragists would seem to be in need of expositors better equipped, or arguments not yet discovered, and of reasons not thus far set forth if it is to make any considerable advance toward success. (Editorial 1908, 12)

Aside from such attitudes, practices, and prejudices, self-interest in other quarters energized opposition to female suffrage. Recall from the previous chapter that, in the pre–Civil War years, the suffrage crusade was an offshoot of the antislavery and temperance movements. Suffrage later became the central goal of many women, but after the end of slavery suffragists retained links with prohibitionists. These were separate movements to be sure. Leaders of the suffrage movement were not the leaders of the temperance movement, especially because far more men were committed to the latter than to the former. Still, many women who favored suffrage were active in temperance causes, and many who favored temperance also favored the vote for women. Understandably, therefore, the Prohibition Party was among the first organizations slating political candidates to advocate full suffrage for women, including such a plank in its platform for the election of 1908. A franchised womanhood would strengthen both the party's cause and the temperance movement generally (Coletta 1971, vol. 3, 2069).

Indeed, without the Women's Christian Temperance Union, the presidential aspirations of the Prohibition Party would doubtless have had less success than they did. (American voters generally have tended to shy away from mainly single-issue parties.) In its best showings in elections between 1884 and 1916, the party never received more than 2.2 percent of the popular vote. By comparison, the Socialist Party received 6 percent in 1912. Nonetheless, the temperance movement was far more successful legislatively. Not only did it have a few of its members elected to Congress, but it managed to convince the legislatures in state after state to "go dry"—to ban the sale of alcoholic beverages. Temperance forces had first been successful in Maine in 1851. By 1917, twenty-seven states were legally dry. (Although dry in law, thanks to enterprising bootleggers and moonshiners, most remained at least "damp" in fact.) Moreover, in others "local option" prevailed whereby cities and counties could decide for themselves whether to outlaw "demon rum" (Morison 1965, 899). Thus, because of the link between temperance and suffrage, manufacturers, distributors, and purveyors of alcoholic beverages were staunchly opposed to extending the vote to women. Industry lobbying reached into the halls of Congress and into state legislative chambers.

Another interest-driven source of opposition were local (and sometimes statewide) political organizations or machines. Tammany Hall—the Democratic Party organization in New York City—was the most famous (some said infamous) and longest-lived of the big city machines, but it was hardly the only one. Found mainly in the large cities of the East and the Midwest such as Boston, Chicago, Philadelphia, Baltimore, and Cleveland, these were usually Democratic in party orientation (but Republican most often in Pennsylvania), and were built upon the support of the largely Roman Catholic, working-class residents, many of whom were immigrants or the sons of immigrants. Such organizations thrived on patronage: government jobs, services, and contracts that were handed out to supporters and contributors. Long the target of good government advocates because of their reliance on patronage and the graft and corruption that such a system encouraged, the machines (whose leaders were rarely found at temperance meetings) hardly wanted to threaten their positions by opening the polls to reform-minded women.

The suffrage movement also stalled because of timing. Although it had little to do with the intrinsic merits or demerits of voting by women, an antidemocratic mood emerged in the United States in the late nineteenth century that looked with skepticism on the franchise as it stood. That is, many had begun to question the nearly universal manhood suffrage then in place. So it was out of the question to consider enlarging it further. In the psychology of marketing and merchandising, they felt the political equivalent of "buyer's remorse." There had been a similar unease during the 1850s, which the Know-Nothings had briefly fed and exploited. Moreover, recall from the previous chapter that, from the perspective of those who favored a broad manhood suffrage, it had been fortuitous that great strides in that direction had already been taken by the time the implications of the demographic and social changes, well underway by midcentury, were fully appreciated. Otherwise, had industrialization and the surge in immigration occurred a few decades earlier, manhood suffrage likely would not have proceeded as far as it did.

[T]here is growing in this country a great skepticism concerning man suffrage," Carrie Chapman Catt told Delaware's constitutional convention in 1897. "If that were not true, our own cause of woman suffrage would grow more rapidly than it is growing" (Keyssar 2000, 201). Catt was referring to those whom one historian has called "tory" antisuffragists, in contrast to the "traditional" antisuffragists who believed in a separate sphere for women and the feminine ideal. Tory antisuffragists favored rule by a paternalistic elite. For them, democracy was "experimental and should be limited to responsible, dutiful citizens who would exercise suffrage in the interest of society, at large." This view was akin to the notion of "virtual representation," highlighted in the debates at Putney and in the rhetoric of the American Revolution, by which the interests of all would be cared for by those in the better classes, even though those in the lesser classes would have no say in the selection of their "betters" who ruled over them. According to one essayist, American democracy was truly government "of the people, but not necessarily of all persons constituting the people" (Graham 1996, 16).

Moreover, most such tories also feared trade unionism and socialism, and found the advocacy of female suffrage by those movements yet another reason to oppose it. "A Vote for Woman Suffrage Will Help Socialism," warned an antisuffrage flier distributed in Virginia (Graham 1996, 16–17). But it was the tide of immigrants that flooded the country in the latter nineteenth century that caused them greatest alarm. Not only would the immigrants sooner or later be voting, but it was among them that labor organizers, anarchists, socialists, and others who frightened the tories recruited followers. Admitting women to the polls would also admit immigrant women, thus making an already tenuous situation worse. "The immigrant woman is a fickle, impulsive creature, irresponsible, very superstitious, ruled absolutely by emotion and intensely personal in her point of view," testified immigration inspector Mary Dean Adams to the Joint Judiciary Committee of the New York state legislature in 1909. "In many things much resembling a sheep," she continued, the immigrant woman "would be as capable of understanding just about as much of political matters as a man deaf and blind would of the opera." The inspector then quoted a labor organizer's response when asked about the effect suffrage would have on immigrant women: "Why, she would sell her vote for a pound of macaroni" (Graham 1996, 17–18). Adams echoed Abraham Kellogg at New York's constitutional convention of 1894: "Before we double twice over the voting population . . . with its untold possibilities of corruption," government was obliged to "bend its efforts towards purifying the Augean stables which we now have to contend with rather than to incur the possibility of new evils which we know not of" (Keyssar 2000, 202).

Some tories even called for a return to property qualifications as a way of saving the republic. Democracy, American style, had yielded corrupt and inefficient government. Restricting the suffrage, not expanding it, would restore honesty and efficiency. "The democratic system in actual operation among us," wrote attorney Alfred Cruikshank as late as 1920, "has been productive of corruption and mismanagement to such an extent as to cause and justify the almost universal verdict that popular misgovernment rather than popular government has been the outcome" (Cruik-shank 1920, 6). To add women to the electorate, therefore, would be to enlarge an electorate that was already too large. For tories, America's problem was too much democracy, not too little.

Adjunct to tory trepidations was the matter of race. Hostility to female suffrage remained strong in southern and border states. It was there that the traditional view of women-on-pedestals was strongest. And it was there that most African Americans lived. From the perspective of the white establishment, therefore, it made sense to oppose efforts to expand suffrage at the state level as well as efforts to secure an expanded suffrage by way of constitutional amendment. The former would double the number of legally enfranchised blacks. The latter would do the same but might also lead to expanded federal oversight of state elections, thus bringing racial discrimination at the polls under greater national scrutiny. Those risks outweighed the claim by some southern suffragists that an expanded franchise would help preserve white supremacy in the South. Southern white men found unpersuasive arguments such as those advanced by Belle Kearney when the NAWSA met in New Orleans in 1903 for its national convention. "The enfranchisement of women would insure immediate and durable white supremacy, honestly attained," she explained, "for upon unquestioned authority it is stated that in every southern State but one there are more educated women than all the illiterate voters, white and black, native and foreign, combined."

As you probably know, of all the women in the South who can read and write, ten out of eleven are white. . . . The South is slow to grasp the great fact that the enfranchisement of women would settle the race question in politics. The civilization of the North is threatened by the influx of foreigners with their imported customs. . . . Just as surely as the North will be forced to turn to the South for the nation's salvation, just so surely will the South be compelled to look to its Anglo-Saxon women as the medium through which to retain the supremacy of the white race over the African. (Buhle and Buhle 1978, 348–349)

In rejecting such arguments, southern legislators may have had thoughts more akin to the candid, if crude, comment by a Mississippi senator who worried that black women, given the matriarchal nature of many African American families at that time, might be more assertive than black men in defending their rights. "We are not afraid to maul a black man over the head if he dares to vote, but we can't treat women, even black women, that way" (Morgan 1973, 96).

Combined, these forces, factors, and views account for "the doldrums" as a time of equilibrium or stasis. Given the pressures against it after 1895 and in the first few years of the twentieth century, woman suffrage had probably moved as far as it could go. The suffrage cause would advance only when circumstances changed.

By 1917, circumstances had changed significantly. First, the campaign for woman suffrage became a mass movement. The NAWSA itself experienced a dramatic increase in membership, from about 100,000 in 1900 to 2 million in 1917. Moreover, the NAWSA was certainly not the only suffrage organization. More militant groups formed as well: the Equality League in 1907, the Woman's Suffrage Party in 1910, the Congressional Union in 1913, and the Woman's Party in 1916. Women paraded and picketed and sometimes got themselves arrested. Some 5,000 marched in a suffrage parade in Washington in 1913, upstaging newly elected President Woodrow Wilson's inauguration (Graham 1996, 55, 82).

Moreover, the NAWSA, women's clubs, and other groups heavily dominated by middle-class women also began to pay more attention to the needs of working-class women. By 1900, women constituted one-fifth of the workforce. Largely outside the organized labor movement, they typically had the lowest-paying jobs and suffered the poorest working conditions. It was not coincidental that the 146 victims of the Triangle Shirtwaist Company fire in lower Manhattan in 1911 were mainly young Italian and Jewish women. Women's clubs, in particular, that had formerly been neutral or even hostile on the suffrage issue, concluded that the urban-centered reforms they hoped to bring about would happen only if they had access to the ballot (Buhle and Buhle 1978, 33).

At the NAWSA convention in 1912, for example, Elsie Cole Phillips emphasized the value of the vote to working women: "Is it to strengthen the hands of the strong? Oh, no; it is to put into the hands of the weak a weapon of self-protection. And who are the weak? Those who are economically handicapped—first of all the working classes in their struggle for better conditions of life and labor. And who among the workers are the weak? Wherever the men have suffered, the women have suffered more."

Aside from the wage-earning woman who would benefit, the country as a whole would profit from the knowledge of the "home-keeping woman, the wife and mother, of the working class.... [W]ho better than she knows what the needs of the workers are in the factories? ... Who, better than the mother who has tried to bring up six or seven children in one room in a dark tenement house, knows the needs of a proper building?" Phillips then turned the "ignorant voter" argument of the antisuffragists on its head:

> The ignorant vote that is going to come in when women are enfranchised is that of the leisure-class woman, who has no responsibilities and knows nothing of what life means to the rest of the world, who has absolutely no civic or social intelligence. But, fortunately for us, she is a small percentage of the women of this land, and fortunately for the land there is no such rapid means of education for her as to give her the ballot and let her for the first time feel responsibilities. (Buhle and Buhle 1978, 376–377)

This cross-class emphasis had been aided by formation in 1903 of the Women's Trade Union League that drew from both the middle and laboring classes. The WTUL's principal objective was unionization of female workers, but it realized that the parallel goals of improved wages and working conditions would be furthered by the ballot. "Behind suffrage," said one organizer, "is the demand for equal pay for equal work." Thus the WTUL helped to convert laboring women to the idea of the vote all the while it tried to persuade them of the need to organize and to bargain collectively. (Sometimes, with Irish and German immigrants in particular, selling the value of woman suffrage was no easy task.) Although the influential American Federation of Labor had officially favored woman suffrage since 1892, its leader Samuel Gompers enthusiastically embraced the idea in 1915 when he urged male trade unionists to make suffrage for women a priority. He saw the link between the rights of labor and the right to vote for women: "Men must join the women in the effort to solve their common problem," he urged in a newsletter, "or else they will find women used against them as competitors" (Keyssar 2000, 205).

The second changed circumstance after 1917 was that the standoff that had prevailed between the pro- and antisuffrage forces since 1895 was broken in favor of the former. Few things energize a cause quite like a victory, and woman suffrage forces could now claim two more. A referendum in Washington in 1910 conferred full suffrage in that state. The following year, Progressive-minded Democrats and Republicans in California took charge in the legislature and submitted a woman suffrage amendment to the male electorate. Out of about 246,000 votes cast, it passed by a margin of only 3,587. Nonetheless, a win was a win. The Washington and California successes had an electrifying effect on the movement, just in time for the elections of 1912, where November ballot questions on woman suffrage in Kansas and Oregon prevailed. Furthermore, Arizona was admitted to the union in the same year with a full-suffrage provision in its constitution. Thus, within just two years, women had been enfranchised in five states. Illinois followed in 1913 with suffrage for women in presidential elections and for certain state and local offices.

Not surprisingly, this flurry of activity between 1910 and 1912 had at least some effects on presidential politics. President William Howard Taft addressed the NAWSA's annual convention in 1910, not only putting his considerable physical mass behind the organization by his presence on the dais but by at least opaquely endorsing a woman's right to vote. When the Republican Party split in 1912, its traditional wing renominated Taft. The Progressive wing bolted and put former President Roosevelt at the head of its Bull Moose ticket. At the Republican convention in June, the draft platform made no mention of woman suffrage. "Our friends being deluged with requests for planks favoring woman suffrage. Will be glad to learn your wishes," Charles Hilles, the president's personal secretary, telegraphed Taft. "I will not make a declaration in the face of the convention on the woman suffrage business any more than I have already done," Taft replied. Later in the summer, in a letter to Hilles, he reiterated his opposition to the amendment route: "I cannot change my view . . . just to suit the exigencies of the campaign, and if it is going to hurt me I think it will have to hurt me. . . . It is really a matter for state action and I would have no right to commit the party to anything beyond the fact that it is a state question" (Pringle 1939, vol. 2, 824–825).

But the Bull Moose Progressive platform stressed the suffrage issue: "The Progressive Party, believing that no people can justly claim to be a true democracy which denies political rights on account of sex, pledges itself to the task of securing equal suffrage to men and women alike" (Schlesinger and Israel 1971, vol. 3, 2187).

A careful reading shows that the language of the plank begged the question whether equal suffrage should be achieved by constitutional amendment or action by the individual states, although many Progressives preferred the former route. Even so, this plank was the first on woman suffrage in the platform of a major American political party. The presence or absence of a plank was (and is) important not because a victorious party always enacts all or even most of its promises, but because a platform is a window into the collective mind of a party. It "suggests where the energy of the party is" (Drew 1985, 588).

As for the Democrats, their platform, taking into account the importance of the party's southern wing, ignored woman suffrage altogether. Moreover, their nominee, Woodrow Wilson, was decidedly cool on the idea of women voting, but, thanks to the split among Republicans, it was Wilson who prevailed. Poor Taft finished in third place in both the popular and electoral vote counts behind Roosevelt, the only occasion in the twentieth century when one of the two major parties finished nationally in neither first nor second place.

The second year of Wilson's presidency, 1914, yielded mixed results on suffrage. Advocates cheered when Montana and Nevada joined the list of the states that had fully enfranchised women, all of them being west of the Mississippi River. Thus, with the grant of partial presidential suffrage in Illinois in 1913, women in twelve states would be eligible to vote in the presidential election of 1916. Moreover, in 1915 the NAWSA recommitted itself to securing a constitutional amendment and reallocated organizational resources accordingly, a change in emphasis no doubt encouraged by some bad news: lop-sided defeats of suffrage proposals in New York, Massachusetts, and Pennsylvania in the same year (Keyssar 2000, 212). Alongside these facts, what role would the suffrage issue play in the upcoming national elections?

In 1916, Democrats readily renominated Wilson for a second term and adopted a platform that mimicked in many ways the Bull Moose platform from 1912. Bull Moose Republicans also held a convention, but when Roosevelt, their standard bearer in 1912, refused a nomination and told them to return to the Republican fold, they did. Reunited and therefore emboldened, Republicans nominated U.S. Supreme Court Justice Charles Evans Hughes, a former New York governor with some Progressive leanings. Despite disagreement on many things, both parties were now officially in agreement on woman suffrage: "We recommend the extension of the franchise to the women of the country by the States upon the same terms as to men," declared the Democratic platform. The Republican platform favored "the extension of the suffrage to women, but recognize[d] the right of each State to settle this question for itself" (Schlesinger and Israel 1971, 2279, 2286). Thus for the first time both major parties took a stand in favor of a vote for women, but also refrained from endorsing a suffrage amendment. In terms of their personal views, however, Hughes was known to favor opening the vote to women by the amendment route; Wilson remained personally lukewarm, although it was said that he had cast a prosuffrage vote in a 1915 referendum in his home state of New Jersey (Graham 1996, 114). And he offered the NAWSA opaque support when he addressed that body's convention in Atlantic City in September of the election year: "I have not come to ask you to be patient, because you have been, but I have come to congratulate you that there has been a force behind you that will beyond any peradventure be triumphant and for which you can afford a little while to wait" (Buhle and Buhle 1978, 434).

Woman suffrage, however, proved not to be a key issue in the race—that was unlikely, in any event, because both major parties outwardly took the identical stance. (As it happened, the Socialists, who were as adamantly in favor of woman suffrage as the Prohibitionists, did only about half as well in 1916 as they did in 1912, in terms of percentage of popular vote received.) Moreover, no third (minor) party was poised to pose a major threat at the polls, and the topic was not one that figured prominently in campaign speeches and literature. Instead, aside from the general competency of Wilson in his first four years, peace was the question that seemed to overshadow all others.

War had broken out in Europe in August 1914, and the conflict quickly engulfed the Continent. By 1916, an uncanny "quiet" had settled onto the western front in France. The French army seemed as incapable of dislodging the Germans as the Germans were of advancing any further. Casualties mounted into the millions, as newly developed tools of warfare like the machine gun, barbed wire, tanks, poison gas, and long-range, railway-transportable artillery took their toll. These new implements of war overwhelmed the underdeveloped capabilities of medical science to cope with the carnage. No previous war provided a parallel. "Its colossal expenditure of blood and treasure, with lasting effects on the life and economy of victor and neutral hardly less than of vanquished, its monstrous inventiveness and efficiency in the field of scientific devastation, were things quite outside the experience of the pre-1914 generation" (Gathorne-Hardy 1964, 14). And there was another difference: the problem presented by the submarine—the U-boat—that Germany used with a vengeance, along with mines, in an effort to counter the blockade of its own ports by putting an ocean-based stranglehold on England and France.

Officially, the United States was neutral in the conflict. Emotionally, there were strong feelings in America for the British, French, and others on their side, except among some of German and Irish birth or descent who hoped for defeat of the Allies. Mainstream suffragist organizations in the United States such as the NAWSA initially took a pacifist position on the war, publicizing a call for peace from women in twenty-six countries. As the NAWSA's *Woman's Journal* declared in 1914, they wanted "to show war-crazed men that between contending armies there stand thousands of women and children who are innocent victims of men's unbridled ambitions; that under the heels of each advancing army are crushed the lives, the hopes, the happiness of countless women whose rights have been ignored" (Buhle and Buhle 1978, 39).

Between 1914 and early 1917, much trade flowed from the United States to England, and here the German submarines posed an ever-mounting problem. Nonetheless, Democrats emphasized in 1916 that America under Wilson's leadership had so far managed to steer the nation clear of the conflict. The keynote speaker at the 1916 Democratic convention cited instance after instance in which the Wilson administration had been able to avert war. After each one, delegates shouted "We didn't go to war!" That refrain became the campaign's theme: "He kept us out of war!" (Morison 1965, 855). Yet Wilson "knew best of all that a German lieutenant looking through a submarine periscope could make nonsense of the slogan" (Smith 1964, 32).

That same theme probably accounted for Wilson's narrow victory over Hughes. It was also a surprise victory: Based on the early returns from California, Wilson went to bed that Tuesday night believing that the Republicans had won, "remarking that it seemed his programs had not been completely understood by the voters" (Smith 1963, 32). But by noon on Wednesday the returns proved otherwise. It was the first time a Democratic president had won a successive second term since Jackson in 1832. (Democrat Grover Cleveland served two terms, but they were bifurcated: 1885–1889, and 1893–1997.)

It was also the first time in American history when voting by women made a difference in a national election. As many as one million women may have voted in 1912, but aside from the phenomenon itself, they made absolutely no difference in the outcome of the election. The election of 1916, however, was far different. Not only were women in more states eligible to vote for president than in 1912, but in 1916 they converted what otherwise would have been a victory for Hughes into a victory for Wilson. Hughes lost because of "the emotional votes of the women, . . . the extreme speeches of Roosevelt, and . . . the besotted comfort of the western farmers," lamented former President Taft (Pringle 1939, 899).

Wilson received 277 electoral votes and 49 percent of the popular vote. Hughes received 254 electoral votes and 46 percent of the popular vote. By contemporary standards, perhaps, those numbers may not seem close. However, in terms of electoral vote, the presidential election of 1916 was the closest since 1876, and with respect to the popular vote, it was among the closest since the end of the Civil War. But the Wilson-Hughes contest was even closer than the overall vote counts suggest. After Arizona and New Mexico were admitted to the Union in 1912, there were 48 states. With 435 members of the House of Representatives and 96 members of the Senate, that meant that the total number of electoral votes in play was 531. To win the presidency, a candidate had to receive a majority of the electoral vote, or 266. Thus, with Wilson's 277 and Hughes's 254, a shift of merely 12 electoral votes from Wilson to Hughes would have given Hughes, not Wilson, the key to the White House.

Aside from the traditionally loyal Democratic South, what were some of the states that Wilson carried? (To "carry" a state means to win a plurality of the vote in that state, and, ordinarily, all of that state's electoral vote.) Among the states that had allowed women to vote in presidential elections, Wilson carried Wyoming with three electoral votes, Utah with four, Colorado with six, Idaho with four, Arizona with three, California with thirteen, Washington with seven, Kansas with ten, Montana with four, and Nevada with three. But, that said, were any of these contests close? There were about 1 million votes cast in California, and Wilson's margin of victory in that state was less than 4,000. Although no exit polls were conducted in 1916, anecdotal evidence indicates that women voted disproportionately for Wilson because of the peace issue, despite the fact that Wilson remained tepid toward woman suffrage. In Washington, Wilson's margin was just under 17,000. Reports suggest that 90,000 of 155,000 women on the registration rolls voted for Wilson, again with peace apparently being the primary issue on their minds. In Kansas, some 70,000 Republican women voted for Wilson (out of 625,000 votes cast) in a race that Wilson won by about 37,000 votes. Had California sided with Hughes instead of Wilson, or had Republicans captured Washington and Kansas, Hughes would have won. Thus the overwhelming evidence is that, for the first time, women made a decisive difference in a presidential election (Link 1965, 161). Henceforth, could politicians in other states fail to notice?

In 1917, two not unrelated developments made prompt full national woman suffrage all but inevitable. The first was America's entry into the war, and the second involved a surprising about-face in New York. Germany's proclamation of unrestricted submarine warfare neutralized America's neutrality, and the Wilson administration broke off diplomatic relations with Germany in February 1917. In a war message to Congress on April 2, the president justified American involvement in the conflict by proclaiming, "The world must be made safe for democracy" (Knock 2001, 843). On April 6, Congress obliged and declared war. In the months that followed, the United States mobilized militarily to an unprecedented extent. Within a year, the nation's armed forces mushroomed from 100,000 to 5 million. Women had a wartime role far beyond anything that had been seen in the Civil War. In addition to the expected voluntary activities like bandage rolling, food distribution, and assistance with the sale of war bonds and stamps, thousands of women served in noncombatant positions in the military and in nongovernmental organizations such as the Red Cross. Moreover, women filled numerous government positions as the size of government grew and as posts fell vacant as men went off to fight. A similar phenomenon occurred in the private sector as 1 million women took factory jobs that hitherto had been reserved for men.

The NAWSA strategically aligned itself with the administration's war policies, with prominent suffragists Carrie Catt and Anna Howard Shaw serving on the Women's Committee of the Council on National Defense. The NAWSA's *Woman's Journal* was retitled the *Woman Citizen*. "No jockeying with the pacifist past can save the world now," it editorialized in June 1917. "However the War may have been intrigued in the beginning, by capital, by secret diplomacy, war is here. And superior to all the intrigue . . . is an ideal that is sustaining the world today—the ideal of democracy." The *Woman Citizen* preached cooperation with, and support for, the government's war aims in service of women's own interests. "[A]n intimate part of ourselves . . . whether its administration wholly satisfied us or not, [the war policy] stands for our own effort to hold ourselves coherently to group action, group control, group progress," the *Citizen* declared in September 1918 (Buhle and Buhle 1978, 39–40). In contrast, more militant suffragists organized picket lines and hunger strikes to protest the war and to excoriate Wilson for pretending to defend democracy abroad but ignoring it at home. Despite such activities that provided plenty of fodder for antisuffragists, participation by most women in the national effort at all levels crippled one of the antisuffragists' oldest arguments: that women should not vote because they did not bear arms.

Seven months after the United States officially threw itself into World War I, the all-male electorate of New York State approved an amendment to the state constitution conferring full suffrage on women, making that state the first one east of the Mississippi River to do so. What had happened to reverse the results of a suffrage defeat in a referendum in the same state only two years before? Major credit belonged to the organizational efforts at the grass roots by a coalition of groups such as the NAWSA, the Woman Suffrage Party, and the Women's Trade Union League. They in effect constructed their own "suffrage machine." As New York State Woman Suffrage Party Chairman Mrs. Norman Whitehouse commented, "the change in sentiment in regard to women, because of the assistance they have given the government at war, has been enormous." The Socialist Party, first generation German Americans, and pacifists joined the coalition on the mistaken theory that enfranchised women would curtail or diminish

American participation in the war. In fact, the still antisuffragist *New York Times* gave the Socialists credit for the victory (Graham 1996, 99, 112–113). The *Times's* opinion aside, the referendum succeeded most probably because Tammany Hall decided to take a "hands-off" position on the question, even though the New York City Democratic leadership had staunchly opposed suffrage. Wives of some machine bosses were recruited into the Woman Suffrage Party and installed as leaders. Suffragists then convinced the top Tammany leadership that Democrats would be held responsible, were the proposal to be defeated, once women did eventually get the vote. To be sure, standing aside was not the same as lending support, but at least the Tammany leadership would not use its considerable muscle by standing in the way.

The wartime mood had its effects elsewhere as well. Four more states (Michigan, Nebraska, North Dakota, and Rhode Island) enfranchised women for presidential elections. In the same year, statutes in Indiana and Ohio to do the same fell victim to judicial invalidation and a referendum, respectively (Keyssar 2000, 389–390). But in the first significant prosuffrage step in the South, Arkansas opened party primaries to women (Graham 1996, 111).

The victory in New York State, however, was probably most important. This is why Carrie Catt called the "battle of New York the Gettysburg of the woman suffrage movement"(Graham 1996, 113). Symbolically, there was now to be full woman suffrage in a state east of the Mississippi—and the largest state at that. Substantively, because of its population, New York had the largest congressional delegation. That would mean more members of Congress attuned to suffrage. As one suffrage lobbyist reported, "Most of those [in the New York delegation] listed as 'doubtful' on our poll promptly changed to supporters, as did several of those previously opposed, because the carrying of New York was accepted by the politically wise as the handwriting on the wall" (Graham 1996, 114). Moreover, there would be ripple effects into presidential politics that few politicians could fail to miss: as a result of the New York referendum, the number of electoral votes from suffrage states jumped from 172 to 215.

Support for a suffrage amendment intensified in Congress. Even though Congress had rejected amendment proposals in 1914 and 1915, the incremental progress of woman suffrage in the states was felt on Capitol Hill by 1917. More representatives and senators were elected from states where women could vote. Step by step, individual states were altering Congress from the outside in, as well as from the inside out. Women were increasingly in a position to reward or to punish both officeholders and a political party because of stands taken on a suffrage amendment. Congressional wives and socially prominent women who had been won over to the suffrage cause aided the NAWSA in its congressional lobbying efforts. In fact its Congressional Committee came to be called the "Front Door Lobby," so named by one reporter because the suffragists never used "backstairs" methods or behind-the-scenes approaches (Graham 1996, 92).

In the fall of 1917, prosuffrage members of the House of Representatives decided to push the amendment as a "war measure," as a way of avoiding a standing congressional dictum against nonemergency legislation. Encouraged by President Wilson, the powerful House Rules Committee declined to oppose creation of a Woman Suffrage Committee that would formally shepherd the amendment. The Rules Committee chair, who had been previously opposed, summed up the new sentiment on the House floor: "A word to the wise is sufficient; this, Mr. Speaker, is a question that will not go down" (Graham 1996, 111).

The amendment had momentum. On January 9, 1918, Wilson announced his support for an amendment in a formal address, but aware of both congressional and party sensitivities, he advocated it as a "war measure." That accorded with the congressional practice that discouraged nonemergency legislation, but it also provided cover for those whose support for an amendment might otherwise be politically risky. In other words, passing a federal suffrage amendment could be described as part of the task of waging war successfully. The challenge was the Constitution's stipulation that amendments be proposed by a *two-thirds* vote by both the House and the Senate. Ordinarily, legislation requires only a simple majority, but constitutional amendments require a supermajority, thus allowing one-third of the members, plus one, in *either* the House or the Senate to block an amendment. The two-thirds requirement is not easily met.

On January 10, the proposed suffrage amendment cleared the two-thirds threshold by the barest of margins when the House voted 274 to 136 in favor of the amendment. One Indiana representative casting an "aye" vote did so from a stretcher. Another member, expected to vote "aye," was literally extracted from a train wreck and rushed to Washington. Others made extraordinary, if less dramatic, efforts to be present for the vote (Graham 1996, 115). The Senate, however, was another matter. The equal basis for representation in that body (two votes per state) and rules that magnified the ability of any one senator or a small group of them to delay or to divert business, gave antisuffrage states, many of which were in the South, additional leverage. (Southern senators remained worried over the added authority the amendment might give to the federal government over elections.) In addition, most probusiness Republican stalwarts like Henry Cabot Lodge of Massachusetts also continued to oppose woman suffrage. So the amendment failed in the Senate in October.

With the new Sixty-sixth Congress convening in the new year, and without Senate passage in the Sixty-fifth Congress, the suffrage amendment process would have to begin afresh in 1919. Still, the November 1918 elections meant that proamendment bloc in the Senate was going to be larger in the new year, and referenda in South Dakota, Michigan, and Oklahoma meant that, for the 1920 presidential elections, there would be even more electors from states where women could vote.

The House repassed the federal suffrage amendment on May 21, 1919, and the Senate agreed to schedule it for debate in June. Senate Republicans held a slim 49–47 majority over their Democratic colleagues, and decided to remain quiet during the debate, leaving it to the Democrats to thrash out the merits and demerits of what the House had done. A favorable 56–25 vote followed on June 4.

Success in Congress, however, marked only step one in the amendment process. Now, suffrage forces would have to secure ratification by legislatures of three-fourths of the states. Although a two-thirds supermajority in both houses of Congress posed an obstacle for any would-be amendment, the three-fourths rule for ratification was an even greater hurdle. Of the forty-eight states, all had bicameral legislatures like Congress at that time. Bicameralism meant that approval had to be achieved in both houses; a negative vote in either house would be a negative vote for ratification. Thus, for suffragists the magic number in a forty-eight-state union was thirty-six. For antisuffragists, the magic number was thirteen—that is, if even one house in as few as thirteen states refused to ratify, the three-fourths stipulation could not be reached. These numbers thirty-six or thirteen pointed to an additional wrinkle in ratification politics. In amending the national Constitution, every state counts equally; the population of a state is irrelevant. Having a large delegation in Congress obviously gives one state an advantage over smaller states in *proposing* amendments, but not in *ratifying* them. In step two of the amendment process in 1919, Vermont and Wyoming, with minimal representation in Congress, counted absolutely the same as New York and Pennsylvania with two of the largest delegations.

Ratification would be a function of two variables: the relative strength in the legislatures between suffrage and antisuffrage forces, and the timing of legislative sessions. Legislatures met at different times of the year, as they still do, and in the early twentieth century some state legislatures met only every other year. Some would have to be called into special session if the amendment was to be voted upon in time for the 1920 elections. The NAWSA of course did not leave the ratification process to chance. Intense lobbying at the state level promptly began in earnest soon after the Senate vote. By September 1919, the NAWSA's tally showed that seventeen states had already ratified the proposed amendment and that seventeen more would nearly certainly ratify when governors summoned their legislatures into special session. Thus the "plus" column totaled thirty-four sure, or nearly sure, states—two short of the necessary number. Of the remaining states, positive results seemed likely to come only from Vermont, New Jersey, Delaware, or Connecticut. "The situation in each of these is pretty bad," Catt confided to a coworker (Graham 1996, 131).

As depicted below in results certified by the states to the secretary of state, ratification moved forward in several stages, depending (1) on enthusiasm for the amendment and (2) upon state legislative scheduling. Within each stage, states are listed alphabetically.

Stage One: Ratification on July 10, 1919 (3 states)
   Illinois
   Michigan
   Wisconsin
Stage Two: Ratification from July 16 to July 28, 1919 (9 states)
   Arkansas
   Iowa
   Kansas
   Massachusetts
   Missouri
   New York
   Ohio
   Pennsylvania
   Texas

Stage Three: Ratification from August 2 to December 15, 1919 (10 states)

California
Colorado
Maine
Minnesota
Montana
Nebraska
New Hampshire
North Dakota
South Dakota
Utah

Stage Four: Ratification from January 6 to March 22, 1920 (13 states)

Arizona
Idaho
Indiana
Kentucky
Nevada
New Jersey
New Mexico
Oklahoma
Oregon
Rhode Island
Washington
West Virginia
Wyoming

Catt was correct in her call about New Jersey, but wrong with respect to hopes in Vermont, Delaware, and Connecticut. Suffragists were correct, however, in predicting little support for the amendment in most southern states. They are noticeably absent from the list above. But that list totals only thirty-five states. Which state was the thirty-sixth to put the amendment "over the top"? It was Tennessee. The Tennessee legislature debated the amendment during the summer of 1920. The resolution passed the senate with little difficulty, but the house proved far more difficult. After two weeks, a vote was called on August 18. A motion to table the amendment resolution was tied, so the speaker called for a final vote. A tie vote on ratification would be a vote against ratification. For suffragists in the gallery, defeat seemed imminent. But neither they nor the antisuffragists had expected the unexpected. A twenty-four-year-old first-term Republican representative from eastern Tennessee named Harry Burn had voted to table the amendment a few minutes before. He sported the red rose in his lapel typically worn by antisuffragists. Both sides therefore felt confident of his final negative vote. Unknown to either side, however, he had promised his suffragist mother that he would vote for the amendment, even though his constituents were strongly opposed, should it come down to a tie. He had a note in his pocket from his mother reminding him, "Don't forget to be a good boy." When his name was called, he shouted "aye," and so sealed ratification of the Nineteenth Amendment (Graham 1996, 144). With official certification of the Tennessee legislature's action in hand, the U.S. secretary of state declared the amendment in force on August 26, 1920.

Two questions on woman suffrage must still be considered. First, what accounts for the rapid acceleration toward suffrage near the end? The war, surely, made a huge difference in a way unlike the Civil War. Then, women expected the vote at the same time full citizenship was being conferred on African Americans. It did not happen. Probably the much larger role that women played in the war effort in 1917 and 1918 was itself a powerful argument for suffrage, especially alongside the incremental progress in suffrage that had already been made. Compared to the immediate post–Civil War period, the position of women in both respects was hardly comparable. Then there was what Alexander Keyssar has called the "endgame" or bandwagon phenomenon: Once impending or even possible victory seemed likely, the "potential cost of a vote against enfranchisement rose dramatically" (Keyssar 2000, 214). The risk of being on the losing side seemed too great. True, but there were also those prepared to take that risk. United States Senator Boies Penrose, Republican chieftain in Pennsylvania and a staunch foe of woman suffrage, was once taunted by a suffragist who advised him to switch sides because woman suffrage was "coming anyway." Penrose's retort was: "So is death, but I don't have to go out and meet it halfway" (Key 1964, 617 n.).

Potent as well were the cumulative effects of persistence. The steady number of suffrage demonstrations and other displays of militant tactics probably took their mental and emotional toll on the resistance. In January 1919, after the House had mustered its two-thirds majority for a suffrage amendment but when it became apparent that the amendment was stalled in the Senate, suffragists organized a massive demonstration at the White House, with each speaker being arrested and hauled away in a police wagon as she arose to talk. This was followed by a hunger strike that resulted in the release of those who had been incarcerated. This process repeated itself several times, with those who had been released boarding a "Prison Special" to tour the country by rail on behalf of the cause. Little wonder, then, that President Wilson by June had persuaded enough senators to relax their opposition to suffrage, if not eagerly to embrace the idea. "The suffragettes may not have had a steamroller, but the steady din of their agitation must have been about as soothing as the rattle of a pneumatic hammer" (Key 1964, 617 n.). In the years before air-conditioning, it was a steady din that must have enveloped the White House with its windows open on warm days.

Also important in the quick reversal of fortune was the influence of prosuffrage forces in states where women had full or partial access to the ballot. There were increasing opportunities for suffragists to wreak retribution at the polls. Moreover, near the end, ratification of the Eighteenth Amendment neutralized the opposition alcoholic beverage interests had mounted against woman suffrage. The "wets" had lost even in the absence of a federal suffrage amendment. Ratification was also probably encouraged by the growing realization among men that enfranchising women did not bring about radical changes. Just as the gradual expansion of the franchise among men in pre–Civil War America had refuted most of the dire predictions of what might happen if ordinary men could vote, so the gradual enfranchisement of women in various states had yielded no radical changes. Family and home life had not disappeared in the suffrage states.

Second, once enfranchisement of women was a reality across the nation, did women change American politics? Aside from the obvious fact that the Nineteenth Amendment doubled the size of the electorate, the conventional account is that little about politics changed, at least in the short term. One reason was that the Eighteenth Amendment had already enshrined prohibition as a national policy objective. Had that issue still been unresolved as of 1920, woman suffrage would probably have pushed it quickly along. Although many reformers had hoped that woman suffrage would result in a sort of purification of American politics, that did not happen. The decade of the 1920s was a return to "normalcy," as President Warren Harding said, not an age of reform (Morison 1965, 918). As two constitutional historians observed more than a half century later, woman suffrage had little or no purifying effect. "It was found that women had for the most part the same political virtues and failings as their menfolk and that they were divided along much the same party, class, and sectional lines" (Kelly and Harbison 1976, 641). Thus the effects on the political system seemed minor. More recent scholarship, however, disputes the view that, because women did not vote distinctly as a bloc differently than men, suffrage failed to produce long-term political gains for women (Alpern and Baum 1985; Lemons 1973; Cott 1987). Instead, from this perspective, the increasing role that women began to play in the life of the nation had more subtle effects. Especially after the NAWSA had reorganized itself as the League of Women Voters, the 1920s proved to be a decade in which "women's pursuits proliferate[d], their social and political commitments expand[ed]. . . . [T]he new generation of women in the twenties set out into a different world—one in which women could assume the rights for which their mothers and grandmothers struggled so hard" (Katzenstein 1992, 86–87). Government became more attuned to the particular concerns of women, especially those affecting the family. Most importantly perhaps, having the vote meant that women henceforth also had a right to act as public persons, expecting leadership roles in both government at all levels and in the private sector and working for objectives in all realms of society and politics.

Race and Voting: Culmination of a Century of Struggle

As the previous section demonstrated, abolishing gender barriers at the polls nationally by way of the Nineteenth Amendment was possible in large part because suffrage efforts were first successful in some states. A political base in favor of woman suffrage thereby became a critical mass that expanded its influence from state to state in one contest and referendum after another. The movement did not begin in Congress, but the movement ended there. Congress was a latecomer to the suffrage issue when it first began to give woman suffrage serious consideration after 1913. In proposing the Nineteenth Amendment in 1919, its members decided that a developing consensus about suffrage in some states should become the law of the land. This revolution in women's rights was at heart the product of a fundamental rethinking by men of the relationship between gender and politics. This rethinking eventually bubbled up and resounded at the top.

In contrast, the abolition of racial barriers at the polls happened in the reverse. As Chapter Two explained, no national consensus in favor of voting by African Americans existed in 1865. Indeed, prevailing opinion, North and South, was very much opposed to the idea. Ratification of the Fifteenth Amendment in 1870, which guaranteed a right to vote free of racial discrimination, came about more as a result of Reconstruction and partisan politics than because of any large-scale change of mind in the general white population about the desirability of political equality for blacks. This revolution in rights for African Americans thus originated not at the grassroots, but at the highest levels of government. It would succeed only if the national government was prepared to commit sufficient resources to make good on the promises of the Fifteenth Amendment, and/or if a consensus in support of those promises eventually took root among ordinary citizens and their state governments. By the late nineteenth century, it became clear that neither of those conditions was in place. The first had petered out and the second had never firmly materialized. It would take a long struggle over the better part of the twentieth century before both were again in place. Indeed, the Fifteenth Amendment is unique among all the statutory and other constitutional extensions of the franchise: Never has so specific a constitutional directive been so plainly evaded for so long.

It was in the ninety-five years between 1870 and 1965 that the nation wrestled with the voting rights of racial minorities (mainly African Americans, but not exclusively so). This time frame conveniently divides itself into three periods: (1) from 1870 until 1893, (2) from 1893 until 1927, and (3) from 1927 until 1965. As Chapter Two suggested, the status of black voting rights in the first period may fairly be characterized by the word "irresolution," by "retreat" in the second, and by "restoration" in the third. The years since 1965 constitute yet a fourth period in voting rights that has been characterized by "clarification."

In the first few years after ratification of the Fifteenth Amendment, the question whether black men would permanently become part of the political community of the United States remained unresolved and unclear. The outlook for black voting was decidedly mixed. Encouraging signs included voting by large numbers of blacks and the election of some of them to public office. Discouraging signs included the emasculation of federal civil rights legislation by the Supreme Court and the return of white Democrats (the "Redeemers") to power in the South.

From the 1890s through about the first quarter of the twentieth century, voting by southern blacks was at, or near, its nadir. With but one exception, the legal and political machinery of the United States seemed incapable or unwilling to apply any corrective measures. Voting rights by blacks were effectively determined not by the Constitution and Congress but by state and local white officials and voters. Only after 1927 does one begin to see evidence of a movement to reclaim the ballot on behalf of African Americans. These efforts resulted in a series of courtroom victories and in passage of the Voting Rights Act in 1965. More than any other single piece of legislation, it converted the promise of the amendment into reality and will be examined in detail later in this section.

Several forces and factors were at work to produce so severe and pervasive a denial of voting rights that it took a massive national effort to restore them. One such factor was racism itself. Hardly unique to the South, it merely manifested itself most noticeably in the states of the old Confederacy because most blacks lived there. In a society dominated by notions of white supremacy and black inferiority, it did not take a giant leap of logic to justify withholding the white person's rights and privileges from the black person. Also contributing were the same class-biased tory ideas that were a hindrance to woman suffrage as well. If the franchise was already too large, as these antisuffragists believed, the ballot should instead be the province only of dutiful, upstanding adults. Black adults were disproportionately poor and uneducated. Many lived in rural areas under conditions as squalid as those of immigrants in the tenements of New York City. So, from this perspective, like immigrants in the Northeast, blacks as a group seemed unworthy of the responsibilities of full citizenship. Compatible with both racism and tory antisuffragism was Social Darwinism that preached "survival of the fittest" in the social realm, even as Darwinists wrote about "natural selection" as an explanation for the origin and development of species (Mason and Leach 1959, 359–361). The principal thrust of Social Darwinism was minimalist government, carrying to an extreme Thomas Paine's Revolutionary-era slogan, "That government is best which governs least" (Morison 1965, 770–771). If government was ill-advised to intervene in the economy to help the masses by smoothing out the rough edges of the industrial revolution, a similar sentiment would weigh against government intervention on behalf of voting rights.

A fourth force in play was the need for national reconciliation among whites in the decades after the Civil War. The Compromise of 1877, discussed in Chapter Two, had led to an end to Reconstruction and a restoration of "home rule" in the South. White southerners accepted the outcome of the war and promised to recognize the status of the recently emancipated blacks. Northern whites promised to leave southern whites in charge of their own affairs. They were indeed left alone, but the black population fell victim to politics. Because blacks tended to vote Republican, disfranchising them eliminated any possibility of a Republican resurgence in the South, where whites voted overwhelmingly Democratic. Moreover, having blacks on the political sidelines meant that no Democratic faction could court their support. Just as politics in the nineteenth and early twentieth centuries was seen as a "man's business," politics in the South rapidly came to be seen as the business of white people, and white people only.

As a symbolic beginning to the national retreat on black voting rights, Congress in 1893 repealed those sections of the 1870 and 1871 Enforcement Acts providing for federal supervision of elections and federal remedies in voting disputes. Party politics again played a role, just as it had in ratification of the Fifteenth Amendment itself. Democrats had been elected in 1892 on a platform of eliminating federal interference in state affairs, and the Republicans had come around to the view that to maintain themselves as a national party, they would have to appeal to southern whites and not just to southern blacks. The House committee report on the repeal was explicit in its objectives: "Let every trace of the reconstruction measures be wiped from the statute books, let the States of this great Union understand that the elections are in their own hands." Moreover, repeal would "eliminate the judiciary from the political arena" (Stephenson 1989, 58). It would be difficult to craft language that was any more explicit as to purpose. And by the turn of the century, disfranchisement of blacks through various devices was well underway. That process was illustrated by several cases that also demonstrated that the judiciary eliminated itself, for a time at least, from a positive role in the voting rights arena. Some attention to the facts of these cases reveals the various schemes that had been devised to minimize voting by African Americans.

Williams v. Mississippi (1898), mentioned briefly in the last chapter, involved a black man's challenge to his murder indictment. Mississippi officials drew the names of grand and petit jurors from the list of registered voters. Williams claimed that the Mississippi Constitution of 1890 had caused wholesale disfranchisement of black voters through literacy tests, taxpaying requirements, and exclusion of those convicted of certain offenses. The laws vested "in the administrative officers the full power . . . to ask all sorts of vain, impertinent questions," Williams claimed. "[T]his officer can reject whomsoever he chooses, and register whomsoever he chooses." Yet because neither state statutes nor the state constitution explicitly discriminated on the basis of race, the Supreme Court found no Fifteenth Amendment violation. As the majority explained, the state's laws "reach weak and vicious white men as well as weak and vicious black men, and whatever is sinister in their intention, if anything, can be prevented by both races by the exertion of that duty which voluntarily pays taxes and refrains from crime." The record showed no "sufficient allegation of an evil and discriminating administration of [the laws]." Evil was possible, but not proven, so the principle of *Yick Wo v. Hopkins* (1886), in which there had been plain evidence of systematic discrimination against Chinese Americans in San Francisco, would not apply.

If *Williams* found the Court disinclined to probe for racially discriminatory schemes in voting, the remarkable case of *Giles v. Harris* (1903) found the Court unwilling to act when voting discrimination all but was admitted. At issue was a provision in the Alabama constitution of 1901, which changed registration requirements effective January 1, 1903. Those who registered before this date were registered for life. Those who registered after this date had to face strict literacy, employment, property, or other tests. Anyone who met certain residency rules, had paid poll taxes, and had served in a war of the United States, including the Civil War, or was a descendant of someone who had served, was allowed to register before January 1. Otherwise, a prospective registrant had to pass good character and understanding tests. The problem, of course, was that few blacks met the military service test. Therefore, most blacks needed an official to certify their good character, thus placing their right to vote in the sole discretion of local officials. Giles's complaint was that the plan disfranchised almost every black voter in Alabama, while making it very easy for most whites to comply.

The majority opinion by Justice Oliver Wendell Holmes acknowledged the racial motivation at work. "[W]e are dealing with a new and extraordinary situation [that] the whole registration scheme of the Alabama constitution is a fraud upon the Constitution of the United States." Yet the Court would not grant relief. If the scheme was a fraud, "how can he make the court a party to [it] . . . by adding another voter to its fraudulent lists?" The Court could not correct the situation by ordering that all blacks be registered, since only a few probably would be. Besides, "it would be a new doctrine in constitutional law that the original invalidity could be cured by an administration which defeated [the Constitution's] intent."

Even more fundamental was the Court's admission that it was *unable* to provide relief. The federal courts had no way to supervise black voting in Alabama. If "the great mass of the white population intends to keep the blacks from voting," Holmes admitted, "a name on a piece of paper will not defeat them." Instead, relief would have to come from the state or from "the legislative and political department of the government of the United States." In short, Holmes acknowledged over three dissents that the Court was powerless, not just because he questioned its authority to act but because he doubted its ability to force its will. To have ruled for Giles would have required more than a negative judgment, as happened when the Court set aside a law. It would have called for a judicially led political revolution and a radically enlarged view of the Court's role.

The following year, Giles was back before the Court in a suit for money damages and a suit in mandamus against the registrars in Montgomery County. (A mandamus is a type of court order to a public official.) Holmes's opinion in *Giles I* had suggested that possibility. But, with only Justice John Marshall Harlan dissenting, the majority turned Giles away a second time because the Alabama Supreme Court had decided the case on independent state grounds. The reasoning satisfied Justice William R. Day and the majority who appeared to be looking for a way to sidestep a staggering social and political problem. If Giles and the others had been kept off the rolls because of race, "no damage has been suffered by the plaintiff, because no refusal to register by a board thus constituted in defiance of the Federal Constitution would have the effect to disqualify a legal voter." And the attempt to add his name by mandamus would not work because, if the state constitution was illegal, "there would be no board to perform the duty sought . . ." (*Giles v. Teasley,* 1904).

Without direct action by Congress and the president or a fundamental change of mind among whites in the southern states, the Fifteenth Amendment by this time seemed practically a nullity. The Supreme Court was not ready to accept the view announced some years later by Justice Felix Frankfurter, that the amendment "nullifies sophisticated as well as simple-minded modes of discrimination" (*Lane v. Wilson,* 1939). Thus, by the second decade of the twentieth century, the remarkable thing was that the Supreme Court had any civil rights cases on its docket at all. The overall record since *United States v. Reese* and *United States v. Cruikshank* in 1876 (see Chapter Two) would have inspired few to look to the federal judiciary as a temple of racial justice.

Nonetheless, hope continued to triumph over experience. In 1915, the Supreme Court decided three cases from two states that presented additional examples of such "sophisticated" discrimination. The lead case was *Guinn v. United States* that called into question the constitutional validity of an amendment to the Oklahoma constitution, put to the voters before the election of 1910. According to Article III, Section 4a, voter registration was now to require a literacy test. Attached to the literacy requirement, however, was a "grandfather clause," a device similar to ones employed in other southern states.

> No person shall be registered as an elector of this State, or be allowed to vote in any election therein, unless he be able to read and write any section of the Constitution of the State of Oklahoma; but no person who was, on January 1st, 1866, or any time prior thereto, entitled to vote under any form of government, or who at that time resided in some foreign nation, and no lineal descendant of such person, shall be denied the right to register and vote because of his inability to so read and write sections of such Constitution. (Stephenson 1988, 60)

As stated, the new amendment allowed almost everyone *but* blacks to avoid the literacy test and thus to be registered. Of 55,684 blacks living in Oklahoma in 1900, only 57 had come originally from any of the six states that permitted blacks to vote in 1866. The grandfather clause thus shielded illiterate whites from the registrar's discretion. The literacy test, however, made that discretion controlling for blacks. Yet, African Americans constituted only 9 percent of the state's population in 1910, so the grandfather clause presumably was not motivated by a fear that blacks would dominate state or local politics. Together with whatever role racism may have played in selecting this device, the real drive for the clause probably came from Oklahoma Democrats who feared a loss of power to Oklahoma Republicans. Black voters might make the margin of difference in the next election. As one local Republican wrote President Taft in 1910, the amendment was adopted "for the express purpose of disfranchising negro voters, not because they are black, but because they vote the Republican ticket" (Bickel and Schmidt 1984, 928).

Officials in the Taft administration concluded that nothing could be done. They were not sure that surviving statutes from the Reconstruction era applied to the Oklahoma situation, and the *Giles* cases from 1903 and 1904 offered no help. Besides, there was reluctance to take on a southern voting law that might look like another example of "bloody shirt" politics that white southerners so detested. Taft Republicans still hoped that the party would eventually appeal to that part of the electorate, too. Yet they also realized that electoral victory in future contests might hinge on a more visible commitment to voting rights (Pringle 1939, II, 80). John Embry, the U.S. attorney in Oklahoma, took advantage of the confusion in Washington and pressed ahead with prosecutions against Oklahoma officials. In the meanwhile, Taft concluded that his renomination at the Republican convention might hinge on support from African American delegates, so he and Attorney General George Wickersham acquiesced at this point in the win-

win expectation that jurors probably would not convict. But they did, on September 29, 1911.

Supreme Court review of the case did not occur until after the Wilson administration had taken office in March 1913. Wilson's solicitor general was John W. Davis of West Virginia, who nearly forty years later would argue in defense of the separate-but-equal racial segregation doctrine of *Plessy v. Ferguson* (1896) on behalf of the southern states in the school segregation litigation of 1954 (*Brown v. Board of Education*). Davis's arguments in *Guinn* against the validity of the grandfather clause were more persuasive than his arguments in *Brown*. The Court in 1915 seemed prepared to meet a plain constitutional challenge and so for the first time applied the Fifteenth Amendment to invalidate a state voting scheme. The decision, decided midway in the amendment's fifth decade, marked an exception to the usual judicial deference that one finds with respect to state voting laws and practices during the second period.

Key to the Court's holding that the Fifteenth Amendment had been violated was the reference date of the grandfather clause: 1866. Only racial exclusion could explain the choice of that year.

> [W]e are unable to discover how, unless the prohibitions of the 15th Amendment were considered, the slightest reason was afforded for basing the classification upon a period of time prior to the 15th Amendment. Certainly it cannot be said that there was any peculiar necromancy in the time named which engendered attributes affecting the qualification to vote which would not exist at another and different period unless the 15th Amendment was in view.

Yet Oklahoma contended that, because the clause made no mention of race as such, it amounted to racial discrimination no more than would a property qualification. For the Court, the date was dispositive. The clause "in substance and effect" lifted prohibited conditions "over to a period of time after the Amendment, to make them the basis of the right to suffrage conferred in direct and positive disregard of the 15th Amendment."

Even so, Chief Justice Edward Douglass White, who as a very young man fought in the Confederate Army, was careful to contain the decision. Without mentioning the *Williams* jury and voting case from Mississippi or others by name, he noted that "no right to question the motive of the state in establishing a standard . . . or to review or supervise the same, is relied upon, and no power to destroy an otherwise valid exertion of authority upon the mere ultimate operation of the power exercised is asserted." That is, the holding was limited to the grandfather clause, and would not extend to literacy tests, good character tests, and other franchise requirements.

On the same day *Guinn* came down, the Court decided *Myers v. Anderson* (1915) and *United States v. Mosley* (1915). In the latter, the majority affirmed a conviction for throwing out ballots cast by African Americans in Oklahoma precincts where the grandfather clause had not strictly been enforced in the 1912 election. The majority went out of its way to include official derelictions within the coverage of a leftover Reconstruction law that appeared on its face to refer only to violence and intimidation of voters. It was the same statutory provision that the Court had relied upon in *Ex parte Yarbrough* (1884), discussed in Chapter Two, but here it was used against an election official. In *Myers*, the Court invalidated a Maryland statute that limited voting to taxpayers owning $500 worth of assessed property, naturalized citizens and their sons, and citizens or their male descendants entitled to vote before 1868. It was the *Guinn*-like grandfather provision, with its date of 1868 (the year of ratification of the Fourteenth Amendment), that brought the statute down.

What accounted for the Court's unusually aggressive posture in 1915, as contrasted with its timidity in 1903? A partial explanation might be that *Guinn* was decided by a somewhat different bench; a majority of the justices had been appointed since *Guinn*. Probably more decisive, however, was the fact that *Guinn,* in contrast to *Giles,* was a criminal prosecution. Because Guinn had been found guilty of violating the Enforcement Act of 1870, his principal basis for challenging the conviction, therefore, was that the grandfather clause was compatible with the Fifteenth Amendment. So the question before the Court in *Guinn,* as in the companion *Myers* and *Mosley* cases, was the application of the Fifteenth Amendment. If there was a violation of that constitutional provision, Guinn's conviction stood. If not, he was innocent. In contrast, *Giles* had presented the Court with an admittedly intolerable but also delicate situation with no practical judicial means at hand to correct it. The Court then in *Giles* had to tolerate the intolerable. *Guinn,* in contrast, was a more conventional case; the holding raised no unusual barriers to normal operation of the judicial process.

May *Guinn* also be explained as an example of Progressive thinking on the bench? Perhaps, but probably not. In 1915, the Court consisted of only one justice (Hughes) who had Progressive leanings. (As noted in the previous section, Hughes would resign in 1916 to accept the Republican nomination for president; Wilson added Louis D. Brandeis and John H. Clarke—both Progressives—to the bench in 1916.) Still it is possible that the remaining members had been affected by some of the Progressive ideas that filled much of the public debate of that day. But that possibility has to be discounted to the degree that many Progressives shared conventional ideas about race relations and so did not place a high value on protecting the civil rights of African Americans. To be sure, the National Association for the Advancement of Colored People (NAACP), which remains a highly influential ethnic advocacy organization even today, had been founded in 1910 by both white and black Progressives. And its attorneys would play a role in nearly every high-profile civil rights legal case thereafter.

Yet, even though quadrennial platforms of the Republican Party typically paid lip service to civil rights, the values of racial equality were near the top of no major party's agenda during this period. Indeed, it was a conspicuous omission from the goals Democrats sought for the nation every four years. Nonetheless, Woodrow Wilson in his successful "New Freedom" campaign for the White House in 1912 had openly appealed for black votes, and the black turnout (largely in the North) for Wilson was the heaviest ever to date for a Democratic presidential candidate. But promptly upon taking office in 1913, he instituted racial segregation in all departments of the federal government (Link 1956, 246–247). And as noted in the previous section, some supporters of woman suffrage (another Progressive value) over the decades seemed to think more in terms of *white* woman suffrage, justifying their claim on grounds of the racial superiority of white women. Indeed, soon after ratification of the Nineteenth Amendment in 1920, the liberal weekly opinion magazine *Nation* published an article outlining the difficulties black women faced in some southern states attempting to exercise their new right (Pickens 1920, 372). The editors then forwarded copies of the article to the 160 members of the National Advisory Committee of the National Women's Party, asking them whether they were concerned about the denial of the vote to black women. Only about one-third responded. Although most of those were "gratifying," wrote the *Nation,* the editors were perplexed by the lack of interest shown by the others, wondering whether, having secured the vote for themselves, they then cared little for those who had yet to enjoy what had been conferred ("White Woman's Burden" 1921, 257).

Although *Guinn* outlawed restrictions on voting that involved variations of the grandfather clause and so was an important symbolic victory, that decision alone was hardly enough to restore voting rights to blacks. Indeed, *Guinn* made little practical difference in the short run. Most states that had adopted such clauses had already abandoned them because they had become such embarrassing subterfuges. Besides, there were still good character, literacy, and/or understanding tests to pass and poll taxes to pay in many places. But the most effective barrier to black voting was the white primary that was in place across the South by the time *Guinn* was decided.

Recall from the first section of this chapter that the direct primary was a political reform that became popular during the Progressive era. It allowed voters, not party leaders, to choose a party's candidates. But the South had become a solidly one-party region, so the primary had taken on new importance in the selection of public officials. Whoever won the Democratic primary had in effect won the election because Republican opposition in the general election was either minimal or nonexistent. Thus, for all practical purposes, the Democratic primary was the election that mattered—the event where the real political choices were made. Limiting participation in the Democratic primary to whites seemed a foolproof way to disfranchise blacks in fact, if not in name. The few blacks who were registered to vote might still vote in the general election, but their ballots would make no difference. Thus, from the perspective of those who wanted to minimize the political influence of blacks, the white primary was a godsend. Yet, if the Fifteenth Amendment foreclosed outright a racially based state voting law, could a political party accomplish the same result by conducting a racially exclusive primary? This question took more than two decades to settle conclusively.

Democratic primaries in Texas had by party rule been closed to blacks for some years, but, by grace of local officials, blacks commonly voted in San Antonio nonetheless. After a losing candidate attributed his defeat in a primary to black voters, he convinced the state legislature in 1923 to make the white Democratic primary a requirement of state law: "In no event," read the statute, "shall a negro be eligible to participate in a Democratic party primary election held in the State of Texas" (Stephenson 1988, 63). Texas thus codified the practice that was already the rule in the southern states, although the Texas law swept more broadly because in practice Mexican Americans were negatively affected, too (Levinson 1963, 3). The first serious constitutional challenge to the white primary in the Supreme Court came through the efforts of Dr. L. A. Nixon, a black man living in El Paso.

Agreeing with Nixon that the white primary statute was unconstitutional, Justice Holmes's opinion rested not on the Fifteenth Amendment but on the equal protection clause of the Fourteenth Amendment. That provision forbids a state to "deny to any person within its jurisdiction the equal protection of the laws."

> We find it unnecessary to consider the 15th Amendment because it seems to us hard to imagine a more direct and obvious infringement of the 14th. . . . States may do a good deal of classifying that it is difficult to believe rational but there are limits, and it is too clear for extended argument that color cannot be made the basis of a statutory classification affecting the right set up in this case. (*Nixon v. Herndon,* 1927)

Why did Holmes rely on the Fourteenth Amendment and not the Fifteenth Amendment? The Court only rarely in those days deemed any legislative classification or distinction among people a violation of equal protection. As Holmes himself commented just a short time later in a case having nothing to do with voting, reliance on equal protection in Supreme Court litigation was the "last resort of constitutional arguments" (*Buck v. Bell,* 1927). A reasonable or rational classification sufficed, and the Court seemed to find reasonableness or rationality nearly everywhere but in Texas's white primary law. Besides, grounding a voting rights judgment on the Fourteenth Amendment seemed novel because of the Waite Court's decision in *Minor v. Happersett* in 1875. It rejected a claim that the "privileges or immunities" of national citizenship, protected by the Fourteenth Amendment against infringement by the states, conferred a right to vote on women. Perhaps Holmes relied on the Fourteenth because it was the path of least resistance to an equitable result. The Texas law, after all, was discriminatory, an issue the Court had addressed in the context of residential racial segregation in *Buchanan v. Warley* (1917) ten years earlier. Resorting to the Fifteenth Amendment would mean equating primaries with elections, a step the Court had not taken, even in matters of election fraud (*Newberry v. United States,* 1921). Indeed, *Newberry* had decreed that because primaries were unknown to the framers of 1787, primaries were beyond the reach of the Constitution.

In any event, *Nixon v. Herndon* marked a shaky beginning to the third, or restoration, period in the story of black voting rights, a period that extended until 1965. More than four decades were required for racial barriers at the polls to be firmly laid aside for at least two reasons. First, various devices in the South that kept black voting to a minimum persisted. White southerners generally remained unwilling to allow significant numbers of blacks to vote, except at the command of a court. Second, it took many years for a national consensus on voting rights to develop that translated into a decision by Congress to act decisively.

So, after *Nixon,* it is hardly surprising that white Texans responded quickly. As reported in the *New York Times,* Governor Dan Moody declared that "some legislation will be necessary to protect the ballot and give that guarantee of good government which the voided statute was designed to offer" (Stephenson 1988, 63). The governor's statement reflected the view, widespread at the time and during the three previous decades, that the disfranchisement of blacks was at heart a reform measure, a way of maintaining the purity of the political process. To this end, the legislature substituted a new plan: "Every political party in this State through its State Executive Committee," read the statute, "shall have the power to prescribe the qualifications of its own members and shall in its own way determine who shall be qualified to vote or otherwise participate in such political party." The executive committee of the Democratic Party of Texas then adopted a resolution declaring "that all white democrats who are qualified under the constitution and laws of Texas . . . and none other, be allowed to participate in the primary elections" (Stephenson 1988, 64). Dr. Nixon then filed another suit to challenge this latest reincarnation of the white primary.

In place of the unanimous bench in *Nixon v. Herndon* was a five-to-four decision, holding—again—that the newly styled white primary was unconstitutional. Like Holmes in *Nixon I,* Justice Benjamin Cardozo based the Court's judgment on the Fourteenth, not the Fifteenth amendment. Concluding that membership in the party was not unconnected to state action as would be membership in a golf club or a Masonic lodge, Cardozo found that the statute was still the source of membership and participation. "Whatever power of exclusion has been exercised by the members of the committee has come to them, therefore, not as the delegates of the party, but as the delegates of the state." The test of state action, and hence the reach of the Fourteenth Amendment, was "whether they [party officials] are to be classified as representatives of the State to such an extent and in such a sense that the great restraints of the Constitution set limits to their action" (*Nixon v. Condon,* 1932).

The white primary, however, was not dead. In the wake of *Nixon II,* the Texas legislature repealed all statutes regulating state primaries, thus attempting to sever the link between the state and the Democratic Party that seemed to direct the outcome in the second white primary case. As anticipated, the Democratic state convention then adopted a rule barring participation by blacks in the primary, and a third legal challenge was underway. This time, in a unanimous judgment, however, the Supreme Court found no constitutional infirmity. The state convention's decision was admittedly discriminatory, but that decision was the result of private action, not action by the state, and constitutional limitations did not (and still do not) reach private individuals or entities except when they are acting under color of law (*Grovey v. Townsend,* 1935).

Texas had latched onto a constitutionally acceptable way to keep party primaries lily white, as could any other state. The two *Nixon* decisions had suggested that an end to racial discrimination at the polls was perhaps in sight. *Grovey* dashed that hope and left prospective black voters where they had been before 1927. Proponents of a racially neutral franchise must have been deeply dismayed. Looking backward from 1940, they could tell that the record of the Fifteenth Amendment had been more an account of what the amendment did not do than what it accomplished. Perhaps the Court's formalistic and myopic opinion in *Grovey* reflected a national consensus that the Constitution should not be taken to mean entirely what it said; that the states should be allowed great latitude in deciding who could vote; and that only the most blatantly discriminatory laws would be struck down. Given the gap between promise and reality that had to be bridged, this was probably as much as could be expected. It was no surprise, then, that in the South at least, black voting remained exceedingly low. In 1940, some 5 million African Americans of voting age lived in the southern states, but of these, only about 150,000—3 percent—were registered to vote. Actual votes cast, of course, were fewer. To be sure, registration by white southerners was below the national average, but not nearly so low as the figures for blacks (Key 1949, 504–535).

Yet, as of 1940, the Fifteenth Amendment could not be branded a complete failure. It did, after all, proclaim a crystal clear constitutional command for those who wanted to hear. It had accomplished what many of its original supporters clearly intended—it generally secured black voting rights *outside* the southern states. And an increasing number of blacks lived in nonsouthern states. The Great Migration during and immediately after World War I had witnessed the relocation of over 1 million African Americans from rural areas in the South mainly into cities in the Northeast and Midwest. Driven by the lure of wartime jobs, many also left because of the devastation of cotton plantations after infestations of boll weevils crept eastward from Texas after 1900. Outside the South blacks still encountered discrimination and more segregation, but in most places they were free to vote, and so created a political base in support of black voting rights over the next several decades. Just as representatives and senators from states that had extended the vote to women before 1920 were understandably among the most outspoken advocates of woman suffrage, so also there would gradually be more members of Congress whose *voting* constituents included African Americans in increasingly significant numbers.

Moreover, *United States v. Classic* (1941) held out the possibility that *Grovey* might not be an insurmountable obstacle on the road to black voting rights. Although *Classic* did not involve a challenge to the white primary, it did involve congressional power over a party primary, the very issue that presumably had been settled in *Newberry*. The Justice Department had charged Louisiana election officials with tampering with ballots in a Democratic congressional primary in September 1940 in violation of civil rights statutes. Citing *Newberry*, their defense was that Congress could not regulate primaries. Overruling *Newberry*, a majority of the Supreme Court concluded that Congress's regulatory authority over elections for federal office encompassed a party primary when the primary had been made an integral part of the electoral machinery of the state.

About a year before *Classic* was decided, a black man named Smith, who lived in Houston, Texas, attempted to vote in the 1940 Democratic primary in that state but was denied a ballot on account of race, as dictated by the 1932 convention. Lower courts, citing *Grovey*, rejected his contention that the Constitution entitled him to vote in the primary. When his case reached the Supreme Court in 1944, Smith's appeal was in the hands of attorneys from the NAACP's Legal Defense Fund that included future Supreme Court Justice Thurgood Marshall. With a dissenting vote cast only by Justice Owen J. Roberts, who had authored the opinion in *Grovey*, the Court reenergized the Fifteenth Amendment by invalidating the white primary. Citing *Classic*, Justice Stanley Reed began with this key assumption: "It may now be taken as a postulate that the right to vote in such a primary for the nomination of candidates without discrimination by the State, like the right to vote in a general election, is a right secured by the Constitution." The question then became whether the state of Texas had engaged in forbidden discrimination, or whether that discrimination occurred only at the hands of the Democratic party. "We think that [the Texas] statutory system for the selection of party nominees for inclusion on the general election ballot makes the party which is required to follow these legislative directions an agency of the state in so far as it determines the participants in a primary election," Reed explained.

> The party takes its character as a state agency from the duties imposed upon it by state statutes; the duties do not become matters of private law because they are performed by a political party. The plan of the Texas primary follows substantially that of Louisiana, with the exception that in Louisiana the state pays the cost of the primary while Texas assesses the cost against candidates. In numerous instances, the Texas statutes fix or limit the fees to be charged. Whether paid directly by the state or through state requirements, it is state action which compels. When primaries become a part of the machinery for choosing officials, state and national, as they have here, the same tests to determine the character of discrimination or abridgement should be applied to the primary as are applied to the general election. If the state requires a certain electoral procedure, prescribes a general election ballot made up of party nominees so chosen and limits the choice of the electorate in general elections for state offices, practically speaking, to those whose names appear on such a ballot, it endorses, adopts and enforces the discrimination against Negroes, practiced by a party entrusted by Texas law with the determination of the

qualifications of participants in the primary. This is state action within the meaning of the Fifteenth Amendment. (*Smith v. Allwright,* 1944)

The white primary was dead, or was it? "[L]ike some ghoul in a late-night horror movie that repeatedly sits up in its grave and shuffles abroad after being repeatedly killed and buried, the *Lemon* test stalks our Establishment Clause jurisprudence." Justice Antonin Scalia's graphic language from a religious freedom case *(Lamb's Chapel v. Center Moriches School District,* 1993) fits nearly perfectly the saga of the white primary. The reader has only to exchange the words "white primary" for "*Lemon* test" and "Fifteenth Amendment" for "Establishment Clause." So, in *Terry v. Adams* (1953), the Court confronted yet another variation of this electoral anomaly.

Since 1889, the Jaybird Democratic Association of Fort Bend County, Texas, had conducted a primary of its own, just ahead of the official Democratic primary. Candidates who prevailed in the Jaybird primary were ordinarily nominated in the official primary without opposition—making the process of candidate selection one extra step removed from the general election. After *Smith,* blacks were eligible to vote in the official primary, but not allowed to vote in the Jaybird primary. Thus they had no say in selecting those persons whose names would appear on the Democratic primary ballot. But the peculiar facts of this case raised the question whether the Fifteenth Amendment applied to an association that was not regulated by the state at all, and that was not a political party but a self-governing voluntary club. For a more egalitarian bench, those facts posed no obstacle to a reaffirmation of *Smith.* "For a State to permit such a duplication of its election processes," answered Justice Hugo Black, "is to permit a flagrant abuse of those processes to defeat the purposes of the Fifteenth Amendment." The Court had come a long way since *Grovey.*

Paralleling the developments on the judicial front in *Smith* and *Terry* were political stirrings. Both major political parties in the 1940s spoke out for racial equality, although the Democrats were in the more awkward position due to their need to balance a desire for black votes in the North with a fear of alienating their white base in the South. And there were northern white liberals to contend with as well. Accordingly, the 1944 Democratic platform asserted that "racial and religious minorities have the right to live, develop and vote equally with all citizens and share the rights that are guaranteed by our Constitution. Congress should exert its full constitutional powers to protect those rights" (Schlesinger and Israel, vol. 4, 3041). In his State of the Union address in January 1948, President Harry Truman announced the goal of "secur[ing] fully the essential human rights of our citizens," and recommended legislation on employment, lynching, and voting rights (Stephenson 1999, 164). Because the message ruffled white southern sensibilities, the White House then delayed introduction of the bills and in its draft of the 1948 Democratic Platform merely drew from the relatively mild reference to civil rights from the 1944 platform. This hesitation caused young Minnesotan (and future senator and vice president) Hubert H. Humphrey, one of the party's most outspoken liberals, to lead a fight at the convention in Philadelphia in July that succeeded in inserting a more vigorous plank. At its adoption, the entire Mississippi delegation and half the Alabama delegation walked out of the convention hall.

We highly commend President Harry S. Truman for his courageous stand on the issue of civil rights. We call upon the Congress to support our President in guaranteeing these basic and fundamental American Principles: (1) the right of full and equal political participation; (2) the right to equal opportunity of employment; (3) the right of security of person; (4) and the right of equal treatment in the service and defense of our nation. (Schlesinger and Israel, vol. 4, 3154)

By the end of the month, Truman issued executive orders to end racial discrimination in the armed forces and the federal civil service.

At about the same time, however, Marshall and others at the Legal Defense Fund (the LDF by this time had become corporately separate from parent NAACP for tax purposes) redirected the focus of the drive for civil rights to segregated schools almost exclusively (Greenberg 1994, 152–162). In retrospect, this strategic decision had grave consequences. The decision represented a departure from the earlier policy that had divided resources between securing the vote and combating the multifarious forms of segregation. Probably the LDF staff thought that the vote was secure as a result of *Smith* and related cases in the lower courts, or at least that the vote would soon be secure. Yet, with the continued operation of other voter qualifications such as literacy tests that could be administered in a racially discriminatory way, this expectation proved unfounded.

To be sure, the shift in emphasis to the eradication of racially segregated education was understandable. Of all forms of segregation, segregated educational facilities were probably the most pernicious because by their very existence they inculcated in each new generation the propriety of a racially segregated society. Yet there was great irony after the LDF gained its greatest victory when the Supreme Court ruled in *Brown v. Board of Education* (1954) that legally mandated racial segregation in public schools (and by inference in any other public facility or program) violated the Fourteenth Amendment's equal protection clause: Some eight years passed before *any* appreciable implementation of that ruling occurred in most states of the former Confederacy.

One principal reason for the delay was that in the locales where resistance to *Brown* was the greatest, blacks were least likely to have access to the polls (Patterson 2001). They had no chance to vote for judges, school board members, county sheriffs, legislators, governors, and others whose behavior in the wake of *Brown* might have been quite different had they been concerned with black constituents who could vote. Access to schools had come ahead of access to ballot boxes—a political example of the cart before the horse. To be sure, the extent of opposition that developed in the wake of *Brown* was wholly unanticipated by many who applauded the ruling in 1954. Nevertheless, had widespread racially unrestricted access to the polls been attained prior to *Brown,* implementation of *Brown* would probably have encountered much less resistance and would have moved more swiftly. There would surely have been fewer elected officials digging in their heels and engaging in a thorough pillorying of *Brown* and the Supreme Court. There might have been no "Southern Manifesto" issued by 77 of the 105 southern members of the U. S. House of Representatives and 19 of 22 senators from the southern states that promised to use "all lawful means to bring about a reversal of this [Brown] decision which is contrary to the Constitution" ("Declaration" 1956, 19). Albeit with laudable intentions, the LDF seemed to have forgotten one of the oldest lessons in the struggle for voting rights: the empowerment (and security) that the vote could provide. And there was a second, and personal, irony as well in the shift of emphasis from voting to education. In 1961, President John Kennedy's nomination of *Brown* counsel Thurgood Marshall for the U.S. Court of Appeals for the Second Circuit proved highly contentious among southern senators largely because, even then, most of their African American constituents still lacked the vote, and hence political power.

Before it integrated many schools, however, *Brown* jumpstarted the modern civil rights movement that attacked segregation in both the public and private sectors (Klarman 2004, 454). Taking a cue from the tactics used in the campaign for woman suffrage early in the twentieth century, civil rights activists, black and white, began in the late 1950s and early 1960s to picket, to organize boycotts and voter registration drives, and to orchestrate mass demonstrations, "freedom rides," and sit-ins—all to dramatize grievances and to attract attention in the national news media. Groups such as the Southern Christian Leadership Conference (SCLC), headed by Martin Luther King Jr., practiced passive, nonviolent methods of protest, modeled after Mohandas (Mahatma) Gandhi's tactics against British rule in India years before. Other groups such as the Student Non-Violent Coordinating Committee (SNCC—pronounced as if it were spelled "snick") preferred more militant, in-your-face, forms of protest more likely to provoke violent backlashes from local authorities. The many-faceted patterns of protest that occurred were the offspring of the "revolution of rising expectations," a phrase coined by U.S. diplomat Harlan Cleveland in 1949 (Safire 1993, 662). His concept was that unrest is most likely, not when conditions are at their worst and appear hopeless, but when even small steps forward hold out the promise for a brighter future.

Not coincidentally during this same period, Congress enacted the first civil rights legislation since 1875. Within a period of seven years, three statutes were passed that addressed voting rights in part. The first and second, in 1957 and 1960, were possible because of a fortuitous confluence of timing, circumstance, and talent. Beginning its second term in 1957, President Dwight Eisenhower's Republican administration favored national civil rights legislation. Democrats controlled both houses of Congress, as they had since 1955. Despite the influence wielded by southern Democrats against any such legislation, both houses were led by men with unusually polished coalition-building skills who thought the time for such legislation had come: Both Texans, Sam Rayburn was Speaker of the House, and Lyndon Johnson was majority leader of the Senate. The fact that each party was officially on record in support of civil rights reduced the political liability that either party might have suffered by going it alone. Southern Democrats might be unhappy with their party's position, but the Republicans offered no alternative haven. With accomplishments on civil rights, Republicans might stem the flow of black voters outside the South into Democratic ranks; Democrats would be able to retain and possibly expand their support among blacks.

The Civil Rights Act of 1957 was significant in three respects. A civil rights unit in the Department of Justice was reconfigured into a full-fledged division, organizationally on the same plane as, say, the antitrust division or criminal division. Accordingly, the new division was also to be headed by an assistant attorney general for civil rights. Moreover, the law established the United States Commission on Civil Rights as a bipartisan agency charged with investigating and reporting to the president and the Congress on civil rights problems in the nation. There was now a fixture in the national government the sole initial mission of which was to highlight manifestations of racial discrimination and to make remedial recommendations. Beyond these institutional changes, the 1957 statute empowered the Department of Justice to institute *civil* actions for equitable (that is, injunctive) relief where the right to vote was threatened or denied. The word *civil* was important. Since Reconstruction it had been a criminal offense for a government official (someone acting "under color of law") to deny someone a federally protected constitutional right. But criminal prosecutions are not easily conducted. At the very least, no conviction can be had unless the government's case is proven "beyond a reasonable doubt." Civil actions are different. A court can render a judgment on behalf of the aggrieved party based upon a "preponderance of the evidence." That is a lower threshold to meet. Under the new law, therefore, upon receiving complaints, the attorney general could institute legal proceedings, thus throwing the full legal authority of the United States into the fray. A finding in favor of the government would then result in a judicial order, called an injunction, to the respective voting officials. Disobedience would subject the officials to punishment for contempt of court (Hamilton 1973, 54–55; Bardolph 1970, 400–403).

The Civil Rights Act of 1960, signed by Eisenhower in the last year of his presidency, instituted additional procedures and

brought the federal judiciary into literal contact with voter registration. First, the government had to obtain a court finding that a
person had been deprived of the right to vote on account of race
and that the denial was part of a "pattern or practice" of similar
denials. Second, for at least twelve months after such finding, persons who were victims of racial discrimination at the polls could
apply for a judicial order declaring them eligible to vote. Third,
the court could hear such applications or could appoint a panel of
registered voters to act as referees. Finally, to assist with findings
of a "pattern or practice," voting records were to be made public
and preserved for at least twenty-two months following a primary
or general election (Hamilton 1973, 65–66; Bardolph 1970,
403–405). This was a cumbersome procedure; moreover, prospective voters still bore the burden of coming forward initially as
complainants, if not litigants. Running afoul of local conventions
that politics was for white people only was often risky. White
landlords, employers, and roughnecks in some places had means
at their disposal to keep assertive blacks in line.

The facts and record in a lawsuit filed in Mississippi in 1961 illustrate some of the hurdles would-be voters had to jump in order
to be registered (*United States v. Lynd,* 1962). Since February
1959, Theron C. Lynd had been the registrar in Forrest County.
There were some 22,000 white adults in the county, most of whom
were registered to vote, but only 25 of the 7,500 black adults were
registered. Between February 1959 and January 1961, no black
person was allowed to apply for registration, although during the
same period, no named white person was turned down. Sixteen
black witnesses testified at the trial that, during this period, they
were "told by a lady [a deputy registrar] at the office to see Mr.
Lynd"; that "Mr. Lynd said he was not set up for registration and
did not know when he would be"; that "Mr. Lynd told me I
would have to come back because he did not have his feet on the
ground"; and that Mr. Lynd said "he did not have time and did not
know when he would have the time" (Hamilton 1973, 129). After

January 1961, some blacks were allowed to apply for registration, but none was registered, apparently because they failed the literacy and/or understanding test. These people included high school teachers, an elementary school principal, and two members of the clergy. Further evidence revealed that prospective white voters were processed by deputies, while all blacks were referred directly to Lynd. Moreover, black applicants were given long and complex passages from the state constitution to interpret, while white applicants, if they were asked a question at all, were quizzed on simpler passages. Deputies assisted white applicants in completing registration forms, but black applicants received no assistance. Any minor error on the form could be grounds for rejection of the application (Hamilton 1973, 129–133).

Registrars in Mississippi and elsewhere "had a bottomless bag of tricks," LDF lawyer Jack Greenberg later recorded, "ranging from violence to switching dates and times of opening and closing—designed to achieve the same end." On one occasion in the 1950s, he noted, Thurgood Marshall complained to the Justice Department about a Mississippi registrar who routinely asked prospective black voters, "How many bubbles in a bar of soap?" When queried about the practice, the registrar desisted, but substituted something else just as clever (Greenberg 1994, 175).

It was in part to confront such practices that Congress passed the Civil Rights Act of 1964. By this time, the tragic murder of President Kennedy in November 1963 had elevated Vice President Lyndon Johnson to the presidency. Much of what passed in 1964 had originally been proposed without success during the Kennedy administration. In fact, despite having had the benefit of black votes in key states in his close win over Republican Vice President Richard Nixon in 1960, Kennedy took office prepared to take few civil rights initiatives. "We must realize the constitutional rights of Negroes in states where they are denied," stated assistant attorney general Burke Marshall, "but we must do so with the smallest possible federal intrusion into the conduct of state affairs" (Garrow

1978, 21–22). Looking forward to the 1964 election and looking backward to the slim margin of victory in 1960, Kennedy could ill afford to upset his party's southern base that had already shown signs of substantial erosion in national elections, especially since states' rights–oriented Republicans were beginning to have a larger say in that party's affairs. As events unfolded, the Kennedy administration indeed had a full civil rights agenda, but little of it was proactive. Instead, it was reactive (Hutchinson 1998, 260–286). Because of state and local defiance of judicial desegregation orders, the Kennedy administration was forced to apply countermeasures by dispatching federal troops to the University of Mississippi in Oxford, by utilizing a heavy federal presence as Governor George C. Wallace stood "in the doorway" (thus fulfilling a defiant promise to block enrollment of black students) at the main administration building at the University of Alabama in Tuscaloosa, and by intervening in other places as well (Doyle 2001; Safire 1993, 752).

However, the shock of Kennedy's assassination, the ceaseless drumbeat of civil rights protests, and the legislative skills of the new president combined to produce the most comprehensive civil rights package that Congress has ever enacted into law. Among other things, the statute banned racial discrimination in privately owned places of public accommodation, such as hotels and theaters, in Title II, and it forbade racial and other forms of discrimination in the workplace in Title VII and in Title VI in programs receiving federal financial assistance. The law's Title I dealt with voting. Henceforth, black and white applicants would be judged by the same registration criteria. No one could be denied the right to vote because of a minor error or omission on a registration form. In states employing literacy tests, the tests would have to be written, not oral, and kept on file for later scrutiny. Furthermore, in any suit to gain access to the ballot, the court was to assume that any applicant who had completed the sixth grade was sufficiently literate, unless the state could prove otherwise. Finally, in voting rights cases, the federal government had the option of requesting that the suit be heard by a three-judge panel, instead of by a single U.S. district judge as was ordinarily the practice (Bardolph 1970, 406). (A decision by a three-judge panel qualifies for a direct appeal by right to the Supreme Court, bypassing the court of appeals.) For voting rights advocates, going before a single judge was one thing if the person was a rights-friendly judge such as Eisenhower-appointee Frank Johnson in Alabama (Gerhardt 2003, 416–419). However, appearing before someone like Kennedy-appointee Harold Cox in Mississippi was another matter altogether. (It had been Cox, sitting as the trial judge in the *Lynd* case, who had denied relief to the prospective black voters.)

Yet even with the changes and presumptions in the 1964 act, voting rights were sure to remain under attack in places where blacks were unwelcome at the polls. Accusations by blacks that they had been improperly turned away from registration offices would have to be investigated by Justice Department officials. If the claims seemed meritorious, then legal proceedings would be launched. This was both a time-consuming and a labor-intensive process, much like that of a fire department putting out fires in a community with a lot of structures built with highly flammable materials. By that analogy, the thinking went, the fire department might better spend its time on fire prevention to address the problem at its source.

Not long after the new Congress convened in January 1965, Johnson insisted on more legislation with far more sweeping reforms. Ironically, additional voting rights measures would not have been enacted so quickly, if at all, without the unintended assistance provided by Governor Wallace and state and local law enforcement officers in Alabama. In early 1965, John Lewis and other leaders of SNCC, which had been attempting to register voters and also engaging in protests in Dallas County, Alabama, decided to move the center of their operations from Selma, the county seat, to Montgomery, the state capital, that lay about fifty miles to the east on U.S. Highway 80. Moreover, they decided to dramatize the move by conducting a "march" from Selma to Montgomery on Sunday, March 7. Governor Wallace promptly issued an order banning the march. With SNCC prepared to march in spite of the ban, a confrontation was in the making. Joined by Hosea Williams, a top aid to Martin Luther King Jr. in the SCLC, Lewis and some 600 demonstrators started out on foot. They walked only about six blocks. As they reached the Edmund Pettus Bridge in Selma over the Alabama River, they met a detachment of 200 state troopers plus a posse organized by Dallas County sheriff Jim Clark, all armed with tear gas, nausea bombs, guns, and clubs. As the group continued forward, law enforcement officers attacked. Mounted officers ran down some demonstrators. Seventeen protestors required hospitalization, while others received emergency treatment at the scene (Greenberg 1994, 354–356). Film and still photographers recorded the mayhem for television and newspapers. Within hours Americans across the country witnessed a replay of scenes usually associated with dictatorships. Not filmed for television was the fate of a white homemaker named Viola Liuzzo, from Detroit, Michigan. She was killed in nearby Lowndes County, as she drove demonstrators from Montgomery toward Selma. (As for the march, it in fact occurred, beginning two weeks later under the protection of federalized Alabama National Guard units.)

The "outrage in Selma," as Johnson and some in Congress and elsewhere called it, made further voting legislation seem imperative. It was at this point that Johnson sent the Voting Rights Act to Congress. It had been in the works for a while. As the president later revealed in his memoirs, he instructed Attorney General Nicholas Katzenbach "to write the god-damnedest, toughest voting right act that you can devise" (Johnson 1971, 161). The efforts of Katzenbach and others surely met the president's expectations. In August 1965, five months after the incident at the Edmund Pettus Bridge, the Voting Rights Act of 1965 became law and launched what might be called a "second Reconstruction."

The Voting Rights Act, like previous statutes, was grounded on Congress's authority to enforce the Fifteenth and Fourteenth amendments, as granted in their sections two and five, respectively. But there the similarity ended. The new statute took an altogether different approach to opening the polls to blacks. Previous measures were at heart litigation driven, in which relief depended upon a judicial finding. Complaints would lead to lawsuits, which would lead to hearings before judges who might or might not grant relief. Either way, appeals might follow, drawing out the process even further. There were more state and local officials prepared to drag their heels on voting rights than there were federal officials deployed to make sure they did not. Provisions of the 1965 act instead enforced voting rights directly, bypassing much of the litigation that had consumed so much time to accomplish relatively little. And, indeed, little progress had been made in the previous seven years, as Attorney General Katzenbach demonstrated when he laid statistics before the House Judiciary Committee as it considered the bill. Between 1958 and 1964, registration of blacks in Alabama had increased 5.2 percent, to a total of 19.4 percent of those eligible by age and residence. For Mississippi, the percentage increase was no more than 2 percent, to a total registration percentage of 6.4 percent. In Louisiana, the percentage had remained about the same, at 32 percent of those blacks qualified by age and residence (Hamilton 1973, 232–235).

The 1965 act addressed voting rights in several ways. First, certain provisions of the law were selectively applied to what were called "covered" jurisdictions. These included any state, or a part of a state, that employed a literacy or similar test *and* where fewer than 50 percent of the voting age population was registered to vote on November 1, 1964. In 1965, covered jurisdictions included Alabama, Georgia, Louisiana, Mississippi, twenty-six counties in North Carolina, South Carolina, Virginia, and Alaska.

In those areas, any use of a literacy, good character, or similar test was forbidden for five years. (In 1969 Alaska was able to remove itself from the list of covered jurisdictions through a procedure provided in the act.) Florida, Texas, and Arkansas fell beneath the 50 percent registration bar but did not qualify as "covered" because no literacy tests were in use. By targeting literacy tests, the statute indirectly highlighted their irony. Even when applied even-handedly, the tests often disadvantaged blacks because they had long been relegated to inferior budget-starved schools. Thus, the same state governments that short-changed their education through segregated schools penalized them through literacy tests for the negative effects of segregated education itself.

For the affected states U.S. marshals and other federal officials were authorized to oversee local registration operations and to register prospective voters directly, if local officials failed to do so. But as drastic as these measures seemed to be, they paled alongside Section 5 of the act, the so-called pre-clearance section. Under Section 5, prior to making any change in "voting qualifications or prerequisites to voting, or standard, practice or procedures with respect to voting," covered jurisdictions were required to receive permission (clearance) from either the attorney general or the U.S. District Court for the District of Columbia. The intent of that provision was to head off any impact of a change in the law, whether intended or not, that might obstruct or discourage voting by blacks or otherwise diminish their voting strength. The Supreme Court upheld all of these provisions by a near unanimous vote in *South Carolina v. Katzenbach* (1966). At first it was unclear what electoral changes required preclearance. Were they limited to changes in voter registration standards or procedures, or did they encompass more? In 1969, the Supreme Court gave Section 5 the broader reading, reaching all modifications of election laws or laws that affected elections (*Allen v. State Board of Elections*).

The principle of retrogression—being worse off than before the change in question—is ordinarily dispositive for Section 5 proceedings. According to *Beer* v. *United States* (1976), "the purpose of § 5 has always been to insure that no voting-procedure changes would be made that would lead to a retrogression in the position of racial minorities with respect to their effective exercise of the electoral franchise." Even in situations where a discriminatory intent might be evident, Section 5 "prevents nothing but backsliding," declared the Court in a Louisiana case challenging voting districts for school board members (*Reno v. Bossier Parish School Board,* 2000).

To illustrate the operation of Section 5, consider the facts of *Rome v. United States* (1980). The city of Rome, Georgia, enlarged its corporate boundaries. The result was that the increased population of the city contained a smaller percentage of black voters than before, thus weakening or diluting their voting influence in city politics. It made no difference whether the plan had been intended to accomplish that result. A Section 5 violation occurred if the alteration of political boundaries had the arithmetic effect, which it did, of vote dilution. As will be seen in Chapter Four, Section 5 has been a prolific source of controversy about "majority-minority" legislative districts that began to bedevil the Supreme Court in the 1990s and that have continued into the twenty-first century.

Yet another part of the law had a more narrow focus than the wide sweep of preclearance for covered jurisdictions. It took aim at New York City to benefit the large Spanish-speaking Puerto Rican population (and the Democratic Party). If prospective voters had at least a sixth-grade education in another language, provided that education had been in an "American flag" school system, the state could not use an English language literacy test to disqualify them. The Supreme Court upheld that restriction in *Katzenbach v. Morgan* (1966), even though the Court had already upheld the use of literacy tests generally in *Lassiter v. Northampton County Board of Elections* (1959).

The 1965 statute addressed voting rights nationally as well. According to its Section 2, "No voting qualification or prerequisite to voting, or standard, practice, or procedure shall be imposed or applied by any State or political subdivision to deny or abridge the right of any citizen of the United States to vote on account of race or color." Initially, this seemed to be merely an amplification of the prohibition already contained within the Fifteenth Amendment. It applied to *existing* laws, procedures, and practices in all jurisdictions, not just to the jurisdictions under the preclearance requirement of Section 5. Also initially, it was thought that Section 2 banned only electoral rules or practices that had a discriminatory *intent* or purpose. Indeed, this was the Supreme Court's construction of Section 2 in *Mobile v. Bolden* (1980). Black residents of Mobile, Alabama, claimed that the existing system of at-large election of members of the Mobile City Commission violated Section 2, as well as the Fourteenth and Fifteenth Amendments, because the at-large system diluted black votes. (A multimember body elected at large means that all voters cast a vote for each position, rather than for a candidate representing only a part of the community. Thus, if blacks composed a minority of the voting population, the majority in an at-large arrangement could determine the outcome for each position.) The record showed that no black had ever been elected to the five-member commission since its creation in 1911. The Court concluded that Section 2 would be violated if and only if claimants could prove that the at-large system had been adopted and maintained *for the purpose of* minimizing the influence of black votes. The presence of a discriminatory *effect* alone would not violate Section 2. Establishing discriminatory intent was not an impossible standard, to be sure, but it was far more difficult to meet than merely demonstrating an electoral system's effects. As noted below, Congress soon "corrected" the Court's reading of Section 2.

Aside from the fact that Section 2 applies nationally and Section 5 applies only to selected jurisdictions, there is an important difference between them in terms of the dynamics of each. The preclearance process of Section 5 may be handled entirely adminis-

tratively. That is, the process involves a dialogue between a state
or locality and, ordinarily, the Department of Justice. The latter
either approves the particular change in question, or it does not.
Litigation comes into play, when a jurisdiction finds the Justice
Department's position unacceptable and wishes to challenge it.
Section 2 issues, by contrast, arise entirely in the context of litigation or the threat of litigation and are dealt with in the courts, not
by the Justice Department.

Amazingly, in contrast to the tedious, drawn-out, and uphill
battle waged for black voting rights before 1965, implementation
of the law proceeded surprisingly well after 1965. Indeed, the effects of the law in most locales were dramatic and almost instanta-
neous. By 1967, black voter registration had doubled in Georgia,
jumped nearly 800 percent in Mississippi, and nearly tripled in Alabama. In the 1968 presidential elections, some 52 percent of all
blacks of voting age in the South cast ballots (compared with 62
percent of whites). Moreover, for the first time since Reconstruction, blacks were being elected to public office in significant numbers, some 400 in the South by 1969 (Bardolph 1970, 421; Davidson 1990, 21, 29–30). Thus implementation and interpretation of
the law since 1965 have focused less on outright denials of the vote
and more on the subtle ways in which electoral procedures can restrict the effects of the votes that are cast.

Several subsequent renewals of the 1965 act have also made important changes. In 1970, the ban on literacy tests in the covered
states was applied to all states, and additional areas were brought
within the terms of covered jurisdictions. In 1975, the act was renewed for seven years, and the nationwide ban on literacy tests was
made permanent. The renewal in 1982, which was for twenty-five
years, was Congress's last revision of the Voting Rights Act. And it
was in the 1982 renewal that Congress modified the Court's reading
of Section 2 in the Mobile city commission case. Because the *Mobile*
decision, with its emphasis on purpose or intent, made it more difficult to prove racial discrimination in voting, Congress specified

that Section 2 was violated even if the electoral practice in question resulted only in a discriminatory effect, the easier standard of proof. "No voting qualification or prerequisite to voting, or standard, practice, or procedure," read the revised Section 2, "shall be imposed or applied by any State or political subdivision *in a manner which results in* a denial or abridgement of the right of any citizen of the United States to vote on account of race or color" (emphasis added). In making that judgment, courts were to take the "totality of circumstances" into account, one such circumstance being the "extent to which members of a protected class have been elected to office in the State or political subdivision." Nonetheless, Congress also made clear that Section 2 was not designed to create a legal right to proportional representation: "[N]othing in this section establishes a right to have members of a protected class elected in numbers equal to their proportion in the population." Ironically, the increase in minority voting strength in the South after 1965 meant that there was more support for the 1982 extension among southern legislators than there had been for the original Voting Rights Act (Kousser 1974, 151).

The Supreme Court's first opportunity to interpret the 1982 amendment came in *Thornburg v. Gingles* (1986), which upheld a district court finding that the use of multimember legislative districts in North Carolina violated Section 2 because they made it more difficult for African American candidates to be elected and otherwise diminished the influence of African American voters. According to the Court, multimember districts would be deemed to impair a group's Section 2 rights if three conditions were met. First, the group "must be sufficiently large and geographically compact to constitute a majority in a single-member district." Second, the group "must be politically cohesive," and, third, the group "must have its preferred candidate out-voted in most instances by a majority that votes as a block." (Other constitutional and legal aspects of legislative districting are examined in the next section.)

The Voting Rights Act will again be on the congressional agenda when the twenty-five-year extension of 1982 expires in 2007. What changes will Congress make? Will electoral arrangements in the southern states again be subjected to special outside review and oversight? Or will Congress conclude that America's struggle with race and voting is, finally, in the past?

Three additional changes in voting rights laws in the mid-1960s that bear at least indirectly on racial discrimination merit attention here. Two were accomplished by constitutional amendment and the other by judicial decision.

The Twenty-third Amendment, proposed in June 1960 and ratified in March 1961, allows residents of the District of Columbia to vote in presidential elections. A city with a largely African American population, Washington has no voting representatives in Congress, a fact that will be addressed in more detail in Chapter Four. The Twenty-third Amendment treated the District as if it were one of the smallest states in population (which it would be if it were a state) and assigned electoral votes no greater than that of the least populous state, which, since 1961, has been three. In terms of the electoral college, the amendment raised the total number of electoral votes in play from 535 to 538, thus allowing for the possibility of a tie. (A tie vote for president is not altogether improbable. In 2000, had Vice President Al Gore won the electoral vote in Florida, as he almost did, and had Governor George Bush won the electoral vote in Pennsylvania, each would have received a total of 269 electoral votes, one short of the constitutional requirement of a majority. Had that happened, the House of Representatives would have elected the 43rd president, with each state delegation casting one vote.)

The other change in the Constitution applied nationally, although its actual effects were largely symbolic. Recall from the previous chapter that, as a broad adult manhood suffrage took hold in the nineteenth century, some states imposed a taxpaying requirement in the form of a poll or head tax. In the twentieth century the poll tax was one of the ways to minimize black voting; indeed, it cut into voting by poor whites as well. Being disproportionately poorer than whites, blacks were less likely to pay the tax, which was usually in the range of one to two dollars. By the early 1960s poll taxes survived in only five states. There was thus little resistance to the Twenty-fourth Amendment, which Congress proposed in August 1962, to abolish the use of poll taxes in elections for federal office. In January 1964 it had been ratified by the necessary three-fourths of the states. With a ban on the use of a poll tax as a voter qualification in some, but not all elections, the tax became an administrative burden and so probably would have eventually collapsed under its own weight. The Supreme Court took no chances, however, and in *Harper v. State Board of Elections* (1966) ruled that a poll tax imposed by a state for any election violated the equal protection clause of the Fourteenth Amendment. "Voter qualifications have no relation to wealth nor to paying or not paying this or any other tax," wrote Justice William O. Douglas for the majority. "We say the same whether the citizen, otherwise qualified to vote, has $1.50 in his pocket or nothing at all, pays the fee or fails to pay it. The principle that denies the State the right to dilute a citizen's vote on account of his economic status or other such actors by analogy bars a system which excludes those unable to pay a fee to vote or who fail to pay." Not quite thirty years before, the Court had found no constitutional defect in a state's use of a poll tax (*Breedlove v. Suttles,* 1937).

Harper and the Twenty-fourth Amendment were thus light-years removed from the consensus in earlier American history that paying a tax or owning property was an essential prerequisite for voting, one that was proof of an individual's stake in the social order. Moreover, *Harper* and the Twenty-fourth Amendment, as well as the Voting Rights Act, were signs of a remarkable transformation going on in the United States during the 1960s. That transformation involved greater emphasis on equality and participation. It revamped not only rules and realities governing access to the ballot box, but, even more fundamentally, representation as well.

THE "POLITICAL THICKET" OF REPRESENTATION

When Earl Warren retired as the fourteenth chief justice of the United States in 1969, journalists asked him to identify his major contribution. The question was potentially difficult because between 1953 and 1969 the Warren Court, with revolutionary effects, had erected landmark decisions across the landscape of American constitutional law. From criminal justice and racial equality to religious freedom and privacy, the Court had left few aspects of American life untouched. Indeed, Warren's tenure had been one of the most judicially active and remarkable in American history. By one count, in the approximately 150 years before Warren's appointment, the Supreme Court had overruled 88 of its precedents. During Warren's 16 years it added another 45 to the list. The revolution that the Warren Court initiated is measured by President Dwight Eisenhower's latter-day lament over Warren's appointment: "The biggest damn fool mistake I ever made" (Mason and Stephenson 2002, 7).

Yet Warren's apparently surprising answer to the reporters' question was categorical: the redistricting and representation cases. Why? The right to vote freely and equitably for the candidates of one's choice is the essence of democracy. Untrammeled exercise of this right, he said, is essential to the preservation of all others—"the bedrock of our political system" (Mason and Stephenson 2002, 200). Warren knew that representation and voting are inseparably linked because representation gives effect to voting; it translates voting into power (White 1982, 337). This is true because of a principal characteristic of American government: it is republican or *representative* government. Laws are made by city council members, state legislators, and members of Congress. The manner in which these individuals are elected, however, largely determines the degree of influence that voters have over their officials, or indeed, whether some voters have more influence than other voters.

To grasp this central point, consider the contrasting systems of representation in the United States Congress. The House of Representatives has 435 members, a figure last set by statute in 1929. The Constitution guarantees every state a least one representative, with the remaining number apportioned among the states on the basis of population. Thus, with 50 seats automatically allocated because there are 50 states, 385 seats are "in play" for reallocation after each decennial census. Based on the 2000 census, California with its population of 34.5 million has 53 representatives, while Wyoming with 494,000 souls has but one. With a population of 21.3 million Texas has 32 representatives, while Delaware with 796,000 has one. Numerically then, the residents of large states such as California and Texas and the interests within those states matter a great deal more in the politics of the House than do the residents and interests of small states like Delaware and Wyoming. In contrast, the apportionment of seats in the Senate is fixed by the Constitution at two per state, meaning that the less populous states, and the citizens and interests within them, count appreciably more in the politics of the Senate than those from the large states. The ratio of senators to population in California is about 1:17,000,000, but in Wyoming the ratio of senators to people is roughly 1:247,000. Per person, therefore, Wyoming is weighted nearly 69 times more heavily than California in the Senate. The voices of small states may be nearly drowned out in the House, but they will be heard in the Senate.

Representation becomes even more complex when one looks not just *between* states but *within* them. All states have an elected legislature, and in all states except Nebraska the legislature is bicameral—that is, with two houses, as found in Congress. (Nebraska adopted its current unicameral system in 1934 [Dobbins 1941, 511].) Except for legislatures in states that are awarded only a single representative, state legislatures are responsible for creating congressional districts within their states from which their representatives are elected. In 1842, Congress specified for the first time that congressional districts were to be single-member districts—that is, voters in each district were to choose one representative. Prior to that time, members of the House were chosen in different ways, depending on the preference of the state legislatures: through at-large voting as well as through multimember and single-member districts. Later statutes allowed some variation in the type of district used, but since 1967, Congress—to prevent vote dilution in the wake of the Voting Rights Act—has required all districts to be single-member districts (Hacker 1964, 18–19; *Congress and the Nation* 1969, 449). Whatever the type of district used, the population of one district relative to another within the same state of course makes a difference in the system of representation that results.

In addition to shaping districts for congressional representation, state legislatures in most states are the bodies that establish districts for themselves. Even if state law assigns that function to another part of the state government, the concern raised with respect to congressional districts still applies: the population and composition of one district, say for the upper house of the state legislature, relative to that of another. Whether the districts are for the state legislature or for the U. S. House of Representatives, large numerical disparities among districts of the same type skew representation and thereby overweight or underweight the votes of some as compared to others.

The Supreme Court first confronted the arithmetic of districting in *Colegrove v. Green* (1946). Illinois residents challenged their state's congressional districting plan because of sharp population disparities among districts—the least populous district had 112,000 people and the most populous 914,000. Indeed, the legislature had last redistricted after the census of 1900. No changes had been made to take account of growth and shifts in population after the censuses of 1910, 1920, 1930, or 1940.

The Illinois districts resembled a reincarnation of the old "rotten boroughs" in England, of which those taking part in the debates at Putney in the seventeenth century had been very much aware. There, under the system then used to allocate seats in the House of Commons, some towns or regions with few inhabitants were represented on or nearly on a par with cities of much larger populations. At the extreme, one man could send two members to Commons to represent the borough of Old Sarum, while the city of London, with one million inhabitants, had but four. "[I]t often comes to pass . . .," observed English philosopher John Locke in 1689, "that in tract of time . . . representation becomes very unequal and disproportionate to the reasons it was first established upon. . . . This strangers stand amazed at, and everyone must confess needs a remedy; though most find it hard to find one, because . . . no inferior power can alter [the legislature]. . . . And, therefore, . . . this inconvenience is thought incapable of a remedy" (Locke 1924, para. 157, 197). At the Philadelphia Convention in 1787, James Madison referred to that abuse as "vicious representation" (Farrand 1966, vol. 1, 464). The question posed by *Colegrove* was whether, in contrast to the intractableness of the problem in the England of the seventeenth century, the U.S. Constitution afforded a remedy to the people of Illinois in the twentieth century.

With only seven justices participating, three were prepared to grant relief under the Fourteenth Amendment's equal protection clause, but three were not. Writing for the latter bloc, Justice Frankfurter termed legislative districting as "peculiarly political" and "therefore not meet for judicial determination." That is, he applied the so-called political question doctrine, discussed in Chapter Two in connection with the Dorr Rebellion in Rhode Island, that assigns certain kinds of constitutional disputes to the "political" (elected) branches of the government. For the unhappy residents from the more populous districts, relief in other words lay elsewhere. They were to turn to the state legislature or Congress, but not to the Court. "Courts ought not to enter this 'political thicket,'" Frankfurter warned. "It is hostile to a democratic system to involve the judiciary in the politics of the people. The remedy for unfairness in districting is to secure state legislatures that will apportion properly, or to invoke the ample powers of Congress." A fourth justice also agreed that the Court should deny relief, but probably because there was insufficient time before the next election for the necessary adjustments to be made. *Colegrove* therefore came to stand for the proposition that federal courts were not to involve themselves in lawsuits involving legislative districting in the states.

It was unlikely, however, that the Illinois legislature would correct the disparities on its own. Its own members had been elected from numerically skewed districts. They had a vested interest in keeping things the way they were. Change would mean that some of them would be voting themselves out of office; moreover, the areas and interests that many of them represented would lose influence. Unless required to do so, elected officials are not accustomed to relinquishing power; that would be an unnatural act.

As for Congress, its most recent apportionment statute in 1929 had left out requirements for compact, contiguous, or equally populated districts that had been a part of some previous census-related enactments. As the years went by, populations of House districts across the nation grew increasingly imbalanced. Indeed, data in the *Colegrove* case showed that, of forty-five states with more than one representative in 1946, thirty-six states contained congressional districts with substantial differences in population, some as imbalanced as those in Illinois. Thus members of the House of Representatives from many states, like the Illinois legislators, had a vested interest in the political status quo and were now unlikely on their own to insist on reform.

In *Gomillion v. Lightfoot* (1960), however, which at heart was a racial voting rights case, the Court took a step that brought it closer to the thorny issue of representation. Involved was an Alabama law that redrew the boundaries of the city of Tuskegee from a simple square into a twenty-eight-sided monster. The result of this exercise in political cartography was the removal from the city of all but a handful of black voters, while leaving white voters unaffected. If blacks were registered to vote, they could not vote in city elections because they now suddenly found themselves living outside the city limits. Justice Frankfurter, in spite of his position in *Colegrove* about political questions, declared that the Fifteenth Amendment guarantee against racial discrimination in voting justified judicial intervention. Left unanswered was the question whether the Fourteenth Amendment's equal protection clause might apply to nonracial discrimination, based on urban versus suburban or rural residence.

An affirmative answer was soon forthcoming. *Baker v. Carr* (1962) was first of several Supreme Court decisions that, within a span of only two years, mandated a reallocation of voting strength (and with it political power) in virtually every state in the Union. *Baker* involved a 1901 Tennessee statute that apportioned legislative seats for the state's ninety-five counties. Residents in some heavily populated, but underrepresented, counties claimed that the legislature's failure subsequently to redistrict the seats to take account of substantial growth and redistribution of the state's population debased their votes and denied them equal protection of the laws as guaranteed by the Fourteenth Amendment. Districts containing 37 percent of Tennessee's population elected twenty of the thirty-three senators; districts containing forty percent of the population elected sixty-three of the ninety-nine representatives. Citing *Colgrove,* the U.S. district court that first heard the suit ruled that it lacked jurisdiction. In the Supreme Court, however, six of the eight participating justices announced that the political question doctrine was no longer a barrier to judicial intervention in such matters. But having opened the thicket of legislative districting and apportionment to the federal courts, the Supreme Court strangely offered little guidance as to the standard judges were to apply. Was *some* population disparity among districts constitutionally acceptable? If so, how much was to be allowed? Indeed, what was "fair representation"?

Frankfurter, author of the plurality opinion in *Colegrove* and now nearly at the end of a judicial career that had begun in 1939, wrote an impassioned dissent that was joined by Justice John Marshall Harlan. "[T]here is not under our Constitution a judicial remedy for every political mischief, for every undesirable exercise of legislative power. The Framers carefully and with deliberate forethought refused so to enthrone the judiciary. In this situation, as in others of like nature, appeal for relief does not belong here. Appeal must be to an informed, civically militant electorate. In a democratic society like ours, relief must come through an aroused popular conscience that sears the conscience of the people's representatives." Moreover, Frankfurter had serious questions about the practical reach of judicial power. Upon a finding that a legislature was unconstitutionally districted, how was a court to enforce an order that would in effect direct many legislators to walk the plank into a sea of political oblivion? "[T]here is nothing judicially more unseemly nor more self-defeating than for this Court to make *in terrorem* pronouncements, to indulge in merely empty rhetoric, sounding a word of promise to the ear, sure to be disappointing to the hope."

The following year, the Court wandered even further into the thicket of state politics and unveiled the standard to be applied. The occasion was *Gray v. Sanders* (1963) that challenged a curious electoral arrangement in Georgia called the county unit system. It was used in the Democratic primary for nominating U.S. senators, the governor, and other statewide officers. Each county had a "unit vote" that was a function of the number of representatives to which that county was entitled in the state house. Of Georgia's

159 counties, the 8 most populous had 3 representatives each, the 30 counties having the next largest population had 2, and the remaining counties had one each. A county's unit vote was equivalent to twice its number of representatives, meaning that the largest counties had 6 unit votes apiece, the next 30 had 4 each, and the others 2 unit votes each. The candidate receiving the most popular votes cast in the primary in a county received all of that county's unit vote. The system meant that voters in the rural counties controlled the outcome in primaries for statewide positions. (The system also minimized the influence of blacks who voted in large numbers in Atlanta.) The population of the largest county (Fulton) was 556,000, or 14 percent of the state's 1960 population; it had 6 votes. The population of the smallest county (Echols) was 1,900, or 0.05 percent of the state total; it had 2 votes. And because Georgia at that time was a heavily Democratic state, the winner of the Democratic primary was virtually guaranteed to be the winner in the general election. The Democratic primary, in short, *was* the election that mattered.

"If a State . . . weighted the male vote more heavily than the female vote or the white vote more heavily than the Negro vote," wrote Justice Douglas for the Court, "none could successfully contend that that discrimination was allowable. How then can one person be given twice or 10 times the voting power of another person in a statewide election merely because he lives in a rural area?" Instead, in sentences with far reaching implications, Douglas maintained,

> Once the geographical unit for which a representative is to be chosen is designated, all who participate in the election are to have an equal vote—whatever their race, whatever their sex, whatever their occupation, whatever their income, and wherever their home may be in that geographical unit. This is required by the Equal Protection Clause of the Fourteenth Amendment. The concept of "we the people" under the Constitution visualizes no preferred class of votes but equality

among those who meet the basic qualifications. . . . The conception of political equality from the Declaration of Independence, to Lincoln's Gettysburg Address, to the Fifteenth, Seventeenth, and Nineteenth Amendments can mean only one thing—one person, one vote.

In early 1964, Georgia was the setting for the Court's third major redistricting decision (*Wesberry v. Sanders*). In dispute was the state's 1931 congressional districting plan that was still in effect. Districts displayed population deviations almost as wide as those contested unsuccessfully in *Colegrove* twenty-eight years before. The Fifth District, the most populous, comprised Fulton County (and within it the city of Atlanta), plus suburban DeKalb County and (then) rural Rockdale County, with a total of 824,000 people. The Ninth District had the fewest number of people, 272,000, with the average of all 10 districts being 394,000. After *Gray*, with its incantation of one person, one vote, the Court's decision was hardly a surprise. "We hold that, construed in the historical context," wrote Justice Hugo Black, "the command of Article I, § 2, that Representatives be chosen 'by the People of the several States' means that as nearly as is practicable one man's vote in a congressional election is to be worth as much as another's." Although the target of the Court's decision in *Baker v. Carr* had been a *state's* districting plan for its own legislature, *Wesberry* had added significance because it dealt with the lower house of the Congress of the United States. Because many states besides Georgia had numerically skewed congressional districts, the Court was in effect not merely questioning the constitutional integrity of a coordinate branch of the national government but pronouncing it practically illegitimate: many, probably most, of its members had been chosen under arrangements that, according to *Wesberry,* violated the Constitution. Understandably, *Wesberry* ruffled sensibilities on Capitol Hill.

In June, the Court went the rest of the distance, completing what it had set in motion in the Tennessee case. On the docket were the state legislative districting plans of Alabama, Colorado, Delaware, Maryland, New York, and Virginia. Challenged specifically in Alabama were three distinct schemes: the existing plan, a proposed plan, and a "stand-by" plan. All contained population variations ranging, at the least, from 31,175 to 634,854 for the 35-member state senate, and from 20,000 to 52,000 for the 106-member house. The Court found each plan constitutionally deficient (*Reynolds v. Sims,* 1964). Similar results followed in the other cases from the other states. Applying the now familiar principle of one person, one vote, the justices called into question the legitimacy not only of the 6 states involved but of least 34 more. This was because *Reynolds* mandated numerically equal districts for *both* legislative chambers, not merely one of them, a test that most states would fail. "Legislators represent people, not trees or acres," declared Chief Justice Earl Warren. "Legislators are elected by voters, not farms or cities or economic interests. . . . [I]t is inconceivable that a state law to the effect that, in counting votes for legislators, the votes of citizens in one part of the State would be multiplied by two, five or 10, while the votes of persons in another area would be counted only at face value, could be constitutionally sustainable," he continued. "Of course, the effect of state legislative districting schemes which give the same number of representatives to unequal numbers of constituents is identical." Therefore, the one person, one vote standard applied to all state legislative districts as well as with congressional districts. "We hold that, as a basic constitutional standard, the Equal Protection Clause requires that the seats in both houses of a bicameral state legislature must be apportioned on a population basis. Simply stated, an individual's right to vote for state legislators is unconstitutionally impaired when its weight is in a substantial fashion diluted when compared with votes of citizens living in other parts of the State."

In so doing, Warren and his Court also rejected the so-called federal analogy. The states had insisted that while population might be the appropriate basis for one legislative chamber, some other basis might properly be used for the second chamber, giving less populated regions a greater say than they would otherwise have, as in the United States Senate. The analogy, Warren said, was inapposite. "Attempted reliance on the federal analogy often appears to be little more than an after-the-fact rationalization offered in defense of maladjusted state apportionment arrangements." The contrasting bases of representation in the two houses of Congress instead arose from unique historical circumstances. It "is one ingrained in our Constitution, as part of the law of the land. It is one conceived out of compromise and concession indispensable to the establishment of our federal republic." In short, what was appropriate nationally in 1787 was no longer appropriate for any member state of the Union.

Although agreeing that the districting plans under review from four of the states violated the Constitution, Justice Potter Stewart dissented in the New York and Colorado cases. Despite the presence of some population disparities, he found their systems of representation acceptable. In explaining his position, Stewart also revealed a deep understanding of the intricacies involved in representation that were glossed over by the chief justice's opinion. "Representative government," reminded Stewart, "is a process of accommodating group interests through democratic institutional arrangements."

> Its function is to channel the numerous opinions, interests, and abilities of the people of a State into the making of the State's public policy. Appropriate legislative apportionment, therefore, should ideally be designed to insure effective representation in the State's legislature, in cooperation with other organs of political power, of the various groups and interests making up the electorate. In practice, of course, this ideal is approximated in the particular apportionment system of any State by a realistic accommodation of the diverse and often conflicting political forces operating within the State.

Stewart rejected the notion "that the requirements of the Equal Protection Clause can be met in any State only by the uncritical, simplistic, and heavy-handed application of sixth-grade arithmetic." Rather, the Constitution required that two standards be met. First, "in the light of the State's own characteristics and needs, the plan must be a rational one. Secondly, . . . the plan must be such as not to permit the systematic frustration of the will of a majority of the electorate of the State." That is, there must be a reasonable justification for the system, and a majority of the people must be in a position to elect a majority of both houses of the legislature. Both could be satisfied, Stewart thought, with something less than the rigidity of one person, one vote.

Stewart made a sound argument. Its weakness lay in the fact that his defense of rational plans based on nonpopulation factors did not itself fit the facts in most states. That is, the districting arrangements challenged in Illinois in 1946 or in Georgia in 1964 were not "planned." They simply happened as a product of legislative inaction. There, as in many states, districts gradually grew more and more lopsided, as population growth and shifts occurred. The greater the variances among districts, the greater the resistance to change by those then advantaged by the status quo.

"As nearly as practicable," the Court declared in *Wesberry*, "one man's vote in a congressional election is to be worth as much as another's." So in applying the one person, one vote standard to districting cases across the nation, what has "[a]s nearly as practicable" meant in practice? The answer depends on whether the Court is judging state legislative or congressional districts. With state legislative districts, the applicable constitutional provision ordinarily is the equal protection clause alone. With them, the Court has routinely accepted small population deviations among districts of at least several percentage points where the deviations have been justified in order to respect the boundaries of political subdivisions such as counties, cities, and townships. In *Mahan v. Howell* (1973), for example, the Court approved a Virginia plan in

which the maximum departure from the ideal (the difference between the most populous and the least populous district) was 16.4
percent and where the average deviation from the norm was plus
or minus 3.89 percent. The outer limit would seem to be illustrated by the unusual circumstances of *Brown v. Thompson*
(1983). In this case a bare majority of the Court approved a districting plan for the Wyoming House of Representatives with an
average deviation of 16 percent and a maximum deviation of 89
percent. Crucial to the decision were the isolation and vast dis-
tances separating some sparsely settled areas of a sparsely settled
state. If one extrapolates from these and other cases, an average
deviation of as much as 10 percent is ordinarily (but not always)
acceptable.

With congressional districts, however, no such latitude is allowed because the Court sees two constitutional mandates that
apply. In addition to the equal protection clause, there is the provision in Article I mandating that the "Members" of the House
are to be "chosen every second Year by the People of the several
States," language that the Court construed in *Wesberry* to require
one person, one vote. Reinforcing that conclusion were the historical data showing that, in the early years of the Republic, most
states conducted House elections at large, meaning that there were
no districts and also that every vote was weighted equally. Moreover, the Court has concluded, fewer countervailing interests,
such as maintaining the integrity of political subdivisions, apply in
the case of congressional districts. As a result, the Court tolerates
only the slightest departures from the norm. This was apparent as
early as *Kirkpatrick v. Preisler* (1969). Missouri's districting plan
was defective because it displayed deviations as wide as 5 percent
from the most populous district to the least. No numerical variance between districts would be considered "negligible," the
Court explained. "Any variance, no matter how small, must be
justified or shown to be unavoidable." Ultimately the Missouri
plan that won approval had variances within plus or minus 0.15

percent. *Kirkpatrick* partly explains *Karcher v. Daggett* (1983) that disallowed congressional districting in New Jersey where the maximum deviation was no more than 1 percent. In the majority's view, the state legislature had nonetheless fallen short of the constitutional standard. But, as explained further below, *Karcher* was distinctive in another way and so posed a second representational problem for the Court.

The judiciary's equation of equal numbers with fair representation, however, obscured the fact that no system of representation is "perfect" in terms of producing results that are necessarily and always an accurate reflection of people's preferences. The widely used single-member district, for instance, is winner-take-all and so injects its own distortion into representation. Regardless of the number of candidates contesting a seat, there can by definition be only one winner, only one representative to be elected. Votes for the losing candidates or parties are wasted and are of no use to anyone. Lines between districts are like fire walls, not addition signs. Votes cast for the second-place party in district A cannot be carried over and tallied with votes the same party receives in district B, and so on.

Similarly, consider a state with ten congressional districts, where Democrats hold approximately a 60–40 percent edge in voter registration in each of the districts. Barring the unexpected, a Democrat will win each of the seats, yielding a congressional delegation of ten Democrats and no Republicans. A different configuration of districts might produce, say, three with Republican majorities, and so could be expected to yield a congressional delegation of seven Democrats and three Republicans. In both examples the one person, one vote standard has been met, yet with strikingly different results in terms of representation. Even so, the Democrats in a majority Republican district, or the Republicans in a majority Democratic single-member district, are effectively disfranchised in the sense that their candidate will almost always lose. Single-member districts can thus be the very antithesis of proportionality in voting strength for majority and minority alike. Moreover, as much as any other institutional device in American politics, they reinforce the two-party system, making it exceedingly difficult for a third (minor) party to win elections on any consistent basis. And in one-party dominant areas of the country, single-member districts help to make sure that the weaker of the two parties remains ineffective.

Until as late as the mid-1980s, alongside single-member districts, many states used multimember districts, which could magnify such distortions in representation. A multimember district, at least as they have usually been arranged in the United States, effectively creates an at-large election within a part of a state. If the ratio of representatives to population in a state is, say, 1:50,000, then a multimember district electing six representatives would contain 300,000 persons. The ratio remains 1:50,000, satisfying the one person, one vote rule. But if the same majority of voters chooses all six representatives (white Republicans, for instance), then the Democrats and/or persons of color who may have voted for other candidates have won nothing, even though their votes might equal a substantial minority of the total votes cast. Indeed, multimember districts historically have been put in place to add to a dominant party's electoral gains or perhaps to minimize the influence of racial minorities such as blacks and Mexican Americans. Although multimember districts, even today, are not unconstitutional per se, even when used in conjunction with single-member districts, their presence amounts to a yellow, if not a red, flag for the judiciary, inviting extra scrutiny.

That was the message the Court sent in *White v. Regester* (1973), involving a Texas plan that mixed the two kinds of districts for its state House of Representatives. The 150 representatives were to be chosen from 79 single-member districts and 11 multimember districts. The Supreme Court upheld findings of the district court that use of multimember districts in Dallas County diluted the votes of African Americans. (Since Reconstruction, there had been only two blacks elected to the state house from Dallas County.)

The use of multimember districts in Bexar County was similarly defective. Mexican Americans constituted 29 percent of the county's population, and they lived largely in twenty-eight contiguous census tracts (the "Barrio") within San Antonio. Lumping them into a much larger district where they thereby became a minority seemed to be one of the reasons why, since 1880, only five Mexican Americans had ever been elected to the state house from Bexar County. The arrangement meant that, like the African Americans in Dallas County, Mexican Americans "had less opportunity than did other residents in the district to participate in the political processes and to elect legislators of their choice," explained the Court.

Multimember districts of course do not have to be deployed as small-scale versions of an at-large election. They can actually be used to enhance representation of racial and political minorities through a system called proportional representation. In use in some European countries, seats in a multimember district can be awarded to candidates in rough proportion to the numbers of votes received by their respective parties. Whereas, in a winner-take-all multimember district, the party that finishes second, third, or fourth wins nothing, with a system of proportional representation, by contrast, a party winning, say, 25 percent of the vote is entitled to about one-fourth of the delegates. Just as the single-member district discourages minor parties from taking hold, proportional representation tends to encourage them, by increasing the chances that they can win at least a small "prize" (such as a legislative seat) in the game of politics.

For a time, the revolution in representation launched by the Warren Court had a dimension wholly apart from litigation over principles of correct districting: a political backlash. As the one person, one vote standard was taking shape in the 1960s, many state legislatures and members of Congress did not view the

Court's handiwork in cases like *Wesberry* and *Reynolds* with favor. Redrawing political maps meant altering the power structure in state after state. Frankfurter's dissent in *Baker v. Carr* had pointedly suggested that by wandering into the political thicket of representation, the judiciary might test the limits of its power. To a degree Frankfurter was correct. First, state legislators complied only reluctantly with the new one person, one vote rule—usually because they found themselves under a directive from a federal district judge to redistrict. Other than the principle of the rule of law, what power did a judge possess to force compliance? Noncompliance ultimately would lead to the awkward situation in which an elected legislature would be deemed lacking in legal authority, meaning that none of its legislation would actually be law. Short of that, and no state went that far, a legislature's failure to redistrict would thrust that job in the judge's hands. And if there was anything more distasteful than redistricting oneself out of a seat, it was the specter of that being done by a judge. So while some redistricting was judicially managed, many legislatures undertook the unpleasant chore themselves.

But as this process got underway after 1964, a two-pronged countermovement developed. Both targeted *Reynolds v. Sims,* the more controversial of the two 1964 districting decisions. Many state legislators and members of Congress could not understand why the Court had not adopted a compromise position that would have demanded representation strictly based on population in one house, but tolerated a more relaxed standard for the other house, as in keeping with the federal analogy that *Reynolds* rejected. Fundamentally, many state legislators, especially, remained convinced that how a state was districted was their business, not the Court's.

One attack on the Court was orchestrated by the Council of State Governments. It urged state legislatures to petition Congress for a constitutional amendment to overturn, or at least to limit, *Reynolds v. Sims.* This strategy relied on a provision in Article V of the Constitution that directs Congress to convene a constitutional convention upon the request by the legislatures of two-thirds of the states. (With a fifty-state union, a minimum of thirty-four states would have to act.) This part of Article V has never been implemented; the United States has witnessed no national constitutional convention since 1787. One reason why the alternate amendment route has never been tried is that no one knows what a convention, once convened, might actually do. So, when there has been agitation within the states for constitutional change, Congress usually short-circuits the movement by debating and perhaps proposing a constitutional amendment itself. Indeed, all twenty-seven amendments to the Constitution have initially been proposed by Congress before being sent to the states for ratification. The Council's goal therefore was to summon a convention and/or to goad Congress to take action against *Reynolds.* The Council also hoped to capitalize on the anti-Court sentiment that existed in many quarters because of the justices' unpopular rulings on other subjects as varied as subversive speech, school prayer, pornography, and criminal justice (Hanson 1966, 90; Stephenson 1999, 172–178).

The second attack was led by Republican Senator Everett McKinley Dirksen of Illinois. (The Senate was the *only* legislative body in the United States not directly covered by the 1964 rulings.) Although supporting the Council's objective, Dirksen was not prepared to wait for an organized uprising among the state legislatures. Instead, he pushed for a constitutional amendment directly.

This was hardly the first time that a representative or senator had attempted to amend the Constitution to overturn or at least modify a Supreme Court decision. Although such efforts only rarely succeed, the justices by the 1960s had been expressly reversed by constitutional amendment on three occasions. The Eleventh Amendment, restricting federal court jurisdiction over the states, overturned *Chisholm v. Georgia* (1793). The Fourteenth Amendment, in part granting both national and state citizenship to "all persons" born in the United States, countered odious language to the contrary in the infamous *Dred Scott* decision (1857). The Sixteenth Amendment, allowing for a national tax on incomes, reversed *Pollock v. Farmers' Loan & Trust Co.* (1895). (A fourth "correction" occurred in 1971 and will be discussed in the next section). Arguably, there were two other such reversals as well. The Nineteenth Amendment, after all, reduced to nothing the holding in *Minor v. Happersett* (1875) that the Fourteenth Amendment was no bar to state laws that excluded women from the franchise. The Twenty-fourth Amendment of 1964 partly displaced the Court's rejection twenty-seven years earlier of a Fourteenth Amendment challenge to poll taxes in *Breedlove v. Suttles.*

Dirksen was determined to add one more amendment to that list. His proposal declared, first, that "the right and power to determine the composition of the legislature of a State and the apportionment of the membership thereof shall remain in the people of that State." The implication was that matters of composition and apportionment (districting) would not be subject to review by the courts. A second component of the Dirksen amendment asserted that nothing in the U.S. Constitution was to prohibit a state from using "factors other than population" in setting up the districts of one house of a bicameral legislature or from giving "reasonable weight" to nonpopulation factors in a unicameral state. Last, any plan based on nonpopulation factors would have to be approved by the voters in a statewide referendum. Thus the thrust of his proposal was a reversal of *Reynolds v. Sims,* but not necessarily a reinstatement of representation schemes in place before the landmark ruling. The people of a state, not the federal courts, would have the ultimate decision about representation within their state.

Dirksen calculated that Senate passage would be more difficult than House passage, especially since the House had already passed a bill to eliminate the Supreme Court's jurisdiction over legislative districting cases entirely. He was correct. In August 1965, the Senate's vote on the amendment was fifty-seven to thirty-nine. That was a majority, to be sure, but the Constitution stipulates that a *two-thirds* vote is needed in each house in order to propose an amendment for ratification by the states (Hanson 1966, 87–101).

Time was definitely not on Dirksen's side, nor was it on the side of the Council that had been urging action within the states. In effect, a race had begun, and time gave proponents of one person, one vote the advantage. As redistricting proceeded in the states, fewer legislatures would be opposed to the new order of things. Legislators elected under one person, one vote plans would now have a vested interest themselves in preserving *Reynolds v. Sims.* Likewise, as time passed, more members of the House of Representatives would be elected from districts redrawn under *Wesberry v. Sanders.* Consequently, the anti-*Reynolds* movements withered away.

Today, litigation over population variances continues, especially after each new census, but the principles of those cases are as permanently fixed as can be in American constitutional law. They now seem entirely unexceptionable and noncontroversial. Today, even politically aware Americans have either forgotten or have never known that those principles redrew the map of voting effectiveness, and hence of political power, in the United States. But that consensus hardly means that representation itself has ceased to be rife with controversy. As already noted, districts can be drawn in a variety of ways, each meeting the test of one person, one vote. That task is far easier today than it was in the 1960s because of computers. Data about census tracts and political subdivisions can be entered into a program, and with just a few keystrokes any number of numerically equal representational patterns emerge in seconds.

Computers have thus only made easier an aspect of districting that is nearly as old as the Republic itself: gerrymandering. The term is an amalgam of Elbridge *Gerry* and sala*mander.* Gerry, a

Democratic-Republican, was in his second term as governor of Massachusetts in 1810–1811. His Jeffersonian followers attempted to retain control of the state legislature by redrawing districts to their advantage and to the disadvantage of the opposition Federalists. This maneuver required several peculiarly shaped districts, at least one of which resembled the amphibian creature called a salamander. The portrait artist Gilbert Stuart is supposed to have looked at a drawing of the oddly shaped districts and pronounced them a "gerrymander" (Stephenson, Bresler, Friedrich, Karlesky 1992, 164). Ever since, the term has remained a fixture in the lexicon of American politics.

If the problem before 1964 was a reluctance by entrenched legislators to engage in much redistricting at all, the judicially mandated redistricting that now must occur after each new census presents an enticing opportunity for a political party, especially if it controls both houses of a state legislature and the governorship, to attempt to strengthen itself politically by skewing districts not numerically but by party. That is, the temptation can be great to produce an arrangement of districts by which the dominant party can gain additional congressional or state legislative seats. This can be done either by assigning the other party to minority status in as many districts as possible ("cracking") or by concentrating the other party in as few districts as possible ("packing"). But is gerrymandering consistent with the Constitution?

Recall the reference earlier in this section to *Karcher v. Daggett*. In that case the Supreme Court invalidated a congressional districting plan that the Democrat-controlled New Jersey legislature had crafted after the 1980 census. Ostensibly the reason the Court gave for striking down the plan was that the population deviation of less than 1 percent was too large. In holding that the state had not made a "good faith effort to achieve population equality," the Court may have been persuaded by the unusually strange shapes of some of the districts. One resembled a swan and took in parts of seven counties. Another looked like a fishhook. The Court may have reasoned that legislators could have come even closer to numerically equal districts had they not been trying to maximize the number of districts likely to be in Democratic hands after the next election. Indeed Republicans had protested the plan as an unconstitutional gerrymander, and Justice Stevens made it clear in a concurring opinion that the "judiciary is not powerless to provide a constitutional remedy in egregious cases" of gerrymandering.

The fact was, however, that the Supreme Court had never held that a partisan gerrymander, in and of itself, violated the Constitution. To be sure, *Gomillion v. Lightfoot* in 1960 had placed the drawing of political boundaries out of bounds when that sought to neutralize black votes, but that case has nothing to do with partisanship. And the constitutional infirmities of the multimember districts thirteen years later in *White v. Regester* arose because of the diluting effects they had on African American and Mexican American voters in Texas, not on voters generally.

Three years after deciding *Karcher,* however, the Court squarely confronted partisan gerrymandering for the first time, and in so doing ventured into yet another political thicket in the forest of representation. Republicans had arguably been the victims in the New Jersey case. Now, in a case from Indiana, Democrats cried foul.

The Indiana legislature has a 100-member house and a 50-member senate. House members serve two-year terms, with elections for all seats every two years. Senators serve four-year terms, with half of the seats up for election every two years. In the 1980s, senators were elected from single-member districts; representatives were elected from a mixture of single-member and multimember districts. After the Republican-controlled legislature drew up a districting plan based on the 1980 census figures, Democrats challenged it as an unconstitutional gerrymander under the equal protection clause. Before the case went to trial in U.S. district court, elections under the new plan were held in November 1982. Democratic candidates for the House received 51.9 percent of the votes cast statewide but only 43 of the 100 seats to be filled. Democratic candidates for the Senate received 53.1 percent of the votes cast statewide, and 13 of the 25 Democratic candidates were elected. In Marion and Allen Counties, however, that were both divided into multimember house districts, Democratic candidates received 46.6 percent of the vote but won only 3 of the 21 seats at stake. Relying primarily on these data, the district court invalidated the 1981 reapportionment plan and ordered the legislature to prepare a new plan.

When the case reached the Supreme Court, however, Democrats fared badly, with only two justices finding the Indiana plan constitutionally defective (*Davis v. Bandemer,* 1986). Yet the decision was highly significant for two reasons. First, six justices did agree that partisan gerrymanders, like numerically imbalanced districts, presented a justiciable, and not a "political," question. Just as *Baker v. Carr* held in 1962 that cases involving population disparities were appropriate for judges to decide, *Bandemer* held that gerrymander claims were also cognizable under the equal protection clause. Having done this, however, the Court announced a standard for determining a constitutionally unacceptable gerrymander that was far less precise than the one-person-one-vote rule that emerged from *Gray v. Sanders, Wesberry v. Sanders,* and *Reynolds v. Sims* in the 1960s. "Unconstitutional discrimination occurs only when the electoral system is arranged in a manner that will consistently degrade a voter's or a group of voters' influence on the political process as a whole." Left in doubt was the kind of evidence and the period of time required to prove an unconstitutional gerrymander. A further complication for any such challenge was the redistricting that would occur after each decennial census. Thus, while leaving the door open to the possibility of an unconstitutional gerrymander, *Bandemer* made it difficult to establish one.

As the twentieth century drew to a close, no districting plan had been invalidated by the Supreme Court as a partisan gerrymander. That fact suggested that the future of judicial oversight of gerrymanders could move in one of three directions. The Court might continue to maintain the status quo, holding out the possibility of an unconstitutional gerrymander as a deterrent to one far more egregious than was challenged in *Bandemer.* Or the Court could abandon *Bandemer* altogether, deciding that the goal of writing standards that distinguish between acceptable and unacceptable gerrymanders is simply unattainable. If so, the Court would vindicate the warning Justice Sandra Day O'Connor issued in the 1986 decision, when she argued that gerrymander claims should be deemed nonjusticiable.

> Vote dilution analysis is far less manageable when extended to major political parties than if confined to racial minority groups. First, an increase in the number of competing claims to equal group representation will make judicial review of apportionment vastly more complex. Designing an apportionment plan that does not impair or degrade the voting strength of several groups is more difficult than designing a plan that does not have such an effect on one group for the simple reason that, as the number of criteria the plan must meet increases, the number of solutions that will satisfy those criteria will decrease. Even where it is not impossible to reconcile the competing claims of political, racial, and other groups, the predictable result will be greater judicial intrusion into the apportionment process.

Alternatively, an abandonment of *Bandemer* might thrust the Court more deeply into the quagmire of partisan politics. The Court might conclude that, because the *Bandemer* test for an unconstitutional gerrymander is too nebulous, a more precise and workable standard is in order. That route might entail some sort of requirement of proportional representation for political parties. In his *Bandemer* opinion, Justice Powell maintained that district lines should be the product of "neutral and legitimate criteria" and that the state "should treat its voters as standing in the same position, regardless of their political beliefs or party affiliation." If so, the only way to assess whether the line-drawing criteria were both neutral and legitimate would be by their results—that parties would win seats approximately in proportion to their strength among the voters statewide. Aside from other consequences, adoption of this standard would surely bring about increased judicial entanglement in the political affairs of the country. Chapter Four outlines the route the Court now seems prepared to take.

A NEW CONSENSUS ON VOTING AGE

By law and custom dating from English practice and the colonial period, the minimum voting age in the United States for more than 150 years was fixed at twenty-one. That was the age at which young men, and later young women, were recognized as having reached their political majority. Indeed, the rule of twenty-one was probably the longest-lasting constant among voting qualifications in all the states. There were variations with respect to other criteria but not to age. This uniformity in law, however, did not mean necessarily that a uniformity of opinion existed. Certainly each time the nation went to war, there were those who argued that one's eligibility to fight, and perhaps die, for one's country should also carry with it a right to a voice in its affairs. Such arguments carried even more urgency when a military draft was in place. In World Wars I and II, for example, the armed forces of the United States consisted of millions of draftees—those who were compelled to serve, whether they chose to or not.

The first official break in the rule of twenty-one came at the end of World War II. In 1945, Georgia ratified its new constitution that fixed the minimum voting age at eighteen. The newly enfranchised voters of the state were able to exercise their right to vote for the first time in the Democratic primary of 1946. Ironically, because of the Supreme Court's decision in *Smith v. Allwright,* discussed earlier in this chapter, this was also the first primary in

Twentieth-Century Issues

Georgia in which black residents of eligible age could participate. The 1946 primary therefore reflected a double enfranchisement of new voters, by age as well as race.

In 1954, Dwight Eisenhower became the first U.S. president formally to endorse a constitutional amendment setting a national voting age of eighteen. The former general was already on record as having equated the responsibilities of voting and military service, reminding his audience that "a man . . . old enough to fight . . . is old enough to vote" (Cultice 1992, 30). Ike's ideas were shared by other prominent leaders. Moreover, the armed services remained large during the Cold War of the 1950s, following the "hot war" in Korea (1950–1953). That, plus the continuation of the draft, kept the link between military service and voting very much alive. Moreover, with most American youth now completing all of high school, the case for a rule of eighteen seemed to be enhanced by the confluence of high school graduation and a presumption that graduates, almost all of whom would be about eighteen, were now ready to assume the responsibilities of full citizenship. Yet even though many in Congress favored the idea, it was not high on their agenda, given other needs that seemed more urgent or that had stronger political backing. For most, there seemed little advantage to be gained from a campaign to enfranchise eighteen-, nineteen-, and twenty-year-olds.

Indeed, some congressional leaders were dead set against lowering the voting age. For example, liberal Democrat Emanuel Celler of Brooklyn, born in 1888, rejected the link between voting and military service, saying that the two were "as different as chalk is from cheese." Soldiers were supposed to be uncritically obedient, he said; that was not what was expected from voters.

> To say that he who is old enough to fight is old enough to vote is to draw an utterly fallacious parallel. No such parallel exists. The ability to choose, to separate promise from performance, to evaluate on the basis of fact, are the prerequisites to good voting. Eighteen to twenty-

one are mainly formative years where the youth is racing forward to maturity. His attitudes shift from place to place. These are the years of the greatest uncertainties, a fertile ground for the demagogues. Youth attaches itself to promises, rather than to performance. These are rightfully the years of rebellion rather than reflection. We will be doing a grave injustice to democracy if we grant the vote to those under twenty-one. (Keyssar 2000, 279)

Exactly what accounted for the transformation of an unqualified twenty-year-old into a qualified twenty-one-year-old, the senior Democrat did not explain. Nor did he explain why his logic might not require disfranchising *all* soldiers, at least those over twenty who remained "uncritically obedient." But Celler's views counted. From 1955 until 1972, he chaired the House Committee on the Judiciary without interruption, and it was through his committee that any proposed constitutional amendment would have to pass. Moreover, southern representatives and senators tended to oppose a national relaxation of the voting age on the familiar ground that it would lead to more congressional control over state election laws. And, as everyone knew, virtually all eighteen-year-olds would become twenty-one within three years. No one was permanently disfranchised. It was a question of being patient for a little while. Discrimination against younger citizens was therefore wholly unlike discrimination based on an immutable racial or gender characteristic. (Sex-change operations were unknown in the years leading up to the Nineteenth Amendment.)

The rule of twenty-one might have persisted in most states for quite some time but for two developments, one cultural and the other military. Perhaps inspired by the civil rights movement of the 1950s and early 1960s, a youth revolution swept the country in the middle and late 1960s. In part this was a product of numbers: the post–World War II "baby boom" generation had gone to college. There was a renewed emphasis on the presumed wisdom of youth. Existing norms on subjects ranging from attire to personal morality were questioned and often jettisoned. On campuses, young men and women demanded, and often received, a relaxation of student rules and a say in curricular policies and faculty hiring. The turbulent sixties were very much the antithesis of the quiescent Eisenhower fifties.

Then after 1964, President Johnson and his administration sharply escalated the war in Vietnam into a conflict that engaged hundreds of thousands of American troops, most of them young draftees. As casualties mounted into the thousands and as victory still seemed remote, the war became increasingly unpopular. Indeed, the inability of prospective draftees to vote lent credibility to those who branded the war as illegitimate. After the assassinations of Martin Luther King Jr. and Senator Robert Kennedy in 1968, even the political process itself seemed to have become corrupted (Kelman 1970, 1–76; Bresler 1999, 55–77).

Understandably perhaps, the drive for a rule of eighteen began to gain momentum. And by this time, Alaska, Hawaii, and Kentucky had also set minimum voting ages below twenty-one: at nineteen, twenty, and eighteen, respectively (*Congress and the Nation* 1973, 1003). Moreover, many Democrats and Republicans, liberals and conservatives alike expected to benefit from an expanded franchise. Age reform also had the support of major civil rights and labor groups. But the first attempt to change the voting age did not come by constitutional amendment, but by statute.

As noted earlier in this chapter, the Voting Rights Act of 1965 had initially been passed for a five-year period. Up for renewal and amendment in 1970, liberal Democrats including Senator Edward Kennedy and the Senate Majority Leader Mike Mansfield inserted a rule of eighteen into the act that would apply to all elections in the United States, state as well as federal. Congress's authority to prescribe a national voting age in elections for national office—even though this had never been done before—seemed at least plausibly grounded in Section 4 of Article I: "The Times, Places and Manner of holding Elections for Senators and Representatives, shall be prescribed in each State by the Legislature thereof; but the Congress may at any time by Law make or alter such Regulations, except as to the Places of chusing Senators." If voting age fell into the category of the "Manner" of holding such elections, then Congress was on firm ground. But to claim authority to do so in elections for state and local offices seemed shaky. Nonetheless the bill easily passed the Senate. (Given initial passage of the Voting Rights Act five years earlier, the southern fear of increased federal control over elections had already been realized, and so that argument against a congressional change in the voting age evaporated.)

However, the House of Representatives still had to act. Chairman Celler of the Judiciary Committee remained hostile to any lowering of the voting age, but he was a strong supporter of the main provisions of the Voting Rights Act, which targeted racial discrimination. If the House approved a voting rights bill without the rule of eighteen inserted by the Senate, the measure would have to be reconsidered by the Senate. No bill, after all, can proceed to the president for signature unless it has been passed by both houses in precisely the same form. But action by a conference committee or reconsideration by the Senate might put other parts of the bill in jeopardy. Celler, therefore, swallowed hard and did what he thought was best for the country in the long run: maintaining the Voting Rights Act in force.

When President Richard Nixon signed the extension of the Voting Rights Act into law, he urged a speedy judicial challenge to the provision that thrust a uniform voting age on the nation by statute. That promptly materialized, and in *Oregon v. Mitchell* (1970), the Supreme Court affirmed Congress's authority to set a voting age in elections for federal officials, but denied its authority to do so in elections for state and local officials. The latter were the province of the individual states, as had always been the case.

The country—especially state election officials—now faced the prospects of an administrative nightmare. As a result of the combination of the 1970 Voting Rights Act amendments and *Oregon v. Mitchell,* eighteen-, nineteen, and twenty-year-olds would be eligible, along with all other eligible voters, to cast ballots for U.S. representatives, senators, and presidential electors in 1972. But in almost all states they remained ineligible to cast ballots for all state and local offices. Were there to be separate ballots, depending upon one's age, or separate elections based on age? State officials promptly pressured Congress for a resolution. The result was the Twenty-sixth Amendment, officially proposed by Congress on March 23, 1971, and quickly ratified by the legislatures of the necessary three-quarters of the states five weeks later on June 30, 1971—the fastest time on record for any constitutional amendment: "The right of citizens of the United States, who are eighteen years of age or older, to vote shall not be denied or abridged by the United States or by any State on account of age." Because of its language, the amendment does not in fact fix the minimum voting age at eighteen. A state remains free, if it chooses, to enfranchise younger residents, although none to date has done so.

In the elections of 1972, the newly enfranchised citizens did not overwhelm the polls as many politicians had expected. Nor did they vote differently in large numbers from their older brothers or sisters between the ages of twenty-one and thirty. Students of voting behavior have long known that voter turnout is directly correlated with age, at least up to about age sixty-five. The overall turnout of eligible voters, including the newly enfranchised, was 55.6 percent, but polling data showed that only 48 percent of those in the eighteen-to-twenty age bracket cast a vote. The highest participation rate belonged to voters between the ages of forty-five and sixty-four, 71 percent of whom went to the polls (*Congress and the Nation* 1973, 1006).

CONCLUSION

The twentieth century witnessed an unprecedented expansion of the American electorate. In 1900, almost all white males could vote throughout the United States. Women were fully enfranchised in only a handful of states and could vote only in certain local elections in some other states. Black males were supposed to be eligible to vote; the Fifteenth Amendment said so. But in practice, especially in the South, access to the ballot was rapidly disappearing. Overall, therefore, politics remained very much a (white) man's business.

Contrast the status of voting rights at the beginning of the century with what transpired over the next ten decades. Women, white women at least, were fully enfranchised nationally by constitutional amendment in 1920. Forty-five years later, Congress took drastic steps to make good on the promise of the Fifteenth Amendment, to make sure that the color of one's skin could no longer determine one's access, or not, to the ballot box. Almost contemporaneously, the United States Supreme Court rewrote constitutional standards for representation, the structure through which voters primarily convey their influence. An unelected and politically unaccountable institution came to the rescue of electoral majoritarianism itself. Through its ruling against the poll tax, the Court also closed the door on any possibility that property or payment of a tax could ever again be considered a valid qualification for voting. Far less controversial, at least at the end, was the lowering of the voting age to eighteen. Taken together, these changes brought about for the first time in American history a national franchise. True, states still conduct elections and there are important differences among the states in their election laws. But in terms of those who are eligible to participate, with few exceptions a national rule now prevails.

Voting and representation nonetheless remain complex phenomena. The changes wrought in the twentieth century have hardly silenced debate about either in the twenty-first.

REFERENCES

Alpern, Sara, and Dale Baum. 1985. "Female Ballots: The Impact of the Nineteenth Amendment." *Journal of Interdisciplinary History* 16: 43.

Bardolph, Richard, ed. 1970. *The Civil Rights Record: Black Americans and the Law, 1849–1970.* New York: Thomas Y. Crowell.

Bickel, Alexander M., and Benno C. Schmidt Jr. 1984. *The Judiciary and Responsible Government 1910–21.* New York: Macmillan.

Blair, Karen J. 2001. "Women's Club Movement." In Paul S. Boyer, ed., *The Oxford Companion to United States History.* New York: Oxford University Press.

Bresler, Robert J. 1999. *Us vs. Them: American Political and Cultural Conflict from WWII to Watergate.* Wilmington, DE: Scholarly Resources.

Bryce, James. 1921. *The American Commonwealth.* 2 vols. New & rev. ed. New York: Macmillan.

Buhle, Mari Jo, and Paul Buhle, eds. 1978. *The Concise History of Woman Suffrage: Selections from the Classic Work of Stanton, Anthony, Gage, and Harper.* Urbana: University of Illinois Press.

Burr, A. R. 1926. *Russell H. Conwell and His Work.* Philadelphia: Winston.

Catt, Carrie C., and Nettie R. Shuler. 1923. *Woman Suffrage and Politics.* New York: Charles Scribner's Sons.

Coletta, Paolo E. 1971. "Election of 1908." In Arthur M. Schlesinger Jr. and Fred L. Israel, eds., *History of American Presidential Elections.* 4 vols. New York: Chelsea House.

Congress and the Nation 1965–1968. 1969. Washington, DC: Congressional Quarterly.

Congress and the Nation 1969–1972. 1973. Washington, DC: Congressional Quarterly.

Cott, Nancy F. 1987. *The Grounding of Modern Feminism.* New Haven, CT: Yale University Press.

Crossen, Cynthia. 2004. "Before Radio, Citizenry Got Culture, Politics from Traveling Troupes." *Wall Street Journal,* July 7, B1.

Cruikshank, Alfred B. 1920. *Popular Misgovernment in the United States.* New York: Moffat, Yard.

Crunden, Robert M. 2001. "Progressive Era." In Paul S. Boyer, ed., *The Oxford Companion to United States History.* New York: Oxford University Press.

Cultice, Wendell W. 1992. *Youth's Battle for the Ballot: A History of Voting Age in America.* Westport, CT: Greenwood.

Davidson, Chandler. 1990. "The Recent Evolution of Voting Rights Law Affecting Racial and Language Minorities." In Chandler Davidson and Bernard Grofman, eds., *Quiet Revolution in the South: The Impact of the Voting Rights Act, 1965–1990.* Princeton, NJ: Princeton University Press.

"Declaration of Constitutional Principles Issues by 19 Senators and 77 Representatives of the Congress." 1956. *New York Times,* March 12: 19.

Dobbins, Harry T. 1941. "Nebraska's One House Legislature—After Six Years." *National Municipal Review.* 30: 511.

Doyle, William. 2001. *An American Insurrection: The Battle of Oxford, Mississippi, 1962.* New York: Doubleday.

Drew, Elizabeth. 1985. *Campaign Journal.* New York: Macmillan.

Editorial. 1893. *New York Times,* October 10: 4.

Editorial. 1908. *New York Times,* December 6: 12.

Farrand, Max. 1966. *The Records of the Federal Convention of 1787.* 4 vols. New Haven, CT: Yale University Press.

Flexner, Eleanor. 1975. *Century of Struggle: The Women's Rights Movement in the United States.* rev. ed. Cambridge, MA: Harvard University Press.

Garrow, David J. 1978. *Protest at Selma: Martin Luther King, Jr., and the Voting Rights Act of 1965.* New Haven, CT: Yale University Press.

Gathorne-Hardy, G. M. 1964. *A Short History of International Affairs 1920–1939.* 4th ed. New York: Oxford University Press.

Gerhardt, Michael J. 2003. "Frank M. Johnson, Jr." In John H. Vile, ed., *Great American Judges: An Encyclopedia.* 2 vols. Santa Barbara, CA: ABC-CLIO.

Graham, Sara Hunter. 1996. *Women's Suffrage and the New Democracy.* New Haven, CT: Yale University Press.

Greenberg, Jack. 1994. *Crusaders in the Courts: How a Dedicated Band of Lawyers Fought for the Civil Rights Revolution.* New York: Basic Books.

Hacker, Andrew. 1964. *Congressional Districting.* Washington, DC: Brookings Institution.

Hamilton, Charles V. 1973. *The Bench and the Ballot: Southern Federal Judges and Black Voters.* New York: Oxford University Press.

Hanson, Royce. 1966. *The Political Thicket: Reapportionment and Constitutional Democracy.* Englewood Cliffs, NJ: Prentice-Hall.

Hutchinson, Dennis J. 1998. *The Man Who Was Once Whizzer White: A Portrait of Justice Byron R. White.* New York: Free Press.

Johnson, Lyndon Baines. 1971. *The Vantage Point: Perspectives of the Presidency, 1963–1969.* New York: Holt, Rinehart and Winston.

Katzenstein, Mary Fainsod. 1992. "Constitutional Politics and the Feminist Movement." In Donald W. Rogers, ed., *Voting and the Spirit of American Democracy.* Urbana: University of Illinois Press.

Kelly, Alfred H., and Winfred A. Harbison. 1976. *The American Constitution: Its Origins and Development.* 5th ed. New York: W. W. Norton.

Kelman, Steven. 1970. *Push Comes to Shove.* Boston: Houghton Mifflin.

Key, V. O., Jr. 1949. *Southern Politics in State and Nation.* New York: Alfred A. Knopf.

———. 1964. *Parties, Politics, and Pressure Groups.* 5th ed. New York: Thomas Y. Crowell.

Keyssar, Alexander. 2000. *The Right to Vote: The Contested History of Democracy in the United States.* New York: Basic Books.

Klarman, Michael J. 2004. *From Jim Crow to Civil Rights: The Supreme Court and the Struggle for Racial Equality.* New York: Oxford University Press.

Knock, Thomas I. 2001. "World War I." In Paul S. Boyer, ed., *The Oxford Companion to United States History.* New York: Oxford University Press.

Kobach, Kris. 1994. "Note: Rethinking Article V: Term Limits and the Seventeenth and Nineteenth Amendments." *Yale Law Journal* 103: 1971.

Kousser, J. Morgan. 1974. *The Shaping of Southern Politics: Suffrage Restriction and the Establishment of the One-Party South.* New Haven, CT: Yale University Press.

Lemons, J. Stanley. 1973. *The Woman Citizen: Social Feminism in the 1920s.* Urbana: University of Illinois Press.

Levinson, Paul. 1963. *Race, Class, and Party: A History of Negro Suffrage and White Politics in the South.* New York: Russell and Russell.

Link, Arthur S. 1956. *Wilson: The New Freedom.* Princeton, NJ: Princeton University Press.

———. 1965. *Wilson: Campaign for Progressivism and Peace 1916–1917.* Princeton, NJ: Princeton University Press.

Locke, John. 1924. *Two Treatises of Civil Government.* W. S. Carpenter, ed. New York: E. P. Dutton.

Mason, Alpheus Thomas, and Donald Grier Stephenson Jr. 2002. *American Constitutional Law: Introductory Essays and Selected Cases.* 13th ed. Upper Saddle River, NJ: Prentice Hall.

Mason, Alpheus Thomas, and Richard H. Leach. 1959. *In Quest of Freedom: American Political Thought and Practice.* Englewood Cliffs, NJ: Prentice-Hall.

Morgan, David. 1973. *Suffragists and Democrats: The Politics of Woman Suffrage in America.* East Lansing: Michigan State University Press.

Morison, Samuel Eliot. 1965. *The Oxford History of the American People.* New York: Oxford University Press.

Myrdal, Gunnar. 1944. *An American Delimma: The Negro Problem and Modern Democracy.* 2 vols. New York: Harper.

Norgen, Jill. 1999. "Before It Was Merely Difficult: Belva Lockwood's Life in Law and Politics." *Journal of Supreme Court History* 23: 16.

Patterson, James T. 2001. Brown v. Board of Education: *A Civil Rights Milestone and Its Troubled Legacy.* New York: Oxford University Press.

Pickens, William. 1920. "The Woman Votes Hit the Color Line." *Nation* 111 (October 6): 372.

Pringle, Henry F. 1939. *The Life and Times of William Howard Taft.* 2 vols. New York: Farrah and Rinehart.

Roosevelt, Theodore. 1912. Address in Chicago, Illinois, August 6. In Arthur M. Schlesinger Jr. and Fred L. Israel, eds., *History of American Presidential Elections.* 4 vols. New York: Chelsea House.

Rotunda, Ronald D. 1996. "The Aftermath of *Thornton.*" *Constitutional Commentary* 13: 201.

Safire, William. 1993. *Safire's New Political Dictionary: The Definitive Guide to the New Language of Politics.* New York: Random House.

Schlesinger, Arthur M., Jr., and Fred L. Israel, eds. 1971. *History of American Presidential Elections.* 4 vols. New York: Chelsea House.

Smith, Gene. 1964. *When the Cheering Stopped: The Last Years of Woodrow Wilson.* New York: William Morrow.

Stephenson, Donald Grier, Jr. 1988. "The Supreme Court, The Franchise, and the Fifteenth Amendment: The First Sixty Years." *UMKC Law Review* 57: 47.

———. 1989. "Choosing Presidential Candidates: Why the Best Man Doesn't Necessarily Win." *USA Today* (Magazine), 117 (March): 15.

———. 1999. *Campaigns and the Court: The United States Supreme Court in Presidential Elections.* New York: Columbia University Press.

Stephenson, Donald Grier, Jr., Robert J. Bresler, Robert J. Friedrich, and Joseph J. Karlesky. 1992. *American Government.* 2d ed. New York: Harper Collins.

Ware, Susan. 1981. *Beyond Suffrage: Women in the New Deal.* Cambridge, MA: Harvard University Press.

Wayne, Stephen J. 1997. *The Road to the White House 1996.* Postelection ed. New York: St. Martin's Press.

White, G. Edward. 1982. *Earl Warren: A Public Life.* New York: Oxford University Press.

"White Woman's Burden." 1921. *Nation* 112 (February 16): 257.

Wilson, Woodrow. 1913. *The New Freedom.* New York: Doubleday.

4

TWENTY-FIRST CENTURY ISSUES

A century can make a lot of difference. In 1901, the franchise in the United States was still closed to more adults than it was open. Women could vote in only a handful of states. African American males had a legal right to vote in all states, but in practice the right to vote for most black men was nonexistent. To be sure, the franchise in 1901 was far more inclusive than it had been at the beginning of the nineteenth century, before the drive to remove property qualifications had made substantial headway. But access to the ballot in 1901 paled alongside the near universal national suffrage that was in place in every state by the start of the twenty-first century. Not only had racial and gender barriers to the polls been relegated to the trash heap of history in fact as well as in law, but, with the abolition of devices such as the poll tax and literacy test, fewer variations in voter qualifications among the states remained. Substantial uniformity has replaced the widely diverse pattern of rules and practices among the states that, for much of American history, determined who could vote. Indeed, the degree of uniformity today would flatly dumbfound Americans of a century ago and even surprise those who had reached their mature years by midcentury. Of course, none of this change happened by chance. It was a product of new political attitudes, constitutional amendments, congressional legislation, and Supreme Court decisions. Moreover, a by-product of this transformation is that the judiciary now has the last word on most major aspects of the electoral process across the nation (Hasen 2003).

Though significant, the uniformity that has been achieved is by no means complete. Elections in the United States are still conducted by state and local governments, not by the federal government, and no state's election laws are exactly like another's. Thus some variations that remain affect what the right to vote may mean *in practice* from state to state. Some of these concerns are the subject of this chapter. But we begin with representation, first introduced in the last chapter, and how that issue has continued to manifest itself in the context of race. In light of the fact that cases on the Supreme Court's docket reflect matters that divide and perplex Americans, it is well to remember that, for the foreseeable future, racially tinted voting rights disputes are likely to command much of the Supreme Court's time.

MAJORITY-MINORITY DISTRICTS: FROM THE THICKET INTO THE MORASS

The Supreme Court first engaged the issue of race and political boundaries in 1960. As Chapter Three explained, the Court found in *Gomillion v. Lightfoot* rampant evidence of a racial gerrymander. The bizarre redrawing of the corporate limits of Tuskegee, Alabama, "removed" nearly all black voters from the city and thereby violated the Fifteenth Amendment, even though there had been no literal denial of anyone's right to vote. Then, passage of the Voting Rights Act in 1965 made it virtually certain that racially tinged examples of political cartography would remain a fixture on the Court's docket. This was true because of Sections 2 and, especially, 5. Recall from the previous chapter that the purpose of the 1965 statute was to prohibit both direct and indirect obstacles to voting by minorities, whether in the form of literacy or good character tests that worked to keep blacks off the registration rolls or in the form of institutional arrangements that undercut the political influence of racial minorities even when they were able to cast ballots.

As amended in 1982, Section 2, which applies in all parts of the nation, bars the adoption of any "voting qualification or prerequisite to voting, or standard, practice, or procedure . . . by any state or political subdivision in a manner which *results* in a denial or abridgement of the right of any citizen of the United States to vote on account of race or color" (emphasis added). Thus Section 2 applies to *existing* laws or arrangements that have a racially discriminatory effect on voting—specifically arrangements that result in a situation in which a protected minority group, in the language of Section 2, has "less opportunity than other members of the electorate to participate in the political process and to elect representatives of their choice."

Section 5 applies only to specific (or covered) jurisdictions, mainly in the South, that had a long history of racial discrimination in voting. In these states or parts of states, *changes* to voting procedures, including redistricting after each decennial census, must be approved in advance by the U.S. Department of Justice or the U.S. District Court for the District of Columbia, to make sure that the changes do "not have the purpose and will not have the effect of denying or abridging the right to vote on account of race or color." The purpose of this "pre-clearance" rule is to make sure that no change in election laws results in retrogression—that is, that no change leaves minority voters with less political influence than before.

If redistricting that reduces the political influence of minority voters violates the Voting Rights Act and the Fifteenth Amendment, what is the legal and constitutional status of districting plans designed to *enhance* minority voting influence? In other words, if districting with racially *invidious* effects is obviously un-acceptable, is districting with racially *ameliorative* effects nonetheless to be allowed?

The Supreme Court first addressed this question in *United Jewish Organizations v. Carey* (1977). The litigation grew out of the New York State legislature's redistricting of itself following the 1970 census. Three counties within New York City (Kings, New York, and Bronx) had been designated covered jurisdictions under Section 5 of the Voting Rights Act, and so the redistricting within them was subject to preclearance. The attorney general objected to redistricting of senate and assembly seats in Kings County (Brooklyn) in the original 1972 plan, and the state sub-mitted a revised plan in 1974. Under the 1972 plan, Kings County had three state senate districts with nonwhite majorities, in per-centage of approximately 91, 61, and 53. Under the revised 1974 plan, there were again three districts with nonwhite majorities, but the three were between 70 and 75 percent nonwhite. As for state assembly districts, both the 1972 and the 1974 plans pro-vided for seven districts with nonwhite majorities. However, un-der the 1972 plan, there were four that ranged between 85 and 95 percent nonwhite, and three with approximately 76, 61, and 52 percent. Under the 1974 plan, the two smallest nonwhite majori-ties were increased to 65 percent and 67.5 percent, and the two largest nonwhite majorities were decreased from greater than 90 percent to between 80 and 90 percent. Thus the overall effect was to create more districts with a substantial nonwhite population. This was deemed desirable because nonwhite voter turnout was usually lower than white voter turnout. A substantial majority of nonwhite voters, therefore, would be needed in a district for nonwhite voters to prevail at the polls in electing someone of their choice.

These 1974 adjustments, however, impacted the Williamsburgh area, where about 30,000 Hasidic Jews lived. Under the 1972 plan, the Hasidic community was located entirely in one assembly district (61 percent nonwhite) and one senate district (37 percent nonwhite). In order to achieve the objectives of the 1974 plan, the Hasidic community was split between two senate and two assembly districts. Hasidic Jews then claimed that, because they had been assigned to electoral districts on the basis of race, the plan violated the Fourteenth and Fifteenth Amendments by diluting their voting influence.

With only one dissenting vote (and with one justice not taking part) the Supreme Court upheld the 1974 plan. Although the case yielded no single opinion that in its entirety commanded the support of a majority of the bench, Justice White's plurality opinion explained that no constitutional violation had occurred and that the 1974 redistricting was appropriate under Section 5 of the Voting Rights Act.

[T]he Constitution does not prevent a State subject to the Voting Rights Act from deliberately creating or preserving black majorities in particular districts in order to ensure that its reapportionment plan complies with § 5.... New York's revision of certain district lines is little different in kind from the decision by a State in which a racial minority is unable to elect representatives from multimember districts to change to single-member districting for the purpose of increasing minority representation. This change might substantially increase minority representation at the expense of white voters, who previously elected all of the legislators but who with single-member districts could elect no more than their proportional share.

Also important to the outcome of the case were the facts that Hasidic Jews were not a protected minority under the Voting Rights Act and that the plan retained white majorities in 70 percent of the senate and assembly districts, even though the white population of Kings County was but 65 percent. Thus the decision in *United Jewish Organizations (UJO)* came to stand for the proposition that, in designing a plan of representation, the Constitution permitted race-based districting to enhance the voting influence of certain racial minorities.

Or so it appeared when the North Carolina legislature redrew districts for the U.S. House of Representatives after the 1990 census. As a result of increased population, the state was now entitled to a twelfth congressional seat. Particularly because no African American had represented North Carolina in Congress since 1901, state legislators recognized from the outset of the redistricting process that the new boundaries would have to include one majority-minority district. Yet, when the state submitted its plan in 1991 to the Justice Department for preclearance as required by Section 5 of the Voting Rights Act, officials in Washington insisted that approval was contingent on there being two such districts. The expectation should not have come as a surprise, for a Supreme Court decision in 1986 on multimember state legislative districts in North Carolina had looked favorably on greater political empowerment for racial minorities (*Thornburg v. Gingles*).

From the state's perspective, however, the Justice Department's goal was more easily set than met. Unlike the densely populated minority neighborhoods that had made it relatively easy for the New York legislature in *UJO* to create several state senate and assembly districts containing a substantial majority of minority voters, blacks in North Carolina were dispersed across many counties in the state, not overwhelmingly concentrated in one or two compact regions. Drawing a second majority-minority district would either endanger a senior Democratic incumbent (and Democrats controlled the North Carolina legislature) or, because of the dispersed nature of the minority population, pose a serious cartographical challenge. To win the Justice Department's approval, legislators chose to confront the latter. And so was born several rounds of litigation that not only stretched over a decade, but consumed the energies, attention, and time of eleven different Supreme Court justices, a phalanx of federal judges, numerous decent and highly principled litigants and attorneys on both sides, both major political parties, and several hundred North Carolina state legislators. The outcomes of this flurry of activity included new constitutional standards on race and representation that in turn begat litigation in other states (Yarbrough 2002).

As shown in Figure 4.1, legislators crafted Districts 1 and 12 to contain a majority of African American voters. Neither district was a model of compactness. The *Wall Street Journal* compared District 1 to a "bug splattered on a windshield." A federal district judge involved in the first round of the legal challenges to the plan likened it to a "Rorschach ink-blot test." Referring to District 12, which snaked along the Interstate 85 corridor between Durham and Charlotte, one state legislator critically observed that "if you drove down [Interstate 85] with both car doors open, you'd kill most of the people in the district" (Yarbrough 2002, 21). Indeed, in some places, in a heroic effect to maintain contiguity among black residential areas, the district was no wider than the interstate highway itself.

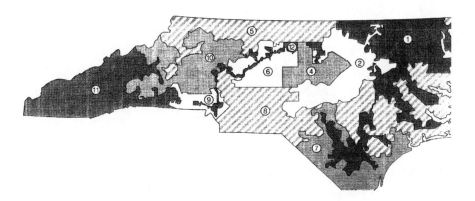

Figure 4.1 North Carolina Congressional Districting Plan Contested in *Shaw v. Reno*

Shaw v. Reno (*Shaw I*) was the Supreme Court's first decision on the North Carolina majority-minority districts. This five-to-four ruling in 1993 was significant because it established for the first time a cause of action—in effect, a new constitutional right—under the Fourteenth Amendment. According to *Shaw,* individuals, regardless of race, have a right to live in a district that has not been drawn primarily for racial reasons—regardless of whether the intent is ameliorative, benign, or invidious. "[A] plaintiff challenging a reapportionment statute under the Equal Protection Clause," explained Justice O'Connor, "may state a claim by alleging that the legislation, though race-neutral on its face, rationally cannot be understood as anything other than an effort to separate voters into different districts on the basis of race, and that the separation lacks sufficient justification." The 1977 decision in *UJO* was not controlling: members of the Hasidic community "did not allege that the [New York] plan, on its face, was so highly irregular that it rationally could be understood only as an effort to segregate voters by race." *Shaw I,* however, did not decide whether the two districts at issue were constitutionally invalid. That determination was left to the trial court, which, on remand, ruled in 1994 that both contested districts conformed with the Voting Rights Act and were a modest, long-overdue measure of power sharing.

Before the district court's validation of North Carolina's districts returned to the Supreme Court, however, a similar and seminal case from Georgia—*Miller v. Johnson* (1995)—had been decided. In 1972, Georgia elected its first African American to the U.S. House of Representatives since Reconstruction, and redistricting after the 1980 census created the state's first majority-minority district. Under the 1990 census, Georgia's population (27 percent of which was black) entitled the state to an additional seat, its eleventh, in Congress. The state's General Assembly approved a districting plan that contained three majority-minority districts after the Justice Department refused to preclear, under Section 5 of the Voting Rights Act, two earlier plans that each contained only two majority-black districts. (Note that 3/11 is approximately 27 percent.) Elections held in November 1992 resulted in the election of black representatives from all three majority-minority districts (Districts 2, 5, and 11).

In 1994, five white voters in the new District 11 (see Figure 4.2) challenged the constitutionality of their district on the ground that it was a racial gerrymander in violation of the equal protection clause as interpreted in *Shaw v. Reno* (1993). District 11 meandered from the rural and impoverished outskirts of Savannah on the coast to the tony suburbs of Atlanta, nearly 200 miles away. A three-judge panel of the U.S. District Court for the Southern District of Georgia agreed, holding that the state legislature's purpose, as well as the district's irregular borders, showed that race was the overriding and predominant factor in the districting determination. (U.S. district judges ordinarily hear cases sitting individually. In voting rights disputes, however, the bench consists of three district judges, and on appeal the case moves directly to the Supreme Court, bypassing the respective court of appeals.) The Supreme Court agreed, five to four. "The congressional plan challenged here," declared Justice Kennedy for the majority, "was not required by the Voting Rights Act under a correct reading of the statute." Because increasing the number of majority-minority districts from one to two (as the state had originally proposed) would hardly violate the nonretrogression principle of Section 5, there was no compelling reason to resort to cartographical contortions to construct a third. Because District 11 could not fairly be explained on any basis other than race, it was unconstitutional. Race was not to be the predominant factor in designing a district. Thus *Miller* cut into the "great potential" of the Voting Rights Act "for leveling the playing field between majority and minority interests" (Hench 1998, 749).

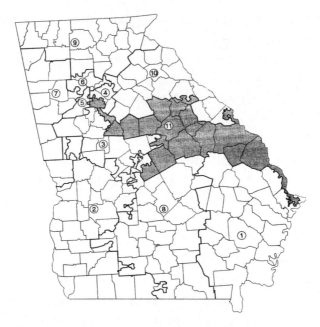

Figure 4.2   The Georgia Congressional Districting Plan Contested in *Miller v. Johnson*

Following the Supreme Court's decision in *Johnson,* the Georgia legislature did not reach agreement on a revised plan by the October 15, 1995, deadline imposed by the district court. The district court then itself redrew the boundaries of the state's eleven congressional districts, leaving only the one majority-minority district (District 5), which roughly corresponded to the district that had been created after the 1980 census around the city of Atlanta. In the November 1996 elections, the black incumbents who had represented the formerly majority-minority Districts 2 and 11 won reelection to the U.S. House of Representatives, as did the incumbent from the surviving majority-minority district, happily indicating, contrary to the conventional wisdom, that many white voters, even southern white voters, do not necessarily turn their backs on nonwhite candidates. In 1997, the Supreme Court upheld the districting plan used in the 1996 elections (*Abrams v. Johnson*).

Bush v. Vera (1996) reinforced *Miller.* Because the 1990 census entitled Texas to three additional congressional seats, and in an attempt to comply with the Voting Rights Act, the Texas Legislature adopted a redistricting plan that, among other things, created District 30 as a new majority African American district in Dallas County and District 29 as a new majority Hispanic district in Harris County, and reconfigured District 18, which was adjacent to District 29, as a majority African American district. After the Department of Justice precleared the plan under Section 5, six Texas voters filed suit claiming that the three districts constituted racial gerrymanders in violation of the Fourteenth Amendment. Although the Supreme Court was unable to agree on a single statement of the law, a majority affirmed the trial court's decision that the districts violated the Constitution. "Our Fourteenth Amendment jurisprudence," wrote Justice O'Connor, "evinces a commitment to eliminate unnecessary and excessive governmental use and reinforcement of racial stereotypes." In other words, race-based districting rested on a premise that the Court did not want to countenance: that persons of a certain race ordinarily voted only for candidates with whom they shared a racial identity.

Meanwhile, the North Carolina litigation, *Shaw v. Hunt* (*Shaw II*), had returned to the Supreme Court. In this 1996 decision, District 1 survived because the plaintiffs had moved elsewhere and so lacked standing to press the suit. District 12, however, was deemed to be a predominantly racial gerrymander that was not narrowly tailored to serve a compelling state interest. After the state legislature went back to work to produce a constitutionally acceptable twelfth district, their handiwork was challenged again. After a round of preliminary skirmishes, the drawing of yet another twelfth district, and a Supreme Court-mandated trial in the district court, five justices voted in 2001 to accept the 1997 plan (*Hunt v. Cromartie*, 2001). They accepted the district court's conclusion that the new District 12 was a predominantly *partisan,* not mainly a *racial,* gerrymander. That is, the compression of black voters within a single district was done not because the voters were black voters but because they were highly reliable Democratic voters. Therefore, under the far more relaxed standard that applied to the partisan gerrymanders under *Davis v. Bandemer,* as discussed in Chapter Three, there was no constitutional violation. Aside from the decision's resolution of North Carolina's strung-out redistricting war, *Cromartie* is significant. Although "predominantly racial" gerrymandering is forbidden, not all consideration of race in the redistricting process is prohibited. If *Cromartie* can be read to allow party preference to be a proxy for race, then the decision may suggest somewhat less frequent judicial intrusions into the politics of race-based districting.

The decade of redistricting confusion in North Carolina also demonstrated that the packing or compression of African Americans into a few districts in southern states invariably confounds partisan politics. Whites in the South in recent decades have tended to vote Republican, especially in elections for national office. (In the 2000 presidential election, for example, Democratic presidential candidate Al Gore carried not a single southern state, not even his home state of Tennessee.) Because African Americans are the most reliable Democratic voters, the presence of majority-minority districts increases the chances of Republican victories in the remaining districts of a state. Many blacks support such districts for the obvious reason that they enable more blacks to be elected or at least to determine who will be elected. Indeed, while initially suspicious of districting that was purposefully not "color blind," blacks, particularly those who are politically aware and active, now favor them in substantial numbers (Tate 2003, 52–53). At the same time, many white Democrats oppose them because they may result in the election of fewer Democrats overall because black (Democratic) voters have been packed into a small number of districts. Indeed, the Republican Party's strength in the U.S.

House of Representatives and in some southern state legislatures during the past decade is partly due to this effect of majority-minority districts on electoral outcomes. Ironically, based on their pre-Court partisan affiliations, justices of the Supreme Court typically take counterintuitive positions. Justices inclined to favor policies ordinarily supported by Democrats find no quarrel with majority-minority districts; Republican-inclined justices usually do.

These dynamics were illustrated by *Georgia v. Ashcroft* (2003), another five-to-four ruling. Following the 2000 census, the Georgia legislature redistricted itself and submitted the plan to the Department of Justice for preclearance under Section 5 of the Voting Rights Act. Significantly, the plan had been supported by both black and white Democrats and opposed by Republicans, meaning that black support was essential for passage. A problematical feature of the plan, however, was the "unpacking" of three existing majority-minority senatorial districts, so that each contained only a bare majority of blacks of voting age as opposed to a substantial majority. The percentage of black voters in District 2 dropped from 60.6 to 50.3, from 55.4 to 50.7 in District 12, and from 62.4 to 50.8 in District 26. Moreover, with the change, the percentage of blacks registered to vote in the three districts was actually under 50 percent. The state maintained that, even though black voters might not necessarily be able to dominate elections in those particular districts, their influence would be greater in a larger number of districts. Thus in place of some minority districts with heavy black majorities were some additional "influence" or "coalitional" districts. With influence districts, lines are drawn to achieve a sizeable minority population across a range of districts, thereby providing notable, if not decisive, influence to produce an increase in the number of legislators sympathetic to the interests of minority voters. Similarly, with coalitional districts, lines are drawn to include predictably supportive nonminority voters.

Yet both the Justice Department and the U.S. district court concluded that the plan violated Section 5 because the unpacking amounted to retrogression. A bare majority of the Supreme Court disagreed. "The ability of minority voters to elect a candidate of their choice is important," explained Justice O'Connor, "but often complex in practice to determine." A statewide perspective was essential "[W]hile the diminution of a minority group's effective exercise of the electoral franchise in one or two districts may be sufficient to show a violation of § 5, it is only sufficient if the covered jurisdiction cannot show that the gains in the plan as a whole offset the loss in a particular district." Thus any reviewing court must engage in a thorough review of the political realities of the state. Under Section 5, a state may "choose to create a certain number of 'safe' districts, in which it is highly likely that minority voters" will prevail. "Alternatively, a State may choose to create a greater number of districts in which it is likely—although perhaps not quite as likely . . .—that minority voters will be able to elect candidates of their choice." Either approach can be acceptable under Section 5.

Georgia v. Ashcroft also illustrated the tension between Section 2 and Section 5 of the Voting Rights Act, at least as construed by the Court (Pildes 2002). A covered jurisdiction may violate the retrogression principle of Section 5 without violating the strictures of Section 2. Likewise, a covered jurisdiction may violate Section 2 while conforming to Section 5. Moreover, actions that go beyond what Section 5 requires may themselves violate the Fourteenth Amendment. As Justice Kennedy's concurring opinion in the Georgia case observed, "[r]ace cannot be the predominant factor in redistricting under our decision in *Miller v. Johnson.* Yet considerations of race that would doom a redistricting plan under the Fourteenth Amendment or § 2 seem to be what save it under § 5."

The case also illustrates the complexities of representation itself. As noted in the last chapter, assuring "fair" or "equal" representa tion involves much more than the "one person, one vote" standard (that is, making sure that districts contain the same number of people). Under a system of single-member districts, an identifiable group might make up, say, 25 percent of the population of a state. Yet if that group is also an equally small minority in every district, members of that group are much less likely to be "represented" in the sense of being able to control or decisively to influence the outcome of an election. Construction of districts containing a majority of minority voters thus gives them an opportunity, which they otherwise might not have, to dictate the results of an election. Except in situations where large numbers of minority voters live in a defined region—in which case ordinary districting principles of compactness and contiguity could yield a majority-minority district—such districts may validly be configured far more easily in a jurisdiction covered by Section 5 than in one that is not.

An alternative to majority-minority districts is a system of multimember districts combined with weighted voting. As explained in Chapter Three, as multimember districts have usually worked in the United States, the dominant group within the district picks the winners. Weighted voting in a district that has, say, five representatives would give each voter five votes. A voter could cast one vote for a candidate for each of the five positions, or could cast as many as five votes for a single candidate. In this way, a racial minority of perhaps 25 percent in a district would still be able to elect a candidate of its choice (Guinier 1994).

Still another alternative that, like weighted voting, might enhance minority representation (and also encourage the growth of third parties) is the single transferable vote (STV). It operates like an instant runoff election. Voters rank all candidates for a particular office, from their first choice to, say, their fourth choice. After first choice votes are tabulated, the last-place candidate is eliminated. But second-choice votes for the eliminated candidate are then distributed to the remaining candidates. Then the next-to-last-place candidate is dropped, and her or his second-choice votes are distributed, and so on. When there are but two candidates still standing, so to speak, the one with a majority of votes is the winner. Thus voters can cast a first-choice vote for a "long shot" candidate without believing that they are throwing their votes away or believing that their votes do not "count" (Abramowitz 2004, 43; Rush and Engstrom 2001).

Nonetheless, for the foreseeable future American electoral politics will continue to rely on the single-member plurality district. The candidate with the most votes wins. Representation thus becomes a function of the composition of the district itself. It is to a district's composition and its effects that the Supreme Court has so frequently addressed itself in recent years. Many of these cases were decided five votes to four. Thus even small changes in the composition of the Court itself over the next few years may greatly shape the future of majority-minority districts.

PARTISAN GERRYMANDERING REVISITED

The Court's wariness of racial gerrymanders, whether invidious or ameliorative, has not carried over to partisan gerrymanders. As Chapter Three explained, six justices (White, Brennan, Marshall, Blackmun, Stevens, and Powell) ruled in *Davis v. Bandemer* (1986) that issues of partisan gerrymandering were justiciable—that is, they did not fall into the category "political questions" and so remained within judicial bounds. But no majority coalesced around a standard for determining when partisan gerrymanders violated the Fourteenth Amendment's equal protection clause. For Justices White, Brennan, Marshall, and Blackmun, an alleged gerrymander violated the Constitution if the "electoral system is arranged in a manner that will consistently degrade a voter's or a group of voters' influence on the political process as a whole." For Justices Stevens and Powell, something approaching proportionality was essential: "[D]istrict lines should be determined in accordance with neutral and legitimate criteria. When deciding where those lines will fall, the state should treat its voters as standing in the same position, regardless of their political beliefs or party affiliation." The plurality standard in *Bandemer* turned out to mean little in practice. Federal courts applying it against alleged gerrymanders set the bar so high that few plaintiffs could satisfy the burden of proof. Because no one believed that *Bandemer* had outlawed *all* partisan influences, the question became one of deciding how much partisanship was *too* much.

So the situation stood until the Pennsylvania legislature was faced with redistricting the state's congressional districts following the 2000 census. The task was made more complicated because the reapportionment of the House of Representatives had cost Pennsylvania two seats, as the state dropped from twenty-one to nineteen representatives. Under the districting plan in place after the 1990 census, the 2000 elections had awarded eleven seats to the Republicans and ten to the Democrats. When the nineteen seats were filled in the November 2002 elections, Republicans won twelve and Democrats just seven. The results only strengthened the insistence by Democrats that Republicans, who held a majority in both houses of the state legislature and controlled the governorship when the post-2000 plan was adopted, of an unconstitutional gerrymander.

After the U.S. District Court for the Middle District of Pennsylvania denied relief, the Supreme Court ruled against the challengers in 2004 (*Vieth v. Jubelirer*). As in *Bandemer*, the Court was again unable to agree on a majority opinion, but this time there were four votes declaring that *Bandemer* had been wrongly decided. Partisan gerrymanders presented a nonjusticiable political question because of a lack of any judicially manageable standards for determining when a violation had occurred. This quartet included Chief Justice Rehnquist and Justice O'Connor who remained consistent with their position in the 1986 case. Justice Kennedy provided the fifth vote for dismissing the Democratic challenge. He agreed that no judicially manageable standards *currently* existed, but refused to rule out the possibility that some might be devised in the future, at which time the Court might be able to adjudicate a partisan gerrymander case in an intelligible fashion. Of the remaining four justices, only Justice Stevens had been on the Court when *Bandemer* was decided. He and Justices Souter, Ginsburg, and Breyer believed that proper standards did exist, although they could not agree among themselves as to what those standards should be.

Indeed a close look at a state's political landscape may demonstrate just how difficult it can be to determine the degree to which a districting plan has penalized a particular political group. Complicating matters is the fact that voters do not always vote according to party registration or preference. In Pennsylvania during the past several decades, for example, Democrats have held a voter registration lead over Republicans of about a half million, sometimes a little more and sometimes a little less. Yet Democrats have not dominated statewide elections. Between 1968 and 2004, both U.S. senators from Pennsylvania were Republican, except for one Democrat who served a partial term between 1991 and 1994. In presidential elections in the past twenty-four years, Republican candidates carried the state in 1980, 1984, and 1988, but Democrats carried the state in 1992, 1996, and 2000. The governorship has alternated between parties, usually every eight years, with Republicans controlling the state legislature in recent years.

What does the Court's decision in *Vieth* mean for future redistricting in other states, as well as in Pennsylvania? If the Court's position on partisan gerrymander remains firm—a big "if" considering the fact that some changes in the Court's personnel are very likely in the near term—the prospects are that *Vieth* will be read as countenancing "anything goes." Justice Kennedy's reservation of course leaves open the possibility for future judicial intervention in the face of a record showing that a legislative majority had truly run amok. Yet, the fact that no more than two justices in the minority were able to agree on a standard suggests that, at most, all the Court might be able to say in some future litigation would be that a plan was unacceptable without being unable to explain why. Therefore, should the Court later decide to reenter this corner of the political thicket, a formidable amount of work would have to be done. Moreover, if a judicial hands-off policy applies to partisan gerrymandering of congressional districts, presumably it would also apply to partisan gerrymandering of state legislative districts. Therefore, it will become all the more critical in each state as to whether one party or another is dominant immediately following the census in 2010.

At the same time, *Vieth* applies only to adjudications under the U.S. Constitution. Nothing in the decision prevents state courts from applying state statutes or constitutions to erect their own barriers against gerrymandering, at least in the context of state legislative districts. Moreover, Congress certainly has authority to intervene into the arena of districting of its own body by virtue of its powers under Article I, Section 4.

"MOTOR VOTER":
ENLARGING THE ELECTORATE

As should be apparent by now, the act of voting entails more than deciding for whom to vote and then casting a ballot. There are two key preliminary steps that must also be taken. One is deciding whether to vote at all. But even prior to waking up on election day and making a decision *to* vote, one ordinarily must previously have registered to vote. Only in a handful of places in the country has anything like "walk-up registration" been tried, whereby registration and voting occur at the same place on the same day. For everyone else, without prior registration an otherwise eligible person may not vote no matter how motivated and energized she or he might be on election day. Some even attribute the decline in voter turnout in recent decades to obstacles in registration, although accounting for diminishing turnout is undoubtedly more complex than that: in 1960, for example, when such things as registration and residency requirements posed greater hurdles to voting than they do today, turnout was substantially higher. Nonetheless it makes sense to conclude that part of the task of "getting out the vote" is to ensure that the pool of registered voters is generally coterminous with the pool of those who *could* be registered. Otherwise eligible unregistered citizens remain nonvoters for as long as they remain unregistered.

Such concerns prompted Congress in the late 1980s to consider legislation to boost registration across the nation, but President George H. W. Bush vetoed such a measure in 1991. The bill required states to allow eligible citizens to register to vote at the same time they applied for or renewed a driver's license, to permit mail-in registration, and to provide voter registration services at various public assistance agencies and military recruitment offices. Fearing openings for fraud and possible coercion, Republicans generally opposed the bill. Taking office in 1993, the Clinton administration made the so-called motor voter bill a priority, and the president signed it into law on May 20. "Voting is an empty promise unless people vote," Clinton said. "Now there is no longer the excuse of the difficulty of registration" ("'Motor Voter'" 1994, 199).

As expected, the National Voter Registration Act (NVRA) swelled the voter registration rolls, with 11.2 million people registering to vote or updating their registration information in the first year alone. By 1998, data provided by the Federal Election Commission on its website (www.fec.gov) indicated that states counted a total of 140,946,508 registered voters, or 70.15 percent of the voting age population—the highest percentage of voter registration since 1970. By 2000, the registration rolls totaled 149,476,705 individuals, about 73 percent of the voting age population. Being registered to vote, however, by no means assures that one will vote. Despite this swelling of the rolls, actual voter turnout has remained relatively flat. Judged against the voting age population, turnout has hovered around 50 percent in the past three presidential elections, and remains well below that in midterm congressional and off-year state elections. Thus, with registration having been made substantially simpler and more convenient by the NVRA, the task in the twenty-first century remains one of energizing the electorate, encouraging a greater sense of civic duty and voter efficacy, and, as addressed below, making the act of voting itself more accurate and less complex.

BUSH V. GORE: COUNTING THE VOTES

Most adults in the United States today surely remember something about the contested presidential election of 2000. Florida became a battleground after November 7, Election Day, even though all agreed that, nationally, Democratic presidential candidate Albert Gore had a lead in the popular vote total of several hundred thousand over Republican candidate George W. Bush. But that national margin made no difference. As matters stood early on the morning of November 8, Gore was sure of 267 electoral votes, and Bush could rightly claim 246. But winning the presidency requires a minimum of 270 electoral votes. What was now to be dispositive was the popular vote in Florida, because the vote count in Florida would determine whether Florida's 25 electoral votes would be awarded to Bush or to Gore. And the candidate receiving those electoral votes would become the forty-third president.

The controversy that ensued over the next several weeks did not arise because citizens lacked the franchise, although some prospective voters did claim that they were turned away from the polls because registration lists had been purged. (Many states periodically purge the registration rolls of inactive voters to guard against a kind of fraud sometimes called the "graveyard vote.") Thus the problem in Florida was not one of *who* could vote. Rather the problem was one of *how* the ballots of those who did vote would be counted, or indeed, whether some would be counted at all. Some ballots could not be read by the machines because some voters who used punch cards did not completely puncture the card, or, if they did, left a piece of paper (a chad) dangling, or left only an impression. These were the so-called "undervotes," and were not counted. Similarly excluded were a smaller number of "overvotes." These occurred when ballots were marked or partially marked for more than one presidential candidate (and nine presidential candidates had qualified for the ballot in Florida). Similar problems had arisen at other times in Florida, but the margins were not as close and the stakes were not as high. Trailing by only 537 votes (out of about 6 million cast) after the legally mandated machine recount, Gore wanted those uncounted ballots read by hand, as allowed by law. Bush feared that any hand count to determine the intention of the voter would inject enough subjectivity into the process to cost him the election. (Although a machine recount discounts many more oddly marked ballots than would a hand recount in determining "intent," it makes no difference to the machine whether a voter "seemed" to vote Democrat or Republican. What matters is whether the ballot is machine readable.)

The U.S. Supreme Court first stopped a hand recount ordered by the Florida Supreme Court and then ruled in *Bush v. Gore* (2000) that hand counting could not proceed without uniform standards to determine the intent of the voter. With voting by the Electoral College just days away, five justices concluded that no constitutionally acceptable hand counting was possible. Otherwise, citing the legislative districting cases (discussed in the last chapter), they reasoned that one person's ballot might be treated differently from another's, thus violating the equal protection clause of the Fourteenth Amendment. This unprecedented decision was noteworthy even beyond the energizing "we-wuz-robbed" effect it had on Democrats in the election of 2004.

First, the Court's intervention in the election of 2000 was only the latest demonstration of the role it can play in the political life of the nation. Between the end of the Civil War in 1865 and 2000, the United States confronted three constitutional crises: (1) the disputed presidential election of 1876; (2) the Court-packing controversy of 1937; and, (3) the Watergate affair of 1972–1974. In each one, justices of the Supreme Court were key players.

In 1974, the Supreme Court virtually dictated President Richard M. Nixon's departure from office, the only instance in American history when a president has stepped down during his term. Its decision in *United States v. Nixon* ordered the president, against a claim of executive privilege, to hand over certain documents and sound recordings to a court in the District of Columbia for use as evidence. The documents and recordings in turn amounted to the proverbial "smoking gun" that revealed the president's complicity in a two-year-long coverup of illegality. The president thus had a choice between vacating the White House voluntarily or facing certain impeachment by the House of Representatives and near-certain conviction, and therefore removal from office, by the Senate.

In 1937, by contrast, the judiciary was on the presidential griddle. It was the Court's own unprecedented obstinacy during 1935 and 1936 in reaction to major economic reforms in the midst of the Great Depression that prompted President Franklin D. Roosevelt's equally unprecedented assault on the structure and composition of the Supreme Court. FDR lost the Court-packing battle, but, because he quickly secured an administration-friendly bench, he won the war.

The justices were also involved in resolving the disputed election of 1876, as Chapter Two explained. The difference was that, in this crisis, the Court institutionally was not a participant. No decision rendered by the highest court in the land decided that election. Instead, the Court was indirectly entangled because five of its nine justices accepted appointment as members of a fifteen-person commission established by Congress to resolve disputes over contested returns. Democratic candidate Samuel Tilden had a comfortable edge in the popular vote over Republican candidate Rutherford B. Hayes. In doubt were twenty electoral votes from Florida, Louisiana, Oregon, and South Carolina. Tilden needed only one additional electoral vote added to his tally in order to claim victory. Hayes needed all twenty. The special electoral commission handed all twenty to Hayes.

Nor was the election of 2000 the first time in American history that the elections had left the identity of the next president in doubt. It was the fourth. In addition to the crisis of 1876, there were two others. They arose in 1800 and 1824 when no candidate received a majority of electoral votes, as Article II of the Constitution requires. As a result, the House of Representatives elected the president on those occasions.

Second, *Bush v. Gore* was noteworthy because the Supreme Court thrust itself into the center of controversy. Aside from the fact that, as would be expected, Republicans defended the Court and Democrats called the decision an outrage, numerous articles and books appeared in print within the next eighteen months probing the question whether the High Court should have intervened at all. "In a country committed to electoral democracy, was it illegitimate for unelected justices for life to decide the election? Did the Court overstep its institutional role and preempt the authority of Congress or a state court" (Schultz 2002, 366)? Nonetheless, a systematic study based on data collected one year after the decision showed that the Court had weathered the partisan and scholarly storm it stirred up rather well. There was little evidence that the Court itself had sustained institutional damage in terms of a diminution in its legitimacy among the American people (Gibson, Caldeira, and Spence 2002, 20–21).

Third, because of the equal protection standards the Court applied in the Florida case, *Bush v. Gore* portends an increased oversight role for the federal judiciary in election controversies.

Fourth, and probably most important for the long-term, *Bush v. Gore* focused unprecedented attention on voting procedures and the administration of elections—how votes are cast and tabulated. For the first time, the medium through which voters express their preferences became a salient national issue. After all, having the right to vote means nothing if one's vote literally goes uncounted or if a particular balloting medium so confuses a voter that the choice recorded is not the choice intended.

In the wake of *Bush v. Gore,* it became painfully obvious that ballot confusion was not merely a Florida problem, but a national one. Election officials and students of voting have long known that there is hardly an election in any state without irregularities or problems of some sort. These range from confusing ballots and overcrowded and understaffed polling places to equipment malfunctions, registration mix-ups, and clerical errors. Indeed, one study estimated that in the 2000 election somewhere between 4 and 6 million votes were "lost" through a combination of such difficulties. That number is equivalent to about 5 percent of the total votes in the election that were actually counted (Gugliotta 2001, A-1).

Although problem-free elections in a country as large as the United States may be an impossibility (there are some 200,000 polling places in the nation), two realities of voting in America increase the chances that voting irregularities will occur and that when they occur they will be managed in different ways: partisanship and decentralization (Abramowitz 2004, 48). In contrast to some other democratic nations, elections here are typically administered and overseen by officials who themselves attained office on a partisan ballot. At the center of the Florida recount, for example, was Katherine Harris, a Republican who as the Florida secretary of state had the responsibility of certifying the results of the election as "official." She was also cochair of the Bush campaign in the Sunshine State. It is no criticism of her to say that, had a Democrat been secretary of state, some decisions might have been made differently. Even the Florida Supreme Court that ordered the hand recount consisted of jurists who had been elected on partisan ballots. Most of them were Democrats. It is no criticism of them to observe that had there been more Republican justices than Democratic ones, the United States Supreme Court might never have become entangled in the election at all because there might have been no dispute between Harris's call and the state's high court. Indeed, even though justices of the U.S. Supreme Court are not themselves elected, they are nominated by a president and confirmed by senators, all of whom are elected on partisan ballots.

Moreover, recall a fact emphasized repeatedly throughout this book that is of overriding importance: Except as modified by constitutional amendment, congressional statute, or Supreme Court decision, voting and elections in the United States are in the hands of state governments. Each state has its own election laws. Again in contrast to most other democratic countries, there have been no uniform national standards for voter registration records, voting equipment, or vote-counting procedures. In some places, instructions on marking ballots are clearly written and in other places not. Sometimes officials are on hand at the polls to explain how one is to cast a ballot or to answer other questions, and at other times not. Tables 4.1 and 4.2 illustrate the variety of media through which Americans have cast ballots in recent presidential elections.

Not only are there variations *among* the states but there are variations *within* some states. In states like Florida, for instance, important decisions about voting equipment, ballot design, and registration procedures were delegated to individual counties along with funding responsibilities. Such variations have consequences. In Florida counties using optical scanning equipment in the 2000 election, for example, ballots without a valid presidential vote totaled about 1 percent of all ballots cast. But in counties using punch-card machines, invalid ballots totaled as many as 6 percent of all ballots cast (Abramowitz 2004, 49). Moreover, some optical scanning equipment will alert a voter immediately to an error, thus allowing correction. The voter might mistakenly have

Table 4.1   Voting Equipment in Presidential Elections 1980–2004, as a Percent of Registered Voters

	1980	1988	1992	1996	2000	2004
Paper	11	6.5	4	2	2	1
Lever	43	31	28	21	16	12
Punch Card	31	41	40	36	31	19
Mixed	12.5	12	11	10	9	7
Optical	1.5	6.5	13	21	30	32
Electronic	1	3	4	10	12	29

Source: Election Data Services. Data for 2004 are estimates.

Table 4.2   Voting Equipment in Presidential Elections 1980–2004, as a Percent of Counties

	1980	1988	1992	1996	2000	2004
Paper	40.5	32	22.5	15	12	9
Lever	36.5	29	26	18	14	8.5
Punch card	18.5	25	26	24	19	10.5
Mixed	3	7	4	5	4	4
Optical	1	5	18.5	30	42	46
Electronic	0.5	2	3	8	9	22

Source: Election Data Services. Data for 2004 are estimates.

voted for two candidates for the same position or might have skipped candidates for a position entirely. And as happened in some areas of Florida in 2000 that used a poorly designed "butterfly ballot," some people mistakenly voted for third-party candidate Pat Buchanan without realizing it. With punch cards, there is no feedback at all. And there are further variations. Even in counties using punch-card machines, invalid ballots were far more likely to have been cast in precincts with concentrations of poor and minority voters than in precincts populated largely by white upper-middle-class voters. Why? Poorer voters tended to have both less education and less experience in voting and so had more difficulty understanding the ballot layout and in following directions. The oldest voters of all races encountered voting difficulties arising from various infirmities. In short, voters cast their ballots with the firm expectation that their votes would be counted, but, depending on equipment, there was no assurance that that would happen. Thus the dilapidated electoral machinery highlighted by the Florida recount controversy—with the resulting electoral train wreck—practically guaranteed that remedial legislation of some kind would be forthcoming eventually from Congress.

If 34 days elapsed between Election Day 2000 and the decision in *Bush v. Gore,* precisely 103 weeks separated Election Day from enactment of the Help America Vote Act (HAVA). Signed into law by President Bush on October 29, 2002, the statute is the most comprehensive voting rights legislation to be passed since the Voting Rights Act of 1965. The product of much partisan wrangling in Congress, it attempts to improve the administration of elections in the United States, primarily through three means: (1) creation of a new agency called the Election Assistance Commission; (2) authorization of funds to enable states to improve election administration and to replace outdated voting systems; and, (3) establishment of certain minimum standards for states to follow in several key areas of administering elections (Abramowitz 2004, 49–50). Combined, the various provisions of the law make significant inroads into the tradition of decentralization that has characterized American elections since the beginning of the Republic.

With only very limited formal rule-making authority, the Election Assistance Commission consists of four persons appointed by the president and confirmed by the Senate. (Because President Bush did not formalize nominations for the commission until October 2003, with the Senate confirming them in December 2003, the commission was late beginning its work.) Among other duties, it serves chiefly (1) to function as a clearinghouse of information on voting equipment; (2) to write voluntary guidelines for states in complying with new election standards; (3) to act as a conduit for annual grants to states; (4) to provide for testing and certification of voting hardware and software; and, (5) to conduct studies on election-related matters such as absentee voting, military and overseas voting, and voter registration by mail (Nather 2002, 2870).

The clearinghouse and testing roles may prove to be the most important, particularly because new electronic voting devices may themselves prove operationally problematical in addition to presenting security concerns. Some computer scientists claim that the systems leave elections vulnerable to hackers (or terrorists), while other critics say that because most electronic voting terminals do not produce paper records, there is no way to ensure accurate recounts. Moreover, with voting via the Internet now an option, other questions will have to be addressed. For example, Internet voting may mean only that the voters go to the polls and cast their votes on electronic machines that in turn transmit the votes to a central location over the Internet. Alternatively, Internet voting can encompass voting that is done remotely, from one's home or, literally, from any location on the planet with Internet access. Clearly security concerns, plus the possibility of voter intimidation, are a greater worry with the latter than with the former. Internet voting could also easily encompass a voting period of more than one day—an election "window" as opposed to a single election day. Moving more in that direction, however, would transgress the principle of temporality. If everyone but absentee voters casts ballots on a single day, all do so on the basis of the same information available at that time. "To the extent that voting takes place simultaneously, elections express the will of a determinate majority rather than the preferences of a series of different majorities" (Thompson 2004, 51).

The statute also provides nearly $3.9 billion over a three-year period to help states train election workers and to "buyout" outdated voting machines such as those using levers and punch cards.

These would be replaced by optical scanning or the newer electronic touch-screen devices. As of early 2004, however, only $650 million had been distributed to the states for this purpose. Because the economic downturn had already left many state governments financially strapped, replacement of older devices with newer and presumably better ones will take several additional years at least ("New Study Shows . . ." 2004, 2).

But the greatest change to be brought about by HAVA lies in the imposition of national standards for election administration. As a result of the "uniform and nondiscriminatory" requirements imposed by HAVA, states must: (1) enable voters to check for and to correct errors on their ballots in a private and independent way; (2) provide a provisional ballot to a voter whose eligibility is in doubt at the polls (such voters would be able to confirm later that their ballots were counted, or not); (3) maintain a uniform, centralized, and computerized statewide voter registration list, with a unique number assigned to each registered voter (upon notice, after a voter's failure to vote in two consecutive federal elections, states are permitted to remove a name from the list); (4) provide at least one voting machine in every precinct that enables disabled voters to cast ballots in a private and independent manner; (5) adopt a "uniform and nondiscriminatory" definition of what will be counted as a legal vote, depending on the voting device in use; (6) operate an election system with an error rate below a percentage to be established by the Election Assistance Commission; and (7) conform to the Voting Rights Act's mandate for multilingual accessibility at the polls (Nather 2002, 2871). As one example of the degree of change that will have to occur, consider these statistics on registration records for the 2000 elections: according to the Federal Election Commission, only ten states had real-time, online access to a centralized statewide voter database, and fifteen other states maintained no statewide registration database at all.

Because these are to be phased in by the states between 2004 and 2007 and because congressional appropriations have lagged, however, some voters in the 2004 elections found themselves voting under conditions practically identical to those in 2000 while other voters encountered major changes (Chapin 2004). Indeed, some states moved ahead on their own toward reform even before HAVA began to be implemented. Understandably sensitive to its newly acquired reputation as the "Recount State," Florida banned the use of punch-card election machines, but still allows a variety of other devices to be used, including paper ballots, optical-scanning and touch-screen units. Perhaps Georgia took the greatest leap, requiring all counties to employ identical touch-screen devices exclusively (Abramowitz 2004, 50).

The Help America Vote Act also puts in place antifraud protections and requires states receiving federal funds under the act to implement grievance procedures for those who believe they have not received treatment to which they are entitled under the statute. Although individuals may not file lawsuits under HAVA, the statute empowers the Justice Department to initiate litigation to compel states to comply with the "uniform and nondiscriminatory" requirements. The law also directs states to centralize absentee voting procedures for persons out of state, in the military, or otherwise living abroad and to provide data to the Election Assistance Commission on the number of applications received from such persons and the number of ballots distributed (Nather 2002, 2871).

Combined, HAVA's provisions portend major changes in election administration. Moreover, without the 2000 voting debacle in Florida or an imbroglio of similar magnitude, it is highly improbable that Congress would have been moved to act on electoral administration as it did in HAVA.

Nonetheless, some Americans have understandably continued to wonder which candidate—Bush or Gore—actually garnered the greater number of votes in Florida. The state's official certification gave Bush the narrowest of leads: 537 votes, meaning that a shift of only 269 votes toward Gore would have altered the outcome of the presidential election. A study sponsored by major news organizations during 2001 inspected some 175,000 ballots that were not included in Florida's certified tally. Of these 175,000, journalists detected as many as 23,799 potentially valid votes for Gore or for Bush. Had the U.S. Supreme Court allowed the hand recount ordered by the state supreme court to continue, the study concludes that Bush still would have carried Florida by a few hundred votes. If, however, the hand recount had proceeded under vote-counting rules on voter intention that were adopted in Florida after the election, Gore probably would have won, although by an even smaller margin. The study emphasized that hand recounts are reliable only if the standards for such recounts are clear and easily applicable to the all ballots at hand (McManus, Drogin, and O'Reilly 2001, A2). Remarkably, the uncertainty from the outset over who "really" prevailed appeared not to have adversely affected George W. Bush's claim on legitimacy to any appreciable degree among the general public. In the wake of the Supreme Court's decision in *Bush v. Gore,* the Gallup Poll organization sampled public opinion between December 15 and 17, asking this question: "Now that George W. Bush has been declared the winner and will be inaugurated next January, will you accept him as the legitimate president or not?" Some 83 percent said "yes," while 16 percent said "no" (Thompson 2002, 1).

With the Florida election crisis now securely embedded in American political history and lore, HAVA looks to the future by introducing a new way of looking at voting in the United States. It will take time to measure its impact fully, and there will be litigation for sure to clarify some of its provisions. But it is now doing for voting and elections across the United States something that no previous act of Congress has ever attempted.

CAPITAL ANOMALY

Consider an adult U.S. citizen who lives on Melrose Street in Chevy Chase, Maryland. Consider another adult U.S. citizen who lives in the Rosslyn section of Arlington County, Virginia. Both individuals are but a few minutes' walk from Washington, District of Columbia. The Maryland resident can easily enter the District by strolling a few blocks south on Connecticut Avenue; the Virginia resident can quickly reach the District by walking across Key Bridge that spans the Potomac River. Each of these individuals is completely enfranchised. The Maryland and Virginia residents are both eligible to vote for a representative in Congress and two United States senators, among other officials. Suppose, however, one of these individuals purchases a house, and takes up residence, about three miles away on Macomb Street, N.W., in Washington. By virtue of that relocation, the person is now completely disfranchised in Congress, because the nation's capital has no voting members of either the House of Representatives or the Senate. Thus the right to vote depends in this instance not on *who* a person is, but on *where* a person lives. Although residents of Washington must pay federal income, inheritance, gasoline, and social security taxes like everyone else, and meet other obligations of citizenship, the District of Columbia persists as a voting rights anomaly. Hence the District's slogan on the license plates it issues: "taxation without representation."

The origin of this situation lies in the Constitution itself. Article I, Section 8, Paragraph 17 empowers Congress to "exercise exclusive Legislation in all Cases whatsoever, over such District (not exceeding ten Miles square) as may, by Cession of particular States, and the acceptance of Congress, become the Seat of the Government of the United States." The purpose of setting aside a special federal district was to make sure that the seat of government would not be subject to the laws of any state and to reduce the probability that any single state would have undue influence on the operation of the national government. Virginia and Maryland soon ceded land to the national government, and the national capital moved from Philadelphia to the new city of Washington in 1800. (Virginia's land was ceded back to the state in 1846, so the present District of Columbia lies entirely in an area that once belonged to Maryland.) Presumably no one at the Constitutional Convention in 1787 gave any thought to the question of representation of persons who would reside in the new district and therefore lie outside the jurisdiction of any state. The Constitution apportioned representation for both the House and the Senate around the states, and around the states alone.

Initially this structure was not a problem, because after the District was created in 1790, residents continued to vote in congressional elections in Virginia or Maryland, depending on whether they lived on one side of the Potomac or the other, just as they always had. That option ended in 1801, however, when Congress set up a local government for the District. In 1878, because Washington had become heavily populated with African Americans, Congress removed all rights of local self-government. It was not until after 1974 that District residents were again able to vote for a mayor and members of a city council. During those ninety-six years, committees in the House and Senate were effectively the governing body for Washington, DC (Gordon 2004, A12). Even with the post-1974 changes in governance, Congress retains authority to rescind council actions. And a National Capital Service Area, which includes most of the major federal office buildings, remains under national control (Peltason 1988, 73).

Thanks to the growth of the national government during the New Deal and World War II eras, by the mid-twentieth century Washington was no longer the sleepy town it had been in the nineteenth century, when members of Congress, present annually for only a few months at most, were far more likely to live in boarding houses than to own residences. By 1960, it had become a major American city, with a population of 763,000, a number greater than the populations of ten of the fifty states. (But Washington remained, as President John F. Kennedy commented in 1961, "a city of Northern charm and Southern efficiency" [Platt 1989, 368].)

To address the apparent inequity in voting, Congress in the same year proposed the "D.C. Suffrage Amendment," which was ratified nine months later in March 1961 as the Twenty-third Amendment. (Tennessee was the only southern state voting to ratify.) The amendment extended the franchise to District residents in presidential elections only, authorizing residents to choose a number of electors equal to that of the least populous state, a stipulation then (and now) that entitles the District to three electoral votes. (Without that stipulation, the District's population would have entitled it to four electoral votes in the 1964 presidential election.) Ever since, at 100 percent, the District has been the most reliably Democratic voting jurisdiction in the United States. Even in 1984, when President Ronald Reagan carried forty-nine states in a landslide reelection, Walter Mondale, his Democratic opponent, received 85 percent of the District vote. Ironically, when the amendment was being considered in Congress, Republican leaders were dubious, suspecting (correctly, it turned out) that the amendment would routinely add three electoral votes to the Democratic column in presidential races. Republicans in the District, however, allayed their fears ("23rd Amendment" 1965, 1516).

Yet, because the Twenty-third Amendment addressed presidential elections only, District residents still lacked representation in Congress. A small step in that direction occurred in 1970, when Congress authorized the District to elect a delegate to the House of Representatives. Although that individual may participate in debates, she or he has no vote. Curiously, provision for a nonvoting House delegate had been part of the D.C. Suffrage Amendment in its original form, but it was dropped from what became the Twenty-third Amendment to assure approval by the House and to expedite ratification. As an example of another might-have-been, when the Kennedy administration submitted draft legislation in 1961 to implement the new amendment, it called for a minimum voting age of eighteen, but as enacted, presidential suffrage in the District adhered to the prevailing twenty-one-year-old rule ("23rd Amendment" 1965, 1516).

What the Twenty-third Amendment did not accomplish, and more, was addressed by a constitutional amendment that Democrats in Congress sent to the states in 1978 for ratification. For purposes of congressional representation, it would treat the District as if it were a state, including two senators. Republicans in Congress and many state legislators looked dimly on the idea. Republicans opposed it on partisan grounds, because with near certainty it would add permanently to Democratic strength in Congress itself. Others opposed it for more principled reasons. Although there was merit to giving the District voting representation in the House, on what grounds did a city deserve two senators as if it were a state? To be sure, in 1960 the District's population was greater than that of ten states, but since that time the District has been losing population in both relative and absolute terms. The 2000 census, for example, recorded a population of 572,000, a drop of nearly 200,000 from the 1960 figure. As such, the District was in a dead-heat race for last place when considered against the populations of the states. Only Wyoming, with 494,000, counted fewer souls. Moreover, by 2000, even among cities Washington was losing ground: as the twenty-third largest city, it was just ahead of Nashville, Tennessee, that had to share Tennessee's two senators with Memphis, Knoxville, and Chattanooga. Moreover, awarding two senators to the District would only further skew the population disparities within that body, making the Senate even less representative of the nation generally. And the District's land area of about 68 square miles adds up to only 1/23rd the size of Rhode Island, the smallest state. The arguments took their toll. By 1985, when the proposed amendment's own seven-year time limit for ratification expired, only sixteen states had approved it. No similar amendment has seriously advanced in Congress since that time.

Even before 1985, however, advocates of the District moved on a different front that would avoid the perilous route of constitutional amendment. District residents in a 1980 referendum voted in favor of statehood, and in 1982 a proposed constitution for the fifty-first state of "New Columbia" was sent to Congress. Only a small federal conclave would remain under the exclusive control of Congress, as required by Article I of the Constitution.

The statehood proposal was appealing because of its apparent simplicity. Congress may admit a state to the Union by way of ordinary legislation, passed by simple majority vote and the president's signature, as it had most recently done with respect to Alaska and Hawaii in 1959 (Peltason 1988, 118). Yet the arguments, partisan and otherwise, made against the proposed constitutional amendment applied with equal force to statehood. With Republicans in control of the Senate between 1981 and 1987, the statehood proposal received little attention. Even after Democrats regained control of both houses in Congress in 1987, little happened because Republican George H. W. Bush was president. Statehood hopes brightened when the 1992 elections left Democrats in charge of both branches, but District statehood was not a priority for the new Clinton administration. From 1995 through at least 2004, Republicans have held one or both houses of Congress, so the statehood movement has gone nowhere, regardless of the party controlling the White House. Still the issue of statehood for the District is one on which many Democrats and Republicans divide. When president, Bill Clinton made sure that "taxation without representation" was displayed on automobiles in the White House fleet; upon taking office in 2001, President George W. Bush had the slogan removed.

More than four decades after ratification of the Twenty-third Amendment, further enfranchisement remains stymied. What else might be done? One suggestion calls for a statute awarding the District a House seat. A second seat (presumably as safely Republican as the other seat would be safely Democratic) would be allocated mathematically to Utah (Gordon 2004, A12). That plan, however, seems to conflict with the Constitution's directive that Representatives be chosen "by the People of the several States."

A more ambitious plan would require a constitutional amendment that, first, would repeal the Twenty-third Amendment and, second, would count residents of the District *as if* they lived in Maryland: "For purposes of voting in federal elections and apportionment only, citizens of the District constituting the seat of government of the United States shall be regarded as being and counted as citizens of the state that ceded the land for such purpose, provided the Legislature of that state so agrees by ratifying this Amendment" (Gordon 2004, A12).

Were this proposal to be implemented, the addition of District citizens to Maryland's population for federal electoral purposes would, at present, entitle Maryland to one more seat in the House and to one more vote in the Electoral College. District residents would thus be able to vote for a voting member of the House as well as for Maryland's two senators. The proposal would have to jump the hurdles of any constitutional amendment but, by not awarding two senators to the District, would avoid the pitfalls that were fatal for the 1978 amendment and later statehood measures.

What are the chances that this solution, or something similar, might come to pass in the foreseeable future? The odds for federally enfranchising District residents still seem long. Recall that the Twenty-third Amendment itself, which was a first and so far the only significant step toward this objective, was born in an era of constitutional reform that was inspired by the civil rights movement. Between 1960 and 1971, four amendments became part of the Constitution, three of them having to do with voting rights. Such moments of constitutional change are rare. Second, enfranchising District citizens has not benefited from forces and factors that combined to enlarge the franchise on previous occasions. War and/or military service helped to remove property qualifications, enfranchise black males and later all women, and lower the minimum voting age. It is difficult to imagine a plausible scenario that would similarly bring District residents fully into the electorate. Nor would many representatives and senators probably benefit directly themselves by supporting such an amendment. Members of Congress are citizens of the states they represent and so already have the right to vote "back home." Even many congressional staff workers live in the Virginia and Maryland suburbs and may establish residency there if they choose. The fact that, compared to the suburban counties in Maryland and Virginia, the District's population is disproportionately both poor and African American suggests that its residents are unlikely themselves to have the leverage and resources to mount the kind of lobbying and public relations effort that might lead to success. Moreover, the 2000 census data for the District reveal a growing immigrant (and noncitizen) population. Nor do the "end game" and "critical mass" factors seem to apply to the District's situation as happened with respect to woman suffrage. Citizens of the District are surely the losers under the current arrangement, but, except for them, who gains if they are given congressional representation? The Democratic party would gain only one congressional seat, and that result might be insufficient to justify the expenditure of the political capital that is always required for successful amendments. One is left with the argument that fully enfranchising the District is "the right thing to do," but that argument, by itself, rarely succeeds in thrusting an issue into the congressional limelight and galvanizing the necessary support. Complete enfranchisement may be an admirable goal whose time is not yet here.

IMMIGRANTS

"The right to vote freely for the candidate of one's choice is of the essence of a democratic society," wrote Chief Justice Warren in

Reynolds v. Sims (1964), "and any restrictions on that right strike at the heart of representative government." Yet, aside from the partly disfranchised citizens of the District of Columbia, there remain two large groups of adults in the United States who are not allowed to vote. Combined, the two groups equal about 10 percent of the voting-age population.

The first group consists of immigrants. By the second half of the nineteenth century, U.S. citizenship had become a qualification for voting in all states, although as late as the early twentieth century declarant aliens could vote in some states (Keyssar 2000, 352–356). Although the federal Constitution does not mandate citizenship as a qualification for voting, states increasingly tended to mandate citizenship as the inflows of the foreign-born surged both before and after the Civil War. Thus aliens are today everywhere excluded from the polls. Given the surge in immigration in the United States during recent decades, this exclusion has meant that an ever-growing number of voting-age individuals are not counted among "We the People of the United States." According to census data, there were 2.7 million adult noncitizens in the country in 1970, or 2.2 percent of the voting-age population. By 2000, that number had grown to 16.2 million, or 8 percent of the voting-age population (Abramowitz 2004, 106). (There are also many aliens illegally present that the census counts routinely miss.) The percentages vary widely by state: West Virginia's noncitizen immigrant population is less than 1 percent, but it is 20 percent in California.

To be sure, many of the legal immigrants will eventually become citizens, but others will not—even though perhaps most will remain here as permanent residents. Indeed, the expanding immigrant segment of the national population partly accounts for the apparent decline in turnout in elections. That is, if turnout is based on the whole number of people of voting age, increasing the fraction ineligible to vote will itself decrease the turnout percentage even if the fraction of eligible persons who vote remains constant

(McDonald and Popkin 2001). In other words, what has been on the rise in recent years has not only been merely nonvoting, but the size of the pool of ineligible adults (Patterson 2002). That fact takes on added significance in view of a fact discussed below: the number of individuals convicted of certain crimes who also fall into the ranks of the ineligible.

Is the citizenship requirement justified? Noncitizen immigrants, after all, pay taxes and must obey the laws like everyone else. Moreover, the United States is a nation of immigrants and of people descended from immigrants. If exclusion were based on animus toward immigrants as a class, the answer to the question would have to be no. If exclusion were based on deficiencies somehow intrinsic only to immigrants, then not only should immigrants be barred from the polls, but citizenship itself should be either placed out of reach entirely or, as the Know-Nothings proposed in the 1850s, delayed for an extended period of time. Yet, if exclusion merely follows from the absence of citizenship, then exclusion seems well founded. Citizenship, after all, is a convenient way of defining those adults who are eligible for full-fledged membership in the political community. It may be a remnant of the old eighteenth- and nineteenth-century concept of a "stake" in society and a permanent interest in the political order. To be sure, there are no doubt citizens who have neither, and there are surely noncitizens who, practically speaking, have both. But possession of citizenship seems to be the clearest and fairest way of making that distinction. Without it, the task of deciding which noncitizens should be eligible and which ones should not would be daunting—unless, of course, one concluded that elections should be open to all adults except those holding diplomatic status or tourist visas.

CRIMINAL DISQUALIFICATION

Convicted felons are the other large group of disfranchised adults. Today, in forty-seven states prisoners convicted of felonies are not allowed to vote (Abramowitz 2004, 106). In thirty-two of those states, convicted offenders may not vote while they are on parole, and twenty-nine of the thirty-two states disfranchise offenders on probation. Fourteen states bar voting by the convicts for some period of time after their incarceration, parole, or probation, and ten of those fourteen disfranchise ex-felons for life. In no other democratic country, apparently, are so many people, absolutely or temporarily, excluded from the franchise because of criminal behavior (Fellner and Mauer 1998, 21). And disfranchisement can happen swiftly and easily. An eighteen-year-old first-time offender who trades a guilty plea for a nonprison sentence may unwittingly forfeit forever his right to vote (Fellner and Mauer 1998, 5). The consequences of disfranchisement, especially when permanent, are severe. As depicted by U.S. District Judge Henry Wingate, "the disenfranchised is severed from the body politic and condemned to the lowest form of citizenship, where voiceless at the ballot box . . . the disinherited must sit idly by while others elect his civil leaders and while others choose the fiscal and governmental policies which will govern him and his family" (*McLaughlin v. City of Canton*, 1995).

Although it is possible for ex-offenders to regain the right to vote, in spite of those barriers, the possibility is more illusion than reality. Upon release, ex-felons are not necessarily told what they must do to have the vote restored and, for those who are told, few have the financial and other resources to proceed. In 1996 and 1997, for example, there were 200,000 ex-felons in Virginia, but of this number only 404 regained the vote (Fellner and Mauer 1998, 5–6). Ironically, any one of these ex-offenders of at least twenty-five years of age could be elected to the U.S. House of Representations (or, if at least thirty, to the U.S. Senate), but in many states the would-be candidates would be ineligible to cast a vote for themselves. The reason for this curious anomaly is that, while states may deny ex-offenders the right to vote and even bar them from holding state or local office, states are powerless to attach qualifications to elected federal offices beyond those stipulated by the Constitution itself (*U.S. Term Limits, Inc. v. Thornton*, 1995).

Criminal disqualification is hardly a recent phenomenon. A few states in the early nineteenth century barred from the polls persons convicted of certain crimes, and by midcentury nineteen of the thirty-four states did so (Fellner and Mauer 1998, 2–3). This pattern of general disfranchisement of convicted felons took hold in most of the rest of the states after the Civil War (Keyssar 2000, 375–380). Losing the vote was thus one of the "civil" consequences of crime, in the same category with other civil penalties such as being barred from jury service or elective state and local office. In part this was a function of the broadening of the franchise to include virtually all adult males. As older barriers fell, some new ones took their place. In southern states especially, criminal disqualification was part of the package of devices to keep voting by blacks at a minimum. In some states, the disqualification was even based on conviction of offenses more common to blacks than whites (Shapiro 1993, 541). The infamous "white supremacy" constitutional convention in Alabama in 1901 made conviction of even nonfelonious crimes of "moral turpitude" (as determined by local officials) cause for disfranchisement. Later estimates were that this provision alone excluded about ten times as many blacks as whites (*Hunter v. Underwood*, 1985).

Yet, what makes criminal exclusion a matter of contemporary urgency is not the number of *states* that exclude, but the number of *persons* who have been excluded plus the racially disproportionate impact that the exclusion has wrought. As of 1998, when the most comprehensive study was done, a total of 3.9 million adults (about 2 percent of the voting-age population) was currently or permanently disfranchised because of a felony conviction. Of that group 1.4 million were black men (a number equal to 13 percent of all black men in the United States)—that is, more than one third of all disfranchised adults were black men (Fellner and Mauer 1998, 8). The figure of 1.4 million gains added significance alongside the fact that no more than 4.6 million black men voted in the presidential elections of 1996 (*Voting and Registration* 1998, 20–504).

Rates of disfranchisement vary significantly by state. In Florida and Alabama, 31 percent of all black men are permanently disfranchised. In Iowa, Mississippi, New Mexico, Virginia, and Wyoming, one in four black men is permanently disfranchised (Fellner and Mauer 1998). Some states that disfranchise only currently incarcerated individuals had rates nearly as high. Locally, some of the statistics are mind-boggling: as of the mid-1990s, in Baltimore, more than half of all black men in their twenties were in prison, on probation, or on parole, and in Washington, D.C., the figure was about 40 percent (Hacker 1995, 46). In part this is a function of the tendency in recent years to levy harsher sentences on certain drug and other forms of street crime that might have been regarded as misdemeanors in an earlier day. And the racially disparate impact may be entirely unintended. But faced with such data, the persistence of the disparate impact has caused some to wonder whether "'unintended' consequences are always unintended" (Verba 2003, 665).

Alongside its extensive involvement in other aspects of voting rights—from legislative districting to the Voting Rights Act itself—it is noteworthy that the disfranchisement of felons, especially given the racial overtones, has largely escaped the Supreme Court's attention. In *Richardson v. Ramirez* (1974), three parolees challenged a California law that disfranchised them because of felony convictions. Their argument was that the disability denied them a fundamental right under the equal protection clause of the Fourteenth Amendment and so had to be judged by the exacting standard of strict scrutiny. The Supreme Court disagreed. Relying on the seldom-cited Section 2 of the same amendment, which penalized states for discriminating against males in voting "except for participation in rebellion, or other crime," the majority reasoned that the amendment assumed that commission of criminal acts could properly be grounds for excluding someone from voting. The equal protection clause "could not have been meant to bar outright a form of disenfranchisement which was expressly exempted from the less drastic sanction of reduced representation which § 2 imposed for other forms of disenfranchisement." Indeed, the Supreme Court's only significant decision in this area was in *Hunter v. Underwood,* referred to above. There, because of the apparent racially discriminatory purpose at work, the Court struck down Alabama's "moral turpitude" exclusion that included misdemeanants, as well as felons. In other words, the racially disparate impact of felony disfranchisement laws violates the Fourteenth Amendment's equal protection clause only in situations where the laws derive from a racially discriminatory *intent.* Proving a racially discriminatory *effect* is not enough. However, Congress could probably intervene statutorily, by deploying its implementation powers under the Fourteenth and Fifteenth Amendments to reach the problem, just as it did with literacy tests in the Voting Rights Act.

It may be entirely understandable why nearly all states today disfranchise current felons. Felonies are offenses that a state deems the most serious (although one might think that committing election fraud is a greater threat to the polity than selling a packet of crack cocaine on the street corner). Committing a felony, like any other criminal offense, is seen as an offense not merely against an individual or a business but against society at large. Hence, in criminal prosecutions, the case is styled *"State v. Jones"* or *"People v. Jones."* The argument is that one has broken the "social contract"—that underpinning of democratic society by which each person forfeits some freedom for the good of all and agrees to live by rules enacted with common consent. In American history, the earliest manifestation of that notion was the Mayflower Compact of 1620.

Short of execution, incarceration for several years or longer represents as great a deprivation of individual liberty as ever happens to anyone in America. Citizens do not lose all their constitutional rights when they become prisoners, but some of those rights are in suspension during the time they are behind bars. Prisoners are, by definition, not free to come and go as they please and on their own terms, even in the most relaxed detention centers. One hesitates even to imagine the consequences of applying the First Amendment's guaranty of freedom of peaceable assembly in any rigorous way in the context of the jailhouse. So denying prisoners a direct influence on the political process seems no more unduly harsh than other deprivations they must endure. Besides, one can imagine the bizarre consequences of a large prison vote in the context of elections in the town or county where the prison might be located. The inmates might then truly find themselves in charge of the asylum.

But, even if one decides that probation or parole is a substitute or extension of confinement, and so merits the same political disabilities, what is the justification for extending the political disability beyond the duration of the sentence, or, indeed, for all of the ex-felon's life? The most common reasons given for extended disfranchisement include (1) protection against voter fraud, (2) preventing harmful changes in the law, and (3) protecting the "purity" of the ballot box. With the first, one wonders what most forms of crime have to do with election crime, unless one supposes that an individual inclined to commit offense A will also be inclined to commit offense B, and so on. Indeed, if disfranchisement is to extend beyond the punishment itself, there might be particular virtue in *limiting* such disability to those whose crime was against the electoral process itself. Someone who stuffs ballot boxes would seem to pose a greater danger to the polity than, say, someone who walks off with expensive golf clubs from a pro shop. The second reason supposes that convicted felons would be in favor of weakening the force of the criminal law. Perhaps. But the assumption is that, after incarceration, the individual remains a menace. If the now ex-felon is still a menace, one can ask why he or she is loose on the streets at all? If release from prison, parole, or probation signifies that the debt to society has now been paid (at a high price of individual liberty), then why does payment of the debt not also include restoration of the vote. The third argument erects a bar of morality for voting and elevates that bar out of the ex-felon's reach. But it seems to have nothing to do with whether, having been in prison, the ex-felon is somehow now incapable of making political decisions that his never-imprisoned friends do every day. This reason has its kindred link with the arguments late in the nineteenth century and early in the twentieth century that blacks should be kept from the polls to assure honesty and uprightness in voting. Moreover, one would suppose that reenfranchising ex-felons would ease their productive reentry into American life—a goal, presumably, that nearly everyone wants. Their exclusion from the body politic for life teaches precisely the wrong lesson: that America is divided between "insiders" and "outsiders" and that they will forever be among the latter.

As Justice Thurgood Marshall maintained in his dissent in *Richardson v. Ramirez,* "It is doubtful . . . whether the state can demonstrate either a compelling or rational policy interest in denying former felons the right to vote. [Ex-offenders] have fully paid their debt to society. They are as much affected by the actions of government as any other citizen, and have as much of a right to participate in governmental decision-making."

Nonetheless, even if Marshall had had his way, society would have had little to fear. Most felons are poor and have little education. Even with full enfranchisement of ex-felons, they are likely to vote at a rate far less than the American average. Their exclusion has consequences probably far more symbolic than real. As matters stand, however, the existing postconfinement disabilities will prove difficult to eradicate legislatively. There is precious little political gain for an elected official in befriending ex-convicts.

CONCLUSION

At the outset of nationhood in 1776, the United States was both blessed and cursed. Americans were blessed because they already

had in place traditions of voting and institutions of self-government. The themes of natural rights and government by the consent of the governed that permeated the Declaration of Independence were hardly North American intellectual inventions.
Among other sources, those themes grew from English roots.
Those themes, after all, had been central to the debates at Putney
at the end of the English Civil War in 1647. Thus the American
political experience since 1776 has been a process of modifying,
refining, and applying those themes, especially in the context of
voting. The concepts of consent, participation, and representation
were like a democratic dynamo. Even when their impulses were
resisted, they kept churning. To shift comparisons, the ideals remained as reckoning points. And the ideological forces had their
effects. The abandonment of property qualifications by the middle of the nineteenth century ushered in a political novelty: an era
of nearly complete white manhood suffrage for the first time in
any country on the face of the globe. Remaining gender barriers at
the polls collapsed in 1920. Even the concept of political adult-
hood itself was readjusted in 1971.

Americans were cursed, however, by the presence of slavery
that deepened its hold on the economic life of the country, especially in the middle Atlantic and southern states, after the Revolution. And the curse of slavery was made worse because the slave
population was racially different. Even after the end of the Civil
War and abolition of slavery in 1865, the status of African Americans—whether free persons or former slaves—was left in doubt.
Racism made equal citizenship an elusive goal. So elusive was the
goal, in fact, that meaningful political participation by blacks was
not a reality in all states of the union until more than a century after emancipation.

Measured by its abundant blessings, America has been a beacon
to the world. The passage in the Declaration of Independence proclaiming government by the consent of the governed is no doubt
the most powerful and influential paragraph ever originally

penned in the English language. Measured against the struggle inflicted by its curse, however, Americans betrayed their own ideals. For too long, America has had to play catch-up democracy. At every point, both those possessing the vote and those denied the vote have recognized the same truth: voting facilitates power and control.

Further complicating the picture of voting in the United States from the beginning has been the principle of selectivity: the constitutional traditions of decentralization and federalism, whereby the definition of the franchise for a long time lay entirely with the states. Stretched across this pattern of fragmented authority has been another political tradition: partisanship. The combination of ideology, decentralization, and partisanship has yielded as many pictures or stories of the evolution of voting as there have been states. The collective story of voting rights has thus been in part a chipping away at the prerogative of states to go their own way, all the while contending partisan forces have competed for votes in the struggle for power.

What this chapter has tried to depict are some of the items that remain on the voting rights agenda—unfinished business, as it were. Whatever direction the voting rights debate takes in the coming years, these are issues that are surely to be present and discussed: systems of representation that do not permit majorities to suffocate minorities; technologies that accurately and honestly record and tabulate the preferences of voters; the still only partly enfranchised residents of the District of Columbia; and the considerable number of Americans whose criminal acts have effectively banished them from the political community. That roster of concerns is a reminder that states remain key players in determining what the right to vote actually means as citizens go to the polls.

In February 1788, during the extended campaign to convince New Yorkers to ratify the Constitution, James Madison published *The Federalist,* No. 57. In it he lay out the link provided by the popularly elected House of Representatives between the people and the proposed national government:

> The aim of every political constitution is, or ought to be, first to obtain for rulers men who possess most wisdom to discern, and most virtue to pursue, the common good of the society; and in the next place, to take the most effectual precautions for keeping them virtuous whilst they continue to hold their public trust. The elective mode of obtaining rulers is the characteristic policy of republican government (Brock 1961, 291).

Madison grasped the essential point that elections function both prospectively and retrospectively. They provide the medium by which the people look forward, as they place their trust in those they wish to lead them. Simultaneously, they allow accountability: through voting citizens approve or reject what their leaders have done in the past. To be sure, Madison would never have used the word "democracy" to describe such an arrangement. In his day the word was synonymous with mob rule and merely another form of tyranny that was to be avoided at all costs. Instead, he and others of his generation used the term "republican" to describe the framers' handiwork. They also called it "free government." More than two centuries later, Americans use all three terms interchangeably.

With that difference in usage in mind, Madison understood clearly what the years since 1788 have plainly shown. A political system may allow voting and may administer elections without being democratic; yet no one has learned how to construct a democratic government without voting and elections. "Democratic institutions are never done," observed Woodrow Wilson over a century ago. "[T]hey are like living tissue—always a-making. It is a strenuous thing, this living of the life of a free people" (Wilson 1893, 116). The future president only echoed the verity that voting, elections, and the franchise are together the central forces of democracy.

REFERENCES

"23ʳᵈ Amendment." 1965. *Congress and the Nation 1945–1964.* Washington, DC: Congressional Quarterly Service.

Abramowitz, Alan. 2004. *Voice of the People: Elections and Voting in the United States.* Boston: McGraw Hill.

Brock, W. R., ed. 1961. *The Federalist.* New York: E. P. Dutton.

Chapin, Douglas. 2004. *Election Reform 2004: What's Changed, What Hasn't and Why.* Washington, DC: Election Reform Information Project.

Fellner, Jamie, and Marc Mauer. 1998. *Losing the Vote: The Impact of Felony Disenfranchisement Laws in the United States.* Washington, DC: The Sentencing Project.

Gibson, James L., Gregory A. Caldeira, and Lester Kenyatta Spence. 2002. "The Supreme Court and the U.S. Presidential Election of 2000: Wounds, Self-Inflicted or Otherwise?" Unpublished paper. St. Louis, MO: Weidenbaum Center on the Economy, Government, and Public Policy at Washington University.

Gordon, John Steele. 2004. "A Senator from D.C.?" *Wall Street Journal,* Jan. 14: A12.

Gugliotta, Guy. 2001. "Study Finds Millions of Votes Lost." *Washington Post,* July 16: A-1.

Guinier, Lani. 1994. *The Tyranny of the Majority: Fundamental Fairness in Representative Democracy.* New York: Free Press.

Hacker, Andrew. 1995. "Malign Neglect: The Crackdown on African-Americans." *Nation,* July 10: 45.

Hasen, Richard L. 2003. *The Supreme Court and Election Law: Judging Equality from* Baker v. Carr *to* Bush v. Gore. New York: New York University Press.

Hench, Virginia E. 1998. "The Death of Voting Rights: The Legal Disenfranchisement of Minority Voters." *Case Western Reserve Law Review* 48: 727.

Keyssar, Alexander. 2000. *The Right to Vote: The Contested History of Democracy in the United States.* New York: Basic Books.

McDonald, Michael P., and Samuel L. Popkin. 2001. "The Myth of the Vanishing Voter." *American Political Science Review* 95: 963.

McManus, Doyle, Bob Drogin, and Richard O'Reilly. 2001. "Counting Method Key to Bush's Florida Win, New Study Says." *Philadelphia Inquirer,* Nov. 12: A2.

"'Motor Voter' Bill Enacted After 5 Years." 1994. *1993 Congressional Quarterly Almanac.* Washington, DC: Congressional Quarterly.

Nather, David. 2002. "Provisions of the Federal Voting Standards and Procedures Law." *Congressional Quarterly Weekly Report,* Nov. 2: 2870.

"New Study Shows . . ." 2004. Washington, DC: Election Data Services, Feb. 12: 1.

Patterson, Thomas E. 2002. *The Vanishing Voter.* New York: Knopf.

Peltason, J. W. 1988. *Corwin and Peltason's Understanding the Constitution.* 11th ed. New York: Holt, Rinehart, and Winston.

Pildes, Richard H. 2002. "Is Voting Rights Law Now at War with Itself?" *North Carolina Law Review* 80: 1517.

Platt, Suzy. 1989. *Respectfully Quoted: A Dictionary of Quotations from the Congressional Research Service.* Washington, DC: Library of Congress.

Rush, Mark E., and Richard L. Engstrom. 2001. *Fair and Effective Representation? Debating Electoral Reform and Minority Rights.* Lanham, MD: Rowman and Littlefield.

Schultz, David. 2002. "Election 2000: The *Bush v. Gore* Scholarship." *Public Integrity* 4: 360.

Shapiro, Andrew L. 1993. "Challenging Criminal Disenfranchisement under the Voting Rights Act: A New Strategy." *Yale Law Journal* 103: 540.

Tate, Katherine. 2003. "Black Opinion on the Legitimacy of Racial Redistricting and Minority-Majority Districts." *American Political Science Review* 97: 45.

Thompson, Dennis F. 2002. *Just Elections: Creating a Fair Electoral Process in the United States.* Chicago: University of Chicago Press.

———. 2004. "Election Time: Normative Implications of Temporal Properties of the Electoral Process in the United States." *American Political Science Review* 98: 51.

Verba, Sidney. 2003. "Would the Dream of Political Equality Turn out to Be a Nightmare?" *Perspectives on Politics* 1: 663.

Voting and Registration in the Election of November 1996. 1998. Washington, DC: U.S. Census Bureau.

Wilson, Woodrow. 1893. *An Old Master and Other Political Essays.* New York: Scribner's.

Yarbrough, Tinsley E. 2002. *Race and Redistricting.* Lawrence: University Press of Kansas.

5

KEY PEOPLE, CASES, AND EVENTS

Anthony, Susan B. (1820–1906)

Probably the most famous of woman suffragists, Anthony was born into a Massachusetts Quaker family and became a teacher in 1837. Never married, she spent her life in pursuit of improved legal, political, and social positions for women, particularly in terms of enabling women to provide support for themselves. Her association with Elizabeth Cady Stanton in antislavery and women's rights causes began in 1850. Like most female suffragists, Anthony combined promotion of rights for African Americans with promotion of rights for all women. The end of the Civil War resulted in new national legal protections for the former, but none for the latter. This reality led to her participation in organization of the National Woman Suffrage Association in 1869. In what may have been her most publicized act, she even arranged to cast an illegal vote in a congressional election in New York in 1872 for which she was fined $100 by Supreme Court Justice Ward Hunt sitting as circuit judge. Anthony was probably the leading suffragist strategist of the late nineteenth century. She was convinced that women would secure the vote only if women organized and persisted in a campaign for a constitutional amendment, without attachment to either major political party. When the two branches of the woman's suffrage movement merged in 1890, Anthony was elected in 1892 to succeed Stanton as president of the National American Woman Suffrage Association.

Articles of Confederation

This document was the compact among the original thirteen states of the Union that functioned as the plan of government for the nation prior to ratification of the Constitution in 1788. Initially drafted by the Continental Congress in Philadelphia in 1776, it was adopted by the Congress in November 1777 (Congress was then meeting in York, Pennsylvania, during the British occupation of Philadelphia) and approved by all states but Maryland by 1779. (Maryland withheld approval until 1781 because of a dispute over western lands.) Members of the one-house congress under the Articles of Confederation were elected by the state legislatures, and every state had an equal vote in the congress. The inadequacies of the central government authorized by the articles—there was no national power to tax, no national power to regulate commerce among the states, and no national power over individuals—led to the call for a convention to propose changes in the articles. That convention met in Philadelphia in 1787 and drafted the Constitution.

Baker v. Carr (1962)

In this watershed six-to-two decision, the U.S. Supreme Court announced that numerical disparities among state legislative districts presented a justiciable issue (that is, a question appropriate for judicial consideration) under the Fourteenth Amendment. Chief Justice Earl Warren later characterized the decision as "the most important case of my tenure on the Court" (Warren 1977, 306). Prior to *Baker*, the Court had steered clear of involvement in the politics of redistricting. With almost all states having population imbalances in at least one house of the state legislature and with population disparities in the congressional districts of most states, *Baker* signaled that federal courts would now become intricately entangled in politics in new ways, but the decision set no standard for federal courts to apply in redistricting cases. That standard— one person, one vote—was forthcoming in the later decisions of *Gray v. Sanders* (1963), *Wesberry v. Sanders* (1964), and *Reynolds v. Sims* (1964).

According to one scholar who had early access to otherwise confidential Court papers of Justice William J. Brennan Jr., *Baker* came close to being a very different decision. An explanation of that fact offers insight into how the Supreme Court decides cases. When *Baker* came down on March 26, 1962, Brennan's majority opinion spoke for six members of the Court. Concurring opinions by Douglas and Clark indicated that they would reach the merits of the case if the allegations of inequality in the suit could be sustained. Stewart also concurred, stating that the merits of the case were not before the Court for review. Frankfurter and Harlan dissented, and Whittaker did not take part. But when the case was initially argued during the 1960 term, the vote in conference vote was four to four, with Clark and Whittaker joining Frankfurter and Harlan.

Stewart, it seemed, was undecided on the issue of jurisdiction—that is, whether the issue of legislative districting was justiciable. And it was at his urging the case was carried over for reargument in October 1961. At the conference on October 13, Chief Justice Earl Warren began the discussion by saying, "This is a violation of equal protection. I don't think we have to decide the merits. . . . All we have to decide is that there is jurisdiction. We don't have to say that the state must give complete equality." By this time Stewart had come around to the view that the Court could take jurisdiction, thus giving a five-to-four vote in favor of the Tennessee plaintiffs. But Stewart emphasized two points: "I can't say whether we can or can't frame appropriate relief. On the merits, I couldn't say that equal protection requires representation approximately commensurate with voting strength. So the state doesn't have to justify every departure from a one-man vote basis." He then added that "the greatest burden of proof [was] on a plaintiff to show an arbitrary and capricious system" (Schwartz 1983, 415).

Warren, Black, Douglas, and Brennan wanted to do more than simply to acknowledge jurisdiction. Going to the merits, they would hold that the Fourteenth Amendment required Tennessee to provide "approximately fair distribution or weight in votes." This was *not* the equality rule the Court later imposed in 1964. Moreover, the four justices favoring "approximately fair weight" were prepared to impose that standard *only* on *one* house of a state legislature. To keep Stewart's vote, however, Brennan (to whom Warren had assigned the opinion in *Baker*) would have to stick to jurisdiction and leave standards alone. After Frankfurter circulated his dissent in February, Clark quickly indicated agreement. Frankfurter then suggested to Clark that he write separately "on failure to exhaust other remedies." Frankfurter, presumably, wanted to make sure that Clark's vote held tight by getting him to convince himself that Tennessee voters had other channels for relief. But the plan backfired. As Clark wrote Frankfurter on March 7,

Preparatory to writing my dissent in this case, along the line you suggested of pointing out the avenues that were open for the voters of Tennessee to bring about reapportionment despite its Assembly, I have carefully checked into the record. I am sorry to say that I cannot find any practical course that the people could take in bringing this about except through the Federal courts. . . . I am sorry to say that I should have to ask you to permit me to withdraw from your dissent. (Schwartz 1983, 423)

Attached to the letter was a copy of Clark's *concurring* opinion. This meant that Stewart's vote was no longer necessary to give Brennan's opinion majority status and that *Baker* could reach beyond the jurisdictional point. But because of Stewart's insistence to go no further, Brennan notified Warren, Black, and Douglas on March 10 that he would not press Stewart on changes. So the opinion Brennan announced in the courtroom on March 26 was basically the opinion he had written before Clark switched his vote. Had Clark sided with Brennan initially, or shortly after reargument in October 1961, it seems highly probable that *Baker* would ultimately have reached the question of standards as well as the question of jurisdiction. And the standard would have been the one of "approximately fair weight" for only one house of a state legislature. Had the case worked out this way, it seems highly improbable that the same justices would have changed their minds to adopt the nearly inflexible rule of numerical equality imposed shortly afterwards (Schwartz 1983, 410–423).

Brown v. Board of Education (1954)

This landmark case in the Warren Court considered the question whether legally mandated racially segregated public schools were consistent with the equal protection clause of the Fourteenth Amendment. Racial segregation in schools and other pubic facilities had long been acceptable under the separate-but-equal doctrine of *Plessy v. Ferguson* (1896). The answer the Court gave in *Brown* would have far-reaching ramifications because a total of seventeen states and the District of Columbia required segregated schools, and another four states permitted it as an option in local communities. "We come ... to the question presented," wrote Chief Justice Earl Warren for a unanimous bench: "Does segregation of children in public schools solely on the basis of race, even though the physical facilities and other 'tangible' factors may be equal, deprive the children of the minority group of equal educational opportunities? We believe that it does. . . . [I]n the field of public education the doctrine of 'separate but equal' has no place. Separate educational facilities are inherently unequal." *Brown* thus not only turned away from *Plessy* and marked the beginning of the end of legally enforced segregated schooling but by implication spelled doom for any other racially segregated public enterprise or policy. *Brown* also inspired much of the civil rights movement that culminated in passage of the Civil Rights Act of 1964.

Bush v. Gore (2000)

This remarkable five-to-four decision by the U.S. Supreme Court effectively picked the forty-third president of the United States. On November 8, 2000, the day after the presidential election, election officials in Florida reported that Governor George W. Bush had a lead of 1,784 votes over Vice President Albert Gore. With Florida's 25 electoral votes, Bush would have a total of 271 electoral votes, one more than the minimum required to win the presidency. Without those 25 electoral votes, Gore's tally stood at 267, three shy of victory. Because Bush's margin was so thin, an automatic machine recount followed, as required by Florida law. The new official totals then showed Bush with a lead of 537 votes. Gore initiated legal proceedings in state court to obtain a hand recount in certain counties. After the Florida Supreme Court left the door open to a manual recount across the state, the U.S. Supreme Court ruled on December 11 that the recount could not proceed without uniform standards by which a legal vote could be determined. Otherwise, one person's ballot might not be treated in the same way as someone else's. With voting by the electoral college just days away, five justices concluded that no constitutionally acceptable hand recount was possible. That left in place Bush's officially certified margin of victory of 537 votes.

Catt, Carrie Chapman (1859–1947)

An educator and a journalist, this second-generation leader in the campaign for woman suffrage was born in Wisconsin and reared in Iowa. By her late twenties she had earned a reputation as a both a hard worker in the cause and as a skilled strategist and tactician. After the National American Woman Suffrage Association was formed in 1890 by the merger of the National Woman Suffrage Association with the American Woman Suffrage Association, she succeeded Susan B. Anthony as president of the combined group, serving in that position in 1900–1904 and in 1915–1920, as the Nineteenth Amendment became part of the law of the land. With woman suffrage achieved, she helped to organize the League of Women Voters with the objective of enabling the newly enfranchised class to exercise greater influence in all aspects and at all levels of the political process.

Civil Rights Act of 1866

This statute was the first of several civil rights laws that Congress enacted during Reconstruction (1865–1877). Passed over President Andrew Johnson's veto, the 1866 statute attempted to assure some measure of equality for the newly freed slaves and other African Americans. Section 1 declared that "all persons born in the United States, and not subject to any foreign power, excluding Indians not taxed," were "citizens of the United States; and such citizens, of every race and color, without regard to any previous condition of slavery or involuntary servitude shall have the same right, in every State and Territory . . ., to make and enforce contracts, to sue, be parties, and give evidence, to inherit, purchase, lease, sell, hold, and convey real and personal property, and to full and equal benefit of all laws and proceedings for the security of person and property, as is enjoyed by white citizens, and shall be subject to like punishment, pains and penalties, and to none other, any law, statute, ordinance, regulation, or custom to the contrary not withstanding." Section 1 of the Fourteenth Amendment (1868), in its declaration of national and state citizenship and guarantee of equal protection of the laws, was intended in part to shore up the constitutionality of the 1866 act. Significantly, neither the 1866 law nor the Fourteenth Amendment protected the right to vote. That would not be affirmatively addressed until ratification of the Fifteenth Amendment in 1870.

Civil Rights Acts of 1870 and 1871

These statutes were usually referred to as the "Enforcement Acts" (or the "Force Acts" by their opponents) because they were intended to "enforce" the terms of the Fourteenth and Fifteenth Amendments. The first one restated some provisions from the Civil Rights Act of 1866 and added voting protections, making it a federal offense to interfere with the right to vote. The 1871 statute, also called the "Ku Klux Act" was aimed at vigilante-style intimidation. It criminalized actions by anyone to deny another person any federally protected right as well as interference with federal law enforcement agents in carrying out the terms of the act. Parts of the 1870 law were invalidated or narrowly construed by the Supreme Court in *United States v. Reese* (1876) and *United States v. Cruikshank* (1876), making it far less effective than Congress had intended.

Civil Rights Act of 1957

The first civil rights legislation passed by Congress since 1875, the statute was modest by later standards but was nonetheless significant in three respects. A civil rights unit in the Department of Justice was reconfigured into a full-fledged division, organizationally on the same plane as, say, the antitrust division. The new division was also to be headed by an assistant attorney general for civil rights. Moreover, the law established the United States Commission on Civil Rights as a bipartisan agency charged with investigating and reporting to the president and the Congress on civil rights problems in the nation. There was now a fixture in the national government the sole initial mission of which was to highlight manifestations of racial discrimination and to make remedial recommendations. Beyond these institutional changes, the 1957 statute empowered the Department of Justice to institute *civil* (as opposed to criminal) actions for equitable (that is, injunctive) relief where the right to vote was threatened or denied by local officials.

Civil Rights Act of 1960

Building on the Civil Rights Act of 1957, this 1960 statute provided additional procedures and brought the federal judiciary into face-to-face contact with voter registration. The government initially had to obtain a court finding that a person had been deprived of the right to vote on account of race and that the denial was part of a "pattern or practice" of similar denials. Second, for at least twelve months after such finding, persons who were victims of racial discrimination at the polls could apply for a judicial order declaring them eligible to vote. Third, the court could hear such applications or could appoint a panel of registered voters to act as referees. Finally, to assist with findings of a "pattern or practice," voting records were to be made public and preserved for at least twenty-two months following a primary or general election.

Civil Rights Act of 1964

This statute remains the most sweeping civil rights legislation ever passed by Congress. Its multifaceted provisions addressed racial and other forms of discrimination on several fronts. Among other things, the statute's Title II banned racial discrimination in privately owned places of public accommodation, such as hotels and theaters. Title VI barred discrimination in any program, such as education, receiving federal financial assistance. Title VII forbade discrimination in the workplace. But symbolically it was Title I that dealt with voting. The fact that further measures were necessary, even after the 1957 and 1960 civil rights laws, was evidence enough that racial discrimination in voting remained entrenched in some states. Henceforth, under Title I black and white applicants would be judged by the same registration criteria. No one could be denied the right to vote because of a minor error or omission on a registration form. In states employing literacy tests, the tests would have to be written, not oral, and kept on file for later scrutiny. Furthermore, in any suit to gain access to the ballot, the court was to assume that any applicant who had completed the sixth grade was sufficiently literate, unless the state could prove otherwise. Finally, in voting rights cases, the federal government had the option of requesting that the suit be heard by a three-judge panel, instead of by a single U.S. district judge as was ordinarily the practice, thus guaranteeing the losing party a direct appeal to the Supreme Court.

Compromise of 1877

The term collectively encompasses acquiescence by Democrats, southern members of Congress in particular, in the decision by the electoral commission of 1877 to award all disputed electoral votes in the 1876 presidential election to Rutherford B. Hayes. The result was to hand the key to the White House door to the Republican nominee, instead of to the Democratic nominee, Samuel Tilden, who had received the most popular votes. Democrats in return received promises of (1) federal subsidies to rebuild devastated southern infrastructure (largely left unfulfilled) and (2) prompt withdrawal of the remaining federal troops that had once occupied most of the former states of the Confederacy since 1865. With fulfillment of the second promise came restoration of "home rule" in the South. African Americans were then almost entirely dependent for protection of voting and other rights on the white Democrat-controlled state governments. By the end of the century, rampant disfranchisement of blacks was underway, and a pervasive system of racial segregation was in place.

Constitutional Convention

Because of the inadequacies of the Articles of Confederation—which resulted in a weak central government with little control over the states—a movement developed in 1786 and 1787 for a convention that would propose changes in the articles. That convention, with delegates from all states except Rhode Island, met in Philadelphia between May and September 1787. Its handiwork—the Constitution—was not a list of proposed changes in the articles but entailed scrapping the articles altogether in favor of a radically different plan of government. Notable features of the new government included three separate branches of government, a bicameral legislature, representation based on population in one house that would be elected by the people, and a significant list of powers that the government under the articles lacked. Because amendments to the articles required approval by the *legislatures* of *every* state, the Constitution maneuvered around that fatal impediment by stating that it would go into effect upon ratification by specially called *conventions* in *nine* states.

Davis v. Bandemer (1986)

In this landmark decision, the U.S. Supreme Court ventured further into the political thicket of legislative districting. In a challenge to a districting plan for the Indiana legislature, the Court concluded that partisan gerrymandering presented a justiciable issue under the equal protection clause of the Fourteenth Amendment. (A gerrymander is a districting plan that purposefully attempts to advantage one party at the expense of another.) Yet for future cases, the Court announced a standard much less precise than one-person-one-vote rule that it had applied in conventional districting cases such as *Wesberry v. Sanders* and *Reynolds v. Sims:* "Unconstitutional discrimination occurs only when the electoral system is arranged in a manner that will consistently degrade a voter's or a group of voters' influence on the political process as a whole." Left in doubt was the kind of evidence and the period of time required to prove an unconstitutional gerrymander. Complicating any such litigation is the redistricting that occurs after each decennial census. Thus, the *Bandemer* decision made it more difficult to establish a constitutionally invalid gerrymander. (*See also Vieth v. Jubelirer.*)

Declaration of Independence

Approved by the Second Continental Congress in Philadelphia, Pennsylvania, on July 4, 1776, this foundational document of American nationhood attempted several goals. First, it announced the formal separation of thirteen English colonies (from Massachusetts to Georgia) from Great Britain. Second, it laid out the philosophical and legal justifications for the separation. This second objective had twin goals itself. The Declaration was both an effort both to convince world opinion that the colonists were justified in their rebellion against the Crown and a device to persuade colonial Americans themselves—many of whom remained dubious about, or opposed to, independence—that the cause was both just and necessary. Third, it introduced the former colonies to the world as the "United States of America." Largely the stylistic handiwork of Thomas Jefferson, the Declaration was drafted by a committee of five: Jefferson, John Adams, Benjamin Franklin,

Roger Sherman, and Robert Livingston. The Declaration remains significant because of its evocation of natural rights and its defense of human rights and of government by the consent of the governed.

Dred Scott Case

See Scott v. Sandford

The Federalist Papers

Published serially between October 1787 and May 1788 in newspapers in New York State, this collection of eighty-five essays by Alexander Hamilton, John Jay, and James Madison (under the pseudonym "Publius") was intended to convince New Yorkers to support ratification of the Constitution. New York was a battleground state in the struggle for ratification and was among the last states to accept the new plan of government. The *Federalist* essays were only a small part of a huge "pamphlet war" that was waged in much of the United States as both supporters and opponents (who were called "Antifederalists") of the proposed plan of the new national government debated the document's supposed strengths and weaknesses. Of all of these writings, the *Federalist* essays remain the most famous; as insight into the structure of the Constitution itself they have acquired nearly official status.

Franchise

Originally, the word *franchise* referred to a privilege, prerogative, freedom, or immunity conferred by the government on an individual or a corporation for certain purposes. Even today the term retains much of its earlier meaning, as when a business, for example, receives a "franchise" from the Department of the Interior to operate a restaurant at a national park. But the word has also referred to voting—those eligible to vote are said to have the franchise or to be enfranchised. This usage explains why voting was long thought not to be, strictly speaking, a right, but a privilege that government could bestow or withhold to advance its own purposes.

Gerrymander

See Davis v. Bandemer and *Vieth v. Jubelirer*

Grandfather Clause

Generally, the term refers to any exemption of a certain group of persons from a requirement that is to be imposed on others in the future. More specifically, the term refers to a device in six southern states in the late nineteenth and early twentieth centuries that exempted from literacy tests or other voting requirements those who were eligible to vote prior to certain date and those who were descended from such persons. The date chosen would be a year in which most blacks were excluded from the franchise. Ironically, the first such grandfather clause was enacted by Connecticut in 1818. It disfranchised blacks, but allowed those already eligible to retain their right to vote. *See also Guinn v. United States.*

Gray v. Sanders (1963)

This eight-to-one decision by the U.S. Supreme Court was the first of three cases the Court announced after *Baker v. Carr* (1962) that dealt with redistricting and representation. At issue in *Gray* was Georgia's bizarre scheme for electing officials in statewide elections whereby the votes of those in rural counties counted far more than the votes of those in urban counties. In striking down the system, Justice Douglas's majority opinion announced that the bedrock principle of political equality meant "only one thing—

one person, one vote." As such, *Gray* was a stepping stone for the Court between *Baker v. Carr* and two decisions in the following year: *Wesberry v. Sanders* and *Reynolds v. Sims.*

Guinn v. United States (1915)

This unanimous decision was one of only a handful prior to the 1940s by the U.S. Supreme Court that protected the rights of African Americans to vote. Ordinarily, the Court adopted a highly formalistic approach by which only a law that expressly denied the vote to blacks because of race would be deemed unconstitutional. States therefore turned to surrogate devices to accomplish much the same thing. In this case Oklahoma exempted from a literacy test for voting all persons and their lineal descendants who had voted on or before January 1, 1866, a date that excluded virtually every black. Because race was the only conceivable explanation for the selection of the 1866 date (prior to ratification of the Fifteenth Amendment), Oklahoma's "grandfather clause" was deemed a transparent violation of that amendment. The effects of the Court's ruling, however, were more symbolic than real. Other states that had adopted such grandfather clauses had already allowed them to expire—they were so transparent as to be an embarrassment. Moreover, Oklahoma, like other southern states, had ample other, and less transparent, devices that were deployed to accomplish the same result.

Help America Vote Act (HAVA)

Signed into law by President Bush on October 29, 2002, the statute is the most comprehensive legislation affecting voting rights to be passed by Congress since the Voting Rights Act of 1965. The product of the voting debacle in Florida in the 2000 presidential election (*see Bush v. Gore*), HAVA attempts to improve the administration of elections in the United States, primarily through three means: (1)

creation of a new agency called the Election Assistance Commission; (2) authorization of funds to enable states to improve election administration and to replace outdated voting systems; and, (3) establishment of certain minimum standards for states to follow in several key areas of administering elections. Combined, the various provisions of the law make significant inroads into the tradition of decentralization that has characterized American elections since the beginning of the Republic.

Jackson, Andrew (1767–1845)

The seventh U.S. president (1829–1837), Jackson remolded American government by founding the Democratic Party, the prototype of modern mass-based political organizations. Without question, he was the dominant White House figure between Thomas Jefferson (1801–1809) and Abraham Lincoln (1861–1865). Born in extreme up-country South Carolina, Jackson was barely more than a child when he saw service in the Revolutionary War. Taken prisoner, he was struck across the face with the flat of a sword after he refused to polish a British officer's boots. Some years later Jackson got revenge (and a hero's persona) when he led the American army at the battle of New Orleans in 1815, where some 2,000 British regulars fell alongside only 13 American soldiers. Between those events, he was admitted to the bar in North Carolina and moved to Tennessee in 1788 where he served in a series of offices: prosecutor, judge, U.S. representative, and U.S. senator. He sparked an international incident when he led troops in an incursion against the Seminoles in Spanish-held Florida in 1818. He was appointed its military governor in 1821 after the region's sale to the United States, and was again elected to the Senate in 1823. After an unsuccessful race for the presidency in 1824 that had to be decided by the House of Representatives, "Old Hickory" beat incumbent John Quincy Adams in 1828 and easily won a second term in 1832 against a challenge by Henry Clay. Jackson was not only the first trans-Appalachian president but also the first "self-made" person to grace that office.

Jackson was an energetic nationalist in terms of expansion of American influence and in resistance to the nullification movement in South Carolina in 1833. Yet, as an advocate of an unobtrusive national government and a defender of states' rights, he vigorously opposed the Second Bank of the United States and vetoed internal improvement legislation. As a party-strengthening device, he perfected the spoils system, whereby loyal party members were rewarded with government jobs. Most of all, he opposed privilege and, in an era when nearly every state had moved far along toward universal white adult-male suffrage, relished (and benefited from) his reputation as champion of the common man. Jackson electrified the electorate, a phenomenon that persisted for a time and infected the opposition as well. According to some estimates, voter turnout among eligible males in some elections during the thirty-two years prior to the Civil War exceeded 80 percent. Indeed, Jackson's belief in government as the people's servant dominated American politics for three decades, leading historians to refer to that period before the Civil War as the "age of Jackson."

Johnson, Lyndon B. (1908–1973)

The thirty-sixth American president was born in the central Texas hill-country community of Stonewall and educated at Southwest Texas State Teachers College. After graduation in 1930, he taught school and studied law. Elected to the U.S. House of Representatives in 1936 as an ardent New Dealer, he won a seat in the U.S. Senate in 1948 in an exceedingly close election that was marred by accusations of voter fraud. (A ballot box mysteriously surfaced in Jim Wells County. Its contents gave Johnson an edge of eighty-seven votes over his opponent and also his nickname: "Landslide Lyndon.") In the Senate Johnson proved to be a masterful leader and tactician. Without his efforts neither the Civil Rights Act of

1957 nor the Civil Rights Act of 1960 would have become law. After fellow Senator John F. Kennedy secured the Democratic presidential nomination in 1960, Johnson was his vice presidential pick. Between the elections of 1960 and 2000, inclusive, that selection is probably the only example of a vice presidential candidate's actually deciding the election. Without Johnson and his strength in Texas and a few other southern states, Kennedy could not have won in the close race he ran against Vice President Richard Nixon, his Republican opponent. Becoming president in November 1963 upon Kennedy's assassination, Johnson was elected in his own right in 1964. In terms of domestic policy, Johnson is remembered for pursuit of what he called the Great Society. It combined an extension of New Deal economic programs and an emphasis on civil rights. The Civil Rights Act of 1964 and the Voting Rights Act of 1965 remain as monuments to the Johnson presidency. His considerable legacy, however, was marred after 1965 by the American quagmire in Vietnam. That stemmed from the military involvement he had inherited from the Kennedy administration which, ironically, had excluded the vice president from many important national security deliberations and decisions.

Lincoln, Abraham (1809–1865)

The sixteenth American chief executive (1861–1865), Abraham Lincoln bore witness to the proposition that presidential greatness is in large measure a product of character and force of circumstance. If Lincoln had not been part of the political scene in 1861, the decade might well have unfolded altogether differently. Had the Civil War not happened on Lincoln's watch, he might today be no better remembered or more highly regarded than a dozen or more fairly mediocre nineteenth-century occupants of the White House.

Lincoln's election precipitated southern secession. The improvident attack on Fort Sumter in Charleston Harbor on April 12,

1816, barely a month after his inauguration, furnished the event Lincoln needed to galvanize the North behind his resolve to preserve the Union. Prior to congressional approval in July of most of his initial steps, Lincoln had called for 75,000 volunteers (after which four more southern states seceded), instituted a naval blockade of southern ports, suspended the writ of habeas corpus in certain areas, and supported his commanders in defying Chief Justice Roger B. Taney's ruling on circuit in *Ex parte Merryman* (1861) that the president had no authority unilaterally to suspend the writ. Never had a president made such use of executive powers. His eventual success in finding generals who were a match for the South's allowed the North's overwhelming advantages in manpower and materiel finally to begin to prevail. Their success assured his reelection on a "Union" ticket in 1864 against a Democratic challenge by General George B. McClellan.

Conclusion of the war came quickly. General Ulysses S. Grant accepted General Robert E. Lee's surrender at Appomattox Courthouse, Virginia, on April 9, 1865, and General Joseph E. Johnston surrendered his army to General William T. Sherman at Durham Station, North Carolina, on April 26. Yet Lincoln's plans for a postwar America characterized by magnanimity toward a defeated South came to naught when he was shot by an assassin on April 14, 1865, and died the next day. His successor, Vice President and Tennessee war Democrat Andrew Johnson, lacked the slain president's stature, magnetic oratorical skills, political astuteness, and leadership abilities. The center of power in Washington consequently shifted to the radical wing of the Republican Party in Congress, which pursued a more extreme Reconstruction.

Majority-Minority District

See Shaw v. Reno

Minor v. Happersett (1875)

In this unanimous decision by the U.S. Supreme Court, the bench addressed the question whether access to the polls was a right inhering in *national* citizenship or a privilege conferred on citizens by the states. Once it became apparent that Congress was not going to include a guarantee of woman suffrage as part of the Reconstruction amendments, a St. Louis woman named Virginia Minor in 1869 insisted that the Fourteenth Amendment, along with a few other provisions in the Constitution, implicitly overrode Missouri's restriction of the suffrage to men. Speaking for the Court, Chief Justice Morrison Waite unanimously rejected her reasoning. Citizenship, he wrote, had to do with "conveying the idea of membership of a nation, nothing more." It certainly did not include voting. In conferring citizenship, as the Fourteenth Amendment expressly did, the Constitution "did not necessarily confer the right of suffrage." Just because a person was counted as a "member" of a country did not presuppose a right to participate in its affairs by voting. That right inhered in one's state citizenship, and rights one possessed by virtue of state (as opposed to national) citizenship were not among the rights that the Fourteenth Amendment safeguarded against state interference.

Motor Voter Law

See National Voter Registration Act

Mott, Lucretia (1793–1880)

Perhaps the most senior of the leading nineteenth-century advocates of woman's suffrage, Mott was born into a Massachusetts sea captain's home. After her marriage in 1811 to businessman and fellow teacher James Mott, the couple settled in Philadelphia where they were active in a variety of Quaker-sponsored causes, ranging from a campaign against slavery to pacifism to promotion of women's rights. Mott herself became a Quaker minister in 1821. Refused admission to an antislavery conference in London in 1840, she nonetheless met Elizabeth Cady Stanton at that time, and began an association that led to their joint efforts in organizing the Seneca Falls Convention in 1848. She presided over the first convention of the American Equal Rights Association in 1866 that promoted equal treatment for African Americans and all women. (*See also* Seneca Falls Convention.)

National Voter Registration Act

Sometimes called the "motor voter law," this 1993 congressional statute was the first nationwide attempt to make voter registration easier, so as to enlarge the rolls of registered voters. It requires states to allow otherwise eligible persons to register to vote at the same time they apply for or renew a driver's license, to permit mail-in registration, and to provide voter registration services at certain public assistance agencies and military recruitment offices. The law has added to the number of registered voters but has not had a significant impact on voter turnout.

Northwest Ordinance (1787)

Also called the Ordinance of 1787, this was most significant piece of legislation passed by Congress under the Articles of Confederation. It organized the Northwest Territory (American land west of New York and Pennsylvania) and provided for the admission of new states into the Union on an equal footing with the original states, in a manner that has generally been followed ever since.

Philadelphia Convention

See Constitutional Convention

Plessy v. Ferguson (1896)

This decision by the Fuller Court is usually cited as the origin of the "separate but equal" doctrine that provided a constitutional rationale for legally enforced segregation of blacks from whites. Yet the Waite Court in *Pace v. Alabama* (1882) had already implicitly adopted the controlling principle of *Plessy* when it upheld a state law punishing interracial adultery and fornication more severely than the same offenses when committed by persons of the same race. The 1896 decision involved a Louisiana statute passed in 1890 that required railroad companies carrying passengers within the state to provide "equal but separate" accommodations for whites and blacks. With only Justice Harlan dissenting, Justice Henry Billings Brown explained for the majority that the law was a reasonable regulation designed to promote "public peace and good order." The Waite Court had held in *Strauder v. West Virginia* (1880) that the equal protection clause of the Fourteenth Amendment conferred on blacks "the right to exemption from unfriendly legislation against them distinctively as colored; exemption from legal discriminations, implying inferiority in civil society, and discriminations which are steps towards reducing them to the condition of a subject race." But that was not the situation here, insisted Brown. "We consider the underlying fallacy of the plaintiff's argument to consist in the assumption that the enforced separation of the two races stamps the colored race with a badge of inferiority. If this be so, it is not by reason of anything found in the act, but solely because the colored race chooses to put that construction upon it." Coupled with a broad disfranchisement of black voters in southern states in the decade after *Plessy*, it soon became clear that, in practice, segregated facilities and services for blacks and whites were merely that: "separate" but hardly "equal." The separate-but-equal doctrine remained a valid part of American constitutional law until it was overturned by *Brown v. Board of Education* (1954).

Progressivism

This intellectual movement also spawned a short-lived political party that fielded candidates for president and vice president in the elections of 1912 and 1924. (The movement had little or nothing to do with another political party by the same name that nominated Henry Wallace for president in 1948.) With origins dating into the 1880s but most effective between about 1900 and 1920, the movement loosely included three kinds of political reformers: agrarian, social, and political. Each element had its own set of goals that sometimes overlapped with those of one of the other two elements. The agrarian component drew from the Populist movement of the 1880s and 1890s that sought relief from overbearing costs and rates imposed by the banks and railroads. The social component, which had an urban focus, stressed the role government could have in improvement of the lives of individuals in terms of health, working conditions, education, and freedom from the tyranny of monopolies (both local and national). Elimination of child labor, for example, was a major objective of this strain of Progressivism, as was Prohibition. The political component emphasized the need for various structural and procedural changes in government itself, ranging from the primary election as a device by which parties would choose their candidates to the popular election of United States senators that was achieved by ratification of the Seventeenth Amendment in 1913. Many Progressives were also advocates of woman suffrage.

Putney Debates

In 1647, at the end of the English Civil War, Parliament attempted to disband its army without either appropriating funds to pay the troops or passing legislation to protect the political rights of the people. Led by Oliver Cromwell, a moderate faction within the army submitted a "Declaration of the Army" that made modest political demands. Unpersuaded, radical elements called "Levelers" drafted the "Agreement of the People" that called for major reforms including manhood suffrage. Discussions between the two factions at Putney produced a wide-ranging give-and-take that highlighted both some consensus but mainly sharply divergent views. To one extent or another, nearly every argument over expansion of voting rights for more than 200 years afterwards echoed the debates at Putney. The debates remain significant as a window onto the landscape of English political ideas at a time when English settlements in what became the United States were flourishing.

Reconstruction

Reconstruction was both an era and a national policy objective. As a period of time, Reconstruction included at least the twelve years after the end of the Civil War when U.S. Army troops occupied most of the states of the defeated Confederacy. As policy, Reconstruction encompassed an amalgam of statutes that were enacted and constitutional amendments that were adopted between 1865 and 1875. Statutorily, Reconstruction began with creation of the Freedman's Bureau in 1865 and passage of the Civil Rights Act of 1866 and ended with passage of the Civil Rights Act of 1875. Constitutionally, Reconstruction was symbolized by ratification of the Thirteenth (1865), Fourteenth (1868), and Fifteenth (1870) Amendments to the U.S. Constitution. Overall, their aim was an outright political, economic, and social transformation of the conquered territory and, secondarily, a reshaping of race relations in the rest of the nation.

Surrender of southern armies in the spring of 1865 was followed by ratification of the Thirteenth Amendment in December that abolished slavery. Yet the newly freed slave population remained in a legally undefined, unprotected, and therefore precarious position. Legislatures in states of the former Confederacy promptly adopted Black Codes that denied the vote and other basic civil and other legal rights to blacks and relegated them to a subservient status–barely a notch above slavery itself. Pushed through Congress by Republicans and largely opposed by Democrats, including Lincoln's successor President Andrew Johnson, Reconstruction measures—now backed by federal troops—overrode the Black Codes and required the southern states to rewrite their laws and constitutions to reflect the new order by enfranchising black males. These men in turn were as reliably Republican at the polls as most southern whites were reliably Democratic. Moreover, reseating of a southern state's congressional delegation was made dependent upon that state's ratification of the Fourteenth Amendment that sought to federalize protection of basic rights. Such demands, coupled with ratification of the Fifteenth Amendment in 1870 that removed race everywhere as a criterion for voting, made Republicans the dominant party in much of the South until after federal troops were withdrawn following Democratic acquiescence in Rutherford B. Hayes's controversial ascension to the presidency in 1877. The close identification between Reconstruction and the Republican Party, combined with a near-total disfranchisement of blacks after the end of the century, helped to assure white Democratic dominance of the politics of the region until well after the middle of the twentieth century.

Reynolds v. Sims (1964)

Preceded by the redistricting and election cases of *Baker v. Carr, Gray v. Sanders,* and *Wesberry v. Sanders,* this eight-to-one decision by the U.S. Supreme Court applied the rule of numerical equality (one person, one vote) from *Gray* and *Wesberry* to both houses of a state legislature. Henceforth, all districts for the lower house of a state legislature would have to contain the same number of people, as would all districts for the upper house of a state legislature. The effects of the decision brought greater representation to urban and suburban counties, at the expense of more sparsely populated regions of a state.

Scott v. Sandford (1857)

The *Dred Scott Case* is nearly universally regarded as the Supreme Court's most disastrous decision. By denying Congress's authority to ban slavery in the territories, the ruling inflamed public opinion on both sides, forced candidates for national office to take a position on one side or the other, split the Democratic Party, and thus helped to precipitate Abraham Lincoln's election as president in 1860. By placing itself on the wrong side of history, the Court badly tarnished its reputation.

Seneca Falls Convention (1848)

The first women's rights convention held in Seneca Falls, New York, in 1848 is usually regarded as the beginning of the campaign for woman suffrage in the United States. Led by women such as Lucretia Mott and Elizabeth Cady Stanton, the convention produced a declaration that detailed numerous examples of discrimination against women, chief among which was the denial of the ballot in every state of the Union.

Shaw v. Reno (1993)

This five-to-four decision by the U.S. Supreme Court established a right under the Fourteenth Amendment for voters to live in legislative districts that had not been drawn principally on racial grounds. At issue were so-called majority-minority districts, created to enhance representation of racial minorities and to enable racial minorities to control the outcome of elections within their districts. Particularly after amendments to the Voting Rights Act in 1982, the Department of Justice had urged the creation of such districts. Since *Gomillion v. Lightfoot* (1960), it had been clear that political boundaries could not be drawn for the purpose of discriminating against racial minorities. But could such boundaries be drawn for racially ameliorative purposes? In *Shaw* and subsequent cases, the Supreme Court ruled that race could ordinarily not be the predominant factor in drawing district lines.

Smith v. Allwright (1944)

This landmark eight-to-one decision by the U.S. Supreme Court laid to rest the white primary and ended seventeen years of vacillating rulings on the question. For nearly a half century it had been the principal means by which African Americans were denied virtually all influence on the political process. After 1896, the South became a one-party region, with Democrats in control. By excluding blacks from the primary that selected the sure-to-win party's nominees for local, state, and congressional offices, any blacks who were eligible to vote in the general election thus had no practical say in its outcome, other than in presidential races. A letter from Justice Robert H. Jackson to Chief Justice Harlan F. Stone, dated January 14, 1944, indicates some of the behind-the-scenes maneuvering as to which justice would speak for the Court in this case.

> I hope you will forgive me for intruding into the matter of assignments . . ., but I wonder if you have not overlooked some of the ugly factors in our national life which go to the wisdom of having Mr. Justice Frankfurter act as the voice of this Court in the matter of *Smith v. Allwright*. It is a delicate matter. We must reverse a recent, well-considered, and unanimous decision [*Grovey v. Townsend,* 1935]. We deny the entire South the right to a white primary, which is one of its most cherished rights. It seems to me very important that the strength which an all but unanimous decision would have may be greatly

weakened if the voice that utters it is one that may grate on Southern sensibilities. Mr. Justice Frankfurter unites in a rare degree factors which unhappily excite prejudice. In the first place, he is a Jew. In the second place, he is from New England, the seat of the abolition movement. In the third place, he has not been thought of as a person particularly sympathetic with the Democratic party in the past. . . . With all humility I suggest that the Court's decision, bound to arouse bitter resentment, will be much less apt to stir ugly reactions if the news that the white primary is dead, is broken to it, if possible, by a Southerner who has been a Democrat and is not a member of one of the minorities which stir prejudices kindred to those against the Negro. (Mason 1956, 615)

Chief Justice Stone promptly withdrew the case from Frankfurter and assigned it to Justice Stanley Reed of Kentucky. (*See also* White Primary.)

Stanton, Elizabeth Cady (1815–1902)

This most prominent women's rights theorist of the late nineteenth century was the daughter of a prominent New York lawyer and educated in a school for girls in Troy, New York. After her marriage to abolitionist Henry Stanton in 1840, she concentrated not only on antislavery causes, alongside rearing seven children, but on improving the legal, political, and social status of women. With Lucretia Mott she organized the first women's rights convention in her hometown of Seneca Falls, New York, in 1848, which placed a special emphasis on female suffrage. In 1866, she ran unsuccessfully for Congress, after realizing that, while New York prohibited women from voting, no gender barriers existed for office holders. With Susan B. Anthony, she founded the National Woman Suffrage Association in 1869, and served as president for the next twenty years. More so than most advocates of female suffrage, she embraced and articulated a broad women's rights agenda, ranging from birth control to women-friendly divorce laws. (*See also* Seneca Falls Convention.)

Stone, Lucy (1818–1893)

A pioneer in women's rights issues, including suffrage, Stone was born in Brookfield, Massachusetts, and educated at Oberlin College. A forceful speaker and politically talented, she addressed legislators in the 1850s on the political and legal status of women and organized groups at the community level to press for change. Like other suffragists before the Civil War, she was active in antislavery organizations as well. After her marriage to Henry Blackwell in 1855, she retained her original family name as a way to highlight the legal impairments women encountered in marriage. When it became evident that Congress would not include female suffrage as part of the Reconstruction-era amendments, Stone broke with Susan B. Anthony and Elizabeth Cady Stanton over strategy to secure the franchise. This schism led to Stone's formation of the American Woman Suffrage Association (juxtaposed to Anthony and Stanton's National Woman Suffrage Association) that stressed organization and action at the state and local level. Stone also wanted little to do with the emphasis Anthony and Stanton placed at times on the superiority of educated white women to the newly enfranchised black male population. Stone also founded *The Woman's Journal* (retitled *The Woman Citizen* in World War I); for sixty years after its first issue in 1870 it chronicled progress and setbacks on the road to full suffrage. Stone's organization reunited with its rival group in 1890.

Suffrage

Originally *suffrage* referred to intercessory prayer, but by the 1600s the word meant "widely shared opinions." Today the word is synonymous with the right to vote, as it has been since the late eighteenth century. As Pennsylvania's James Wilson asked in his law lectures in the 1790s, "who shall be entitled to suffrage? This darling privilege of freemen should certainly be extended as far as considerations of safety and order will possibly admit. The correct theory and the true principles of liberty require, that every citizen, whose circumstances do not render him necessarily dependent on the will of another, should possess a vote in electing those, by whose conduct his property, his reputation, his liberty, and his life, may be all most materially affected" (McCloskey 1967, vol. 1, 406–407). Suffrage is also used interchangeably with "franchise."

Vieth v. Jubelirer (2004)

In contrast to *Davis v. Bandemer* (1986), this Supreme Court decision practically removes federal courts from the realm of deciding cases alleging partisan gerrymandering, or the deliberate shaping of legislative districts to enhance a party's strength at the expense of the opposition.

Voting Rights Act of 1965

This statute remains the most important voter legislation ever enacted by Congress. Its measures (such as a ban on literacy tests) were extreme, but so were the evils it sought to correct. Upheld by the U.S. Supreme Court in *South Carolina v. Katzenbach* (1966), the law has done more than any other legislation to end racial discrimination in voting, particularly in southern states. Indeed, in the South today, blacks vote in percentages that almost equal those for whites.

Three sections of the 1965 act are especially noteworthy. Section 2 repeats the Fifteenth Amendment's prohibition against racial discrimination in voting and applies throughout the United States. An amendment to Section 2 in 1982 expressly prohibits voting regulations that *result* in a denial of the right to vote on account of race. A violation of Section 2 occurs when the "totality of circumstances" reveals that minority voters have less opportunity than others to elect officials "of their choice." Section 4 sets up a triggering mechanism for determining which parts of the country (mostly in the South) are subject to Section 5. Section 5 requires that any change in a "standard, practice, or procedure with respect to voting" can take effect only after being cleared by the attorney general or by the U.S. District Court for the District of Columbia. The Supreme Court has interpreted "standard, practice, or procedure" to include any changes in a locale's electoral system. This preclearance requirement is satisfied only if the jurisdiction proposing the change can demonstrate that the change neither has the purpose nor will have the effect of "denying or abridging the right to vote on account of race or color." Black voting strength, therefore, cannot be weakened or diluted by a change in local election practices. For example, the Supreme Court decided that Section 5 is violated if a city covered by the act enlarges its boundaries in such a way that blacks become a smaller percentage of the voting population (*Rome v. United States,* 1980). Thus, retrogression—being worse off than before—is ordinarily dispositive for Section 5 violations. "[T]he purpose of § 5 has always been to insure that no voting-procedure changes would be made that would lead to a retrogression in the position of racial minorities with respect to their effective exercise of the electoral franchise" (*Beer v. United States,* 1976). Congress will confront the Voting Rights Act again in 2007, the year in which the law's twenty-five-year extension in 1982 expires.

Warren Court

Earl Warren (1891–1974) was chief justice of the United States between 1953 and 1969. His Court was one of the most active and remarkable in American history. By one count, in the approximately 150 years before Warren's appointment, the Court had overruled eighty-eight of its precedents. In Warren's sixteen years it added another forty-five to the list. Hardly an aspect of public life went untouched by landmark decisions on race discrimination, voting, and the Bill of Rights. The Warren Court truly initiated a revolution that is measured by President Dwight Eisenhower's latter-day lament over the chief justice's appointment: "The biggest damn fool mistake I ever made."

Wesberry v. Sanders (1964)

Preceded by the redistricting and election cases *Baker v. Carr* (1962) and *Gray v. Sanders* (1963), this seven-to-two decision by the U.S. Supreme Court applied *Gray's* one person, one vote standard to congressional districts. Henceforth, the principle of numerical equality would apply for all states with more than one congressional district. *Wesberry* effectively redrew the map of political power within the U.S. House of Representatives.

White Primary

The Supreme Court decreed in *United States v. Reese* (1876) that the Fifteenth Amendment on its on terms conferred the right to vote on no one. Instead, it barred race as a criterion for voting. Around the beginning of the twentieth century, after the South had become a one-party region almost entirely, states began to exclude blacks from voting in primaries. The legal question thus became whether voting in a primary implicated a right protected by the Constitution. In *Nixon v. Herndon* (1927), the Supreme Court held that the Texas white primary violated the Fourteenth Amendment's equal protection clause. The Court reached a similar result in *Nixon v. Condon* (1932) after the state tried to maneuver around the strictures of the amendment. In *Grovey v. Townsend* (1935), however, the Court found no constitutional violation when the exclusion of black votes seemed entirely to result from a decision made not by the state but by the Democratic Party. *United States v. Classic* (1941) portended a shift in the other direction when, in an election fraud case, the primary itself was deemed to be in effect an election. *Smith v. Allwright* (1944) adopted the *Classic* logic and decreed an end to the white primary. *Terry v. Adams* (1953) blocked a circumvention of the *Smith* decision. The victory over the white primary, however, did not result in a resurgence of voting by blacks because other hurdles remained in place. The legal forces in the NAACP's Legal Defense Fund that helped to defeat the white primary did not remain resolute in its defense of voting by blacks, but shifted resources to knocking down racial barriers in public education. Even the latter goal would not be significantly implemented until the former goal of an expanded franchise was achieved legislatively in the mid-1960s. (See also *Smith v. Allwright.*)

Willard, Frances (1839–1898)

This university educator and reformer was born in Churchville, New York, and reared in Wisconsin. In 1874, she became active in the Women's Christian Temperance Union, one of the first national reform-minded organizations for women. Heading the WCTU after 1878, she focused hers and the WCTU's efforts not only on the evils of strong drink but on woman suffrage, penal and labor betterment, public health, and improved sexual morality. In her view, elevating the status of women and the quality of home life required action across a broad front. She even made an unsuccessful attempt in 1892 to unite the WCTU with the Knights of Labor and the Populist Party to form a new political party.

Wilson, (Thomas) Woodrow (1856–1924)

The twenty-eighth American president was the only national chief executive to date whose principal professional experience prior to the White House was in the academy. Born into the home of a Presbyterian minister in Staunton, Virginia, Wilson spent most of his boyhood years in South Carolina and Georgia during the Reconstruction era. After a year at Davidson College, he matriculated at Princeton, from which he graduated in 1879. Law study at the University of Virginia led to a brief practice in Atlanta, after which Wilson entered graduate school at Johns Hopkins University, earning a Ph.D. in 1886 in history and the new discipline of political science. He returned to Princeton as a member of the faculty and was elected its first nonclerical president in 1902. After losing a tussle with his graduate school dean over the location of a graduate residence facility, Wilson left Princeton in a huff and successfully ran as a Democrat for the New Jersey governorship. By 1912, it became clear that incumbent President William Howard Taft was unelectable. When "Old Guard" Republicans renominated him anyway, more liberal Republicans bolted, formed the Progressive (or Bull Moose) Party, and nominated former president Theodore Roosevelt. This division opened the door to victory for Democratic nominee Woodrow Wilson who, as governor, had also both professed and practiced Progressivism. Wilson, however, owed a debt to chance even in securing the nomination. But for a party rule that required a two-thirds vote for nomination, Democrats would have instead selected House Speaker Champ Clark of Missouri, who was decidedly less reform-minded than Wilson.

Wilson's policy agenda was known as the New Freedom. It differed from Roosevelt's New Nationalism chiefly in that the former was flatly opposed to industrial and financial trusts, while the latter found them acceptable if under federal regulation. The Federal Reserve System was born in Wilson's first term, as was the Federal Trade Commission and the first income tax following ratification of the Sixteenth Amendment. For the first time in sixty years, protectionist tariffs ceased to be a cornerstone of federal policy, as rates were dropped to pre–Civil War levels. World War

I and its aftermath dominated Wilson's second term, after his victory in 1916 over Republican Charles Evans Hughes. After the Armistice in November 1918, Wilson campaigned for nearly a year for American participation in the League of Nations. He exhausted himself on that issue both physically and politically: he suffered a massive stroke in October 1919 that left him an invalid for the remainder of his term, and the Senate rejected the League Covenant. It was during his second term that the Nineteenth Amendment, enfranchising women, became part of the Constitution.

6

DOCUMENTS

ARTICLES AND AMENDMENTS,
U.S. CONSTITUTION

Article I

Section 2

The House of Representatives shall be composed of Members chosen every second Year by the People of the several States, and the Electors in each State shall have the Qualifications requisite for Electors of the most numerous Branch of the State Legislature. . . .

Representatives and direct Taxes shall be apportioned among the several States which may be included within this Union, according to their respective Numbers, which shall be determined by adding to the whole Number of Free Persons, including those bound to Service for a Term of Years, and excluding Indians not taxed, three fifths of all other persons. The actual Enumeration shall be made within three Years after the first Meeting of the Congress of the United States, and within every subsequent Term of ten Years, in such Manner as they shall by Law direct. The Number of Representatives shall not exceed one for every thirty thousand, but each State shall have at least one Representative; and until such enumeration shall be made, the State of New Hampshire shall be entitled to chuse three, Massachusetts eight, Rhode Island and Providence Plantations one, Connecticut five, New York six, New Jersey four, Pennsylvania eight, Delaware one, Maryland six, Virginia ten,

North Carolina five, South Carolina five, and Georgia three. [But see Amendment XIII and Amendment XIV, Section 2, below.]

Section 3

The Senate of the United States shall be composed of two Senators from each State, chosen by the Legislature thereof, for six Years; and each Senator shall have one Vote. [But see Amendment XVII below.— Au.]

Section 4

The Times, Places and Manner of holding Elections for Senators and Representatives, shall be prescribed in each State by the Legislature thereof; but the Congress may at any time by Law make or alter such Regulations, except as to the Places of chusing Senators.

Section 8

. . . To exercise exclusive Legislation in all Cases whatsoever, over such District (not exceeding ten Miles square) as may, by Cession of particular States, and the acceptance of Congress, become the Seat of the Government of the United States. . . .

Article II

Section 1

The executive Power shall be vested in a President of the United States of America. He shall hold his Office during the Term of four Years, and, together with the Vice-President, chosen for the same term, be elected, as follows.

Each State shall appoint, in such Manner as the Legislature thereof may direct, a number of Electors, equal to the whole number of Senators and Representatives to which the State may be entitled in the Congress; but no Senator or Representative, or Person holding an Office of Trust or Profit under the United States, shall be appointed an Elector.

The Electors shall meet in their respective States, and vote by Ballot for two persons, of whom one at least shall not be an Inhabitant of the same State with themselves. And they shall make a List of all the Persons voted for, and of the Number of Votes for each; which List they shall sign and certify, and transmit sealed to the Seat of the Government of the United States, directed to the President of the Senate. The President of the Senate shall, in the Presence of the Senate and House of Representatives, open all the Certificates, and the Votes shall then be counted. The Person having the greatest Number of Votes shall be the President, if such Number be a Majority of the whole Number of Electors appointed; and if there be more than one who have such Majority, and have an Equal Number of Votes, then the House of Representatives shall immediately chuse by Ballot one of them for President; and if no Person have a Majority, then from the five highest on the List the said House shall in like Manner chuse the President, but in chusing the President, the Votes shall be taken by States, the Representation from each State having one Vote; a quorum for this Purpose shall consist of a Member or Members from two-thirds of the States, and a Majority of all the States shall be necessary to a Choice. In every Case, after the Choice of the President, the Person having the greatest Number of Votes of the Electors shall be the Vice-President. But if there should remain two or more who have equal Votes, the Senate shall chuse from them by Ballot the Vice-President. [But see Amendment XII below.—Au.]

The Congress may determine the Time of chusing the Electors, and the Day on which they shall give their Vote; which Day shall be the same throughout the United States.

Article IV

Section 4

The United States shall guarantee to every State in this Union a Republican Form of Government, and shall protect each of them against Invasion; and on Application of the Legislature, or of the Executive (when the Legislature cannot be convened) against domestic Violence.

Article V

The Congress, whenever two-thirds of both Houses shall deem it necessary, shall propose Amendments to this Constitution, or, on the Application of the Legislatures of two-thirds of the several States, shall call a Convention for proposing Amendments, which, in either Case, shall be valid to all Intents and Purposes, as part of this Constitution, when ratified by the Legislatures of three-fourths of the several States, or by Conventions in three-fourths thereof, as the one or the other Mode of Ratification may be proposed by the Congress; Provided that no Amendment which may be made prior to the Year One thousand eight hundred and eight shall in any Manner affect the first and fourth Clauses in the Ninth Section of the first Article; and that no State, without its Consent, shall be deprived of its equal Suffrage in the Senate.

Article VII

The Ratification of the Conventions of nine States shall be sufficient for the Establishment of this Constitution between the States so ratifying the Same. . . .

Amendment I (1791)

Congress shall make no law respecting an establishment of religion, or prohibiting the free exercise thereof; or abridging the freedom of speech, or of the press; or the right of the people peaceably to assemble, and to petition the Government for a redress of grievances.

Amendment XII (1804)

The Electors shall meet in their respective states and vote by ballot for President and Vice-President, one of whom, at least, shall not be an inhabitant of the same state with themselves; they shall name in their ballots the person voted for as President, and in distinct ballots the person voted for as Vice-President, and they shall make distinct lists of all persons voted for as president, and all persons voted for as Vice-President, and of the number of votes for each, which lists they shall sign and certify, and transmit sealed to the seat of the government of the United States, directed to the President of the Senate;—The President of the Senate shall, in the presence of the Senate and House of Representatives, open all the certificates and the votes shall then be counted;—The person having the greatest number of votes for President, shall be the President, if such number be a majority of the whole number of Electors appointed; and if no person have such majority, then from the persons having the highest numbers not exceeding three on the list of those voted for as President, the House of Representatives shall choose immediately, by ballot, the President. But in choosing the President, the votes shall be taken by states, the representation from each state having one vote; a quorum for this purpose shall consist of a member or members from two-thirds of the states, and a majority of all the states shall be necessary to a choice. And if the House of Representatives shall not choose a President whenever the right of choice shall devolve upon them, before the fourth day of March next following, then the Vice-President shall act as President, as in the case of the death or other constitutional disability of the President.—The person having the greatest number of votes as Vice-President, shall be the Vice-President, if such number be a majority of the whole number of Electors appointed, and if no person have a majority, then from the two highest numbers on the list, the Senate shall choose the Vice-President; a quorum for the purpose shall consist of two-thirds of the whole number of Senators, and a majority of the whole number shall be necessary to a choice. But no person constitutionally ineligible to the office of the President shall be eligible to that of Vice-President of the United States.

Amendment XIII (1865)

Section 1

Neither slavery nor involuntary servitude, except as a punishment for crime whereof the party shall have been duly convicted, shall exist within the United States, or any place subject to their jurisdiction.

Section 2

Congress shall have power to enforce this article by appropriate legislation.

Amendment XIV (1868)

Section 1

All persons born or naturalized in the United States and subject to the jurisdiction thereof, are citizens of the United States and of the State wherein they reside. No State shall make or enforce any law which shall abridge the privileges or immunities of citizens of the United States; nor shall any State deprive any person of life, liberty, or property, without due process of law; nor deny to any person within its jurisdiction the equal protection of the laws.

Section 2

Representatives shall be apportioned among the several States according to their respective numbers, counting the whole number of persons in each State, excluding Indians not taxed. But when the right to vote at any election for the choice of electors for President and Vice-President of the United States, Representatives in Congress, the Executive and Judicial Officers of a State, or the members of the Legislature thereof, is denied to any of the male inhabitants of such State, being twenty-one years of age, and citizens of the United States, or in any way abridged, except for participation in rebellion, or other crime, the basis of representation therein shall be reduced in the proportion which the number of such male citizens shall bear to the whole number of male citizens twenty-one years of age in such State.

Section 3

No person shall be a Senator or Representative in Congress, or elector of President and Vice-President, or hold any office, civil or military, under the United States, or under any State, who, having previously taken an oath, as a member of Congress, or as an officer of the United States, or as a member of any State legislature, or as an executive or judicial officer of any State, to support the Constitution of the United States, shall have engaged in insurrection or rebellion against the same, or given aid or comfort to the enemies thereof. But Congress may by a vote of two-thirds of each House, remove such disability.

Section 5

The Congress shall have power to enforce, by appropriate legislation, the provisions of this article.

Amendment XV (1870)

Section 1

The right of citizens of the United States to vote shall not be denied or abridged by the United States or by any State on account of race, color, or previous condition of servitude.

Section 2

The Congress shall have the power to enforce this article by appropriate legislation.

Amendment XVII (1913)

The Senate of the United States shall be composed of two Senators from each State, elected by the people thereof, for six years, and each Senator shall have one vote. The electors in each State shall have the qualifications requisite for electors of the most numerous branch of the State legislatures.

When vacancies happen in the representation of any State in the Senate, the executive authority of such State shall issue writs of election to fill such vacancies: Provided, That the legislature of any State may empower the executive thereof to make temporary appointments until the people fill the vacancies by election as the legislature may direct.

This amendment shall not be so construed as to affect the election or term of any Senator chosen before it becomes valid as part of the Constitution.

Amendment XIX (1920)

The right of citizens of the United States to vote shall not be denied or abridged by the United States or by any State on account of sex.

Congress shall have power to enforce this article by appropriate legislation.

Amendment XXII (1951)

Section 1

No person shall be elected to the office of the President more than twice, and no person who has held the office of President, or acted as President, for more than two years of a term to which some other person was elected President shall be elected to the office of President more than once. But this Article shall not apply to any person holding the office of President when this Article was proposed by the Congress, and shall not prevent any person who may be holding the office of President, or acting as President, during the term within which this Article becomes operative from holding the office of President, or acting as President during the remainder of such term.

Section 2

This article shall be inoperative unless it shall have been ratified as an amendment to the Constitution by the legislatures of three-fourths of the several States within seven years from the date of its submission to the States by the Congress.

Amendment XXIII (1961)

Section 1

The District constituting the seat of Government of the United States shall appoint in such manner as the Congress may direct:

A number of electors of President and Vice-President equal to the whole number of Senators and Representatives in Congress to which the District would be entitled if it were a State, but in no event more than the least populous State; they shall be in addition to those appointed by the States, but they shall be considered, for the purposes of the election of President and Vice-President, to be electors appointed by a state; and they shall meet in the District and perform such duties as provided by the twelfth article of amendment.

Section 2

The Congress shall have power to enforce this article by appropriate legislation.

Amendment XXIV (1964)

Section 1

The right of citizens of the United States to vote in any primary or other election for President or Vice-President, for electors for President or Vice-President, or for Senator or Representative in Congress, shall not be denied or abridged by the United States or any State by reason of failure to pay any poll tax or other tax.

Section 2

The Congress shall have power to enforce this article by appropriate legislation.

Amendment XXVI (1971)

Section 1

The Right of Citizens of the United States, who are eighteen years of age or older, to vote shall not be denied or abridged by the United States or any State on account of age.

Section 2

The Congress shall have the power to enforce this article by appropriate legislation.

SMITH V. ALLWRIGHT (1944)

By the time this case was decided, all members of the Court who participated in Grovey v. Townsend, *except Chief Justice Harlan Stone and Justice Owen J. Roberts, had left the bench. Also, readers should review the entry on* Smith v. Allwright *in Chapter Five. It explains the unusual circumstances that influenced Stone to assign the task of writing the opinion of the Court in this important case to Justice Stanley Reed of Kentucky.*

JUSTICE REED delivered the opinion of the Court.

The State of Texas by its Constitution and statutes provides that every person, if certain other requirements are met which are not here in issue, qualified by residence in the district or county "shall be deemed a qualified elector." . . . Primary elections for United States Senators, Congressmen and state officers are provided for by Chapters Twelve and Thirteen of the statutes. Under these chapters, the Democratic party was required to hold the primary which was the occasion of the alleged wrong to petitioner. . . . These nominations are to be made by the qualified voters of the party.

The Democratic party of Texas is held by the Supreme Court of that State to be a "voluntary association," protected by §27 of the Bill of

Rights, Art. 1, Constitution of Texas, from interference by the State except that: "In the interest of fair methods and a fair expression by their members of their preferences in the selection of their nominees, the State may regulate such elections by proper laws."

That court stated further:

> Since the right to organize and maintain a political party is one guaranteed by the Bill of Rights of this State, it necessarily follows that every privilege essential or reasonably appropriate to the exercise of that right is likewise guaranteed,—including, of course, the privilege of determining the policies of the party and its membership. Without the privilege of determining the policy of a political association and its membership, the right to organize such an association would be a mere mockery. We think these rights,—that is, the right to determine the membership of a political party and to determine its policies, of necessity are to be exercised by the state convention of such party, and cannot, under any circumstances, be conferred upon a state or governmental agency. . . .

Texas is free to conduct her elections and limit her electorate as she may deem wise, save only as her action may be affected by the prohibitions of the United States Constitution or in conflict with powers delegated to and exercised by the National Government. The Fourteenth Amendment forbids a State from making or enforcing any law which abridges the privileges or immunities of citizens of the United States and the Fifteenth Amendment specifically interdicts any denial or abridgement by a State of the right of citizens to vote on account of color. Respondents appeared in the District Court and the Circuit Court of Appeals and defended on the ground that the Democratic party of Texas is a voluntary organization with members banded together for the purpose of selecting individuals of the group representing the common political beliefs as candidates in the general election. As such a voluntary organization, it was claimed, the Democratic party is free to select its own membership and limit to whites participation in the party primary. Such action, the answer asserted, does not violate the Fourteenth, Fifteenth or Seventeenth Amendments as officers of government cannot be chosen at primaries and the Amendments are applicable only to general elections where governmental officers are actually elected. . . .

Since *Grovey v. Townsend* and prior to the present suit, no case from Texas involving primary elections has been before this Court. We did decide, however, *United States v. Classic* [1941]. . . . We there held that §4 of Article I of the Constitution authorized Congress to regulate primary as well as general elections, "where the primary is by law made an integral part of the election machinery." Consequently, in the *Classic* case, we upheld the applicability to frauds in a Louisiana primary of §§19 and 20 of the Criminal Code. . . . *Classic* bears upon *Grovey v. Townsend* not because exclusion of Negroes from primaries is any more or less state action by reason of the unitary character of the electoral process but because the recognition of the place of the primary in the electoral scheme makes clear that state delegation to a party of the power to fix the qualifications of primary elections is delegation of a state function that may make the party's action the action of the State. When *Grovey v. Townsend* was written, the Court looked upon the denial of a vote in a primary as a mere refusal by a party of party membership. As the Louisiana statutes for holding primaries are similar to those of Texas, our ruling in *Classic* as to the unitary character of the electoral process calls for a reexamination as to whether or not the exclusion of Negroes from a Texas party primary was state action. . . .

It may now be taken as a postulate that the right to vote in such a primary for the nomination of candidates without discrimination by the State, like the right to vote in a general election, is a right secured by the Constitution. . . . By the terms of the Fifteenth Amendment that right may not be abridged by any State on account of race. Under our Constitution the great privilege of the ballot may not be denied a man by the State because of his color.

We are thus brought to an examination of the qualifications for Democratic primary electors in Texas, to determine whether state action or private action has excluded Negroes from participation. Despite Texas' decision that the exclusion is produced by private or party action . . . federal courts must for themselves appraise the facts leading to that conclusion. It is only by the performance of this obligation that a final and uniform interpretation can be given to the Constitution, the "supreme Law of the Land." . . .

Primary elections are conducted by the party under state statutory authority. The county executive committee selects precinct election officials and the county, district or state executive committees, respectively, canvass the returns. These party committees or the state convention certify the party's candidates to the appropriate officers for inclusion on the official ballot for the general election. No name which has not been so certified may appear upon the ballot for the general election as a candidate of a political party. No other name may be printed on the ballot which has not been placed in nomination by qualified voters who must take oath that they did not participate in a primary for the selection of a candidate for the office for which the nomination is made.

The state courts are given exclusive original jurisdiction of contested elections and of mandamus proceedings to compel party officers to perform their statutory duties.

We think that this statutory system for the selection of party nominees for inclusion on the general election ballot makes the party which is required to follow these legislative directions an agency of the State in so far as it determines the participants in a primary election. The party takes its character as a state agency from the duties imposed upon it by state statutes; the duties do not become matters of private law because they are performed by a political party. The plan of the Texas primary follows substantially that of Louisiana, with the exception that in Louisiana the State pays the cost of the primary while Texas assesses the cost against candidates. In numerous instances, the Texas statutes fix or limit the fees to be charged. Whether paid directly by the State or through state requirements, it is state action which compels. When primaries become a part of the machinery for choosing officials, state and national, as they have here, the same tests to determine the character of discrimination or abridgement should be applied to the primary as are applied to the general election. If the State requires a certain electoral procedure, prescribes a general election ballot made up of party nominees so chosen and limits the choice of the electorate in general elections for state offices, practically speaking, to those whose names appear on such a ballot, it endorses, adopts and enforces the discrimination against Negroes, practiced by a party entrusted by Texas law with the determination of the qualifications of participants In the primary. This is state action within the meaning of the Fifteenth Amendment. . . .

The United States is a constitutional democracy. Its organic law grants to all citizens a right to participate in the choice of elected officials without restriction by the State because of race. This grant to the people of the opportunity for choice is not to be nullified by a State through casting its electoral process in a form which permits a private organization to practice racial discrimination in the election. Constitutional rights would be of little value if they could be thus indirectly denied. . . .

In reaching this conclusion we are not unmindful of the desirability of continuity of decision in constitutional questions. However, when convinced of former error, this Court has never felt constrained to follow precedent. In constitutional questions, where correction depends upon amendment and not upon legislative action this Court throughout its history has freely exercised its power to reexamine the basis of its constitutional decisions. This has long been accepted practice, and this practice has continued to this day. This is particularly true when the decision believed erroneous is the application of a constitutional principle rather than an interpretation of the Constitution to extract the principle itself. Here we are applying, contrary to the recent decision in *Grovey v. Townsend,* the well-established principle of the Fifteenth Amendment, forbidding the abridgement by a State of a citizen's right to vote. *Grovey v. Townsend* is overruled.

Judgment reversed.

JUSTICE FRANKFURTER concurs in the result.

JUSTICE ROBERTS:

In *Mahnich v. Southern Steamship Co.* [1944], I have expressed my views with respect to the present policy of the court freely to disregard and to overrule considered decisions and the rules of law announced in them. This tendency, it seems to me, indicates an intolerance for what those who have composed this court in the past have conscientiously and deliberately concluded, and involves an assumption that knowledge and wisdom reside in us which was denied to our predecessors. I shall not repeat what I there said for I consider it fully applicable to the instant decision, which but points the moral anew. . . .

The reason for my concern is that the instant decision, overruling that announced about nine years ago, tends to bring adjudications of this tribunal into the same class as a restricted railroad ticket, good for this day and train only. I have no assurance, in view of current decisions, that the opinion announced today may not shortly be repudiated and overruled by justices who deem they have new light on the subject. In the present term the court has overruled three cases.

In the present case, as in *Mahnich v. Southern S.S. Co.,* the court below relied, as it was bound to, upon our previous decision. As that court points out, the statutes of Texas have not been altered since *Grovey v. Townsend* was decided. The same resolution is involved as was drawn in question in *Grovey v. Townsend.* Not a fact differentiates that case from this except the names of the parties.

It is suggested that *Grovey v. Townsend* was overruled *sub silentio* in *United States v. Classic.* . . . If so, the situation is even worse than that exhibited by the outright repudiation of an earlier decision, for it is the fact that, in the *Classic* case, *Grovey v. Townsend* was distinguished in brief and argument by the Government without suggestion that it was wrongly decided, and was relied on by the appellees, not as a controlling decision, but by way of analogy. The case is not mentioned in either of the opinions in the *Classic* case. Again and again it is said in the opinion of the court in that case that the voter who was denied the right to vote was a fully qualified voter. In other words, there was no question of his being a person entitled under state law to vote in the primary. The offense charged was the fraudulent denial of his conceded right by an election officer because of his race. Here the question is altogether different. It is whether, in a Democratic primary, he who tendered his vote was a member of the Democratic party. . . .

It is regrettable that in an era marked by doubt and confusion, an era whose greatest need is steadfastness of thought and purpose, this court, which has been looked to as exhibiting consistency in adjudication, and a steadiness which would hold the balance even in the face of temporary ebbs and flows of opinion, should now itself become the breeder of fresh doubt and confusion in the public mind as to the stability of our institutions.

COLEGROVE V. GREEN (1946)

This case involved a challenge under the Fourteenth Amendment's equal protection clause to the congressional districting plan in Illinois, which had last been revised in 1901. With only seven justices participating, the Court divided four to three against those challenging the plan. Justice Robert H. Jackson did not take part because he was serving as chief prosecutor at the Nuremberg war crimes trials in Germany following World War II. Chief Justice

Stone had died, and his successor, Fred M. Vinson, had not been confirmed.

JUSTICE FRANKFURTER announced the judgment of the Court and an opinion in which JUSTICE REED and JUSTICE BURTON concurred.

We are of opinion that the appellants ask of this Court what is beyond its competence to grant. This is one of those demands on judicial power which cannot be met by verbal fencing about "jurisdiction." It must be resolved by considerations on the basis of which this Court, from time to time, has refused to intervene in controversies. It has refused to do so because due regard for the effective working of our Government revealed this issue to be of a peculiarly political nature and therefore not meet for judicial determination. . . .

Of course no court can affirmatively re-map the Illinois districts so as to bring them more in conformity with the standards of fairness for a representative system. At best we could only declare the existing electoral system invalid. The result would be to leave Illinois undistricted and to bring into operation, if the Illinois legislature chose not to act, the choice of members for the House of Representatives on a state-wide ticket. The last stage may be worse than the first. The upshot of judicial action may defeat the vital political principle which led Congress, more than a hundred years ago, to require districting. This requirement, in the language of Chancellor Kent, "was recommended by the wisdom and justice of giving, as far as possible, to the local subdivisions of the people of each state, a due influence in the choice of representatives, so as not to leave the aggregate minority of the people in a state, though approaching perhaps to a majority, to be wholly overpowered by the combined action of the numerical majority, without any voice whatever in the national councils." . . . Nothing is clearer than that this controversy concerns matters that bring courts into immediate and active relations with party contests. From the determination of such issues this Court has traditionally held aloof. It is hostile to a democratic system to involve the judiciary in the politics of the people. And it is not less pernicious if such judicial intervention in an essentially political contest be dressed up in the abstract phrases of the law. . . .

The one stark fact that emerges from study of the history of Congressional apportionment is its embroilment in politics, in the sense of party contests and party interest. The Constitution enjoins upon Congress the duty of apportioning representatives "among the several States . . . according to their respective Numbers. . . ." Yet, Congress has at times been heedless of this command and not apportioned according to the requirements of the Census. It never occurred to anyone that this Court could issue mandamus to compel Congress to perform its mandatory duty to apportion. . . .

To sustain this action would cut very deep into the very being of Congress. Courts ought not to enter this political thicket. The remedy for unfairness in districting is to secure State legislatures that will apportion properly, or to invoke the ample powers of Congress. The Constitution has many commands that are not enforceable by courts because they clearly fall outside the conditions and purposes that circumscribe judicial action. Thus, "on demand of the executive authority," Art. IV, § 2, of a State it is the duty of a sister State to deliver up a fugitive from justice. But the fulfilment of this duty cannot be judicially enforced. The duty to see to it that the laws are faithfully executed cannot be brought under legal compulsion. . . . Violation of the great guaranty of a republican form of government in States cannot be challenged in the courts. The Constitution has left the performance of many duties in our governmental scheme to depend on the fidelity of the executive and legislative action and, ultimately, on the vigilance of the people in exercising their political rights.

Dismissal of the complaint is affirmed.

JUSTICE RUTLEDGE, concurred in the result.

JUSTICE BLACK dissented.

It is difficult for me to see why the 1901 State Apportionment Act does not deny appellants equal protection of the laws. The failure of the Legislature to reapportion the congressional election districts for forty years, despite census figures indicating great changes in the distribution of the population, has resulted in election districts the populations of which range from 112,000 to 900,000. One of the appellants lives in a district of more than 900,000 people. His vote is consequently much less effective than that of each of the citizens living in the district of 112,000. And such a gross inequality in the voting power of citizens irrefutably demonstrates defensible discrimination against appellants and all other voters in heavily populated districts. The equal protection clause of the

Fourteenth Amendment forbids such discrimination. It does not permit the States to pick out certain qualified citizens or groups of citizens and deny them the right to vote at all.

It is contended, however, that a court of equity does not have the power, or even if it has the power, that it should not exercise it in this case. To do so, it is argued, would mean that the Court is entering the area of "political questions." I cannot agree with that argument. There have been cases, such as *Coleman v. Miller* [1938], where this Court declined to decide a question because it was political. In the *Miller* case, however, the question involved was ratification of a Constitutional amendment, a matter over which the Court believed Congress had given final authority. To have decided that question would have amounted to a trespass upon the Constitutional power of Congress. Here we have before us a state law which abridges the Constitutional rights of citizens to cast votes in such a way as to obtain the kind of Congressional representation the Constitution guarantees to them.

It is true that voting is a part of elections and that elections are "political." But as this Court said in *Nixon v. Herndon* [1927], it is a mere "play on words" to refer to a controversy such as this as "political" in the sense that courts have nothing to do with protecting and vindicating the right of a voter to cast an effective ballot. The *Classic* case, among myriads of others, refutes the contention that courts are impotent in connection with evasions of all "political" rights.

... What is involved here is the right to vote guaranteed by the Federal Constitution. It has always been the rule that where a federally protected right has been invaded the federal courts will provide the remedy to rectify the wrong done. Federal courts have not hesitated to exercise their equity power in cases involving deprivation of property and liberty. ... There is no reason why they should do so where the case involves the right to choose representatives that make laws affecting liberty and property. ...

JUSTICE DOUGLAS and JUSTICE MURPHY joined in this dissent.

REYNOLDS V. SIMS (1964)

The climax of a series of cases involving challenges to state apportionment arrangements came in 1964, when the Court invalidated the legislative apportionments of Alabama, Colorado, Delaware,

Maryland, New York, and Virginia. Challenged specifically in Alabama were three distinct apportionment schemes: the existing plan, a proposed plan, and a "stand-by" plan. All contained population variations ranging, at the least, from 31,175 to 634,854 for the 35-member state senate, and from 20,000 to 52,000 for the 106-member state house. A three-judge panel of the U.S. District Court for the Middle District of Alabama found each plan constitutionally deficient. The majority opinion in Reynolds v. Sims *(the Alabama case) sets forth the basic principles applied in each of the six cases.*

CHIEF JUSTICE WARREN delivered the opinion of the Court.

Plaintiffs below alleged that the last apportionment of the Alabama Legislature was based on the 1900 federal census, despite the requirement of the State Constitution that the legislature be reapportioned decennially. They asserted that, since the population growth in the State from 1900 to 1960 had been uneven, Jefferson and other counties were now victims of serious discrimination with respect to the allocation of legislative representation. . . .

Legislators represent people, not trees or acres. Legislators are elected by voters, not farms or cities or economic interests. As long as ours is a representative form of government, and our legislatures are those instruments of government elected directly by and directly representative of the people, the right to elect legislators in a free and unimpaired fashion is a bedrock of our political system. It could hardly be gainsaid that a constitutional claim had been asserted by an allegation that certain otherwise qualified voters had been entirely prohibited from voting for members of their state legislature. And, if a State should provide that the votes of citizens in one part of the State should be given two times, or five times, or 10 times the weight of votes of citizens in another part of the State, it could hardly be contended that the right to vote of those residing in the disfavored areas had not been effectively diluted. It would appear extraordinary to suggest that a state could be constitutionally permitted to enact a law providing that certain of the state's voters could vote two, five, or 10 times for their legislative representatives, while voters living elsewhere could vote only once. And it is inconceivable that a state law to the effect that, in counting votes for legislators, the votes of citizens in one part of the State would be multiplied by two, five or 10, while the votes of persons in another area would be counted only at face value, could be constitutionally sustainable. Of course, the effect of state legislative districting schemes which give the same number of representatives to unequal numbers of constituents is identical. . . .

Logically, in a society that is ostensibly grounded on representative government, it would seem reasonable that a majority of the people of the State could elect a majority of that State's legislators. To conclude differently, and to sanction minority control of state legislative bodies, would appear to deny majority rights in a way that far surpasses any possible denial of minority rights that might otherwise be thought to result. Since legislatures are responsible for enacting laws by which all citizens are to be governed, they should be bodies which are collectively responsive to the popular will. And the concept of equal protection has been traditionally viewed as requiring the uniform treatment of persons standing in the same relation to the governmental action questioned or challenged. With respect to the allocation of legislative representation, all voters, as citizens of a State, stand in the same relation regardless of where they live. Any suggested criteria for the differentiation of citizens are insufficient to justify any discrimination, as to the weight of their votes, unless relevant to the permissible purposes of legislative apportionment. Since the achieving of fair and effective representation for all citizens is concededly the basic aim of legislative apportionment, we conclude that the Equal Protection Clause guarantees the opportunity for equal participation by all voters in the election of state legislators. . . .

To the extent that a citizen's right to vote is debased, he is that much less a citizen. The fact that an individual lives here or there is not a legitimate reason for overweighting or diluting the efficacy of his vote. The complexions of societies and civilizations change, often with amazing rapidity. A nation once primarily rural in character becomes predominantly urban. Representation schemes once fair and equitable become archaic and outdated. But the basic principle of representative government remains, and must remain, unchanged—the weight of a citizen's vote cannot be made to depend on where he lives. Population is, of necessity, the starting point for consideration and the controlling criterion for judgment in legislative apportionment controversies. A citizen, a qualified voter, is no more nor no less so because he lives in the city or on the farm. This is the clear and strong command of our Constitution's

Equal Protection Clause. This is an essential part of the concept of a government of laws and not men. This is at the heart of Lincoln's vision of "government of the people, by the people, [and] for the people." The Equal Protection Clause demands no less than substantially equal state legislative representation for all citizens, of all places as well as of all races.

We hold that, as a basic constitutional standard, the Equal Protection Clause requires that the seats in both houses of a bicameral state legislature must be apportioned on a population basis. Simply stated, an individual's right to vote for state legislators is unconstitutionally impaired when its weight is in a substantial fashion diluted when compared with votes of citizens living in other parts of the State. Since, under neither the existing apportionment provisions nor under either of the proposed plans was either of the houses of the Alabama Legislature apportioned on a population basis, the District Court correctly held that all three of these schemes were constitutionally invalid. . . .

Much has been written since our decision in *Baker v. Carr* about the applicability of the so-called federal analogy to state legislative apportionment arrangements. After considering the matter, the court below concluded that no conceivable analogy could be drawn between the federal scheme and the apportionment of seats in the Alabama Legislature under the proposed constitutional amendment. We agree with the District Court and find the federal analogy inapposite and irrelevant to state legislative districting schemes. Attempted reliance on the federal analogy often appears to be little more than an after-the-fact rationalization offered in defense of maladjusted state apportionment arrangements. The original constitutions of 36 of our States provided that representation in both houses of the state legislatures would be based completely, or predominantly, on population. And the Founding Fathers clearly had no intention of establishing a pattern or model for the apportionment of seats in state legislatures when the system of representation in the Federal Congress was adopted. Demonstrative of this is the fact that the Northwest Ordinance, adopted in the same year, 1787, as the Federal Constitution, provided for the apportionment of seats in territorial legislatures solely on the basis of population.

The system of representation in the two Houses of the Federal Congress is one ingrained in our Constitution, as part of the law of the land. It is one conceived out of compromise and concession indispensable to the establishment of our federal republic. Arising from unique historical circumstances, it is based on the consideration that in establishing our type of federalism a group of formerly independent States bound themselves together under one national government. . . .

We do not believe that the concept of bicameralism is rendered anachronistic and meaningless when the predominant basis of representation in the two state legislative bodies is required to be the same—population. A prime reason for bicameralism, modernly considered, is to insure mature and deliberate consideration of, and to prevent precipitate action on, proposed legislative measures. Simply because the controlling criterion for apportioning representation is required to be the same in both houses does not mean that there will be no differences in the composition and complexion of the two bodies. Different constituencies can be represented in the two houses. One body could be composed of single-member districts while the other could have at least some multimember districts. The length of terms of the legislators in the separate bodies could differ. The numerical size of the two bodies could be made to differ, even significantly, and the geographical size of districts from which legislators are elected could also be made to differ. . . . [T]hese and other factors could be, and are presently in many States, utilized to engender differing complexions and collective attitudes in the two bodies of a state legislature, although both are apportioned substantially on a population basis. . . .

[W]e affirm the judgment below and remand the cases for further proceedings consistent with the views stated in this opinion.

It is so ordered.

JUSTICE HARLAN dissented.

These decisions also cut deeply into the fabric of our federalism. What must follow from them may eventually appear to be the product of State Legislatures. Nevertheless, no thinking person can fail to recognize that the aftermath of these cases, however desirable it may be thought in itself, will have been achieved at the cost of a radical alteration in the relationship between the States and the Federal Government, more particularly the Federal Judiciary. Only one who has an overbearing impatience with the federal system and its political processes will believe that the cost was not too high or was inevitable. . . .

[T]hese decisions give support to a current mistaken view of the Constitution and the constitutional function of this Court. This view, in a nutshell, is that every major social ill in this country can find its cure in some constitutional "principle," and that this Court should "take the lead" in promoting reform when other branches of government fail to act. The Constitution is not a panacea for every blot upon the public welfare, nor should this Court, ordained as a judicial body, be thought of as a general haven for reform movements. The Constitution is an instrument of government, fundamental to which is the premise that in a diffusion of governmental authority lies the greatest promise that this Nation will realize liberty for all its citizens. This Court, limited in function in accordance with that premise, does not serve its high purpose when it exceeds its authority, even to satisfy justified impatience with the slow workings of the political process. For when, in the name of constitutional interpretation, the Court adds something to the Constitution that was deliberately excluded from it, the Court in reality substitutes its view of what should be so for the amending process. . . .

JUSTICE STEWART AND JUSTICE CLARK dissented [in the New York and Colorado cases].

Simply stated, the question is to what degree, if at all, the Equal Protection Clause of the Fourteenth Amendment limits each sovereign State's freedom to establish appropriate electoral constituencies from which representatives to the State's bicameral legislative assembly are to be chosen. The Court's answer is a blunt one, and, I think, woefully wrong. The Equal Protection Clause, said the Court, "requires that the seats in both houses of a bicameral state legislature must be apportioned on a population basis." . . .

With all respect, I think that this is not correct, simply as a matter of fact. It has been unanswerably demonstrated before now that this "was not the colonial system, it was not the system chosen for the national government by the Constitution, it was not the system exclusively or even predominantly practiced by the States at the time of adoption of the Fourteenth Amendment, it is not predominantly practiced by the States today." . . .

The Court's draconian pronouncement, which makes unconstitutional the legislatures of most of the 50 States, finds no support in the words of the Constitution, in any prior decision of this Court, or in the 175-year political history of our Federal Union. With all respect, I am convinced these decisions mark a long step backward into that unhappy era when a majority of the members of this Court were thought by many to have convinced themselves and each other that the demands of the Constitution were to be measured not by what it says, but by their own notions of wise political theory. . . .

What the Court has done is to convert a particular political philosophy into a constitutional rule, binding upon each of the 50 States, from Maine to Hawaii, from Alaska to Texas, without regard and without respect for the many individualized and differentiated characteristics stemming from each State's distinct history, distinct geography, distinct distribution of population, and distinct political heritage. My own understanding of the various theories of representative government is that no one theory has ever commanded unanimous assent among political scientists, historians, or others who have considered the problem. But even if it were thought that the rule announced today by the Court is, as a matter of political theory, the most desirable general rule which can be devised as a basis for the make-up of the representative assembly of a typical State, I could not join in the fabrication of a constitutional mandate which imports and forever freezes one theory of political thought into our Constitution, and forever denies to every State any opportunity for enlightened and progressive innovation in the design of its democratic institutions, so as to accommodate within a system of representative government the interests and aspirations of diverse groups of people, without subjecting any group or class to absolute domination by a geographically concentrated or highly organized majority.

Representative government is a process of accommodating group interests through democratic institutional arrangements. Its function is to channel the numerous opinions, interests, and abilities of the people of a State into the making of the State's public policy. Appropriate legislative apportionment, therefore, should ideally be designed to insure effective representation in the State's legislature, in cooperation with other organs of political power, of the various groups and interests making up the electorate. In practice, of course, this ideal is approximated in the particular apportionment system of any State by a realistic accommodation of the diverse and often conflicting political forces operating within the State. . . .

The Court today declines to give any recognition to these considerations and countless others, tangible and intangible, in holding unconstitutional the particular systems of legislative apportionment which these States have chosen. Instead, the Court says that the requirements of the

Equal Protection Clause can be met in any State only by the uncritical, simplistic, and heavy-handed application of sixth-grade arithmetic.

But legislators do not represent faceless numbers. They represent people, or, more accurately, a majority of the voters in their districts— people with identifiable needs and interests which require legislative representation, and which can often be related to the geographical areas in which these people live. The very fact of geographic districting, the constitutional validity of which the Court does not question, carries with it an acceptance of the idea of legislative representation of regional needs and interests. Yet if geographical residence is irrelevant, as the Court suggests, and the goal is solely that of equally "weighted" votes, I do not understand why the Court's constitutional rule does not require the abolition of districts and the holding of all elections at large. . . .

I think that the Equal Protection Clause demands but two basic attributes of any plan of state legislative apportionment. First, it demands that, in the light of the State's own characteristics and needs, the plan must be a rational one. Secondly, it demands that the plan must be such as not to permit the systematic frustration of the will of a majority of the electorate of the State. I think it is apparent that any plan of legislative apportionment which could be shown to reflect no policy, but simply arbitrary and capricious action or inaction, and that any plan which could be shown systematically to prevent ultimate effective majority rule, would be invalid under accepted Equal Protection Clause standards. But, beyond this, I think there is nothing in the Federal Constitution to prevent a State from choosing any electoral legislative structure it thinks best suited to the interests, temper, and customs of its people. . . .

MILLER V. JOHNSON (1995)

In 1972, Georgia gained its first African American member of Congress since Reconstruction, and redistricting after the 1980 census created the state's first majority-minority district. Under the 1990 census, Georgia's population (27 percent of which is black) entitled the state to an additional representative in Congress. The state's General Assembly approved a districting plan that contained three majority-minority districts after the Justice Department refused to preclear, under § 5 of the Voting Rights Act, two

*earlier plans that each contained only two majority-black districts.
Elections held in November 1992 resulted in the election of black
representatives from all three majority-minority districts. In 1994,
five white voters in the new Eleventh District challenged the constitutionality of their district on the ground that it was a racial
gerrymander in violation of the equal protection clause as interpreted in* Shaw v. Reno *(1993). A three-judge panel of the U.S.
District Court for the Southern District of Georgia agreed, holding
that the state legislature's purpose, as well as the district's irregular
borders, showed that race was the overriding and predominant
force in the districting determination. The lower court assumed
that compliance with the Voting Rights Act would be a compelling
interest justifying the district, but found that the plan was not narrowly tailored to meet that interest because the law did not require
three majority-minority districts.*

JUSTICE KENNEDY delivered the opinion of the Court.

The Equal Protection Clause's . . . central mandate is racial neutrality
in governmental decisionmaking. . . . Laws classifying citizens on the basis of race cannot be upheld unless they are narrowly tailored to achieving a compelling state interest. . . .

In *Shaw v. Reno* we recognized that these equal protection principles
govern a State's drawing of congressional districts, though, as our cau-
tious approach there discloses, application of these principles to electoral
districting is a most delicate task. . . .

This case requires us to apply the principles articulated in *Shaw* to the
most recent congressional redistricting plan enacted by the State of
Georgia.

In 1965, the Attorney General designated Georgia a covered jurisdiction under § 4(b) of the Voting Rights Act. In consequence, § 5 of the
Act requires Georgia to obtain either administrative preclearance by the
Attorney General or approval by the United States District Court for
the District of Columbia of any change in a "standard, practice, or procedure with respect to voting" made after November 1, 1964. The preclearance mechanism applies to congressional redistricting plans, and requires that the proposed change "not have the purpose and will not have

the effect of denying or abridging the right to vote on account of race or color." "[T]he purpose of § 5 has always been to insure that no voting-procedure changes would be made that would lead to a retrogression in the position of racial minorities with respect to their effective exercise of the electoral franchise." . . .

Twice spurned [by the Justice Department], the General Assembly set out to create three majority-minority districts to gain preclearance. Using the A[merican] C[ivil] L[iberties] U[nion]'s "max-black" plan as its benchmark, the General Assembly enacted a plan that "bore all the signs of [the Justice Department's] involvement." The new plan . . . connect[ed] the black neighborhoods of metropolitan Atlanta and the poor black populace of coastal Chatham County, though 260 miles apart in distance and worlds apart in culture. . . . [T]he social, political and economic makeup of the Eleventh District tells a tale of disparity, not community. . . .

[Appellants] contend that evidence of a legislature's deliberate classification of voters on the basis of race cannot alone suffice to state a claim under *Shaw*. They argue that, regardless of the legislature's purposes, a plaintiff must demonstrate that a district's shape is so bizarre that it is unexplainable other than on the basis of race, and that appellees failed to make that showing here. Appellants' conception of the constitutional violation misapprehends our holding in *Shaw*. . . .

Our observation in *Shaw* of the consequences of racial stereotyping was not meant to suggest that a district must be bizarre on its face before there is a constitutional violation. . . . Shape is relevant not because bizarreness is . . . the constitutional wrong . . ., but because it may be persuasive circumstantial evidence that race for its own sake, and not other districting principles, was the legislature's dominant and controlling rationale in drawing its district lines. The logical implication, as courts applying *Shaw* have recognized, is that parties may rely on evidence other than bizarreness to establish race-based districting. . . .

In sum, we make clear that parties alleging that a State has assigned voters on the basis of race are neither confined in their proof to evidence regarding the district's geometry and makeup nor required to make a threshold showing of bizarreness. Today's case requires us further to consider the requirements of the proof necessary to sustain this equal protection challenge.

Federal court review of districting legislation represents a serious intrusion on the most vital of local functions. . . . Redistricting legislatures will, for example, almost always be aware of racial demographics; but it does not follow that race predominates in the redistricting process. . . . The distinction between being aware of racial considerations and being motivated by them may be difficult to make. This evidentiary difficulty, together with the sensitive nature of redistricting and the presumption of good faith that must be accorded legislative enactments, requires courts to exercise extraordinary caution in adjudicating claims that a state has drawn district lines on the basis of race. The plaintiff's burden is to show, either through circumstantial evidence of a district's shape and demographics or more direct evidence going to legislative purpose, that race was the predominant factor motivating the legislature's decision to place a significant number of voters within or without a particular district. To make this showing, a plaintiff must prove that the legislature subordinated traditional race-neutral districting principles, including but not limited to compactness, contiguity, respect for political subdivisions or communities defined by actual shared interests, to racial considerations. Where these or other race-neutral considerations are the basis for redistricting legislation, and are not subordinated to race, a state can "defeat a claim that a district has been gerrymandered on racial lines." . . .

In our view, the District Court applied the correct analysis, and its finding that race was the predominant factor motivating the drawing of the Eleventh District was not clearly erroneous. The court found it was "exceedingly obvious" from the shape of the Eleventh District, together with the relevant racial demographics, that the drawing of narrow land bridges to incorporate within the district outlying appendages containing nearly 80% of the district's total black population was a deliberate attempt to bring black populations into the district. . . .

As a result, Georgia's congressional redistricting plan cannot be upheld unless it satisfies strict scrutiny, our most rigorous and exacting standard of constitutional review.

To satisfy strict scrutiny, the State must demonstrate that its districting legislation is narrowly tailored to achieve a compelling interest. . . . The State does not argue, however, that it created the Eleventh District to remedy past discrimination, and with good reason: there is little doubt that the State's true interest in designing the Eleventh District was creating a third majority-black district to satisfy the Justice Department's preclearance demands. . . . Whether or not in some cases compliance with the Voting Rights Act, standing alone, can provide a compelling interest independent of any interest in remedying past discrimination, it cannot do so here. . . . The congressional plan challenged here was not required by the Voting Rights Act under a correct reading of the statute. . . .

Georgia's drawing of the Eleventh District was not required under the Act because there was no reasonable basis to believe that Georgia's earlier enacted plans violated § 5. . . . Georgia's first and second proposed plans increased the number of majority-black districts from 1 out of 10 (10%) to 2 out of 11 (18.18%). These plans were "ameliorative" and could not have violated § 5's nonretrogression principle. Acknowledging as much, the United States . . . [objects] that Georgia failed to proffer a nondiscriminatory purpose for its refusal in the first two submissions to take the steps necessary to create a third majority-minority district.

The Government's position is insupportable. . . . The State's policy of adhering to other districting principles instead of creating as many majority-minority districts as possible does not support an inference that the plan "so discriminates on the basis of race or color as to violate the Constitution," and thus cannot provide any basis under § 5 for the Justice Department's objection.

"[T]he purpose of § 5 has always been to insure that no voting-procedure changes would be made that would lead to a retrogression in the position of racial minorities with respect to their effective exercise of the electoral franchise." The Justice Department's maximization policy seems quite far removed from this purpose. We are especially reluctant to conclude that § 5 justifies that policy given the serious constitutional concerns it raises. . . .

The Voting Rights Act, and its grant of authority to the federal courts to uncover official efforts to abridge minorities' right to vote, has been of vital importance in eradicating invidious discrimination from the electoral process and enhancing the legitimacy of our political institutions. Only if our political system and our society cleanse themselves of that discrimination will all members of the polity share an equal opportunity to gain public office regardless of race. . . . It takes a shortsighted and unauthorized view of the Voting Rights Act to invoke that statute, which has played a decisive role in redressing some of our worst forms of discrimination, to demand the very racial stereotyping the Fourteenth Amendment forbids.

The judgment of the District Court is affirmed, and the case is remanded for further proceedings consistent with this decision.

It is so ordered.

JUSTICE O'CONNOR concurred.

JUSTICE STEVENS dissented.

JUSTICE GINSBURG, JUSTICE STEVENS, and JUSTICE BREYER dissented (JUSTICE SOUTER joined in part).

[T]he fact that the Georgia General Assembly took account of race in drawing district lines—a fact not in dispute—does not render the State's plan invalid. To offend the Equal Protection Clause, all agree, the legislature had to do more than consider race. How much more, is the issue that divides the Court today. . . .

The record before us does not show that race . . . overwhelmed traditional districting practices in Georgia. Although the Georgia General Assembly prominently considered race in shaping the Eleventh District, race did not crowd out all other factors. . . .

In contrast to the snake-like North Carolina district inspected in *Shaw*, Georgia's Eleventh District is hardly "bizarre," "extremely irregular," or "irrational on its face." . . .

Along with attention to size, shape, and political subdivisions, the Court recognizes as an appropriate districting principle, "respect for . . . communities defined by actual shared interests." The Court finds no community here, however, because a report in the record showed "fractured political, social, and economic interests within the Eleventh District's black population."

But ethnicity itself can tie people together, as volumes of social science literature have documented—even people with divergent economic interests. . . .

To accommodate the reality of ethnic bonds, legislatures have long drawn voting districts along ethnic lines. Our Nation's cities are full of districts identified by their ethnic character—Chinese, Irish, Italian, Jewish, Polish, Russian, for example. . . . The creation of ethnic districts reflecting felt identity is not ordinarily viewed as offensive or demeaning to those included in the delineation. . . .

In adopting districting plans, . . . States do not treat people as individuals. Apportionment schemes, by their very nature, assemble people in groups. States do not assign voters to districts based on merit or achievement, standards States might use in hiring employees or engaging contractors. Rather, legislators classify voters in groups—by economic, geographical, political, or social characteristics—and then "reconcile the competing claims of [these] groups."

That ethnicity defines some of these groups is a political reality. Until now, no constitutional infirmity has been seen in districting Irish or Italian voters together, for example, so long as the delineation does not abandon familiar apportionment practices. If Chinese-Americans and Russian-Americans may seek and secure group recognition in the delineation of voting districts, then African-Americans should not be dissimilarly treated. Otherwise, in the name of equal protection, we would shut out "the very minority group whose history in the United States gave birth to the Equal Protection Clause."

Under the Court's approach, judicial review of the same intensity, i.e., strict scrutiny, is in order once it is determined that an apportionment is predominantly motivated by race. It matters not at all, in this new regime, whether the apportionment dilutes or enhances minority voting strength. As very recently observed, however, "[t]here is no moral or constitutional equivalence between a policy that is designed to perpetuate a caste system and one that seeks to eradicate racial subordination."

Special circumstances justify vigilant judicial inspection to protect minority voters—circumstances that do not apply to majority voters. . . . The majority, by definition, encounters no such blockage. White voters in Georgia do not lack means to exert strong pressure on their state legislators. The force of their numbers is itself a powerful determiner of what the legislature will do that does not coincide with perceived majority interests. . . .

The Court's disposition renders redistricting perilous work for state legislatures. . . . Only after litigation—under either the Voting Rights Act, the Court's new *Miller* standard, or both—will States now be assured that plans conscious of race are safe. . . . This enlargement of the judicial role is unwarranted. . . .

Accordingly, I dissent.

VIETH V. JUBELIRER (2004)

As a result of the 2000 census, Pennsylvania's representation in the U.S. House of Representatives dropped from twenty-one to nineteen. Following adoption of a new redistricting plan in January 2002 (Act 1), several registered Democrats challenged the validity of the plan as a violation of the one-person, one-vote rule and as an unconstitutional gerrymander containing districts that were "meandering and irregular," and that "ignor[ed] all traditional redistricting criteria, including the preservation of local government boundaries, solely for the sake of partisan advantage." A three-judge panel of the U.S. District Court for the Middle District of Pennsylvania dismissed the political gerrymander claim but ruled in favor of the plaintiffs on other grounds. On April 18, 2002, Governor Mark Schweiker signed into law Act 34, a remedial plan that the state General Assembly had passed to cure the deficiencies of Act 1. The plaintiffs then challenged the revised plan as constituting an unconstitutional political gerrymander like its predecessor, a claim that the district court denied. In the November 2000 elections (prior to the redistricting), Republican candidates for Congress won eleven seats and Democratic candidates ten. In the November 2002 elections, Republican candidates for Congress won twelve seats, and Democratic candidates seven.

JUSTICE SCALIA announced the judgment of the Court and delivered an opinion, in which CHIEF JUSTICE REHNQUIST, JUSTICE O'CONNOR, and JUSTICE THOMAS joined.

Plaintiffs-appellants Richard Vieth, Norma Jean Vieth, and Susan Furey challenge a map drawn by the Pennsylvania General Assembly establishing districts for the election of congressional Representatives, on the ground that the districting constitutes an unconstitutional political gerrymander. In *Davis v. Bandemer* (1986), this Court held that political gerrymandering claims are justiciable, but could not agree upon a standard to adjudicate them. The present appeal presents the questions whether our decision in *Bandemer* was in error, and, if not, what the standard should be. . . .

Political gerrymanders are not new to the American scene. One scholar traces them back to the Colony of Pennsylvania at the beginning of the 18th century. . . . The political gerrymander remained alive and well (though not yet known by that name) at the time of the framing. There were allegations that Patrick Henry attempted (unsuccessfully) to gerrymander James Madison out of the First Congress. And in 1812, of course, there occurred the notoriously outrageous political districting in Massachusetts that gave the gerrymander its name–an amalgam of the names of Massachusetts Governor Elbridge Gerry and the creature ("salamander") which the outline of an election district he was credited with forming was thought to resemble. "By 1840 the gerrymander was a recognized force in party politics and was generally attempted in all legislation enacted for the formation of election districts. It was generally conceded that each party would attempt to gain power which was not proportionate to its numerical strength."

It is significant that the Framers provided a remedy for such practices in the Constitution. Article 1, §4, while leaving in state legislatures the initial power to draw districts for federal elections, permitted Congress to "make or alter" those districts if it wished. . . .

The power bestowed on Congress to regulate elections, and in particular to restrain the practice of political gerrymandering, has not lain dormant. In the Apportionment Act of 1842, Congress provided that Representatives must be elected from single-member districts "composed of contiguous territory." Congress again imposed these requirements in the Apportionment Act of 1862, and in 1872 further required that districts "contai[n] as nearly as practicable an equal number of inhabitants." In the Apportionment Act of 1901, Congress imposed a compactness requirement. The requirements of contiguity, compactness, and equality of population were repeated in the 1911 apportionment legislation, but were not thereafter continued. Today, only the single-member-district-requirement remains. Recent history, however, attests to Congress's awareness of the sort of districting practices appellants protest, and of its power under Article I, §4 to control them. Since 1980, no fewer than five bills have been introduced to regulate gerrymandering in congressional districting.

Eighteen years ago, we held that the Equal Protection Clause grants judges the power—and duty—to control political gerrymandering. It is to consideration of this precedent that we now turn.

As Chief Justice Marshall proclaimed two centuries ago, "[i]t is emphatically the province and duty of the judicial department to say what the law is." Sometimes, however, the law is that the judicial department has no business entertaining the claim of unlawfulness—because the question is entrusted to one of the political branches or involves no judicially enforceable rights. . . .

In *Baker v. Carr* (1962), we set forth six independent tests for the existence of a political question:

"[1] a textually demonstrable constitutional commitment of the issue to a coordinate political department; or [2] a lack of judicially discoverable and manageable standards for resolving it; or [3] the impossibility of deciding without an initial policy determination of a kind clearly for nonjudicial discretion; or [4] the impossibility of a court's undertaking independent resolution without expressing lack of the respect due coordinate branches of the government; or [5] an unusual need for unquestioning adherence to a political decision already made; or [6] the potentiality of embarrassment from multifarious pronouncements by various departments on one question."

These tests are probably listed in descending order of both importance and certainty. The second is at issue here, and there is no doubt of its validity. "The judicial Power" created by Article III, §1, of the Constitution is not *whatever* judges choose to do, or even *whatever* Congress chooses to assign them. It is the power to act in the manner traditional for English and American courts. One of the most obvious limitations imposed by that requirement is that judicial action must be governed by *standard,* by *rule.* Laws promulgated by the Legislative Branch can be inconsistent, illogical, and ad hoc; law pronounced by the courts must be principled, rational, and based upon reasoned distinctions.

Over the dissent of three Justices, the Court held in *Davis v. Bandemer* that, since it was "not persuaded that there are no judicially discernible and manageable standards by which political gerrymander cases are to be decided," such cases *were* justiciable. The clumsy shifting of the burden of proof for the premise (the Court was "not persuaded" that standards do not exist, rather than "persuaded" that they do) was necessitated by the uncomfortable fact that the six-Justice majority could not discern what the judicially discernable standards might be. There was no majority on that point. Four of the Justices finding justiciability believed that the standard was one thing; two believed it was something else. The lower courts have lived with that assurance of a standard (or more precisely, lack of assurance that there is no standard), coupled with that inability to specify a standard, for the past 18 years. In that time, they have considered numerous political gerrymandering claims; this Court has never revisited the unanswered question of what standard governs.

Nor can it be said that the lower courts have, over 18 years, succeeded in shaping the standard that this Court was initially unable to enunciate. They have simply applied the standard set forth in *Bandemer*'s four-Justice plurality opinion. This might be thought to prove that the four-Justice plurality standard has met the test of time—but for the fact that its application has almost invariably produced the same result (except for the incurring of attorney's fees) as would have obtained if the question were nonjusticiable: judicial intervention has been refused. As one commentary has put it, "[t]hroughout its subsequent history, *Bandemer* has served almost exclusively as an invitation to litigation without much prospect of redress." The one case in which relief was provided (and merely preliminary relief, at that) did *not* involve the drawing of district lines; in *all* of the cases we are aware of involving that most common form of political gerrymandering, relief was denied. . . . To think that this lower-court jurisprudence has brought forth "judicially discernible and manageable standards" would be fantasy. . . .

Lacking them, we must conclude that political gerrymandering claims are nonjusticiable and that *Bandemer* was wrongly decided.

We begin our review of possible standards with that proposed by Justice White's plurality opinion in *Bandemer* because, as the narrowest ground for our decision in that case, it has been the standard employed by the lower courts. The plurality concluded that a political gerrymandering claim could succeed only where plaintiffs showed "both intentional discrimination against an identifiable political group and an actual discriminatory effect on that group." As to the intent element, the plurality acknowledged that "[a]s long as redistricting is done by a legislature, it should not be very difficult to prove that the likely political consequences of the reapportionment were intended." However, the effects prong was significantly harder to satisfy. Relief could not be based merely upon the fact that a group of persons banded together for political purposes had failed to achieve representation commensurate with its numbers, or that the apportionment scheme made its winning of elections more difficult. Rather, it would have to be shown that, taking into account a variety of historic factors and projected election results, the group had been "denied its chance to effectively influence the political process" as a whole, which could be achieved even without electing a candidate It would not be enough to establish, for example, that Democrats had been "placed in a district with a supermajority of other Democratic voters" or that the district "departs from pre-existing political boundaries." Rather, in a challenge to an individual district the inquiry would focus "on the opportunity of members of the group to participate in party deliberations in the slating and nomination of candidates, their opportunity to register and vote, and hence their chance to directly influence the election returns and to secure the attention of the winning candidate." A statewide challenge, by contrast, would involve an analysis of "the voters' direct *or indirect* influence on the elections of the state legislature as a whole" (emphasis added [by Justice Scalia]). With what has proved to be a gross understatement, the plurality acknowledged this was "of necessity a difficult inquiry." ...

In the lower courts, the legacy of the plurality's test is one long record of puzzlement and consternation.... Because this standard was misguided when proposed, has not been improved in subsequent application, and is not even defended before us today by the appellants, we decline to affirm it as a constitutional requirement.

Appellants take a run at enunciating their own workable standard based on Article I, §2, and the Equal Protection Clause. We consider it at length not only because it reflects the litigant's view as to the best that can be derived from 18 years of experience, but also because it shares many features with other proposed standards, so that what is said of it may be said of them as well. Appellants' proposed standard retains the two-pronged framework of the *Bandemer* plurality—intent plus effect—but modifies the type of showing sufficient to satisfy each.

To satisfy appellants' intent standard, a plaintiff must "show that the mapmakers acted with a *predominant intent* to achieve partisan advantage," which can be shown "by direct evidence or by circumstantial evidence that other neutral and legitimate redistricting criteria were subordinated to the goal of achieving partisan advantage." As compared with the *Bandemer* plurality's test of mere intent to disadvantage the plaintiff's group, this proposal seemingly makes the standard more difficult to meet—but only at the expense of making the standard more indeterminate.

"Predominant intent" to disadvantage the plaintiff political group refers to the relative importance of that goal as compared with all the other goals that the map seeks to pursue—contiguity of districts, compactness of districts, observance of the lines of political subdivision, protection of incumbents of all parties, cohesion of natural racial and ethnic neighborhoods, compliance with requirements of the Voting Rights Act of 1965 regarding racial distribution, etc. Appellants contend that their intent test *must* be discernible and manageable because it has been borrowed from our racial gerrymandering cases. To begin with, in a very important respect that is not so. In the racial gerrymandering context, the predominant intent test has been applied to the challenged district in which the plaintiffs voted. Here, however, appellants do not assert that an apportionment fails their intent test if any single district does so. Since "it would be quixotic to attempt to bar state legislatures from considering politics as they redraw district lines," appellants propose a test that is satisfied only when "partisan advantage was the predominant motivation *behind the entire statewide plan* (emphasis added [by Justice Scalia]). Vague as the "predominant motivation" test might be when used to evaluate single districts, it all but evaporates when applied statewide. Does it mean, for instance, that partisan intent must outweigh all other goals–contiguity, compactness, preservation of neighborhoods, etc.—*statewide*? And how is the statewide "outweighing" to be determined? If three-fifths of the map's districts forgo the pursuit of partisan ends in favor of strictly observing political-subdivision lines, and only two-fifths ignore those lines to disadvantage the plaintiffs, is the observance of political subdivisions the "predominant" goal between those two? We are sure appellants do not think so.

Even within the narrower compass of challenges to a single district, applying a "predominant intent" test to *racial* gerrymandering is easier and less disruptive. The Constitution clearly contemplates districting by political entities, and unsurprisingly that turns out to be root-and-branch a matter of politics. . . . By contrast, the purpose of segregating voters on the basis of race is not a lawful one, and is much more rarely encountered. Determining whether the shape of a particular district is so substantially affected by the presence of a rare and constitutionally suspect motive as to invalidate it is quite different from determining whether it is so substantially affected by the excess of an ordinary and lawful motive as to invalidate it. Moreover, the fact that partisan districting is a lawful and common practice means that there is almost *always* room for an election-impeding lawsuit contending that partisan advantage was the predominant motivation; not so for claims of racial gerrymandering. . . . For these reasons, to the extent that our racial gerrymandering cases represent a model of discernible and manageable standards, they provide no comfort here.

The effects prong of appellants' proposal replaces the *Bandemer* plurality's vague test of "denied its chance to effectively influence the political process," with criteria that are seemingly more specific. The requisite effect is established when "(1) the plaintiffs show that the districts systematically 'pack' and 'crack' the rival party's voters, *and* (2) the court's examination of the 'totality of circumstances' confirms that the map can thwart the plaintiffs' ability to translate a majority of votes into a majority of seats." This test is loosely based on our cases applying § 2 of the Voting Rights Act. But a person's politics is rarely as readily discernible—and *never* as permanently discernible—as a person's race. Political affiliation is not an immutable characteristic, but may shift from one election to the next; and even within a given election, not all voters follow the party line. We dare say (and hope) that the political party which puts forward an utterly incompetent candidate will lose even in its registration stronghold. These facts make it impossible to assess the effects of partisan gerrymandering, to fashion a standard for evaluating a violation, and finally to craft a remedy.

Assuming, however, that the effects of partisan gerrymandering can be determined, appellants' test would invalidate the districting only when it prevents a majority of the electorate from electing a majority of representatives. Before considering whether this particular standard is judicially manageable we question whether it is judicially discernible in the sense of being relevant to some constitutional violation. Deny it as appellants may (and do), this standard rests upon the principle that groups (or at least political-action groups) have a right to proportional representation. But the Constitution contains no such principle. It guarantees equal protection of the law to persons, not equal representation in government to equivalently sized groups. It nowhere says that farmers or urban dwellers, Christian fundamentalists or Jews, Republicans or Democrats, must be accorded political strength proportionate to their numbers.

Even if the standard were relevant, however, it is not judicially manageable. To begin with, how is a party's majority status to be established? Appellants propose using the results of statewide races as the benchmark of party support. But as their own complaint describes, in the 2000 Pennsylvania statewide elections some Republicans won and some Democrats won.... Moreover, to think that majority status in statewide races establishes majority status for district contests, one would have to believe that the only factor determining voting behavior at all levels is political affiliation. That is assuredly not true....

But if we could identify a majority party, we would find it impossible to assure that that party wins a majority of seats—unless we radically revise the States' traditional structure for elections. In any winner-take-all district system, there can be no guarantee, no matter how the district lines are drawn, that a majority of party votes statewide will produce a majority of seats for that party....

For these reasons, we find appellants' proposed standards neither discernible nor manageable.

For many of the same reasons, we also reject the standard suggested by Justice Powell in *Bandemer.* He agreed with the plurality that a plaintiff should show intent and effect, but believed that the ultimate inquiry ought to focus on whether district boundaries had been drawn solely for partisan ends to the exclusion of "all other neutral factors relevant to the fairness of redistricting." Under that inquiry, the courts should consider numerous factors, though "[n]o one factor should be dispositive." The most important would be "the shapes of voting districts and adherence to established political subdivision boundaries." "Other relevant considerations include the nature of the legislative procedures by which the apportionment law was adopted and legislative history reflecting contemporaneous legislative goals." ...

While Justice Powell rightly criticized the *Bandemer* plurality for failing to suggest a constitutionally based, judicially manageable standard, the standard proposed in his opinion also falls short of the mark. It is essentially a totality-of-the-circumstances analysis, where all conceivable factors, none of which is dispositive, are weighed with an eye to ascertaining whether the particular gerrymander has gone too far—or, in Justice Powell's terminology, whether it is not "fair." "Fairness" does not seem to us a judicially manageable standard. Fairness is compatible with noncontiguous districts, it is compatible with districts that straddle political subdivisions, and it is compatible with a party's not winning the number of seats that mirrors the proportion of its vote. Some criterion more solid and more demonstrably met than that seems to us necessary to enable the state legislatures to discern the limits of their districting discretion, to meaningfully constrain the discretion of the courts, and to win public acceptance for the courts' intrusion into a process that is the very foundation of democratic decisionmaking. . . .

We conclude that neither Article I, §2, nor the Equal Protection Clause, nor (what appellants only fleetingly invoke) Article I, §4, provides a judicially enforceable limit on the political considerations that the States and Congress may take into account when districting.

Considerations of *stare decisis* do not compel us to allow *Bandemer* to stand. That case involved an interpretation of the Constitution, and the claims of *stare decisis* are at their weakest in that field, where our mistakes cannot be corrected by Congress. They are doubly weak in *Bandemer* because the majority's inability to enunciate the judicially discernible and manageable standard that it thought existed (or did not think did not exist) presaged the need for reconsideration in light of subsequent experience. And they are triply weak because it is hard to imagine how any action taken in reliance upon *Bandemer* could conceivably be frustrated—except the bringing of lawsuits, which is not the sort of primary conduct that is relevant.

While we do not lightly overturn one of our own holdings, "when governing decisions are unworkable or are badly reasoned, 'this Court has never felt constrained to follow precedent.'" Eighteen years of essentially pointless litigation have persuaded us that *Bandemer* is incapable of principled application. We would therefore overrule that case, and decline to adjudicate these political gerrymandering claims.

The judgment of the District Court is affirmed.

It is so ordered.

JUSTICE KENNEDY concurred.

A decision ordering the correction of all election district lines drawn for partisan reasons would commit federal and state courts to unprecedented intervention in the American political process. The Court is correct to refrain from directing this substantial intrusion into the Nation's political life. While agreeing with the plurality that the complaint the appellants filed in the District Court must be dismissed, and while understanding that great caution is necessary when approaching this subject, I would not foreclose all possibility of judicial relief if some limited and precise rationale were found to correct an established violation of the Constitution in some redistricting cases. . . .

JUSTICE STEVENS dissented.

JUSTICE SOUTER AND JUSTICE GINSBURG dissented.

The plurality says, in effect, that courts have been trying to devise practical criteria for political gerrymandering for nearly 20 years, without being any closer to something workable than we were when *Davis* was decided. While this is true enough, I do not accept it as sound counsel of despair. For I take it that the principal reason we have not gone from theoretical justiciability to practical administrability in political gerrymandering cases is the *Davis* plurality's specification that any criterion of forbidden gerrymandering must require a showing that members of the plaintiff's group had "essentially been shut out of the political process." That is, in order to avoid a threshold for relief so low that almost any electoral defeat (let alone failure to achieve proportionate results) would support a gerrymandering claim, the *Davis* plurality required a demonstration of such pervasive devaluation over such a period of time as to raise real doubt that a case could ever be made out. *Davis* suggested that plaintiffs might need to show even that their efforts to deliberate, register, and vote had been impeded. This standard, which it is difficult to imagine a major party meeting, combined a very demanding burden with significant vagueness; and if appellants have not been able to propose a practical test for a *Davis* violation, the fault belongs less to them than to our predecessors. . . .

Since this Court has created the problem no one else has been able to solve, it is up to us to make a fresh start. There are a good many voices saying it is high time that we did, for in the years since *Davis,* the increasing efficiency of partisan redistricting has damaged the democratic process to a degree that our predecessors only began to imagine. . . .

I would therefore preserve *Davis*'s holding that political gerrymandering is a justiciable issue, but otherwise start anew. I would adopt a political gerrymandering test analogous to the summary judgment standard crafted in *McDonnell Douglas Corp. v. Green* (1973), calling for a plaintiff to satisfy elements of a *prima facie* cause of action, at which point the State would have the opportunity not only to rebut the evidence supporting the plaintiff's case, but to offer an affirmative justification for the districting choices, even assuming the proof of the plaintiff's allegations. My own judgment is that we would have better luck at devising a workable *prima facie* case if we concentrated as much as possible on suspect characteristics of individual districts instead of state-wide patterns. . . .

For a claim based on a specific single-member district, I would require the plaintiff to make out a *prima facie* case with five elements. First, the resident plaintiff would identify a cohesive political group to which he belonged, which would normally be a major party, as in this case and in *Davis.* There is no reason in principle, however, to rule out a claimant from a minor political party (which might, if it showed strength, become the target of vigorous hostility from one or both major parties in a State) or from a different but politically coherent group whose members engaged in bloc voting, as a large labor union might do. The point is that it must make sense to speak of a candidate of the group's choice, easy to do in the case of a large or small political party, though more difficult when the organization is not defined by politics as such.

Second, a plaintiff would need to show that the district of his residence paid little or no heed to those traditional districting principles whose disregard can be shown straightforwardly: contiguity, compactness, respect for political subdivisions, and conformity with geographic features like rivers and mountains. Because such considerations are already relevant to justifying small deviations from absolute population equality, and because compactness in particular is relevant to demonstrating possible majority-minority districts under the Voting Rights Act of 1965, there is no doubt that a test relying on these standards would fall within judicial competence.

Indeed, although compactness is at first blush the least likely of these principles to yield precision, it can be measured quantitatively in terms of dispersion, perimeter, and population ratios, and the development of standards would thus be possible. It is not necessary now to say exactly how a district court would balance a good showing on one of these indices against a poor showing on another, for that sort of detail is best worked out case by case.

Third, the plaintiff would need to establish specific correlations between the district's deviations from traditional districting principles and the distribution of the population of his group. For example, one of the districts to which appellants object most strongly in this case is District

6, which they say "looms like a dragon descending on Philadelphia from the west, splitting up towns and communities throughout Montgomery and Berks Counties." To make their claim stick, they would need to point to specific protuberances on the draconian shape that reach out to include Democrats, or fissures in it that squirm away from Republicans. They would need to show that when towns and communities were split, Democrats tended to fall on one side and Republicans on the other. Although some counterexamples would no doubt be present in any complex plan, the plaintiff's showing as a whole would need to provide reasonable support for, if not compel, an inference that the district took the shape it did because of the distribution of the plaintiff's group. . . .

Fourth, a plaintiff would need to present the court with a hypothetical district including his residence, one in which the proportion of the plaintiff's group was lower (in a packing claim) or higher (in a cracking one) and which at the same time deviated less from traditional districting principles than the actual district. . . . This hypothetical district would allow the plaintiff to claim credibly that the deviations from traditional districting principles were not only correlated with, but also caused by, the packing or cracking of his group. Drawing the hypothetical district would, of course, necessarily involve redrawing at least one contiguous district, and a plaintiff would have to show that this could be done subject to traditional districting principles without packing or cracking his group (or another) worse than in the district being challenged.

Fifth, and finally, the plaintiff would have to show that the defendants acted intentionally to manipulate the shape of the district in order to pack or crack his group. In substantiating claims of political gerrymandering under a plan devised by a single major party, proving intent should not be hard, once the third and fourth (correlation and cause) elements are established, politicians not being politically disinterested or characteristically naïve. . . .

If the affected group were not a major party, proof of intent could, admittedly, be difficult. It would be possible that a legislature might not even have had the plaintiff's group in mind, and a plaintiff would naturally have a hard time showing requisite intent behind a plan produced by a bipartisan commission.

A plaintiff who got this far would have shown that his State intentionally acted to dilute his vote, having ignored reasonable alternatives consistent with traditional districting principles. I would then shift the burden to the defendants to justify their decision by reference to objectives other than naked partisan advantage. They might show by rebuttal evidence that districting objectives could not be served by the plaintiff's hypothetical district better than by the district as drawn, or they might affirmatively establish legitimate objectives better served by the lines drawn than by the plaintiff's hypothetical. . . .

JUSTICE BREYER dissented.

Chronology

1430	England establishes a forty-shilling freehold as a qualification for voting for members of the House of Commons.
1607	A permanent settlement at Jamestown, Virginia, begins English colonization of the east coast of North America.
1647	Debates take place over voting rights, among other topics, at Putney, England, at the end of the English Civil War.
1733	The colony of Georgia is founded on the east coast of North America. It is the last to be settled of the original thirteen English colonies that later become the United States.
1775	The first shots are fired in what becomes the Revolutionary War (or War of Independence) between the thirteen colonies and Great Britain.
1776	The Declaration of Independence is adopted by the Continental Congress in Philadelphia.
1777	The Articles of Confederation are adopted by the Continental Congress meeting in York, Pennsylvania.
1781	The British surrender at Yorktown, Virginia, ends most fighting in the Revolutionary War.
1783	The Treaty of Paris between the United States and Great Britain formally brings the Revolutionary War to a close.

1787　　The Congress of the Confederation enacts the North-west Ordinance, which provides for territories west of the original thirteen colonies (now states) to enter the Union as states on an equal basis with the others. The Constitutional Convention convenes in Philadelphia to consider how to address weaknesses in the Articles of Confederation and ends up creating an entirely new form of government embodied in a new Constitution for the entity to be known as the United States. The Congress of the Confederation refers the proposed Constitution to the states for ratification. Alexander Hamilton, John Jay, and James Madison begin writing *The Federalist,* a series of eighty-five essays published in newspapers in New York State late in the year and early in 1788 that urge approval of the Constitution.

1788　　Ratification of the Constitution is completed.

1789　　Government under the Constitution commences. The Constitution leaves definition of the franchise, even for federal elections, to the states. Congress proposes twelve amendments to the Constitution; ten are ratified by 1791 as the Bill of Rights.

1790　　Most states maintain a property requirement for voting, although in some ownership of property other than real estate suffices; in a few, a taxpaying requirement replaces the property requirement.

1792　　The first American party system begins to take shape, with competition between the Federalists and Antifederalists, later called Democratic-Republicans.

1800　　By this time, all of the American states have abandoned the English rule of primogeniture, by which an estate passed entirely into the hands of the eldest son.

1804　　Ratification of the Twelfth Amendment requires presidential electors to cast separate votes for president and vice president.

1807	New Jersey stipulates that only "free, white male citizen[s]" may vote, thus ending a practice, dating from the Revolution, that allowed some women to vote.
1812	The War of 1812 begins. It concludes with the Treaty of Ghent in 1815.
1821	A constitutional convention in New York State results in abolition of the property requirement for most residents.
1824	The second party system begins to take shape, with competition between the Democrats and National Republicans, later called Whigs.
1828	Democratic candidate Andrew Jackson is elected president and serves until 1837; his presidency begins what some historians call the "age of Jackson" that persists until the Civil War.
1829	A constitutional convention convenes in Virginia to debate abolition of the property requirement for voting in that state.
1830	A quarter century of high rates of immigration to the United States of largely Catholic Europeans begins.
1841	The Dorr Rebellion begins in Rhode Island and concludes in 1842; it results in abolition of the property requirement for voting in that state.
1848	The first women's rights Convention takes place in Seneca Falls, New York, with calls for full woman suffrage.
1849	The Order of the Star-Spangled Banner is founded in New York State as a secret, anti-immigrant, oathbound fraternal order. Its members come to be called "Know-Nothings," and later the American Party.
1856	The third party system begins to take shape, with competition between the Democrats and Republicans.
1860	By this time, property or significant taxpaying requirements for voting have been abolished in all states, ush-

ering in an era of nearly universal white male suffrage; twenty-six of the thirty-one states still prohibit African Americans from voting.

1861   The Civil War begins after several states secede from the Union and after South Carolina troops fire on Fort Sumter in the harbor in Charleston.

1863   President Abraham Lincoln delivers an address at a battlefield in Gettysburg, Pennsylvania.

1865   The Civil War ends. Lincoln is assassinated. Ratification of the Thirteenth Amendment abolishes slavery and the Reconstruction era begins.

1866   The Civil Rights Act becomes law. It is designed to augment the Thirteenth Amendment's abolition of slavery and it declares all persons born in the United States to be national citizens. The statute also seeks to remove discrimination against blacks in contractual rights and in the criminal justice system but does not address voting.

1868   Ratification of the Fourteenth Amendment imposes broad, but undefined, restrictions on the states and threatens states with partial loss of representation in Congress if any otherwise eligible adult "male inhabitants" are denied the right to vote.

1869   The National Woman Suffrage Association (NWSA) and American Woman Suffrage Association (AWSA) are organized; the NWSA and AWSA pursue different strategies toward woman suffrage. Wyoming Territory becomes the first large political jurisdiction to enfranchise women.

1870   Ratification of the Fifteenth Amendment bars the use of race as a criterion for voting; the Enforcement Act is passed to implement its provisions.

1873   The Supreme Court decision in the *Slaughterhouse Cases* minimizes the scope of the Fourteenth Amendment. *Bradwell v. Illinois* upholds Illinois's exclusion of women from the practice of law. Susan B. Anthony is fined for voting in a federal election.

1874   The Women's Christian Temperance Union (WCTU) is organized.

1875   Rejecting the argument that women have a constitutionally protected right to vote, the Supreme Court decision in *Minor v. Happersett* rules that the Fourteenth Amendment confers the right to vote on no one.

1876   The Supreme Court decision in *United States v. Reese* invalidates part of the Enforcement Act of 1870 and makes it more difficult to protect voting rights, especially in state and local elections; *Cruikshank v. United States* renders a narrow construction of another part of the Enforcement Act, invalidating indictments because the defendants were not charged with violating rights actually protected by the Constitution. The presidential election between Democrat Samuel J. Tilden and Republican Rutherford B. Hayes yields inconclusive results because of disputed election returns in four states.

1877   President Ulysses S. Grant signs the bill creating a special electoral commission to resolve the disputed presidential returns. It consists of five members of the House of Representatives, five members of the Senate, and five justices of the Supreme Court. The electoral commission resolves all disputed returns in favor of Hayes, who wins the White House by a margin of one electoral vote, even though Tilden won a clear majority of the national popular vote. Withdrawal of the last of occupying federal troops from some southern states marks the formal end of Reconstruction.

1884   The decision in *Ex parte Yarbrough* becomes the only Supreme Court decision in the nineteenth century in full support of federal protection of voting rights where race is a factor.

1885   The Supreme Court decision in *Murphy v. Ramsey* upholds a congressional statute disfranchising polygamists and their wives in Utah (which had granted women the right to vote in 1870).

1890   The NWSA and the AWSA merge to form the National American Woman Suffrage Association (NAWSA).

1893   Congress repeals those sections of the 1870 and 1871 Enforcement acts providing for federal supervision of elections and federal remedies in voting disputes; as a result there are now fewer safeguards against racial discrimination in voting.

1895   "Tory" attitudes about voting retard the advance of woman suffrage.

1896   The fourth party system begins to take shape, with competition between the ascendant Republicans and the Democrats. The Supreme Court decision in *Plessy v. Ferguson* approves a "separate but equal" formula that permits states to mandate segregation of the races. Southern states begin systematic disfranchisement of African American men. A fifteen-year period of stalled progress that woman suffragists call "the doldrums" begins.

1900   The Progressive era begins to affect American politics and culture and remains highly influential until about 1920.

1903   The Women's Trade Union League organizes and draws from both the middle and laboring classes. Initially stressing improved wages and working conditions, it soon sees the advantages to be gained from woman suffrage. The Supreme Court decision in *Giles v. Harris* refuses to provide a remedy against the wholesale denial of black voting rights brought about by Alabama's Constitution of 1901.

1910 The National Association for the Advancement of Colored People (NAACP) is organized and becomes the nation's preeminent civil rights group.

1911 A fire at the Triangle Shirtwaist Company in New York City's lower Manhattan claims 146 victims, mainly young Italian and Jewish women.

1912 Democrats nominate Woodrow Wilson for president; Progressive Republicans nominate former president Theodore Roosevelt on the "Bull Moose" ticket; regular Republicans nominate incumbent President William Howard Taft. The presidential primary begins to become significant in the process by which delegates to the national conventions of the parties are chosen. Wilson wins the presidential election, only the third win to that office for a Democrat since 1856.

1913 Ratification of the Sixteenth Amendment gives validity to a federal tax on incomes, a key Progressive objective. Ratification of the Seventeenth Amendment introduces direct popular election of United States senators, another key Progressive institutional objective.

1914 World War I begins in Europe.

1915 *Guinn v. United States* invalidates Oklahoma's use of a grandfather clause in setting voter qualifications. The American Federation of Labor enthusiastically embraces the cause of woman suffrage.

1916 President Wilson wins reelection by defeating Republican nominee Charles Evans Hughes. The presidential election is the first in which votes by women in a handful of states may actually have been decisive.

1917 The United States enters World War I. Large numbers of women join the work force and support the war effort in various ways. Male voters in New York State approve a constitutional amendment conferring full suffrage on women.

1918 The U.S. House of Representatives approves a constitutional amendment for woman suffrage. An armistice in November brings the fighting in World War I to an end.

1919 The U.S. House of Representatives reapproves a constitutional amendment for woman suffrage; the U.S. Senate does so several months later and the amendment is referred to the state legislatures for consideration. Approval by thirty-six states is necessary for the amendment to become part of the Constitution. Ratification of the Eighteenth Amendment begins the era of Prohibition in the United States that lasts until the Twenty-first Amendment repeals the Eighteenth in 1933.

1920 On August 18, Tennessee becomes the thirty-sixth state to ratify the woman suffrage amendment. Ratification of the Nineteenth Amendment removes sex as a qualification for voting and marks the end of the decades-long campaign for woman suffrage in the United States.

1921 The Supreme Court decision in *Newberry v. United States* holds that primaries are not elections and so are not subject to federal constraints that apply to the latter.

1927 The Supreme Court decision in *Nixon v. Herndon* invalidates the white primary that had been mandated by Texas law.

1929 A Congressional apportionment statute leaves out requirements for compact, contiguous, or equally populated districts that had been a part of some previous census-related enactments.

1932 In the depths of the Great Depression, the fifth party system begins to take shape, with competition between

	the ascendant Democrats and the Republicans. *Nixon v. Condon* invalidates the second attempt by Texas to maintain a white Democratic primary.
1935	The Supreme Court decision in *Grovey v. Townsend* fails to invalidate the white primary in Texas that was now the product of party rule, not state law.
1941	The Supreme Court decision in *United States v. Classic* overrules *Newberry v. United States* (1921) and holds that a party primary may be considered legally the equivalent of an election.
1944	The Supreme Court decision in *Smith v. Allwright* overturns *Grovey v. Townsend* (1935) and invalidates Texas's white primary.
1945	Georgia is the first state to set the minimum voting age at eighteen.
1946	The Supreme Court decision in *Colegrove v. Green* holds that suits challenging legislative apportionment and districting do not raise proper questions under the federal Constitution's Fourteenth Amendment.
1948	President Harry Truman calls for national legislation to protect voting rights.
1953	The Supreme Court decision in *Terry v. Adams* invalidates the use of an informal white primary held prior to the regularly scheduled party primary. Republican Dwight D. Eisenhower is elected president.
1954	The Supreme Court decision in *Brown v. Board of Education* invalidates state laws requiring racial segregation in public schools, overturns *Plessy v. Ferguson* (1896), and inspires the civil rights movement.
1956	Marking the start of "massive resistance" to school integration in the South, 77 of the 105 southern members of the U.S. House of Representatives and 19 of 22 senators from the southern states issue a "Southern Manifesto" that promises to use "all lawful means to bring

about a reversal of this [*Brown*] decision which is contrary to the Constitution."

1957   Civil rights legislation passed by Congress is the first since 1875; it establishes the Civil Rights Commission and enables the Department of Justice to intervene on behalf of persons denied the right to vote because of race.

1960   Civil rights legislation passed by Congress stiffens the provisions of the 1957 civil rights legislation. The Supreme Court decision in *Gomillion v. Lightfoot* invalidates, as a violation of the Fifteenth Amendment, a redrawing of city boundaries that effectively moves all black voters out of the city limits. Democrat John F. Kennedy is elected president with Lyndon B. Johnson as his vice president.

1961   Ratification of the Twenty-third Amendment allows residents of the District of Columbia to vote in presidential elections and effectively awards the District three electoral votes.

1962   The Supreme Court decision in *Baker v. Carr*, in contrast to *Colegrove v. Green* (1946), holds that the federal courts may properly entertain challenges to population imbalances among legislative districts.

1963   Civil rights demonstrations for voting and against racial segregation occur throughout the South. The Supreme Court decision in *Gray v. Sanders* strikes down Georgia's county unit system for electing U.S. senators and state officials because it underweights votes cast in urban counties; in *Gray*, Justice William O. Douglas announces the one person, one vote standard. President Kennedy is assassinated; Lyndon Johnson becomes president.

1964   Ratification of the Twenty-fourth Amendment bans the use of poll taxes as a requirement for voting in federal elections. The Supreme Court decision in *Wesberry v. Sanders* requires numerically equal districts in electors for the U.S. House of Representatives; *Reynolds v. Sims* mandates numerically equal districts for both houses of a state legislature. President Johnson launches his "Great Society" proposals and is able to push through Congress a multifaceted civil rights bill that is the most comprehensive since Reconstruction.

1965   After attacks on voting rights advocates in Selma, Alabama, Johnson pushes through Congress a comprehensive voting rights bill that sweeps away most legal impediments to voting by blacks. Section 5 of the act applies to certain jurisdictions only (mainly in the South) and bans any change in election laws or practices that diminishes the voting influence of protected racial minorities (the no-retrogression principle).

1966   The Supreme Court decision in *South Carolina v. Katzenbach* upholds the Voting Rights Act of 1965; *Harper v. State Board of Elections* bans the use of poll taxes as a requirement for voting in state and local elections.

1968   The fifth party system disintegrates, followed by a sixth or indeterminate system in which neither Democrats nor Republicans clearly dominate the executive and legislative branches for any extended period of time.

1970   A congressional extension of the Voting Rights Act sets a minimum voting age of eighteen for federal *and* state elections, but the Supreme Court decision in *Oregon v. Mitchell* strikes down that part of the statute mandating a minimum age for *state* elections. Congress authorizes residents of the District of Columbia to elect one *nonvoting* delegate to the U.S. House of Representatives.

1971   Ratification of the Twenty-sixth Amendment in record time mandates a minimum voting age of eighteen for all elections, state and federal.

1973   The Supreme Court decision in *White v. Regester* invalidates a system of multimember legislative districts in Texas that resulted in representational discrimination against blacks and Mexican Americans.

1977   The Supreme Court decision in *United Jewish Organizations v. Carey* approves the creation of majority-minority districts to enhance the representation of African Americans, even though the redistricting decreased the influence of some Hasidic Jewish voters.

1978   Congress sends to the states a proposed constitutional amendment that, for purposes of representation, would treat the District of Columbia as a state, entitling it to two senators as well as to at least one representative. The amendment fails to be ratified.

1980   District of Columbia residents in a referendum vote in favor of statehood for the District.

1982   In a renewal of the 1965 Voting Rights Act for twenty-five years, Congress amends its Section 2 to make clear that the statute bans any voting or election rule or practice that *results* in a denial or restriction of the right to vote. Previously the Supreme Court had required that a violation of Section 2 be predicated on a discriminatory *intent,* a more difficult standard to meet. The District of Columbia petitions Congress to be admitted to the Union as "New Columbia," the fifty-first state, but the proposal makes no progress.

1986   The Supreme Court decision in *Davis v. Bandemer* announces that partisan gerrymandering presents a question cognizable under the Fourteenth Amendment's equal protection clause, but left in doubt is the kind of evidence and the period of time required to prove an unconstitutional gerrymander.

1993   The Supreme Court decision in *Shaw v. Reno* establishes a constitutional right to reside in a legislative district that has not been drawn primarily on racial grounds.

1995   The Supreme Court decision in *Miller v. Johnson* reinforces *Shaw v. Reno* (1993) by invalidating a congressional districting plan in Georgia in which race was the predominant factor in accounting for the shape of one district.

2000   The Supreme Court in *Bush v. Gore* effectively decides the presidential election by halting a recount of votes in Florida. The voting controversy in Florida focuses new attention nationwide on ballot design and voting devices.

2001   The Supreme Court decision in *Hunt v. Cromartie* upholds a majority-minority congressional district in North Carolina where there was substantial evidence that the state's intent was to create a predominantly Democratic, not a predominantly black, district.

2002   Congress enacts the Help America Vote Act (HAVA) to improve the administration of elections in all fifty states.

2003   The Supreme Court decision in *Georgia v. Ashcroft* approves a state legislative districting plan under Section 5 of the Voting Rights Act, even though several districts had smaller black majorities, because black influence was thereby increased in other districts. The successful California gubernatorial recall election of 2003 features 135 candidates on the ballot.

2004   The Supreme Court decision in *Vieth v. Jubelirer* practically eliminates partisan gerrymandering as a justiciable federal constitutional issue; four justices would overturn *Davis v. Bandemer* (1986) outright. Al Quaeda terrorists threaten to disrupt elections in the United States.

TABLE OF CASES

Giles v. Harris, 189 U.S. 475 (1903)
Giles v. Teasley, 193 U.S. 146 (1904)
Gomillion v. Lightfoot, 364 U.S. 339 (1960)
Gray v. Sanders, 372 U.S. 368 (1963)
Grovey v. Townsend, 295 U.S. 45 (1935)
Guinn v. United States, 238 U.S. 347 (1915)
Harper v. State Board of Elections, 383 U.S. 663 (1966)
Heart of Atlanta Motel v. United States, 379 U.S. 241 (1964)
Hunt v. Cromartie, 532 U.S. 234 (2001)
Hunter v. Underwood, 471 U.S. 222 (1985)
Jones v. Van Zandt, 46 U.S. (5 How.) 215 (1847)
Karcher v. Daggett, 462 U.S. 725 (1983)
Katzenbach v. Morgan, 384 U.S. 641 (1966)
Kirkpatrick v. Preisler, 394 U.S. 526 (1969)
Lamb's Chapel v. Center Moriches School District, 508 U.S. 384 (1993)
Lane v. Wilson, 307 U.S. 268 (1939)
Lassiter v. Northampton County Board of Elections, 360 U.S. 45 (1959)
Luther v. Borden, 48 U.S. (17 How.) 1 (1849)
Mahan v. Howell, 410 U.S. 315 (1973)
McLaughlin v. City of Canton, 947 F. Supp. 954 (S.D. Miss. 1995)
Miller v. Johnson, 515 U.S. 900 (1995)
Minor v. Happersett, 88 U.S. 162 (1875)
Mobile v. Bolden, 446 U.S. 55 (1980)
Murphy v. Ramsey, 114 U.S. 15 (1885)
Myers v. Anderson, 238 U.S. 268 (1915)
New York Times Co. v. Sullivan, 376 U.S. 254 (1964)
Newberry v. United States, 256 U.S. 232 (1921)
Nixon v. Condon, 286 U.S. 83 (1932)
Nixon v. Herndon, 273 U.S. 536 (1927)
Oregon v. Mitchell, 400 U.S. 112 (1970)
Pace v. Alabama, 106 U.S. 583 (1883)
Plessy v. Ferguson, 163 U.S. 537 (1896)

ANNOTATED
BIBLIOGRAPHY

BOOKS AND ARTICLES

Abramowitz, Alan. 2004. *Voice of the People: Elections and Voting in the United States.* Boston: McGraw-Hill.

    Concise and current overview of most aspects of American electoral politics.

Adams, Charles Francis. 1856. *The Works of John Adams, Second President of the United States.* Boston: Little, Brown.

    One important source for the papers of the second American president, who had very definite views on the need to maintain a restricted male franchise.

Aldrich, John H. 1995. *Why Parties?* Chicago: University of Chicago Press.

    Examines the purposes, origins, and development of political parties in the United States.

Alpern, Sara, and Dale Baum. 1985. "Female Ballots: The Impact of the Nineteenth Amendment." *Journal of Interdisciplinary History* 16: 43.

    Analysis of voting patterns of women and the impact of woman suffrage.

Alvarez, P. Michael, and Thad Hall. 2004. *Point, Click, and Vote: The Future of Internet Voting.* Washington, DC: Brookings Institution.

    The advantages and possible perils of voting by way of the Internet; advocates wider experimentation with Internet voting in various trial projects.

Anders, George. 2004. "Common Knowledge." *Wall Street Journal,* May 25, D-8.

Review of *The Wisdom of Crowds* by James Surowiecki. See the entry on this book below.

Annbinder, Tyler. 1992. *Nativism and Slavery: The Northern Know-Nothings and the Politics of the 1850s.* New York: Oxford University Press.

Study of the movement (the Know-Nothings) that became a political party for a short time in the 1850s and advocated a highly restricted suffrage as far as immigrants were concerned.

Bardolph, Richard, ed. 1970. *The Civil Rights Record: Black Americans and the Law, 1849–1970.* New York: Thomas Y. Crowell.

Eminently valuable collection of cases, statutes, and other documents on civil rights generally; much of the contents relates to voting rights.

Basler, Roy P., ed. 1953. *The Collected Works of Abraham Lincoln.* 9 vols. and supp. New Brunswick, NJ: Rutgers University Press.

Standard collection of speeches and other papers of the sixteenth American president.

Bickel, Alexander M., and Benno C. Schmidt Jr. 1984. *The Judiciary and Responsible Government 1910–21.* New York: Macmillan.

A volume in the Holmes Devise *History of the Supreme Court of the United States;* includes material on the grandfather clause voting rights case of *Guinn v. United States* (1915).

Blair, Karen J. 2001. "Women's Club Movement." In Paul S. Boyer, ed., *The Oxford Companion to United States History.* New York: Oxford University Press.

Summary of the role played by women's clubs in the nineteenth and early twentieth centuries, including their relation to the woman suffrage movement.

Bresler, Robert J. 1999. *Us vs. Them: American Political and Cultural Conflict from WWII to Watergate.* Wilmington, DE: Scholarly Resources.

Commentary, analysis, and documents relating to cultural divisions in the United States after World War II.

———. 2004. *Freedom of Association: Rights and Liberties under the Law.* Santa Barbara, CA: ABC-CLIO.

A multifaceted study in the America's Freedoms Series of the political and social importance of freedom of association and how it has developed as a constitutional right.

Brock, W. R., ed. 1961. *The Federalist.* New York: E. P. Dutton.

One of any number of editions of this classic from the founding era of the United States; contains the eighty-five essays by Alexander Hamilton, John Jay, and James Madison urging ratification of the proposed

Constitution; each essay was published in newspapers in New York State in late 1787 and early 1788.

Bryce, James. 1921. *The American Commonwealth.* 2 vols. New & rev. ed. New York: Macmillan.

Written by a British historian and diplomat who was ambassador to the United States between 1907 and 1913; his commentaries on American political institutions in these volumes, originally published in 1888, are still highly regarded.

Buhle, Mari Jo, and Paul Buhle, eds. 1978. *The Concise History of Woman Suffrage: Selections from the Classic Work of Stanton, Anthony, Gage, and Harper.* Urbana: University of Illinois Press.

Invaluable source of documents and speeches by participants over several decades in the drive for women suffrage; the volume draws selections from the classic six-volume *History of Woman Suffrage* that was compiled by Susan B. Anthony and others beginning in 1881 and concluding in 1922.

Burnham, Walter Dean. 1967. "Party Systems and the Political Process." In William Nisbet Chambers and Walter Dean Burnham, eds., *The American Party Systems.* New York: Oxford University Press.

A look at the development of American political parties through the chronological lens of the concept of party systems.

———. 1970. *Critical Elections and the Mainsprings of American Politics.* New York: W. W. Norton.

Develops the concept of critical or realigning elections that mark the transition from one party system to the next.

Burr, A. R. 1926. *Russell H. Conwell and His Work.* Philadelphia: Winston.

Published in the year after Conwell's death, a fulsome account of Conwell's life, with an emphasis on his lectures and ideas.

Catt, Carrie C., and Nettie R. Shuler. 1923. *Woman Suffrage and Politics.* New York: Charles Scribner's Sons.

Timely perspectives on the drive for woman suffrage written by two stalwarts in the movement.

Chapin, Douglas. 2004. *Election Reform 2004: What's Changed, What Hasn't and Why.* Washington, DC: Election Reform Information Project.

Report on changes in voting procedures and the administration of elections after the election controversy of 2000.

Chute, Marchette. 1969. *The First Liberty: A History of the Right to Vote in America, 1619–1850.* New York: E. P. Dutton.

Useful account of voting rights in the colonial and early American national periods, through the demise of most property requirements.

Coletta, Paolo E. 1971. "Election of 1908." In Arthur M. Schlesinger Jr. and Fred L. Israel, eds., *History of American Presidential Elections.* 4 vols. New York: Chelsea House.

Analysis of the presidential election that placed William Howard Taft in the White House.

Congress and the Nation 1965–1968. 1969. Washington, DC: Congressional Quarterly.

Encyclopedic recounting of congressional business between 1965 and 1968, in both chronological and topical formats.

Congress and the Nation 1969–1972. 1973. Washington, DC: Congressional Quarterly.

Encyclopedic recounting of congressional business between 1969 and 1972, in both chronological and topical formats.

Cornwell, Nancy C. 2004. *Freedom of the Press: Rights and Liberties under the Law.* Santa Barbara, CA: ABC-CLIO.

Analysis in the America's Freedoms Series of the historical development and contemporary scope of press freedoms in America; emphasizes the importance of various media including the Internet.

Cott, Nancy F. 1987. *The Grounding of Modern Feminism.* New Haven, CT: Yale University Press.

The links between the woman suffrage movement, postsuffrage ideas, and modern feminist thought.

Crossen, Cynthia. 2004. "Before Radio, Citizenry Got Culture, Politics from Traveling Troupes." *Wall Street Journal,* July 7, B1.

Overview of the influence of the traveling Chautauqua events in the early twentieth century, during which time Russell H. Conwell was one of the most popular lecturers.

Cruikshank, Alfred B. 1920. *Popular Misgovernment in the United States.* New York: Moffat, Yard.

A Tory polemic, published just as the Nineteenth Amendment was ratified, that argued against an extended franchise and in favor of a return to more substantial qualifications for voting.

Crunden, Robert M. 2001. "Progressive Era." In Paul S. Boyer, ed., *The Oxford Companion to United States History.* New York: Oxford University Press.

Summary of the various dimensions of the Progressive movement as well as its impact in American history.

Cultice, Wendell W. 1992. *Youth's Battle for the Ballot: A History of Voting Age in America.* Westport, CT: Greenwood.

Account of the efforts to include eighteen-, nineteen-, and twenty-year-olds within the electorate; culminates with ratification of the Twenty-sixth Amendment in 1971.

Cummings, Homer S., and Carl McFarland. 1937. *Federal Justice: Chapters in the History of Justice and the Federal Executive.* New York: Macmillan.

Important source for the early history of federal prosecutions and the Department of Justice; the lead author was attorney general during the first six years of the administration of President Franklin D. Roosevelt.

Currie, David P. 1985. *The Constitution in the Supreme Court: The First Hundred Years, 1789–1888.* Chicago: University of Chicago Press.

The first of a two-volume study of American constitutional history, with a heavy emphasis on the Supreme Court. The second volume, subtitled *The Second Century 1888–1986,* was published by the same press in 1990.

Davidson, Chandler. 1990. "The Recent Evolution of Voting Rights Law Affecting Racial and Language Minorities." In Chandler Davidson and Bernard Grofman, eds., *Quiet Revolution in the South: The Impact of the Voting Rights Act, 1965–1990.* Princeton, NJ: Princeton University Press.

Overview of advances in voting rights after passage of the Voting Rights Act in 1965.

Davidson, Chandler, and Bernard Grofman, eds. 1994. *Quiet Revolution in the South: The Impact of the 1965 Voting Rights Act, 1965–1990.* Princeton, NJ: Princeton University Press.

Collection of essays on the impact of the Voting Rights Act during the quarter century after its enactment.

de Tocqueville, Alexis. 1966. *Democracy in America.* J. P. Mayer and Max Lerner, eds.; George Lawrence, trans. New York: Harper and Row.

One of many editions of this classic work by a French aristocrat who toured America early in the nineteenth century and recorded his perceptive observations, many of which remain true today.

"Declaration of Constitutional Principles Issues by 19 Senators and 77 Representatives of the Congress." 1956. *New York Times,* March 12: 19.

This "Southern Manifesto" marked the beginning of the massive resistance to integration of public schools following the Supreme Court's decision in *Brown v. Board of Education* (1954).

Dobbins, Harry T. 1941. "Nebraska's One House Legislature—After Six Years." *National Municipal Review.* 30:511.

Analysis of the short-term political consequences following adoption of Nebraska's unique unicameral state legislature.

Doyle, William. 2001. *An American Insurrection: The Battle of Oxford, Mississippi, 1962.* New York: Doubleday.

Reviews the resistance thrown up against efforts to integrate the student body of the University of Mississippi that ultimately required intervention by federal troops.

Drew, Elizabeth. 1985. *Campaign Journal.* New York: Macmillan.

Journalistic memoir of, and reflections on, the 1984 presidential election.

DuBois, Ellen Carol. 1978. *Feminism and Suffrage: The Emergence of an Independent Women's Movement in America.* Ithaca, NY: Cornell University Press.

One of the first modern accounts of the woman's suffrage movement by a leading feminist scholar.

———. 1992. "Taking Law into Their Own Hands: Voting Women during Reconstruction." In Donald W. Rogers, ed., *Voting and the Spirit of American Democracy: Essays on the History of Voting and Voting Rights in America.* Urbana: University of Illinois Press.

Recounts the dramatic extralegal and even illegal actions of women during Reconstruction in their efforts to secure the vote at a time when Congress and the nation were extending the vote to African American males.

Dunne, Finley Peter. 1898. *Mr. Dooley in Peace and War.* Boston: Small, Maynard.

One of several volumes of the sayings of the fictional Irish bartender character "Mr. Dooley" about public affairs; wildly popular around the turn of the twentieth century.

Eaton, Clement. 1964. *The Mind of the Old South.* Baton Rouge: Louisiana State University Press.

A collection of essays about various aspects of life and culture in the southern states prior to the Civil War.

Elliott, Ward E. Y. 1974. *The Rise of Guardian Democracy: The Supreme Court's Role in Voting Rights Disputes, 1845–1969.* Cambridge, MA: Harvard University Press.

A study of how voting rights reforms came about both before and after the Supreme Court began intervening in voting rights issues, especially after 1937; explores the effects of the Court's involvement on American democracy.

Farrand, Max, ed. 1966. *The Records of the Federal Convention of 1787.* 4 vols. New Haven, CT: Yale University Press.

Originally published in 1911, this is the standard source for the debates and records of the Philadelphia Convention that produced the Constitution; the debates are found in the first two volumes; documents and correspondence fill volumes three and four.

Fellner, Jamie, and Marc Mauer. 1998. *Losing the Vote: The Impact of Felony Disenfranchisement Laws in the United States.* Washington, DC: The Sentencing Project.

Standard and most recent analysis of the impact of laws that temporarily or permanently disfranchise those convicted of serious crimes.

Firth, C. H., ed. 1891. *The Clarke Papers.* New series XLIX, vol. 1. London: The Camden Society.

The only easily accessible source for the complete Putney Debates. Readers are forewarned, however, that this publication maintains the original mid-seventeenth spelling of the text of the debates, so some words will appear strangely unfamiliar to most readers today. As quoted in Chapter Two in this book, however, the spelling in the debates has been modernized.

Fischer, David Hackett. 1994. *Paul Revere's Ride.* New York: Oxford University Press.

Entertaining and highly readable account of early hostilities in the American Revolution in the Boston area and of those who took part.

Flexner, Eleanor, and Ellen Fitzpatrick. 1975. *Century of Struggle.* Enl. ed. Cambridge, MA: Harvard University Press.

Essential source for information about woman suffrage and other aspects of women's rights.

Friedman, Lawrence M. 2002. *Law in America: A Brief History.* New York: Modern Library.

Brief overview of the development of law and legal institutions in the United States, especially in arenas outside those of constitutional law.

Garrow, David J. 1978. *Protest at Selma: Martin Luther King, Jr., and the Voting Rights Act of 1965.* New Haven, CT: Yale University Press.

Dramatic recounting of the circumstances surrounding the catalytic event for passage of the Voting Rights Act of 1965.

Gathorne-Hardy, G. M. 1964. *A Short History of International Affairs 1920–1939.* 4th ed. New York: Oxford University Press.

Although the focus is on post-1920 international relations, the book also provides a concise summary of the unique aspects of World War I (1914–1918) and how it so stunned its nation-combatants.

Gerhardt, Michael J. 2003. "Frank M. Johnson, Jr." In John H. Vile, ed., *Great American Judges: An Encyclopedia.* 2 vols. Santa Barbara, CA: ABC-CLIO.

Biographical essay about an important federal judge in Alabama during some of the most trying moments of the civil rights movement.

Gibson, James L., Gregory A. Caldeira, and Lester Kenyatta Spence. 2002. "The Supreme Court and the U.S. Presidential Election of 2000: Wounds, Self-Inflicted or Otherwise?" Unpublished paper. St. Louis, MO: Weidenbaum Center on the Economy, Government, and Public Policy at Washington University.

Analysis of the impact on the institutional legitimacy of the Supreme Court in the wake of the Court decision in *Bush v. Gore* (2000).

Gordon, John Steele. 2004. "A Senator from D.C.?" *Wall Street Journal,* Jan. 14: A12.

One proposal on fully enfranchising voters in the District of Columbia that avoids awarding two senators to the city of Washington.

Graber, Doris A. 2000. *Media Power in Politics.* 4th ed. Washington, DC: Congressional Quarterly.

Analysis of the role the mass media, especially television, have come to play in the American political system.

Graham, Sara Hunter. 1996. *Women's Suffrage and the New Democracy.* New Haven, CT: Yale University Press.

How the woman suffrage movement achieved its goal by forging a highly organized and centrally controlled interest group, the National American Woman Suffrage Association (NAWSA); examines the tactics and ideology of the NAWSA and discusses what they reveal about interest group politics, women's rights, and American democracy.

Greenberg, Jack. 1994. *Crusaders in the Courts: How a Dedicated Band of Lawyers Fought for the Civil Rights Revolution.* New York: Basic Books.

Written by a participant in the story the author describes, a memoir-styled account of the courtroom battles fought on behalf of civil rights by the attorneys of the Legal Defense Fund, an offshoot from the National Association for the Advancement of Colored People.

Gugliotta, Guy. 2001. "Study Finds Millions of Votes Lost." *Washington Post,* July 16: A-1.

A report on the number of ballots cast in the presidential election of 2000 that were not counted for various reasons.

Guinier, Lani. 1994. *The Tyranny of the Majority: Fundamental Fairness in Representative Democracy.* New York: Free Press.

The representational deficiencies of the plurality single-member district and a proposal for weighted voting to enhance the power of racial minorities; the author was President Clinton's unsuccessful nominee as assistant attorney general for civil rights in 1993.

Hacker, Andrew. 1964. *Congressional Districting.* Washington, DC: Brookings Institution.

Analysis, in historical perspective, of the then-current districting situation on the eve of the Supreme Court's monumental rulings of 1964 in *Wesberry v. Sanders* (on congressional districting) and *Reynolds v. Sims* (on state legislative redistricting).

———. 1995. "Malign Neglect: The Crackdown on African-Americans." *Nation,* July 10: 45.

Disproportionate impact of felony disfranchisement laws on black Americans.

Hamilton, Charles V. 1973. *The Bench and the Ballot: Southern Federal Judges and Black Voters.* New York: Oxford University Press.

Vivid portrayal of the role of U.S. district and appeals judges in southern states in voting rights cases, mainly in the late 1950s and 1960s; demonstrates the difficulties prior to the Voting Rights Act of 1965 of ridding the nation of racial discrimination in voting.

Handlin, Oscar, and Mary Flug Handlin. 1966. *The Popular Sources of Political Authority: Documents on the Massachusetts Convention of 1780.* Cambridge, MA: Harvard University Press.

Standard source for the proceedings of the state constitutional convention that produced the charter that remains the oldest American state constitution still in force.

Hanson, Royce. 1966. *The Political Thicket: Reapportionment and Constitutional Democracy.* Englewood Cliffs, NJ: Prentice-Hall.

Engaging play-by-play description of the political counterattack to the Supreme Court's redistricting decisions of the early 1960s, especially *Reynolds v. Sims* (1964).

Hasen, Richard L. 2003. *The Supreme Court and Election Law: Judging Equality from* Baker *v.* Carr *to* Bush *v.* Gore. New York: New York University Press.

Demonstrates how the Supreme Court has routinely engaged various kinds of voting rights issues during the past four decades.

Hench, Virginia E. 1998. "The Death of Voting Rights: The Legal Disenfranchisement of Minority Voters." *Case Western Reserve Law Review* 48: 727.

Critical examination of recent Supreme Court decisions affecting the voting rights of racial minorities.

Hoerder, Dick. 1985. *Labor Migrations in the Atlantic Economies: The European and American Working Classes during the Period of Industrialization.* Westport, CT: Greenwood Press.

Useful account of immigration in pre–Civil War America.

Holt, Michael F. 1973. "The Antimasonic and Know Nothing Parties." In Arthur Schlesinger Jr., ed., *History of U.S. Political Parties.* 4 vols. New York: Chelsea House.

Concise account of the rise and dissolution of the American or Know-Nothing Party in the 1850s.

Hutchinson, Dennis J. 1998. *The Man Who Was Once Whizzer White: A Portrait of Justice Byron R. White.* New York: Free Press.

Biography of the first of President John Kennedy's two appointments to the U.S. Supreme Court. Prior to his elevation to the bench, White served as deputy attorney general (the number two official in the Department of Justice) and as such was the Kennedy administration's "point man" to try to defuse civil rights crises in the South.

Isenberg, Nancy. 2001. "Women's Rights Movements." In Paul S. Boyer, ed., *The Oxford Companion to United States History.* New York: Oxford University Press.

Concise overview of the drive for women's rights in American history in its various stages.

Johnson, Lyndon Baines. 1971. *The Vantage Point: Perspectives of the Presidency, 1963–1969.* New York: Holt, Rinehart and Winston.

Memoirs by the thirty-sixth president of the United States, with emphasis on Johnson's "Great Society" initiatives, including protection of voting rights.

Karlan, Pamela S. 2002. "Exit Strategies in Constitutional Law: Lessons for Getting the Least Dangerous Branch out of the Political Thicket." *Boston University Law Review* 82: 669.

Argues for greater legislative discretion in creating majority-minority districts.

———. 2004. "*Georgia v. Ashcroft* and the Retrogression of Retrogression." *Election Law Journal* 3: 21.

Identifies a possible new direction from *Georgia v. Ashcroft* (2003) in interpretation of Section 5 of the Voting Rights Act.

Katzenstein, Mary Fainsod. 1992. "Constitutional Politics and the Feminist Movement." In Donald W. Rogers, ed., *Voting and the Spirit of American Democracy.* Urbana: University of Illinois Press.

One of nine essays on voting rights in this volume, it examines the long-term effects of the woman suffrage victory on women's place in American society.

Kelly, Alfred H., and Winfred A Harbison. 1976. *The American Constitution: Its Origins and Development.* 5th ed. New York: W. W. Norton.

Standard source on American constitutional development, from the colonial era to modern times; a seventh edition, with Herman Belz as a third author, was issued in two volumes by the same publisher in 1991; not all of the material in earlier editions carried over to the 1991 edition, however.

Kelly, Selby, and Bill Crouch Jr., eds. 1982. *The Best of Pogo.* New York: Simon and Schuster.

A collection of newspaper comic strips about the astute alligator of Georgia's Okefenokee Swamp.

Kelman, Steven. 1970. *Push Comes to Shove.* Boston: Houghton Mifflin.

A memoir of campus turmoil at Harvard University in the late 1960s, as seen through the eyes of an astute undergraduate at the time.

Kersch, Ken I. 2003. *Freedom of Speech: Rights and Liberties under the Law.* Santa Barbara, CA: ABC-CLIO.

Historically organized study in the America's Freedoms Series of the development of free speech in the United States, especially in the context of political movements and social change.

Key, V. O., Jr. 1949. *Southern Politics in State and Nation.* New York: Alfred A. Knopf.

Classic study of politics in the southern states at a time when southern politics was a world entirely unto itself; shows the role of race as the ever-present and all-pervading factor.

———. 1964. *Parties, Politics, and Pressure Groups.* 5th ed. New York: Thomas Y. Crowell.

A comprehensive presentation of partisan and otherwise political life in the United States into the era of the fifth party system.

Keyssar, Alexander. 2000. *The Right to Vote: The Contested History of Democracy in the United States.* New York: Basic Books.

Sets the modern-day standard for books on voting rights; comprehensive; contains a wealth of detail, especially in the nearly fifty pages of tables in the appendix.

Klarman, Michael J. 2004. *From Jim Crow to Civil Rights: The Supreme Court and the Struggle for Racial Equality.* New York: Oxford University Press.

An encyclopedic account of civil rights in the United States that emphasizes the period from the late nineteenth century through the 1960s. Addresses the role of courts in setting civil rights policy in the context of whether the judiciary, especially the U.S. Supreme Court, is more follower than leader.

Kleppner, Paul. 1992. "Defining Citizenship: Immigration and the Struggle for Voting Rights in Antebellum America." In Donald W. Rogers, ed., *Voting and the Spirit of American Democracy: Essays on the History of Voting and Voting Rights in America.* Urbana: University of Illinois Press.

One of nine essays on voting rights; focuses on problems for voting rights posed by increased immigration prior to the Civil War.

Knock, Thomas I. 2001. "World War I." In Paul S. Boyer, ed., *The Oxford Companion to United States History.* New York: Oxford University Press.

Concise review of the origins, campaigns, and effects (especially in the United States) of the "war to end all wars."

Kobach, Kris. 1994. "Note: Rethinking Article V: Term Limits and the Seventeenth and Nineteenth Amendments." *Yale Law Journal* 103: 1971.

Demonstrates how the Seventeenth and Nineteenth amendments were propelled by action at the state level, either in providing popular input to state legislative election of U.S. senators or in granting woman suffrage.

Kousser, J. Morgan. 1974. *The Shaping of Southern Politics: Suffrage Restriction and the Establishment of the One-Party South.* New Haven, CT: Yale University Press.

Depicts the use of race-based voting restrictions around the turn of the twentieth century in the building of a strong one-party region under Democratic control.

———. 1999. *Colorblind Injustice: Minority Voting Rights and the Undoing of the Second Reconstruction.* Chapel Hill: University of North Carolina Press.

A comparison of the first Reconstruction to the second; shows the importance of rules and institutions in protecting civil rights of racial minorities; critical of most of the Supreme Court's decisions involving majority-minority districts.

Kraditor, Aileen S. 1973. "The Liberty and Free Soil Parties." In Arthur M. Schlesinger, ed., *History of U.S. Political Parties.* 4 vols. New York: Chelsea House.

Concise account of the first antislavery third parties in pre–Civil War America and their impact on the political system.

Kutler, Stanley I. 1968. "Ward Hunt." In Leon Friedman and Fred L. Israel, eds., *The Justices of the United States Supreme Court 1789–1969: Their Lives and Major Opinions.* 4 vols. New York: Chelsea House.

Biographical essay about the Supreme Court justice who, sitting as circuit judge in New York, presided over the trial of Susan B. Anthony for illegally voting in a federal election.

Labbé, Ronald M., and Jonathan Lurie. 2003. *The Slaughterhouse Cases: Regulation, Reconstruction, and the Fourteenth Amendment.* Lawrence: University Press of Kansas.

The only modern book-length case study of the Supreme Court litigation that resulted in the first authoritative interpretation of the Fourteenth Amendment; the Supreme Court's decision in the *Slaughterhouse Cases* of 1873 helped to shape the institution's attitude toward voting rights issues for the balance of the nineteenth century.

Lemons, J. Stanley. 1973. *The Woman Citizen: Social Feminism in the 1920s.* Urbana: University of Illinois Press.

Thinking about the status of women, especially in the United States, in the decade after ratification of the Nineteenth Amendment.

Levinson, Paul. 1963. *Race, Class, and Party: A History of Negro Suffrage and White Politics in the South.* New York: Russell and Russell.

Depicts the importance of race and class in southern politics, especially in the late nineteenth and early twentieth centuries.

Link, Arthur S. 1956. *Wilson: The New Freedom.* Princeton, NJ: Princeton University Press.

A volume in the author's five-volume biography of the twenty-eighth president of the United States; this one covers the beginning of Wilson's administration and the launch of his "New Freedom" agenda; the author is also the principal editor of the sixty-nine volumes of *The Papers of Woodrow Wilson,* also published by Princeton University Press.

———. 1965. *Wilson: Campaign for Progressivism and Peace 1916–1917.* Princeton, NJ: Princeton University Press.

A volume in the author's five-volume biography of the twenty-eighth president of the United States; this one mainly covers the period immediately preceding American entry into World War I.

Litwack, Leon F. 1961. *North of Slavery: The Negro in the Free States, 1790–1860.* Chicago: University of Chicago Press.

   Landmark study on the legal and cultural status of free blacks in states outside the South prior to the Civil War.

Locke, John. 1924. *Two Treatises of Civil Government.* W. S. Carpenter ed. New York: E. P. Dutton.

   Probably more than any other English writer, this seventeenth-century philosopher had a profound impact on the thinking of the founders of the American republic; the *Two Treatises,* originally published in 1690, are available in several editions.

Lunt, W. E. 1957. *History of England.* 4th ed. New York: Harper and Brothers.

   One of several standard works on the political and constitutional history of England.

Maltz, Earl M. 1996. "The Waite Court and Federal Power to Enforce the Reconstruction Amendments." In Jennifer M. Lowe, ed., *The Supreme Court and the Civil War.* Washington, DC: Supreme Court Historical Society.

   A probing examination of some of the decisions by the Waite Court (1874–1888) dealing with civil rights; concludes that the Waite bench was not as hostile to civil rights as sometimes suggested in the literature.

Manza, Jeff, and Clem Brooks. 1999. *Social Cleavages and Political Change: Voter Alignment and U.S. Party Coalitions.* New York: Oxford University Press.

   A sociological study of the changing nature of social cleavages and their effect on political allegiances and voting behavior in the United States since the 1950s; maintains that social cleavages continue to have important partisan consequences.

Mason, Alpheus Thomas, 1956. *Harlan Fiske Stone: Pillar of the Law.* New York: Viking.

   Biography of only the second sitting associate justice of the Supreme Court to have been named chief justice of the United States. Altogether, Stone sat on the Court from 1925 until his death in 1946, years that encompass the beginning of the Court's modern-day scrutiny of voting rights policies. Mason's biography was noteworthy at the time of its publication because it was the first to utilize internal Court memoranda written by justices still sitting on the bench.

———. 1962. *The Supreme Court: Palladium of Freedom.* Ann Arbor: University of Michigan Press.

Originally presented as a series of lectures, the volume is a concise look at, and justification for, the role of the Supreme Court as a defender of individual liberty.

———. 1965. *Free Government in the Making: Readings in American Political Thought.* 3d ed. New York: Oxford University Press.

Classic work on American political thought; contains insightful essays and key documents, ranging from excerpts from the Putney Debates to the early 1960s.

Mason, Alpheus Thomas, and Donald Grier Stephenson Jr. 2002. *American Constitutional Law: Introductory Essays and Selected Cases.* 13th ed. Upper Saddle River, NJ: Prentice Hall. The 14th edition (2005) was published while this book was in production.

One of several textbooks on most topics of American constitutional law and interpretation; essays on each topic are followed by excerpts from leading cases, including some related to voting rights. The 14th edition is scheduled for publication in 2005.

Mason, Alpheus Thomas, and Richard H. Leach. 1959. *In Quest of Freedom: American Political Thought and Practice.* Englewood Cliffs, NJ: Prentice-Hall.

A book that complements the lead author's *Free Government in the Making;* a narrative and analysis of the development of American political ideas; especially strong for the eighteenth- and nineteenth-century periods.

McCloskey, Robert Green, ed. 1967. *The Works of James Wilson.* 2 vols. Cambridge, MA: Harvard University Press.

With a forty-eight-page introduction by the editor, this set is the most useful collection of the writings of one of the nation's founders, who was also one of the first members of the U.S. Supreme Court. The work includes Wilson's law lectures at the University of Pennsylvania.

McCullough, David. 2001. *John Adams.* New York: Simon and Schuster.

The most recent, and probably the best biography of the Massachusetts statesman who became the second American president.

McDonald, Michael P., and Samuel L. Popkin. 2001. "The Myth of the Vanishing Voter." *American Political Science Review* 95: 963.

Argues that much of the apparent decline in voter turnout in recent years has been due to an increase in the number of adults who, for various reasons, are ineligible to vote at all.

McManus, Doyle, Bob Drogin, and Richard O'Reilly. 2001. "Counting Method Key to Bush's Florida Win, New Study Says." *Philadelphia Inquirer,* Nov. 12: A2.

A press report distributed by the Associated Press that concludes that the "real" winner of the electoral vote in Florida in 2000 would depend on which standards were applied in a hand recount of votes.

Morgan, David. 1973. *Suffragists and Democrats: The Politics of Woman Suffrage in America.* East Lansing: Michigan State University Press.

Examines the links between the woman suffrage movement and how it was affected positively and negatively by the party system.

Morison, Samuel Eliot. 1965. *The Oxford History of the American People.* New York: Oxford University Press.

Sweeping and grand account of American history from the years of colonial settlement to the early 1960s.

"'Motor Voter' Bill Enacted After 5 Years." 1994. *1993 Congressional Quarterly Almanac.* Washington, DC: Congressional Quarterly.

Step-by-step account of the machinations in Congress over a five-year period that led to passage, and a presidential signing, of the National Voter Registration Act, sometimes called the "motor voter" bill.

Myrdal, Gunnar. 1944. *An American Delimma: The Negro Problem and Modern Democracy.* 2 vols. New York: Harper.

Highly influential study of race relations in the United States, on the eve of the rebirth of the civil rights movement.

Nather, David. 2002. "Provisions of the Federal Voting Standards and Procedures Law." *Congressional Quarterly Weekly Report,* Nov. 2: 2870.

Summary of the various objectives of the Help America Vote Act (HAVA) that Congress passed in 2002 to address problems in election administration that surfaced so vividly, especially in Florida, in the presidential election of 2000.

"New Study Shows . . ." 2004. Washington, DC: Election Data Services, Feb. 12: 1.

Report on advances in voting-machine technology in the wake of the enactment of the Help America Vote Act; what changes have been made and what remains the same.

Nicolay, John G., and John Hay, eds. 1905. *Complete Works of Abraham Lincoln.* 12 vols. New York: Tandy.

One of the first comprehensive scholarly collections of the papers of the sixteenth American president.

Norgen, Jill. 1999. "Before It Was Merely Difficult: Belva Lockwood's Life in Law and Politics." *Journal of Supreme Court History* 23: 16.

Engaging essay about one of the first female attorneys in Washington, D.C., and in 1880 the first to argue a case before the U.S. Supreme Court.

Patterson, James T. 2001. Brown v. Board of Education: *A Civil Rights Milestone and Its Troubled Legacy.* New York: Oxford University Press.

A review of this landmark civil rights decision and its impact nearly a half century after it came down.

Patterson, Thomas E. 2002. *The Vanishing Voter: Public Involvement in an Age of Uncertainty.* New York: Knopf.

Argues that the decline in voter turnouts over the past four decades has causes in addition to the increase in the percentage of the adult population that is ineligible to vote.

Peltason, J. W. 1988. *Corwin and Peltason's Understanding the Constitution.* 11th ed. New York: Holt, Rinehart, and Winston.

An annotation of each section of the United States Constitution, noting where applicable the current construction by the Supreme Court; the sixteenth edition was published in 2004 by Wadsworth of Belmont, California.

Pickens, William. 1920. "The Woman Votes Hit the Color Line." *Nation* 111 (October 6): 372.

One of the first articles to emphasize that woman suffrage did not necessarily mean black woman suffrage.

Pildes, Richard H. 2000. "Democracy, Anti-Democracy, and the Canon." *Constitutional Commentary* 17: 295.

Provides detailed information and analysis of the Supreme Court's anti–voting rights decision in *Giles v. Harris* (1904).

———. 2002. "Is Voting Rights Law Now at War with Itself?" *North Carolina Law Review* 80: 1517.

Highlights tensions within the Voting Rights Act, given constructions of it by the Supreme Court.

Platt, Suzy. 1989. *Respectfully Quoted: A Dictionary of Quotations from the Congressional Research Service.* Washington, DC: Library of Congress.

Marvelously useful compilation of quotations on virtually every aspect of political life in the United States, and more.

Plucknett, Theodore F. T. 1956. *A Concise History of the Common Law.* 5th ed. London: Butterworth.

"Concise" only in its title, the book is a lengthy and exhaustive study of the early evolution of the common law and political institutions in England.

Porter, Kirk Harold. 1971. *A History of Suffrage in the United States.* New York: AMS Press.

A reprint of the 1918 edition published by the University of Chicago Press; essential source on the colonial and early national period with respect to property qualifications for voting; written shortly before ratification of the Nineteenth Amendment and at a time when most African American males remained disfranchised.

Price, Polly J. 2003. *Property Rights: Rights and Liberties under the Law.* Santa Barbara, CA: ABC-CLIO.

A volume in the America's Freedoms Series, the book depicts the evolution of property rights in the United States, particularly showing the importance of property as a measure of standing in the early nineteenth century.

Pringle, Henry F. 1939. *The Life and Times of William Howard Taft.* 2 vols. New York: Farrah and Rinehart.

The prosecution that resulted in *Guinn v. United States* (1915) was first initiated in the last year of Taft's presidency; Taft is also the only president to have served as chief justice of the United States (1921–1930).

Richardson, James D. 1917. *A Compilation of Messages and Papers of the Presidents, 1789–1902.* 20 vols. New York: Bureau of National Literature.

Standard source for presidential pronouncements, from George Washington into the administration of Theodore Roosevelt.

Roche, John P. 1961. "The Founding Fathers: A Reform Caucus in Action." *American Political Science Review* 55: 799–816.

Classic piece on the Philadelphia Convention of 1787 that produced the Constitution; argues that virtually all framers wanted some change in the plan of government in existence under the Articles of Confederation and that the framers were well aware of the limits on their options that were imposed by the political realities of the day.

Rogers, Donald W. 1992. "Introduction—The Right to Vote in American History." In Donald W. Rogers, ed., *Voting and the Spirit of American Democracy: Essays on the History of Voting and Voting Rights in America.* Urbana: University of Illinois Press.

Concise overview of voting rights across American history; the essay serves as the introduction to this volume of eight other essays.

Rogers, Donald W., ed. 1992. *Voting and the Spirit of American Democracy: Essays on the History of Voting and Voting Rights in America.* Urbana: University of Illinois Press.

Useful collection of nine essays on various aspects of voting rights; several of the essays are cited separately in this book.

Roosevelt, Theodore. 1912. Address in Chicago, Illinois, August 6. In Arthur M. Schlesinger Jr. and Fred L. Israel, eds., *History of American Presidential Elections.* Vol. 3. New York: Chelsea House.

Roosevelt, the Bull Moose (Progressive) candidate, finished second to winner Woodrow Wilson in the presidential election of 1912; this speech reveals much of the former president's political thought.

Rotunda, Ronald D. 1996. "The Aftermath of *Thornton.*" *Constitutional Commentary* 13: 201.

The title's reference is to the Supreme Court's decision in *U.S. Term Limits, Inc. v. Thornton* (1995), which held that states could not impose term limits on persons elected to Congress.

Rush, Mark E., and Richard L. Engstrom. 2001. *Fair and Effective Representation? Debating Electoral Reform and Minority Rights.* Lanham, MD: Rowman and Littlefield.

Lays out the connections that exist among schemes of representation, other voting issues, and the efficacy of voting by members of racial minorities.

Safire, William. 1993. *Safire's New Political Dictionary: The Definitive Guide to the New Language of Politics.* New York: Random House.

Entertaining and highly informative source describing the origin, development, and usage of many terms and idioms in the American political lexicon.

Schier, Steven E. 2003. *You Call This an Election? America's Peculiar Democracy.* Washington, DC: Georgetown University Press.

A critical look at the unique features of democracy, American style, and their effects on political stability, the accountability of elected officials, and voter turnout.

Schlesinger, Arthur M., Jr., and Fred L. Israel, eds. 1971. *History of American Presidential Elections.* 4 vols. New York: Chelsea House.

An exhaustive and invaluable collection of essays, party platforms, addresses and other documents relating to each American presidential election through 1968.

Schultz, David. 2002. "Election 2000: The *Bush v. Gore* Scholarship." *Public Integrity* 4: 360.

Review essay of several books that were published in the wake of the Supreme Court's intervention into the Florida voting recount dispute; helpful in distinguishing balanced appraisals of the intervention from those that are almost entirely polemical.

Schwartz, Bernard. 1983. *Super Chief: Earl Warren and His Supreme Court.* New York: New York University Press.

Study of Supreme Court decision making during the chief justiceship of Earl Warren (1953–1969), a period of Court history marked, among other things, by important voting rights decisions, especially in the area of representation.

Shapiro, Andrew L. 1993. "Challenging Criminal Disenfranchisement under the Voting Rights Act: A New Strategy." *Yale Law Journal* 103: 540.

An attempt to make felony disfranchisement a subject for litigation under the preexisting provisions of the Voting Rights Act of 1965.

Smith, Gene. 1964. *When the Cheering Stopped: The Last Years of Woodrow Wilson.* New York: William Morrow.

Although the emphasis is on the postwar and tragic years of Wilson's presidency, the book provides a concise look at the administration's efforts in 1916 to remain removed from the conflict in Europe.

Smith, Page. 1962. *John Adams.* 2 vols. Garden City, NY: Doubleday.

One of several modern biographies of the second American president.

Stephenson, Donald Grier, Jr. 1988. "The Supreme Court, The Franchise, and the Fifteenth Amendment: The First Sixty Years." *UMKC Law Review* 57: 47.

Reviews the constitutional history of the Fifteenth Amendment from its ratification through the initial white primary cases.

———. 1989. "Choosing Presidential Candidates: Why the Best Man Doesn't Necessarily Win." *USA Today* (Magazine), 117 (March): 15.

Examines the various ways in which presidential candidates have been selected, from the first years of the republic through the late 1980s.

———. 1999. *Campaigns and the Court: The United States Supreme Court in Presidential Elections.* New York: Columbia University Press.

Studies the effect of presidential elections on the Supreme Court, and the effect of the Court on presidential elections.

Stephenson, D. Grier, Jr., Robert J. Bresler, Robert J. Friedrich, and Joseph J. Karlesky. 1992. *American Government.* 2d ed. New York: Harper Collins.

One of any number of standard surveys of American politics and political institutions.

Surowiecki, James. 2004. *The Wisdom of Crowds.* New York: Doubleday.

A defense of the wisdom of the voting multitude in democracies and so a modern-day defense of universal adult suffrage. He concludes that if voters do not always know the facts, they more often than not will elect officials who do.

Swinney, Everette. 1962. "Enforcing the Fifteenth Amendment, 1870–1877." *Journal of Southern History* 1962: 202–218.

Important for depicting the difficulties in making the Fifteenth Amendment a reality during the last seven years of Reconstruction; helpful in seeing the impact of Supreme Court decisions on protection of voting rights.

Sydnor, Charles S. 1962. *American Revolutionaries in the Making: Political Practices in Washington's Virginia.* New York: Collier.

Readable and entertaining account of political life in early Virginia, especially in relation to voting and elections.

Szymanski, Ann-Marie E. 2003. *Pathways to Prohibition: Radicals, Moderates, and Social Movement Outcomes.* Durham, NC: Duke University Press.

Examines the organization, goals, tactics, and composition of the various elements of the prohibition movement in the United States that culminated in ratification of the Eighteenth Amendment in 1919.

Tate, Katherine. 2003. "Black Opinion on the Legitimacy of Racial Redistricting and Minority-Majority Districts." *American Political Science Review* 97:45.

Analysis of public opinion among African Americans concerning majority-minority districts.

Thompson, Dennis F. 2002. *Just Elections: Creating a Fair Electoral Process in the United States.* Chicago: University of Chicago Press.

A comprehensive philosophical look at aspects of voting in the United States that lend integrity to the voting process and those that do not.

———. 2004. "Election Time: Normative Implications of Temporal Properties of the Electoral Process in the United States." *American Political Science Review* 98: 51.

Although few people give much thought to the idea of a single election day, the author shows that timing of elections—when people cast ballots—is an important ingredient in a fair election.

"23rd Amendment." 1965. *Congress and the Nation 1945–1964.* Washington, DC: Congressional Quarterly Service.

Step-by-step account of the shaping of the Twenty-third Amendment that allowed residents of the District of Columbia to participate in presidential elections.

Verba, Sidney. 2003. "Would the Dream of Political Equality Turn out to Be a Nightmare?" *Perspectives on Politics* 1: 663.

Focuses on the idea of equality of political participation and the arguments for and against it; concludes that the reasons to fear political equality are outweighed by the problems associated with inequality among citizens.

Voting and Registration in the Election of November 1996. 1998. Washington, DC: U.S. Census Bureau.

Official vote and registration data from the 1996 presidential election.

Ware, Susan. 1981. *Beyond Suffrage: Women in the New Deal.* Cambridge, MA: Harvard University Press.

Focuses on the role of women in government in the decade following their enfranchisement.

Warren, Earl. 1977. *The Memoirs of Earl Warren.* Garden City, NY: Doubleday.

Posthumously published memoirs of the fourteenth chief justice of the U.S. Supreme Court, whose tenure from 1953 to 1969 was marked by a host of notable rulings including those on representation and districting and the grafting of the "one person, one vote" principle onto the Constitution.

Wattenberg, Martin P. 2002. *Where Have All the Voters Gone?* Cambridge, MA: Harvard University Press.

Emphasizes the link between the complexity of American elections, brought about by a decline in the strength of political parties and an increase in candidate-centered campaigns; suggests that democracy would be improved if American elections were made more user-friendly.

Wayne, Stephen J. 1997. *The Road to the White House 1996.* Postelection ed. New York: St. Martin's Press.

Helpful guide to the politics of presidential elections; a new edition typically appears just in advance of each quadrennial campaign.

Whichard, Willis P. 2000. *Justice James Iredell.* Durham, NC: Carolina Academic Press.

The most complete biography of one of the first justices on the United States Supreme Court.

White, G. Edward. 1982. *Earl Warren: A Public Life.* New York: Oxford University Press.

Judicial biography of the fourteenth chief justice of the United States, whose tenure (1953–1969) was marked by a series of revolutionary decisions in constitutional law that affected virtually all aspects of American life.

"White Woman's Burden." 1921. *Nation* 112 (February 16): 257.

A reminder to women that the Nineteenth Amendment had not extended the franchise to all women in fact, that African American women were as excluded from the ballot box in many places as were black males.

Wilentz, Sean. 1992. "Property and Power: Suffrage Reform in the United States, 1787–1860." In Donald W. Rogers, ed., *Voting and the Spirit of American Democracy: Essays on the History of Voting and Voting Rights in America.* Urbana: University of Illinois Press.

Alongside eight other essays on voting rights, this one reviews the demise of the property qualification for voting and the arrival of nearly universal white adult-male suffrage.

Williamson, Chilton. 1960. *American Suffrage from Property to Democracy 1760–1860*. Princeton, NJ: Princeton University Press.

Probably the most thorough look at property and related qualifications for voting; exhaustive use of colonial and later state and local historical sources.

Wills, Garry. 2003. *"Negro President": Jefferson and the Slave Power*. Boston: Houghton Mifflin.

Dramatic account of political developments in the United States early in the nineteenth century, particularly showing the political importance of slavery.

Wilson, Woodrow. 1893. *An Old Master and Other Political Essays*. New York: Scribner's.

Political and constitutional essays and commentary by the only Ph.D. to become president of the United States; as the twenty-eighth president, Wilson was in his second term at the time of ratification of the Nineteenth Amendment.

———. 1913. *The New Freedom*. New York: Doubleday.

A statement of the twenty-eighth president's political values and agenda in the first year of his presidency.

Woodward, C. Vann. 1966. *The Strange Career of Jim Crow*. 2d rev. ed. New York: Oxford University Press.

Emphasizes the legal and cultural status of blacks in the South after the Civil War, highlighting cross currents and contradictions in laws and practices; helpful data on the contraction of voting rights that occurred around the turn of the twentieth century.

Yarbrough, Tinsley E. 2002. *Race and Redistricting: The* Shaw-Cromartie *Cases*. Lawrence: University Press of Kansas.

Superb case study of the majority-minority districting controversy in North Carolina that began with *Shaw v. Reno* (1993) and concluded with *Hunt [Easley] v. Cromartie* (2001).

Zall, Paul M. 1981. *Ben Franklin Laughing: Anecdotes from Original Sources by and about Benjamin Franklin*. Berkeley: University of California Press.

Comprehensive compilation of material by and about this prominent early American statesman and sage.

Zelden, Charles L. 2002. *Voting Rights on Trial: A Handbook with Cases, Laws, and Documents.* Santa Barbara, CA: ABC-CLIO.

The essays and supporting materials provide a concise yet comprehensive overview of the various dimensions of voting rights, both in terms of historical development and contemporary problems.

SUPREME COURT DECISIONS AND RELATED LEGAL SOURCES

Decisions by the United States Supreme Court are available in printed form in several editions and are widely available on the Internet.

(1) *United States Reports.* This is the official edition, now published by the Government Printing Office. Until 1875, the reports were cited according to the name of the Reporter of Decisions, with the reporter's name sometimes abbreviated. Beginning with volume 91 in 1875, the reports have been cited only by the designation "U.S." For example, a case cited as 444 U.S. 130 is located in volume 444 of the *U.S. Reports,* beginning on page 130.

1789–1800 Dallas (1–4 Dallas = 1–4 U.S.)
1801–1815 Cranch (1–9 Cranch = 5–13 U.S.)
1816–1827 Wheaton (1–12 Wheaton = 14–25 U.S.)
1828–1842 Peters (1–16 Peters = 26–41 U.S.)
1843–1860 Howard (1–24 Howard = 42–65 U.S.)
1861–1862 Black (1–2 Black = 66–67 U.S.)
1863–1874 Wallace (1–23 Wallace = 68–90 U.S.)
1875–(91– U.S.)

(2) *United States Supreme Court Reports, Lawyers' Edition* (until 1996 published by Lawyers' Cooperative Publishing Company; now published by Lexis-Nexis). The advantage of this complete edition lies in the inclusion of summaries of briefs of counsel plus notes and annotations on various topics of constitutional law. *Lawyers' Edition* is cited as L. Ed. (e.g., 96 L. Ed. 954). Decisions since 1956 appear in a second series (e.g., 118 L. Ed. 2d 293).

(3) *Supreme Court Reporter* (until 1996 published by West Publishing Company; now published by West Group). This is similar in concept to *Lawyers' Edition* but includes decisions only since 1882. Thus for cases in volumes 1–105 U.S., one must consult one of the other editions. It is cited as S. Ct. (e.g., 58 S. Ct. 166).

(4) Decisions of lower federal courts. Until 1879, many opinions issued by U.S. district and circuit courts were published in *Federal Cases* (abbrevi-

ated Fed. Cas.). Beginning in 1880, opinions issued by the circuit courts (and after 1891 the courts of appeals) appeared in the *Federal Reporter* (abbreviated F., F.2d, and F.3d), as did opinions issued by district courts until 1932. Since 1932 the latter have been published in the *Federal Supplement* (abbreviated F. Supp. and F. Supp. 2d).

(5) Internet access. Supreme Court decisions are accessible through Westlaw and Lexis-Nexis (both available through many college and university libraries or by subscription), on CD-ROM, and at various locations on the World Wide Web. As of this writing, the sites listed below are available at no charge. Be advised that any Web address (or Universal Resource Locator, abbreviated URL) is subject to change.

(a) The LII and Hermes: The Legal Information Institute and Project Hermes provide decisions since May 1990 through Cornell University. Decisions are ordinarily accessible within hours of their announcement by the Supreme Court. Several hundred selected decisions prior to 1990 are available from LII at the second address.

http://supct.law.cornell.edu/supct/html
http://supct.law.cornell.edu/supct/cases/historic.htm

(b) FindLaw: FindLaw Internet Legal Resources includes decisions since 1791. The FindLaw site also archives selected decisions by the lower federal courts.

http://www.findlaw.com/casecode/supreme.html

(c) The Supreme Court's website: This official site features the High Court's current docket, calendar, court rules, decisions, orders, and press releases.

http://www.supremecourtus.gov/index.html

OTHER INTERNET RESOURCES

Almost everyone above the age of five knows that the Internet contains vast resources. What some may not know, however, is that the Internet is particularly valuable for, and suitable to, anyone interested in voting rights and elections. This is because voting rights and elections are not static but ongoing and recurring matters. They involve many issues, many separate events, and many individuals, institutions, and groups acting either independently or in concert. There is always yet another development unfolding at the moment, and others about to happen. The Internet connects the student of voting rights and election administration about as close as one can get to the subject in real time. The Internet offers huge advantages in terms of timeliness, the quantity and variety of data that are available, and the ease with which all of that can be located, identified, evaluated, collected, and assimilated. Information obtainable a decade or so ago only at major research libraries, and then often only after a considerable wait because of publication lag times, much page turning, note taking, and a considerable expenditure of time, is now easily and quickly accessible from any point on the globe where there is a computer with access to the Internet.

The most important official sites relating to voting and elections are those maintained by the Federal Election Commission (www.fec.gov), the Department of Justice through the Voting Section of the Civil Rights Division (http://www.usdoj.gov/crt/voting/intro/intro.htm), and the Library of Congress (http://www.loc.gov/law/guide/us.html). The first also contains several databases of voting and election statistics. Information about current litigation involving voting rights and elections in which the U.S. government is a party or in which the government has an interest is accessible through the Solicitor General's office: http://www.usdoj.gov/osg. A section of the Library of Congress site noted above also contains links to information about voting election laws in each of the fifty states, and so is the best starting point for an overview of the variety of electoral practices in the United States (http://www.loc.gov/law/guide/usstates.html).

For information on election administration and vote tabulation, consult http://electiondataservices.com/home.htm maintained by Election Data Services, Inc., as well as http://www.electionline.org/index.jsp maintained by the Election Reform Information Project. The former site also includes material on legislative reapportionment and redistricting. The *Election Law Journal*, published since 2001 by Mary Ann Liebert, Inc., focuses exclusively on voting rights, campaign regulation, and elections. The table of contents for each quarterly issue is accessible at http://www.liebertpub.com/elj.

The Web pages of national newspapers such as the *New York Times* (www.nytimes.com), the *Washington Post* (www.washingtonpost.com), and the *Los Angeles Times* (http://www.latimes.com) frequently contain articles and links on voting rights and elections, as do other news sites such as www.cnn.com, www.foxnews.com, and www.msnbc.com. Search engines such as www.google.com and www.yahoo.com are useful tools not only for locating information but for ferreting out any number of additional sites.

Other useful sites include those maintained by voter advocacy groups. These are useful as clearinghouses and are timely sources to identify current voting rights issues and to track recent developments. Typically, the homepage of each advocacy site explains the basis of its interest and concern regarding voting rights. Anyone accessing the web pages (or published literature, for that matter) of such groups should therefore remember that, by definition, an advocacy group is not (and is not supposed to be) a neutral observer of political affairs. The National Voting Rights Institute site (http://www.nvri.org) contains an online legal library with a particular interest in campaign finance and how that affects voting rights. The voting rights section of the American Civil Liberties Union (http://www.aclu.org/VotingRights/VotingRightsMain.cfm) provides a comprehensive look at the work of one of the nation's oldest organizations that exists primarily to advance civil liberties on a broad front. The Center for Voting and Democracy (http://www.fairvote.org/vra) strives not only to protect voting rights but to promote equality in other aspects of the electoral process. The Voting Rights Project of the Lawyers' Committee for Civil Rights Under Law (http://www.lawyerscomm.org/projects/votingrights.html) litigates voting rights cases, monitors U.S. Justice Department enforcement efforts (including enforcement of the National Voter Registration Act) through legal representation, advocacy, and public education. The National Association for the Advancement of Colored People (NAACP) has long been in the front lines of efforts to combat racial discrimination at the ballot box and across American society. A section of its Internet site deals expressly with election reform and voting rights: http://www.naacp.org/work/voter/voting_rights.shtml. The Voting Rights Action Center (http://www.civilrights.org/issues/voting) is a joint effort of the Leadership Conference on Civil Rights and the Leadership Conference on Civil Rights Education Fund, umbrella organizations for some 180 civil rights groups. The site promises relevant and up-to-the-minute news and information relating to voting rights. Working Assets sponsors a site that facilitates online voter registration: http://yourvotematters .org, while www.teenvote.us is a grassroots arm of Teen Vote, an organization devoted to extension of the franchise to include those fifteen, sixteen, and seventeen years of age. Finally, the National Voting Rights Museum and Institute in Selma, Alabama, provides information not only about the galvanic events at Selma in 1965 but other voting rights data as well: http://www.voterights.org.

As is always the case, the Universal Resource Locator (abbreviated URL) or address of any of these and other sites may change. Sometimes a site that is no longer functioning will conveniently provide a link to the new URL, but not always. Those presented here are accurate as of mid-2004.

Index

About the Author

Donald Grier Stephenson Jr. is Charles A. Dana Professor of Government at Franklin and Marshall College. A graduate of Davidson College (1964), he received the M.A. and Ph.D. degrees from Princeton University in 1966 and 1967, respectively. Between 1968 and 1970 he served in the United States Army, completing his military duty at the rank of captain. He is general editor of ABC-CLIO's America's Freedoms series and is author of *Campaigns and the Court: The U.S. Supreme Court in Presidential Elections* (Columbia University Press, 1999); *The Waite Court: Justices, Rulings, and Legacy* (ABC-CLIO, 2003); and coauthor of *American Constitutional Law: Introductory Essays and Selected Cases* 14th ed. (Prentice Hall, 2005).